Writing College English

A Composition Handbook
for Speakers of English as
a Second Language

April Lambert Levy

HARCOURT BRACE JOVANOVICH, PUBLISHERS
San Diego   New York   Chicago   Austin   Washington, D.C.
London   Sydney   Tokyo   Toronto

Preface

In 1979, I inherited three freshman composition courses for ESL students from a fellow instructor. I also inherited her textbook assignments. For a semester I struggled to make the texts she had chosen work for my students, many of whom had arrived in the United States only six months earlier. I struggled in vain.

The textbooks were too complicated. Their vocabulary was unfamiliar and often eccentric. Sample sentences touched on such topics as electromagnetism, horticulture, and unicorns. Moreover, the texts assumed a familiarity with American culture that my students lacked. And rarely did their authors address the sort of issues that held special interest for my students, such as cross-cultural comparisons, foreign travel experiences, and learning a new language.

In the following semesters, I looked for a text that would be satisfactory for college-level ESL students. I never found one. The existing ESL handbooks on composition, though in many cases useful for students preparing for college entrance, were not suitable for college-level work. Too often, they encouraged simplistic thinking, dictated pat essay structure, blurred important grammatical distinctions, and omitted or gave short shrift to topics essential for students in college composition classes—namely, the summary, the research paper, the essay question, and plagiarism. More surprisingly, a number of them employed sample essays that seemed little more attuned to the needs of international students than did those in traditional college composition texts.

It was during that time that the ideas behind *Writing College English* blossomed. The techniques in this text were developed and tested during several years of classroom teaching. Time has passed, but the gap in the literature I perceived during those years has persisted. *Writing College English* fills that gap by providing a college-level composition text that works for ESL students.

I have made an effort to ensure that neither the style nor the content of *Writing College English* will interfere with student understanding. Language and sentence structure in the text are straightforward. The text avoids obscure and highly specialized vocabulary. It explains essential technical terms. In the grammar section, model sentences employ repetitive vocabulary and deal with everyday topics so the grammatical principles they illustrate are not obscured by difficult language. Sample essays—the great majority of them written by international students—have been chosen to appeal to ESL students. Many of them deal with cross-cultural experiences. Others help acclimate students to life in the United States without assuming that the reader has prior knowledge of the country. Moreover, the number and length of professional essays are kept to a minimum, and the same essays are used as examples or in exercises more than once, in recognition of the time ESL students frequently require for reading English texts.

Conceptual sophistication, however, has not been sacrificed. Complex ideas underlie many of the student and professional essays used in the text. Many of the sample essays are analyzed in depth. And the text encourages students to think and write in a sophisticated manner. The text includes a detailed chapter on argumentation, including an explanation of argumentative fallacies and deductive reasoning. It allows for stylistic variations often proscribed by other texts—for example, the implicit thesis. It promotes variety in essay, paragraph, and sentence structure. It treats grammatical matters such as punctuation and agreement precisely and comprehensively. Moreover, *Writing College English* treats thoroughly those special forms—the summary, the research paper, and the essay question—that are so important for students writing essays for college classes. *Writing College English* is at once accessible and challenging to the international students it addresses.

I would like to thank Stephen Spector, former director of English composition at the University of Bridgeport, where the ideas for this text were first formulated, for giving me the opportunity to create my own curriculum and to experiment with class texts of my own choosing. I also thank Doris Betts, then director of the freshman English program at the University of North Carolina, Chapel Hill, as well as the composition teaching staff in general, for guidance and support in my first experience teaching college composition. They provided a solid grounding in the fundamentals of good writing. I also thank William F. Young and other members of the reference staff at the library of the State University of New York at Albany, as well as the reference staff of the Bethlehem Public Library, for their help in obtaining information included in the chapter on the research paper.

Most importantly, I wish to thank the many students with whom I worked at the University of Bridgeport. It was their enthusiasm, their willingness to make mistakes and try again, and their creativity that inspired me to write this book. It is their efforts at essay writing that give the book much of its special pertinence to international students. The book is about them and, to a large extent, by them.

Finally, I would like to thank my husband, Dan, who urged me to carry out this project, and my children, Morris and Aaron, who often urged me not to. I know that they have forgiven the many missed playtimes, hectic Sundays, and ordered-out dinners because they realize how much I love them and depend on them for their love and support.

April Lambert Levy

A Note to Instructors

In addition to the accessibility to foreign students and the appropriateness to college-level work mentioned in the Preface, *Writing College English* attempts to make another contribution to the teaching of college composition to ESL students: organizaton by subject matter. Unlike many ESL composition texts, which are divided into polyglot lessons comprising in one chapter a bit of rhetoric, a bit of essay structure, a bit of grammar, and so forth, *Writing College English* treats rhetoric, methodology, structure, and grammar as separate topics. This organization allows instructors freedom to construct lesson plans that conform to their students' needs, their departments' requirements, and their own preferences.

Some instructors, however, may desire guidance in combining material from different parts of the text into coherent lesson plans. Frequent cross-references are available to help them make connections between concepts located in different sections of the text. In addition, a sample syllabus is offered on the pages that follow. This syllabus is offered as a suggestion only: some instructors may prefer to treat each unit separately and integrally; others may choose to combine material from different parts of the text in a way distinct from the one offered here.

The syllabus outlined in the following pages represents a weekly summary of material covered in a typical two-semester college course, meeting for three or four hours per week. It could, however, be adapted to courses operating on a variety of schedules. In general, the syllabus follows the outline of the first two units of the text because it is in these introductory and rhetorical units that most of the composition exercises, which are intended as the major course assignments, are to be found. Material from other parts of the text concerned with methodology (Part Three), essay structure (Part Four), and grammar (Part Six) has been inserted where it seems to me most relevant.

I have covered the basic structural principles early in the syllabus because students' success in performing writing assignments may depend on their familiarity with them. As a result, greater course time has been accorded to some of the earlier rhetorical patterns than to some of the later ones. This imbalance, however, provides beginning students with the time they need to adjust to a new environment and to new techniques as they tackle writing assignments early in the term.

In certain cases, especially in the earlier weeks of each semester, I have advised that only some material from a methodological or grammatical chapter be introduced when a class is focusing on a particular rhetorical pattern. In such cases, I have frequently suggested that this material be reviewed when that chapter is dealt with as a whole. For example, I have suggested that the subsection "Subject, Topic, Thesis" be read during the weeks in which narration is treated. I have suggested a review of this subsection during the discussion of analysis, when the chapter in which the subsection occurs is fully treated. ESL students, even more than others, benefit by frequent review of basic principles. In light of this, I have urged that some of the methodological, structural, and grammatical material assigned in the first semester be reassigned during the second.

Unlike many college composition syllabuses, which require research papers to be written during each semester of a two-semester course, the syllabus here defers the writing of the research paper to near the end of the second semester. Some instructors may have good reason for doing it differently. Having tried it both ways, I find this a more effective and less stressful way to assign research writing to students whose limited grasp of English often makes the requisite reading and restating of others' ideas a too-potent temptation to plagiarize.

Due to space constraints, the text could not deal with the fundamentals of grammar—the parts of speech and parts of the sentence. Some students will be adequately versed in these areas by the time they enroll in a college composition section. For those who are not, this material could be covered either in a separate course on the basic principles of English or at some point early in a one- or, more typical, a two-semester course. Instructors should refer to any of a number of fine grammar handbooks available for ESL courses to help their students master this necessary background material.

With all this in mind, I offer the following as one possible way to assign material from *Writing College English*.

First Semester

Weeks 1 and 2:	Chapter 1, all
	From Chapter 21, "Punctuating Dates and Places"
	From Chapter 23, "Capitalization," "Articles," "Word Division (Syllabication),"
	From Chapter 18, "Plagiarism"
Weeks 2 to 4:	Chapter 2, all
	Chapter 13, all
Weeks 5 and 6:	Chapter 3, all
	From Chapter 9, "Subject, Topic, Thesis"
	From Chapter 10, "Informal Outlining"
	Chapter 11, all
Week 7:	Chapter 12, all (concurrent with revision of narration)
	Chapter 14, all
Weeks 8 and 9:	Chapter 4, all
	Chapter 16, all
Weeks 10 and 11:	Chapter 5, all
	Chapter 15, all
	From Chapter 21, "Sentences and Nonsentences," "Combining Clauses, Phrases, and Words"

Week 11:   Chapter 6, all
                         From Chapter 21, "Punctuating Parenthetical Elements," "Elimi-
                             nating Unnecessary Commas," "Introducing a Series or
                             Equivalent Statement"

Weeks 12 and 13:   Chapter 7, all
                         From Chapter 9, "Sentence Agreement"

Weeks 13 and 14:   Chapter 17, all
                         From Chapter 10, "Formal Outlining," "Changing the Outline"
                         From Chapter 21, "Quotation Punctuation," "Punctuation Format"
                         From Chapter 18, "Plagiarism"

Second Semester

Weeks 1 and 2:   Chapter 17, all
                         From Chapter 10, "Formal Outlining"
                         From Chapter 21, "Quotation Punctuation"
                         From Chapter 18, "Plagiarism" (review)

Weeks 2 and 3:   Chapter 12, all (concurrent with revision of summary)

Weeks 3 to 6:   Chapter 8, all
                         Chapter 9, all
                         From Chapter 1, "Audience, Purpose, and Tone"

Weeks 7 and 8:   From Chapter 18, "Gathering Information"
                         Chapter 9, all (review)
                         From Chapter 10, "Formal Outlining" (review)

Weeks 9 to 11:   From Chapter 18, "Documentation," "Plagiarism" (review), "Us-
                             ing Foreign Language Sources"
                         From Chapter 21, "Quotation Punctuation" (review)
                         From Chapter 23, "Italics," "Abbreviations," "Writing Numbers"
                         Chapter 19, all

Weeks 11 and 12:   From Chapter 10, "Changing the Outline"
                         Chapter 12, all (review, concurrent with revision of research pa-
                             per)

Weeks 13 and 14:   Chapter 20, all
                         From Chapter 10, "Informal Outlining"

Contents

Preface   **iii**

Part One The Essay   **1**

Chapter 1. *What Is an Essay?*   **2**

     Essay Length   **3**

     Subject Matter   **4**

     Essay Patterns   **4**

     Audience, Purpose, and Tone   **5**

Chapter 2. *Thesis and Supporting Details*   10

     Thesis   **10**

        excerpt from *North Toward Home* by Willie Morris   **11**

     Supporting Details   **12**

Part Two Patterns for Essays   **19**

Chapter 3. *Narration*   **20**

     Selecting Narrative Details   **21**

     Arranging Narrative Details   **22**

Chapter 4. *Description*   **29**

     Selecting Descriptive Details   **29**

     "Musée des Beaux Arts" by W. H. Auden   **30**

     Arranging Descriptive Details   **34**

     Advantages That the Foreign Student Has in Writing
        Description   **35**

Chapter 5. *Illustration*   **41**

     Balancing Theme and Supporting Details   **42**

Chapter 6. Definition **47**
  Parts of the Definition **47**
  Definition Length **48**
  Avoiding Common Errors in Definition **50**
  Examples of Definition **51**
Chapter 7. Analysis **55**
  Classification **56**
  Subdivision **60**
  Comparison and Contrast **64**
  Cause and Effect **68**
  Process **71**
Chapter 8. Argument **75**
  Elements of Argument **77**
  Tone in Argument **81**
  Analysis of an Argument **82**
  Organization of the Argumentative Essay **84**
  Argumentative Fallacies **85**
  Testing Arguments **86**
Part Three Writing the Essay **93**
Chapter 9. Getting Started **94**
  Subject, Topic, Thesis **95**
  From Subject to Topic **95**
  From Topic to Thesis **96**
Chapter 10. Organizing the Material **99**
  Informal Outlining **99**
  Formal Outlining **101**
  Changing the Outline **106**
Chapter 11. Writing It Out **109**
  The First Draft **109**
  The Introduction **110**
  The Conclusion **112**
  The Title **114**
Chapter 12. Revising **119**
  The Writer as Critic **119**

Revising After Criticism   **122**
The Final Draft   **122**

Part Four   Units of the Essay   129

Chapter 13. Paragraphs   130
Paragraph Unity   **131**
Theme Sentence   **133**
Paragraph Order   **134**
Final Position   **137**
Paragraph Completeness   **138**

Chapter 14. Sentences   147
Variety   **150**
Subordination   **152**
Economy   **154**

Chapter 15. Transitions   160
Indicating Continuity   **160**
Indicating Change   **161**

Chapter 16. Words   167
Building Vocabulary   **168**
Level of Diction   **170**
Concreteness and Specificity   **172**
Connotation   **178**
Figurative Language   **180**
Cognates and False Cognates   **182**

Part Five   Special Forms   191

Chapter 17. The Summary   192
"Velva, North Dakota" by Eric Sevareid   **193**
"Alienation and Affection: Undergraduate Liberal Arts Education" by Craufurd D. Goodwin and Michael Nacht   **199**

Chapter 18. The Research Paper   203
Gathering Information   **204**
Documentation   **218**
Plagiarism   **224**
Using Foreign Language Sources   **227**

Chapter 19. A Sample Research Paper   **233**
Chapter 20. Answering Essay Questions   **251**
  Considering the Question   **251**
  Planning the Essay   **257**
Part Six Grammatical Conventions   261
Chapter 21. Punctuation   **262**
  Sentences and Nonsentences   **262**
  Combining Clauses, Phrases, and Words   **266**
  Punctuating Parenthetical Elements   **271**
  Eliminating Unnecessary Commas   **272**
  Punctuating Dates and Places   **273**
  Introducing a Series or Equivalent Statement   **274**
  Quotation Punctuation   **274**
  Long Quotations   **275**
  Punctuation Format   **280**
Chapter 22. Sentence Agreement   **284**
  Predication   **284**
  Number   **285**
  Person   **288**
  Tense   **288**
  Form   **291**
  Structure   **292**
  Comparison   **293**
  Possession   **295**
Chapter 23. Other Conventions   **299**
  Capitalization   **299**
  Italics   **302**
  Abbreviations   **303**
  Writing Numbers   **306**
  Word Division (Syllabication)   **308**
  Articles   **309**
Glossary   317
Index   327

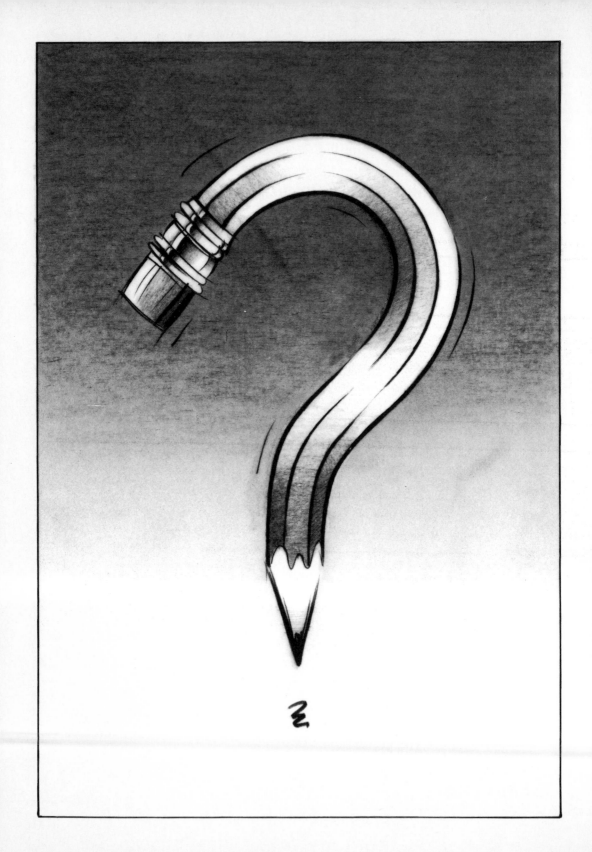

Part One

The Essay

Chapter 1

What is an Essay?

Whatever your field of study—whether engineering, health, computer science, business, or education—from time to time in your college career it is likely that you will be required to write essays. An *essay* is a unified piece of writing on one theme. The essay may be of various lengths and may take various forms or *patterns*, but it is always *unified*—that is, all of the parts of the essay relate to one another, go together. Such *unity* is achieved when the writer includes in the essay only ideas that belong to a central *thesis*,* or main idea. Any idea that does not belong to this thesis does not belong in the essay.

For instance, in the following pieces of writing, two students have described their first day in the United States. Only one of these pieces of writing is a successful essay because in only one of them do all the ideas relate to the central thesis. Here is the first example:

---

*In this text, we use the terms *theme* and *thesis* interchangeably.

Example 1.

> I came to the United States on September 5, 1982. The plane landed at Kennedy Airport at 4:00 p.m. I got off and followed the people to the Immigration Office. Then I got my bags. Then I went to customs. Later I took a limousine to the campus. I got a room at the Holiday Inn. I had a good supper in the hotel restaurant. I went to sleep after dinner.

Here there is no main idea. The details consist of a list of the writer's activities on his first day in the United States. They are not related to one another by any controlling idea (an idea that controls which details a writer includes in his essay). This example is not a successful essay.

Let us look at the second piece of writing:

Example 2.

> The day I came to the United States was very tiring. I hardly slept at all the night before I left. When my father woke me at 6:00 a.m. to take me to the airport, I could not believe it was already morning. We drove for two hours to the airport. When we arrived there, I learned that the plane had been delayed and I would have to wait another two hours before leaving. The flight to the U.S. took eight long hours. And after I got off the plane I had to go through immigration, baggage pick-up, and customs. By the time I had finished answering everyone's questions, I barely had the strength to look for a taxi. Finally arriving at the hotel, I was too tired even to have dinner. I fell asleep on the bed in my room still dressed in the clothes I had put on in my own room that morning.

Here, too, the writer recounts many events, but all the activities are related to the controlling idea that *his first day in the United States was very tiring*. This clause is the thesis of the essay. *Hardly sleeping the night before, being awakened at 6:00 a.m., the eight-hour trip, going through immigration*, and so forth, and *going to bed without either eating or undressing* are all details related to this thesis—details that show that the day was tiring. In the second piece of writing, all parts are related to a clear thesis and, thus, to one another. The second piece of writing is a successful essay.

Essay Length

Examples 1 and 2 are short essays, only one paragraph in length. Essays may be of various lengths, from one or a few paragraphs to many pages—right up to the very long, book-length essays called theses and dissertations. No matter how short or long, an essay must fulfill the same requirement to be successful: its parts must all be related to one another by belonging to a clear thesis; all details must be controlled by one main idea. The length is determined largely by the breadth or scope of an essay's topic, the complexity or difficulty of its thesis, and the number and complexity of the details needed to support the thesis. Often, an instructor's assignment or the time allotted to the writing of an in-class essay will set a limit on the length of a given essay. Thus, an instructor may ask for a *term paper* on a given subject and specify that it be about 2 pages long or about 10 or 20 or more pages in length. Similarly, if a student is given one class period in which to write an answer to an *essay question*, he or she should plan the length of the essay so that it can be completed—and perhaps *proofread*—during this period of time.

Subject Matter

Just as essays can vary in length, so can they vary infinitely in subject matter. Although college essays are perhaps most often associated with the humanities—literature, languages, history—courses in social sciences, such as political science and sociology, and in sciences, such as psychology, chemistry, physics, and biology—as well as professional courses in business, engineering, or medicine—may require the writing of essays. Your college writing instructor will probably ask you to write essays on a variety of subjects. Some may be personal essays, asking you to tell about an experience you have had or to explore your feelings about a given subject. Others may be impersonal essays, some requiring you to support your thesis with materials written by other authors. The methods and rules you learn in writing essays on the subjects chosen by your writing instructor can generally be applied to the writing of essays on other subjects and for other courses.

Essay Patterns

In addition to length and subject matter, the pattern of essays varies. An *essay pattern* is the structure on which a writer organizes his material. These patterns will be discussed in detail in Part Two. They are subdivided in different ways by various authorities on writing. In this text, we will subdivide the patterns for essays into the following categories: narration, description, illustration, definition, analysis (classification, subdivision, comparison and contrast, cause and effect, and process), and argument.

To understand what "patterns" means, we might look again at the essay discussed earlier in this chapter, the one in which the writer wished to show that the day he came to the United States was tiring (see Example 2). This pattern of essay is called a *narrative*. A narrative is a series of events—what happened first, second, third, and so on. In Example 2, the writer recounts what happened to him, what he did on the day he came to the United States. But the writer might have written an essay demonstrating the same main idea—that he was exhausted on the day he came to the United States—by writing a *description* of the way he looked after the day's events:

Example 3.

> After the long trip from my country to the U.S. and up to campus, I was exhausted. Looking at myself in the hotel room mirror, I saw red eyes, their lids half closed, with big, dark circles of skin under them. My hair was rumpled, and my clothes were as wrinkled as my skin felt underneath them. Everything about my appearance seemed to say, "Put me to bed!"

As we can see, the main idea of Example 3 is the same as that of Example 2. In Example 3, however, the writer supports his thesis with details of his *tired appearance* after the tiring day rather than with details of the day's tiring events.

Of course, an essay may employ more than one pattern; indeed, rarely will an essay use only one pattern. Examples 2 and 3, for instance, could easily be combined into one longer essay. But generally, one pattern will predominate—that is, one pattern will be more fundamental and more obvious than the others used in the essay. It is likely that, for the purpose of an exercise, your instructor will ask you to write an essay organized on a particular pattern. If you are asked to do so, be sure to follow directions carefully. If your instructor asks you to write a description, even if you include some narrative details or some details of comparison and contrast, make sure your essay is predominantly a description.

Audience, Purpose, and Tone

Finally, essays vary in audience, purpose, and tone. The *audience* consists of those whom the writer wishes to address—her essay's intended readers. In various situations, the audience might consist of her fellow students, of her native countrymen, of university administrators, of family members or close friends. The *purpose* of an essay is the writer's aim in composing it: the effect the writer wishes to have on her audience. A writer may wish to amuse her readers, to make them laugh. Or she may wish to shock or surprise them, to move them emotionally, to persuade, or simply to inform. *Tone* is the way an essay sounds, the manner of expression with which a writer addresses her audience. Like audience and purpose, tone may vary. It may be light, sentimental, serious, or angry, among others.

Audience, tone, and purpose are closely interrelated. Clearly, a tone suited to one group of readers might be inappropriate for another. Take this passage from a student's letter to a friend:

> Dear Lee,
>   Slide Hall is terrific. You wouldn't believe the incredible parties we have on my floor—the "fabulous fourth"—every weekend. Unbelievable! I've already met more girls than I can count!

We would hardly expect to find this passage in a letter to the student's parents. To them, the student might write as follows:

> Dear Mom and Dad,
>   My residence at Slide Hall has been great. The weekend social events sponsored by the fourth floor, where I'm living, have given me the opportunity to meet lots of students and make many friends.

As we can see, the writer's tone varies in response to his audience and the effect he wants his words to have on it.

Unless otherwise instructed, the beginning college student should direct her essays at an audience made up of typical members of the academic community: students and professors in various disciplines at various institutions. Of course, as she advances, the student's audience will likely narrow, and she will direct at least some of her writing at specialists in her particular field. Generally, however, the student should resist the temptation to write directly to the professor or to the students in her particular class. Essays addressed to such a narrow audience may tend to be overpersonal in tone and content.

The purpose of most college essays will be to inform or persuade. However, occasional writing assignments may indicate that a particular essay should be written to amuse or entertain readers. Obviously, tone will vary accordingly. Generally, however, the tone of college essays should be restrained and serious, like the tone of articles in serious journals.

Whether the writer is interested in achieving the lighter tone of some personal essays or the relative restraint required in most academic writing, it is necessary for the student writer to control her tone, to modulate it in accordance with her audience and the effect she wishes her essay to have on it.

Summary

We have seen that an essay can vary in subject matter, length, pattern, and considerations of audience, purpose, and tone. We have also seen that, to be successful, an essay must be unified—that is, all of its parts must relate to a thesis. In the following chapter, we will look more closely at how a writer makes the parts of his essay relate to a thesis.

Exercises

For Consideration

Exercise 1.   In the following pair of essays, which essay is successfully unified by a clear thesis? Can you state its theme in one sentence? What details support the thesis? Are there any details that do not belong to the thesis? Can you make any specific suggestions to improve the unsuccessful essays?

A.
My Life

I was born in Kuwait on December 12, 1964. I was the youngest of three children, all boys. My father and mother owned a business in the city. They traveled a lot for work. I used to spend a lot of my time with them on their travels. In 1972 we moved to England. Then I decided I wanted to come to the U.S. to study. And in September of 1982 I enrolled at the university here. I haven't decided on a major yet. Right now I'm thinking about medicine, but I'm not sure.

B.
Wandering

I guess you could say I am a nomad. From the time I was born I have been moving from place to place, never quite sure of my home. I was born in Kuwait in 1964, but even as a young child I spent much of my time traveling with my parents, who traveled as part of the business they owned in the capital. Indeed, my two older brothers and I spent as much time out of Kuwait as in it.

Later, my family left Kuwait and went to England, changing schools, friends, languages. The restless spirit seems to have become a part of me, for I decided to leave England to attend a university in the United States. And even now, here at the university, I seem unable to settle down to one major. Today it's medicine; tomorrow, who knows?

Exercise 2. Read the following piece of writing and explain why it is or is not a successful essay.

Some Information About Persia

During the 1930s, the name of Persia was changed to Iran. Iran is the name always used by Iranians. The Iranian solar year begins at the beginning of spring, but the Iranian calendar is 621 years behind the Gregorian calendar. Thus, A.D. 1985 is approximately 1364 on the Iranian calendar. The currency of Iran is the rial. Iran is still a developing country and it is attempting to raise the standard of living of its population.

Exercise 3. In the following essays, students relate the events of their first day in the United States. Are the essays successful or unsuccessful? What are their strengths and weaknesses? Make a list of the events mentioned in each essay. Are the events unified by a controlling idea? Explain.

A.

My First Day in the United States

My first day in the U.S. was something that I will never forget. First of all, the landing at Kennedy Airport took place during a terrible storm. Then in the terminal I couldn't find my baggage, so I spent more than an hour finding it. Once I was out of the customs room, I didn't know what to do or where to go; I didn't even know how to say, "Can you help me?" in English. Finally, I found a Puerto Rican man who helped me. He told me where to get the limousine that would take me to my university. But that day I didn't want to go to the university; the real thing I wanted to do was to know New York City.

It was 6:30 when I asked the man how to get to Manhattan, and he told me that he could take me there because he was a taxi driver. The idea of seeing New York City, with all its skyscrapers and crazy people excited me. During the ride, the driver asked me if I wanted to go to a fancy hotel or to a medium one. I told him that I didn't want to go to a hotel at all because I had an aunt who lived in Queens, New York. So I decided to go to my aunt's house before going to Manhattan.

Once at my aunt's house the taxi driver said to me that the ride cost $8.30. I paid without complaining. My aunt saw me from the window and quickly opened the door of the house. I got into the house and, after having put the baggage in one room, we started talking about my trip. My aunt asked me if I was hungry, and I answered that I was very hungry. She made me something to eat while I was resting on the sofa. I went to New York the next day.

B.

First Visit to New York

In Iran I always dreamed of visiting the great cities of the world, especially New York, which I knew only from books, movies, and TV.

After I arrived in the United States, I went to stay with Iranian friends who were living in New York. I asked them about all the places I had heard about and wanted to visit. They were full of warnings about being alone in the city. Attending a show or the cinema or going shopping, they said, could be a bad experience because the areas around theaters and shops might be full of addicts, purse snatchers, muggers, or prostitutes. They told me to guard my money and to look out for strangers.

That day we visited some of the places I had always wanted to see: Fifth Avenue, Central Park, museums. The streets were crowded during the day or night. They were not clean as I had expected them to be. People were too busy to answer our questions. My friends and I were afraid of walking on many streets even during the day.

I completely lost my feeling of freedom in New York. Poor people, dirty streets, and the way people behaved completely disappointed me.

C.

Visit to New York

Last year, when I first came to the U.S.A., I arrived at Kennedy Airport. I had a bad experience at first. I could not find a taxi, but when I found one I forgot about everything. I went to a hotel in Manhattan. I was amazed when I saw New York's skyscrapers.

The next day I went into the streets. I wanted to see the Empire State Building first because I had heard so much about it when I was at home. I went to the top of the building and looked over the city. The first thing I noticed was the crowded streets and the smoke in the air. When I went down into the street, I was on Thirty-Fourth Street, a street full of dirt and garbage. I had been told that the city was dangerous, but fortunately, I did not have a problem. I stayed in New York for three days. I think New York is exciting and a very nice place to visit, but I wouldn't want to live there!

For Composition

Exercise 4. Write a one- or a two-paragraph essay about what you hope to learn in your composition class. You might include comments on your background in English, your particular weaknesses, or your anticipated need for English composition skills in your future endeavors. Whatever you include, make sure your essay is unified by a controlling idea and that all parts of the essay relate to that idea.

Exercise 5. Write a brief autobiographical essay—an essay about your life—in three or four paragraphs. Of course, since the essay must be brief, you will not be able to include every fact about yourself or every event you have experienced. Rather, choose the facts and events that will make your essay *unified*. To achieve unity, decide before you begin writing on the main idea (thesis) you want to present to the reader. This idea will control which facts and events you choose to write about.

Remember, this is not just a list of your *vital statistics*. For instance, it is probably not important for the reader to know the exact date of your birth, your father's first name, the date on which you arrived in the United States. Focus on the facts and events that will get your main idea across to the writer.

Some possibilities for a controlling idea might be the following:

- I have led a sheltered life so far.
- My life has always been cosmopolitan.
- I have always been a lonely person.
- I am an achiever; nothing can stand in my way.
- I am running hard through life, but I don't know where I'm going.
- I am a nomad.

Chapter 2

Thesis and Supporting Details

As we discussed in Chapter 1, a successful essay must have a main idea to which all its parts are related. The main idea is called the thesis and the related parts are the details that support it, the details that the writer uses to convince the reader of the idea expressed in the theme.

Thesis

The thesis or main idea cannot be fully expressed in a word or a phrase. An idea can only be fully expressed in a complete sentence. Thus, the writer should always be able to express the thesis of his essay in one sentence. This sentence may or may not appear in the essay itself. Whether it does or not, however, the idea should be clear from the supporting details included in the essay.

We might illustrate this with the following passage written by the professional writer Willie Morris. In this passage, Morris reports on something he witnessed while riding a train from New York City home to the suburbs. At one point in the journey, the train is "elevated"—that is, lifted several feet above street level. This elevated train passes by the windows of tenements (run-down apartment buildings) in some of the poorer sections of New York—Harlem and the South Bronx. The writer looks first at the windows of the train and the apartments, and then, as the train slows down, his attention is drawn to a terrible scene on the train tracks opposite him. Here is what the writer witnesses:

> One afternoon in late August as the summer's sun streamed into the car and made little jumping shadows on the windows, I sat gazing out at the tenement[1] dwellers, who were themselves looking out of their windows from the gray crumbling buildings along the tracks of upper Manhattan. As we crossed into the Bronx, the train unexpectedly slowed down for a few miles. Suddenly from out of my window I saw a large crowd near the tracks, held back by two policemen. Then, on the other side from my window, I saw a sight I would never be able to forget: a little boy almost severed[2] in halves, lying at an incredible angle near the track. The ground was covered with blood, and the boy's eyes were opened wide, strained and disbelieving in his sudden oblivion.[3] A policeman stood next to him, his arms folded, staring straight ahead at the windows of our train. In the orange glow of the late afternoon the policeman, the crowd, the corpse of the boy were for a brief moment immobile, motionless, a small tableau[4] to violence and death in the city. Behind me, in the next row of seats, there was a game of bridge.[5] I heard one of the four men say as he looked out at the sight, "God, that's horrible." Another said, in a whisper, "Terrible, terrible." There was a momentary silence, punctuated only by the clicking of the wheels on the track. Then, after the pause, I heard the first man say: "Two hearts."[6,7]

The writer describes the scene in some detail, but he does not describe it for its own sake. The writer is interested in telling us this story because it illustrates an idea: the idea is the writer's thesis. The thesis is not stated in the essay; it must be *inferred*—understood by the reader from the details provided by the writer. Can you infer the writer's thesis? We might express it in any of several ways:
- The bad experiences of others are not always real to one viewing them from the outside.
- People may not be deeply affected by the bad experiences of other people.
- Life goes on despite the tragedies of others.

The thesis is not stated outright, but only *implied*—that is, it is suggested by the details the writer supplies. When the writer includes no sentence stating the thesis directly, we say that the thesis is *implicit*. When the writer includes a sentence that states his thesis outright, we say that it is *explicit*. The writer can choose to make his thesis either implicit or explicit, but in either case he must be certain that it will be clear to his reader.

[1] substandard apartment house
[2] cut through
[3] forgetfulness; unconsciousness
[4] picture
[5] card game
[6] bid in bridge game
[7] Excerpted from Willie Morris, *North Toward Home* (Oxford, MS: Yoknapatawpha Press, 1967), p. 423.

Supporting Details

The thesis is made clear to the reader by the supporting details. In the essay above, the writer needs details to support two ideas: first, that a terrible tragedy has occurred; second, that those who witness it are not deeply affected by the tragedy. To support the first idea, the writer gives many details of the dead body of the boy who has been hit by the train: there is blood all over; the body is bent at an angle the human body cannot normally take; his eyes are wide open, yet can see nothing. All this adds up to a scene of extreme horror and makes the tragedy that has occurred more intense. To show that those witnessing the tragedy are not deeply affected, the writer finishes his story by turning his attention from the terrible scene to the response of others inside the train. For a moment, these witnesses look up from their card game and express their shock at the horrible view outside the train. Then, after a short pause, they return to their game, forgetting the dead boy on the tracks.

These details are key in convincing the reader of the thesis that people may not be deeply affected by the tragedies of others. But many other details in the essay—details which may seem at first to be unrelated to the theme—help to support the writer's thesis. The essay is full of windows, and windows here are like barriers: they allow us to look through them and see others' tragedies, but they prevent us from being touched deeply by those tragedies. The writer, as he rides along the elevated track, looks through his window into the windows of tenements, the run-down homes of the poor. The people in the tenements, in turn, look through their windows at the windows of the train. Eyes are all gazing, staring, but no one is doing, reaching out for involvement. It is not even clear that the eyes that are staring are really focusing on or seeing what they are staring at. One policeman, for example, stares *blankly* at the windows of the train. And even the dead boy is staring in *oblivion*—that is, without consciousness of what it is he is staring at.

There are other barriers to people's involvement with one another as well. One policeman holds the crowd back, away from the dead boy. Another policeman stands with his own arms folded, as if holding himself back from greater involvement. And the idea that life goes on despite others' tragedies is supported several times by the continued forward motion of the train. Even as it passes the body of the boy, the train slows down, but it never fully stops; and even in the "moment of silence," the "click-click" of the wheels turning on the tracks continues.

Thus we see how the writer has constructed a unified essay, one in which the details are clearly related to a central theme. We might also note that these details are all *concrete*—that is, details the reader can see or hear—can experience physically in his imagination. We will discuss concreteness more fully in Chapter 16. Here it will be enough to get an idea of the difference between the concrete and the *abstract*. Concrete details are what the reader can perceive with his five physical senses—details he can see, hear, touch, taste, or smell. The blood on the boy's shirt and on the tracks, the windows, the folded arms of the policeman, the sound of the train wheels and the "sound" of silence—all these the reader perceives in a physical way. Indeed, in the entire paragraph, there is only one phrase that is not concrete, but rather an abstract idea: "violence and death in the big city." Of course, we could make *violence* concrete, by imagining someone shooting someone, for instance, or by kicking over a chair (as I used to do in my classes to show just how concrete a term like *violence* might be made). But the word *violence* itself is abstract, an idea rather than a picture.

A successful essay will not overuse abstract terms, but will use concrete details to make its ideas clear. This is because concrete details are easier for a reader to see or hear or feel—to appreciate. Thus, a successful essay will include as many concrete details as necessary to support its thesis, but will omit any details that do not support its theme.

Each of the two paragraphs below is a poorly written version of the essay we have just been analyzing. Each suffers from a different kind of error. See if you can figure out what the problem is in each.

Version 1.

When I moved to Bridgeport recently, I began to take the commuter train to New York every day to go to my office on Sixth Avenue. On the train I always sit by the window because I don't like to read on moving vehicles (it gives me headaches) and it is boring to look around the car. There is a lot to see on the trip, especially when the train passes through Harlem and the South Bronx. It goes right next to the windows of buildings. I can see people talking, and doing laundry, and many other things. On August 24th of this year, after the train had crossed over the river, the train slowed down to about ten miles per hour from about the bridge to Sixtieth Street in the Bronx. I didn't know why it had stopped. I thought maybe it was a power failure. Then I saw two policemen, one tall and one somewhat shorter, holding back about fifteen people. Near them, a little boy of about eight years of age and dressed in a white tee-shirt and blue jeans was on the track, his body bent at a 250-degree angle or so. There was an old policeman near him. Four men who had been playing bridge since we had left Penn Station were sitting behind me. One of the men said in a deep voice that it was horrible, and his friend whispered his agreement. Then there was silence until the first man said his next bid of two hearts. He didn't even say anything else about the boy. By the way, the man with the deep voice won that hand.

Too many irrelevant details

Version 2.

I would like to tell you about an experience that I had which gave me a new understanding about human nature. Often something that a person sees makes him perceive the nature of human beings more deeply. This happened to me during a train trip home. The train I was on passes near scenes of extreme poverty, so I had an opportunity to observe many unfamiliar events. One such event involved a tragic accident affecting a youngster. My observations made me realize that when the train passed such an event, most of the passengers remained unaffected and unresponsive. Although the evidence of the tragedy was right before us, people continued their usual activities. Indeed, observation can lead to understanding.

Too Abstract

Too few details

As you have probably realized, Version 1 is unsuccessful because it includes many irrelevant details—details, that is, that do not support the thesis. These details are not only unhelpful, they are actually confusing to the reader. The reader begins to wonder just what the thesis is. Even the writer seems confused, continuing beyond the effective final detail of the good version, the players' returning to their card game, to add another irrelevant detail that spoils the effect entirely. The writer here has misunderstood his purpose. He has chosen to report everything that happened instead of selecting only the details that support his thesis.

In Version 2, the writer has provided almost no details and, thus, almost no support. This version is almost completely abstract. Since there are no supporting details to convince the reader of the thesis, the writer feels he has to repeat the theme over and over again in different abstract terms. However, no matter how often he repeats the abstract idea, without the concrete supporting details of the original essay, his essay will continue to be unconvincing, ineffective, and thus, unsuccessful.

Summary

We can see, therefore, that to be successful an essay must have sufficient supporting concrete details to convince the reader of its thesis, but no irrelevant details that might confuse or bore the reader.

Exercises

For Consideration

Exercise 1. In the following paragraphs, the thesis is expressed in the first sentence (theme sentence). Underline all details that do not support the theme of that paragraph.

A.   The *tortilla*, a flat cake made of ground corn or wheat, is the basis of a great variety of Mexican dishes. Indeed, tortilla dishes could provide almost a menu in themselves. There are dishes made of fried tortillas stuffed with a variety of fillings. These are delicious, but rather high in calories. There are tortillas dipped in sauce, filled and baked with more sauce and toppings. There are soups with a tortilla garnish and tortilla appetizers layered with beans and cheese. And, of course, there are plain, fresh tortillas served like bread to be dipped in sauce and eaten with meals or as a snack. As they contain calcium and other minerals and vitamins, tortillas are very nutritious.

B.   The international student population in U.S. colleges and universities is large and growing. In 1984–85, 342,113 foreign students were reported to be attending college in the United States, a .09 percent increase over the previous academic year. Moreover, a report by the American Council on Education outlined in the *Chronicle of Higher Education* predicted that by 1990 there could be over a million foreign college students in the United States. Foreign students enroll mainly in certain technical fields: engineering, business, mathematics, and computer science. Indeed, at some small schools, foreign students constitute a major percentage of the entire student body.

C.   One of the things I like best about living in a dorm is the freedom it gives me. I enjoy the freedom of being able to arrange my room as I want to. I enjoy being able to come and go as I like. Rooming at the dorm costs about $2500 per semester—about the same as a small apartment off campus would cost in this area.

D.   The thing I dislike most about living in a dorm is the lack of privacy I *Rewrite* feel. My roommate spends nearly all her time in the dorm, so I have no *this* time alone in our room. She uses my cosmetics and asks to wear my clothes: *Paragraph* there is nowhere to hide something I want to keep for myself. She has lots of things of her own. Her father must be wealthy, for she has a closet full of clothes, a big collection of jewelry, a TV, and a radio. At night, when I try to sleep, her radio invades my dreams.

E.   How strange everything at the airport was! I arrived at the airport after a twelve-hour journey. I was on my way to the university where I would be studying for the next four years. The faces around me didn't look like the faces at home. The people's dress and manners were different, too. The air was filled with a strange new sound—a language which I had studied, but had never heard spoken like this before. Everything was so strange that I was almost not surprised when, as I opened my bag for the custom's officer, its contents looked unfamiliar to me. Then I realized, I had picked up the wrong suit case!

Exercise 2.   What is the thesis of the following student essay? Is it explicit or implicit? What details does the writer use to support the thesis? Are there any irrelevant details the writer should have omitted? Might the writer have included other details to make the theme stronger?

The Broken Pickle Jar

Oh no! I could recognize the smell which was spreading through the airport. Someone's mango pickle jar must have broken open in the airplane. Who else would be bringing mango pickles to the United States? But even as I looked around at the strange faces about me, I knew the mango pickles had to be mine, the ones my mother had packed back in Fiji.

A yellow-stained box, crushed on one side, came down the luggage ramp, making the smell of spices even stronger. I looked hopefully for something that might tell me it was not mine, but as I went closer to the box, I knew it was. Everyone was looking at that box, and I was embarrassed to pick it off the ramp. On the other hand, I was tempted by the smell to take the pickles out right then and eat them. I was already nervous on my first day in the United States, and the broken pickle jar was making me even more nervous. Embarrassed, I picked up the wet package with the rest of my luggage and walked toward the customs office.

There were not many people going through customs at 2 o'clock in the morning, so I got my things checked quickly. The customs officer, about to check my luggage, said with a smile: "Is that the smell of mango pickles?" I was surprised, but glad that someone else here knew about mango pickles. Then I realized that everyone had to go through customs and possibly the officer had seen, even smelled, mango pickles before. I opened the stained box and saw that all the other things in it were soaked with yellow oil—even my mathematics notes, pages of calculus and trigonometry diagrams turned bright yellow.

Now, six months later, I look at my mathematics notes, and the smell is still there. And I laugh at a broken jar of mango pickles which, in my first moments in this new country, had filled me with such surprise and fear.

For Composition

Exercise 3. Follow the steps below to outline and revise your autobiographical essay (see Chapter 1, Exercise 5).

Step 1:   Make a list of all the facts and events you included in your autobiographical essay.

Step 2:   Write the theme (main idea) of the essay in one sentence.

Step 3:   Eliminate any items from your list of autobiographical facts and events that cannot be used to support your thesis.

Step 4:   Revise your autobiographical essay using the materials assembled in Steps 1–3.

Exercise 4. Make an informal "outline" for an essay about your first day in the United States by following the steps listed below.

Step 1:   Write one sentence to express how you felt on your first day in the United States. Express *one* feeling only: either I *was excited* or I *was confused* or I *was homesick* or I *was lonely* or I *was tired*—not all five! This sentence will be your thesis.

Step 2:   List all the events of that first day that either made you feel this way or showed that you felt this way. This is your list of possible supporting details.

Exercise 5. Write a three- to five-paragraph essay about your first day in the United States, using the materials assembled in Exercise 4. Add any details that will help support your theme. Eliminate details that do not support it. Above all, be sure your theme is clear to your reader throughout your essay.

Part Two

Patterns
for
Essays

Chapter 3

Narration

Narration is probably the most familiar of the patterns for essays. Narration is the recounting of a series of events with a beginning, a middle, and an end. It is what most of us probably think of when we talk about writing. Narration is storytelling, familiar to us from childhood through listening, reading, watching movies and TV. It is the pattern we use to inform someone who asks us, "What happened?" It is the pattern of history.

Yet, though narration is familiar, it is not without difficulties for the writer. When a writer recounts a series of events, he must make choices about which events to include. He must decide how far back to begin and how far forward to continue and just what details to include along the way. If he includes too much, his essay will probably be tedious to read and his thesis may be lost in irrelevant details. If he includes too little, he may fail to make his thesis clear or convincing.

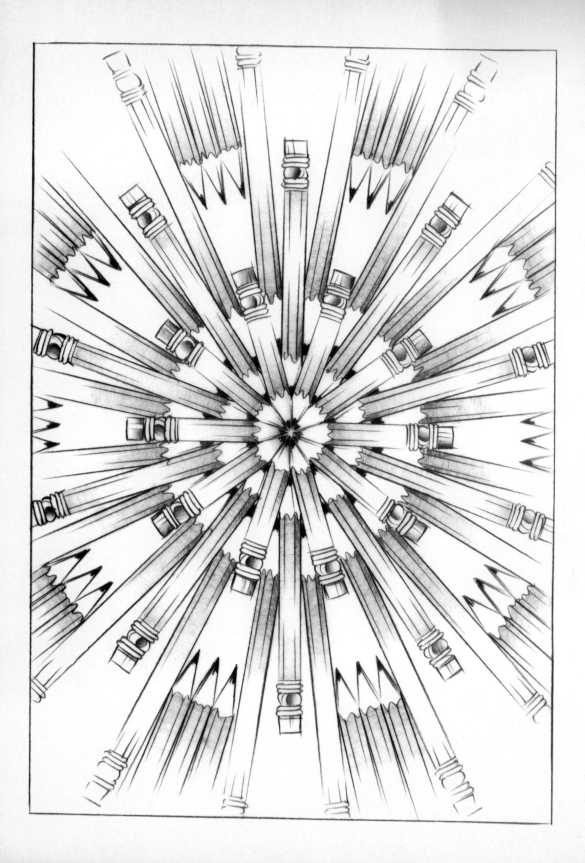

Selecting Narrative Details

Probably all of us have had the experience of listening to someone tell us a story in such detail that we became bored and wished he would come to the point. And we may also have struggled to understand the story that left so much out that we had to keep asking the storyteller for missing details. Probably we have tried to be polite and let such speakers go on with their stories although we lost interest. A reader does not have to be polite, and he cannot stop the writer to ask him a question. If you bore the reader or leave important questions unanswered, he may simply stop reading.

We have already seen examples of successful and unsuccessful narration. In Chapter 1, several essays narrate the events of a student's first day in the United States and others narrate briefly the events of a student's life (autobiography) before arriving in the United States. In Chapter 2, a writer narrates events he witnessed while riding a commuter train. In each case, the successful narration selects and shapes details to make a point. The writer on the train does not need to tell us how many years ago he started riding the train or at what station his office is located. He does not need to tell us who wins the game of cards after the men start playing again. He does not need to tell us how the accident that killed the boy occurred. To make his point, he must tell the reader only that a boy has been horribly killed and that life continues for the onlookers: the train keeps moving, the card players return to their game.

In narration the writer must select from all the details, large and small, that actually occurred in the course of an event only those that are essential to making his point convincingly. This is especially important for the writer to remember when narrating a personal experience, something that happened to her or to someone she knows. Probably she will know a great many details about the event. But she does not need to tell the reader everything. She must omit details that are not relevant. If she wishes, and if her essay does not deal with the sort of material for which factual accuracy is demanded, but only with personal experience, she might even add or change details to make her thesis clearer. The reader of a personal essay is not looking for *literal* accuracy, but for *literary* accuracy. It generally does not matter to the reader whether or not all the details are true. But it does matter that they seem true and are relevant to the thesis.

The following narration was written by a student in response to an assignment to recount a personal experience that led him to an insight—a realization about himself, others, or life in general. This student writer, probably inspired by the Willie Morris passage discussed in Chapter 2, remembered an incident that occurred on his first train ride in the United States.

A Revealing Train Ride

Before I came to the United States, I had often heard that Americans were uncaring people—that they wouldn't help a stranger in trouble. As the crowds pushed past me on my first day in New York, I was convinced that my friends had been right.

That night I took the train from New York to Bridgeport. After each stop, a trainman passed down the aisle without a word to anyone, punching the tickets of new passengers. On one such trip, he stopped by a seat near mine. The woman who had just gotten on didn't have a ticket. The trainman asked her for the fare, but she had no money either.

The trainman bent down to her and asked if there was anything wrong. The woman started to cry. She told the trainman that she and her husband had had a fight and that she was going to her parents' house in New Haven.

The trainman tried to calm the woman. He told her everything would be all right. Then he reached into his own pocket and paid her fare. An old couple in a nearby row of seats came over to sit beside the woman. The old woman offered her a handkerchief and a thermos of coffee. The old man told her that he and his wife had fought the same way once. "In a week you won't remember it happened," he assured her. Soon the trainman was telling jokes and the young woman was laughing.

When things were quiet, I sat back and looked out the window at this new, strange land. Perhaps I had better wait and see before judging the Americans, I thought.

This is a brief essay, only about 250 words. But the writer has made his point clearly and powerfully. What is the thesis of this essay? It is suggested in the final sentence. We can generalize it thus: a person should wait before judging the people of a country that is new to him or her. What are the incidents that bring this insight to the writer? After deciding from his experience among the pushing crowds in New York that Americans are "uncaring people," he sees an example of several Americans coming to the aid of a stranger. Surely, there were other events that occurred during this experience. The writer could have told us what it felt like to buy his first train ticket, how much it cost, the trouble he had finding the station, what the train looked like. But he wisely omits these details and focuses only on those that support his thesis.

Arranging Narrative Details

After the writer has selected the details she needs to support her thesis, she faces another challenge. She must arrange the details as effectively as possible. In narration, the writer will often proceed in chronological order—that is, according to the natural order of events in time: earliest events at the beginning of the essay, last event at the end. But occasionally a writer will use a different arrangement, starting in the middle of events and looking back into the past. In this arrangement, the earliest events may appear somewhere in the middle of the essay (see, for example, Exercise 2B at the end of this chapter). Whichever order she chooses, the writer must keep the time scheme clear enough in her essay so that the reader will not be confused.

Summary

Narration is the recounting of a series of events with a beginning, a middle, and an end. Like any essay, a narrative must have a thesis and supporting details. The writer must include in his narrative only those events that support his or her thesis. In addition, the writer must arrange the events in an effective order, which may or may not be chronological.

Exercises

For Consideration

Exercise 1. Read the following essay. What is its thesis? List the details that support the thesis. Are they sufficient? Has the writer included any details that are irrelevant? How does the essay compare to "A Revealing Train Ride" in terms of convincing the reader of the thesis? Explain.

Journey by Car

After we had finished our classes, my boyfriend, another friend, and I decided that it would be a good idea to go to some other place far away from our university. Thus, we could rest, see other places and have a good time, all at the same time. *Thesis*

So we went to a rent-a-car agency and rented a car—not too big, not too small—and started going towards Washington, D.C.

Our first plans were to go to California, but thinking it over very carefully, we agreed that it would be too long to drive and too expensive because of the cost of the fuel and hotels.

Therefore, we remade our plans and chose Colorado Rocky Mountains National Park as our final destination. We went all across the southern part of the country, through Maryland, Virginia, North Carolina, Tennessee, etc., as far as Colorado, and came back all across the northern part: Chicago, Cincinnati, Indianapolis, Niagara Falls, etc.

It was a wonderful trip. The places I liked most were Washington, D.C., and all the cities in Colorado. Sincerely, Colorado is a marvelous state. It has the most fascinating places and people. Coloradans are not the indifferent people we have been used to seeing all around here, the area near New York City. On the contrary, they are very cordial and attentive even to the smallest details, for example, in asking how one's hamburger is or whether one wants a little more coffee in a restaurant.

Their considerateness changed my opinion about the indifference of the American people. Now I know by my own experience that it is the same as in any country; one finds different kinds of people in different kinds of places.

[handwritten margin notes: Compare with "A Revealing Train Ride." The Point being made. The thesis & Irrelevant details]

Exercise 2. The essays that follow are two versions—a first draft and a revision—of a student's response to the assignment to write about a personal experience that led to an insight. Read both versions. Then, for each version of the essay, list all the details mentioned by the writer in the order in which he has included them. Finally, answer the following questions:

1. Does the first version of the essay have a clear thesis? Is it implicit or explicit? Can you write it in a single sentence?

2. What details in your list for Version A support the thesis? Are they sufficient?

3. What details seem irrelevant?

4. Do there seem to be any gaps (missing events) in the narrative (Version A)? What events need to be included to fill these gaps?

5. The thesis of Version B is implicit. Try to state it in one sentence. Does the writer make it sufficiently clear? Should he have stated it explicitly in the essay? Where? How would an explicit theme affect the essay as a whole?

6. What details of Version A has the writer eliminated from Version B of his essay? Do any irrelevant details remain in Version B? List them.

7. Has the writer added details to Version B that help support his thesis? What are they?

8. The writer uses the following details in both versions of his essay:
   - the "l" for learner
   - the character of the white Fiat being suited to his mother
   - the examiner's sitting beside the writer in the second part of the exam.

   In which essay are these details used more effectively? Explain.

9. The events in Version A are ordered chronologically. In Version B, the writer starts with an event in the middle and looks back to earlier events before proceeding to the end. Which order seems more effective for this narrative? Why?

Version A

The Traffic License

One day last winter, I decided to learn how to drive a car. I had spare time and my mother was willing to give me lessons.

There were two parts to obtaining a traffic license from the Ministry of Transportation. The first step was to pass a written examination concerning the traffic rules from an officially recognized traffic school.

The first class was held on the day I registered, in the late afternoon. To my surprise, I met my best friend in the classroom; but the majority were elderly people. It was a special class in the sense that the teacher was also the translator. The textbook was published in French, as the country we were living in was French-speaking. But the students were mostly English-speaking people from multinational companies.

The course at the school lasted three months. We learned the traffic rules on the blackboard from pictures and from multiple-choice questions which were tried on us.

Meanwhile, I was preoccupied with the gears and the steering wheel on the weekends, with my mother on the next seat. The learning process depended completely on the patience of me and my mother. The place was about a ten-minute drive from our apartment. It was a supermarket parking lot. I cut out the letter "l" for learner and placed it on the back window of the car.

I believe that every car has a character of its own with relation to its owner. In this case, the owner was my mother and the car was a white Fiat 126. It was an ideal car for a beginner: compact and fuel efficient.

On rainy days, I drove in circles, around sharp corners. I practiced parking forwards and backwards. I learned to use the brake at determined markers. I familiarized myself with the dashboard and the seat-belts. I learned how to use the clutch when changing gears.

Although my mother always instructed me correctly, we argued a lot. I realize now that I made her nervous for nothing very often.

We went to the Ministry of Transportation for an appointment for the driving test. I was told that there were two steps in the traffic test: the first in a designated area filled with traffic signs and white lines that the driver must follow, the second on city roads with an instructor pointing the directions.

Naturally, on the examination date, I was showing signs of nervousness. For the first part, I was alone in the car. While the car was at a standstill, the officer gave orders constantly about the dashboard. Then I parked backwards and passed through a very narrow lane.

Everything went fine. Once my mother and the officer were in the car, an extra mirror was put up for the back view and no communication was permitted except by the officer. All the roads were marked with traffic signs. There were many intersections. I drove very carefully and smoothly while the officer marked his exam book. This process continued until I was instructed to make a right turn. I slowed down to first, looked around, put on my indicator, and drove away. The officer sighed and shook his head.

After some more driving we came to a stop outside the Ministry. With my mother I waited quite a while in front of the desk in the waiting room. Then the officer appeared and told me explicitly that I had failed. It was quite a shock and a surprise for both my mother and me. The expression on our faces was unforgettable.

I felt quite weak for a while, but then my anger rose up against the injustice. It was a day in one of these authoritarian places where anxieties run high. My mother was most affected. We drove away talking intermittently.

Version B   ## The Traffic License

It was the day of the appointment for my driving test at the Ministry of Transportation. Unlike my mother, who was moving swiftly around the house, I sat at the table feeling weak. My throat was squeezing and I had difficulty in swallowing my breakfast.

As I sat silently, I looked back on the long three months of weekend practice sessions with my mother. Every Sunday she and I drove to an empty parking lot and practiced driving in circles, turning sharp corners, using the brake at a determined spot, parking. We argued and argued about everything. Sometimes I felt that she would never let me forget that big white "l" for learner that I'd had to cut out and put on the back window. She began to remind me of her car—a white Fiat—compact, tough, and efficient. It took all my patience to get me through those weekend sessions. To myself, I kept saying I would show her at last—just wait for the exam.

My mother drove me to the Ministry of Transportation for the exam. I met with the examiner on the grounds. He was about my mother's age, rather grim looking, his hair combed backwards and held with grease. He wore a black raincoat. In his hand was a little notebook.

For the first stage of the test, I was left alone in the car. I followed the examiner's instructions to park, signal and turn, pass through a narrow passage. During the second stage of the examination, the examiner sat next to me while my mother sat in the back seat. This time, instead of hearing my mother's voice nagging me about my mistakes, I heard the examiner ticking away at his notebook, inhaling deeply. The sweat from my hands made the steering wheel slippery. I began to lose my concentration. I felt weak and dizzy.

I continued driving until we reached the Ministry again. Then the instructor told me that I had failed the test. I stood still for a moment. Then I nodded. In confusion, I wanted to hide my sadness with a smile. But the examiner's black coat, his little book, and the severe lines of the Ministry compelled me to embrace my mother like a child.

Exercise 3. In the three essays that follow, students have narrated events that happened to them in their first days at an American college.

    a.   Do the essays present clear theses? State the thesis of each essay in a complete sentence.

    b.   Are there sufficient relevant details to support the thesis? Are there any irrelevant details that should be deleted? Can you think of any detail the writer might have added to strengthen the thesis?

    c.   Is the arrangement of details logical and orderly? Do you notice any gaps in the sequence of events that need to be filled?

A Lesson in Another Culture

A.

One day, while I was talking with my new American friends in my dorm room, some old friends from my country, Algeria, arrived for a visit. I got up to greet them. We shook hands and then kissed each other on the cheek. In my culture, this is the proper way to greet an old friend that one hasn't seen in a long time.

As we started kissing each other, my American friends stared at us and began to giggle. They seemed shocked at what we did. Probably they had never had a chance to see two males kissing each other. Maybe they wondered about our relationship. I did not mind their laughter. I felt sorry for them because they had never had a chance to experience another culture. For them, it seemed, the only culture was American culture.

A few weeks later, in order to see their reactions, I asked a friend from my country to kiss me on the cheek when he came to the dorm. This time there was no reaction from my American friends. They had learned a lesson about another culture.

Culture Shock

B.

I sat down in my seat, fastened the seat belt, and the plane took off. Fear of the unknown made me wonder what to expect of the people I would meet when the plane landed. I knew only one thing for sure: they would speak another language.

After landing, I took a taxi from the airport to my school. I noticed the driver of the taxi was sitting in the passenger's seat. But then all the drivers around me were doing the same thing—and they were driving on the wrong side of the road! It felt as if I was looking at the road through a mirror.

I entered the housing office, where a nice young man received me politely. "Hi, what's your name?" he asked—or at least, that is how I understood it. "Hani," I answered. I held out my hand to shake his; he ignored the gesture and asked me to have a seat, then directed me to my room. I wondered whether people in the United States shook hands or not—or whether it was just this young man who was different.

In my room I put my suit on, making sure I looked neat before going to dinner, as one always does in my country. The moment I entered the dining hall, it seemed all the people turned to stare at me. Some were smiling and some were laughing. Others just looked and returned to their dinner. It took me a while to realize what they were staring at: it was my suit. I was the only one in the hall in formal dress. Everyone else was wearing jeans and sport clothes. I was embarrassed. My hand began to tremble causing my tray to fall, making me even more embarrassed. I rushed to my room and then to the bathroom to wash up. The bathroom was fairly long with twelve round shower stalls. While I was taking off my clothes, I saw there were a couple of girls in the next stall. I almost fell down! In my country one would never see girls and boys taking showers in the same room. But then, when I think about it—really think about it—I'm not in my country, am I?!?

C.

From Pessimism to Optimism

In my first days of classes and meeting my roommate at the university, I felt pessimistic about building friendships with American students. I wished to practice my English as well as to learn something about American students' lives and beliefs. But, especially when I met my roommate for the first time and, after saying "hi," he turned over on his bed and went to sleep, I felt disappointed. For many days we didn't say anything to each other except "hello" or "see you later." Neither could I seem to make any friends in my classes.

It was only last week that things began to change. My roommate started a conversation and we found out we had some common interests. He invited me to use anything he had. A few days later we played soccer and, more recently, Ping-Pong. Besides, by then I had another friend in one of my classes. We met in communications class, which was appropriate, because he likes to talk. We've had many long conversations and are getting to know one another. At last, I'm becoming more optimistic about having friends among American students.

Exercise 4. Make an informal "outline" (see page 99) of one of the essays in Exercise 3 by writing the thesis of the essay in one sentence and listing all the events the writer mentions, whether or not they support the theme. Using your "outline," respond again to the questions asked by Exercise 3 for the essay you have chosen.

For Composition

Exercise 5. Write a brief essay relating an important event in the history of your country. Choose a single event of narrow scope—an event that occurred over a period of a few hours or days and that can be covered adequately in three to five paragraphs.

Decide on your theme before you start writing. What does the event express about your country, government, or people? What is its meaning? In writing your essay, focus on only the details that support your thesis.

Exercise 6. Follow the steps below.

Step 1: Make a list of everything you can remember happening to you on your first day at the university.

Step 2: Write in one sentence (theme) how you felt on that day; limit yourself to *one* feeling.

Step 3: Eliminate from your list all the events that do not support your thesis. Add any events that will help support the thesis.

Exercise 7. Using the materials assembled in Exercise 6, write a three- or four-paragraph essay about your first day at the university.

Exercise 8. Write a three- to five-paragraph essay relating an experience that happened to you that led you to an insight—a realization about yourself, another person or persons, or life in general. Your insight will be your thesis; the details of the experience will be the support for the thesis.

Whether or not your thesis is expressed in your essay, write the thesis in one sentence separate from the essay itself.

Chapter 4

Description

Narration reports a series of events. Description tells about an object. Whereas narration tells what happens over time, in description, time generally stands still. We look at an object—a person, place, or thing—as if it were frozen in time.

Yet description poses the same basic problem as narration for the writer. In writing a descriptive essay, the writer must select details to support a thesis. Of course, there might be instances in which one would want to give a complete, almost photographic description of something or someone, without omitting a detail (in describing a thief who just robbed you, for instance). But generally a description will focus on certain details in order to make a special point.

Selecting Descriptive Details

Let's look at this poem by the English poet W. H. Auden. Although its form and manner of expression are poetic, its message could easily be written in essay form.

Musée des Beaux Arts

About suffering they were never wrong,
The Old Masters: how well they understood
Its human position; how it takes place
While someone else is eating or opening a window or just
     walking dully along.
How, when the aged are reverently,[1] passionately waiting
For the miraculous birth,[2] there always must be
Children who did not specially want it to happen, skating
On a pond at the edge of the wood:
They never forgot
That even the dreadful martyrdom[3] must run its course
Anyhow in a corner, some untidy spot
Where the dogs go on with their doggy life and the
     torturer's[4] horse
Scratches its innocent behind on a tree.

In Brueghel's *Icarus*, for instance: how everything turns away
Quite leisurely from the disaster; the ploughman may
Have heard the splash, the forsaken[5] cry,
But for him it was not an important failure; the sun shone
As it had to on the white legs disappearing into the green
Water; and the expensive delicate ship, that must have seen
Something amazing, a boy falling out of the sky,
Had somewhere to get to and sailed calmly on.

The second part of this poem is a description. It describes a painting entitled *Icarus* (actually, *The Fall of Icarus*) that hangs in the Musées Royaux des Beaux Arts, an art museum in Brussels. The painting depicts a scene from a well-known Greek myth: the inventor Daedalus has fashioned wings of wax and feathers. Wearing a pair of these wings, his son Icarus flies too near the sun; the wax melts, and Icarus falls into the sea and is drowned.

Even without knowing the painting, we can get some idea of it from the poet's description. Someone has fallen into the sea and there is evidence of the fall in the "splash" and in the "white legs disappearing into the green water." The sun is shining on the legs and there is a ship sailing by. Looking at the painting (see Figure 4-1), we can see the elements that the poet has described: the tiny legs disappearing beneath the great expanse of sea, the "expensive delicate ship" sailing by, the ploughman turning away from the scene of the accident, the sun.

The thesis of the poem is expressed explicitly in the first four lines of the poem. We can express it more simply in our own words:

---

[1] respectfully
[2] the Messiah; a birth considered a supernatural gift of God
[3] giving one's life for a cause
[4] one who gives pain to punish
[5] abandoned; forgotten

Figure 4-1 Brueghel's *The Fall of Icarus*

As the great painters realized, life goes on despite others' tragedies;

or

People are not affected by the tragedies of others.

The poet, then, is expressing the same theme with his description that essayist Willie Morris expressed in his narrative about the commuter train. In the description, the white legs and the splash take the place of the bloodied body of the boy on the tracks. Instead of witnesses expressing horror and then returning to a card game as in the narration, we have the sun continuing to shine and a ship sailing "calmly on."

Of course, there are many differences between these writings, but one major difference is that in Morris's narration, events occur one after another, over time, while in Auden's poem, a description, the object being described, a painting, is timeless. The narrative events happen. The painting simply is. We should note that both pieces of writing include elements of narration and description. In the commuter train passage, the sights on the track form a "tableau"—a picture—for the writer, whereas in "Musée des Beaux Arts," the painting is a depiction of a narrative tale, a myth in which a man falls from the sky in trying to fly too near the sun.

Avoiding Irrelevant and Abstract Detail

The writer's job is much the same in writing description as in writing narration. He must select details, omitting any that do not support his thesis, selecting only those he needs to make his point. We can see how Auden has done this, by looking more closely at the painting he describes in his poem (see Figure 4-1). Truly, the theme of life going on is present in the painting, as Auden says. The white legs of Icarus are there in the painting. But they are tiny. Indeed, *The Fall of Icarus* is an accurate title for the painting, for Icarus (or his lower half) occupies only a tiny portion of the large canvas. Auden might have mentioned this fact, but he did not need to. He has made his point with the details of the ship's sailing on and the sun's shining "as it had to." (The sun, in fact, is somewhat more important in Auden's poem than it is in Brueghel's painting, where it is setting on the horizon and hardly prominent.)

There is a good deal more in Brueghel's *Icarus*. There are three large human figures, a ploughman, a shepherd, and a fisherman, all going on with their tasks, as well as a flock of sheep, a dog, and a bird perched on a branch. And there is much "scenery"—hills, trees, buildings, other ships. Auden included none of this. He did not need to. He makes his point effectively because he omits all these irrelevant details.

Thus, just as with narration, with description the writer must avoid including too much detail or any irrelevant detail. Yet he must also be sure to include enough relevant, concrete detail to support his thesis. To see just how well the poet has done his job here, let us look at two versions of the Auden description that fail to accomplish these goals.

Version A

That human suffering occurs while others are engaging in their normal activities is quite clear in Brueghel's painting *Icarus*. In this painting, everything turns from the main event with no response. Despite possible awareness of the occurrence, workmen are involved in their usual activities because for them the event is of little significance. Nature is unchanged by the experience of a single being, however unfortunate. And other witnesses to the extraordinary phenomenon similarly comply with their ordinary responsibilities with no apparent reaction to the main character of the design.

Here, of course, there is almost no concrete detail. Without having seen the painting, the reader would be unaware even that it depicts a boy's drowning. Since the reader sees nothing, he remains completely unaffected. This is hardly a description at all.

Version B

Brueghel's *Icarus* is an oil panel, 24¾″ × 35½″, which hangs in the Musées Royaux des Beaux Arts, Brussels. Icarus himself—or rather, the lower part of his body, which is still visible above the water—occupies a small portion of the canvas, near the lower-right corner. The rest of the canvas is occupied with a sea-side landscape on which a ploughman pushes his plough, a shepherd and his dog tend a flock of black and white sheep, and a fisherman fishes. There are several ships on the water, sailing toward the setting sun, away from the Icarus figure. The sky is pale, the water a deeper shade lined here and there with the white of gentle waves. There are several rocky promontories reaching up into the sky; some are dotted with tiny, pale buildings. There are several trees in the foreground. On the branch of one of them a large bird is perched.

This might serve for a museum catalogue, but it is hardly successful as an essay. The writer has no theme at all. He simply lists detail after detail without trying to make any point.

Avoiding Vague Modifiers

Finally, with description there is one other error that a writer may commit. This is the frequent use of vague qualifiers—adjectives such as *good, nice, interesting, pretty, beautiful, terrific*. These qualifiers do not describe specifically enough to give the reader a picture of an object. The student writer should take care not to write a description that sounds like the following:

Version C

Brueghel's *Icarus* is a beautiful painting. There are many interesting details on a lovely canvas: a gorgeous ship sailing on a splendid sea, a beautiful sun, a nice farmer. There is, however, one awful feature: a boy is in a terrible situation and there isn't much happening to change that. It's really horrible.

If a writer's thesis is that a certain object is beautiful, he must make his reader appreciate its beauty by showing it clearly. The "gorgeous ship" in Brueghel's painting appears more beautiful when Auden describes it as "expensive" and "delicate" than it does in the vague description of Version C above. A "lovely sunset" is lovelier when described as "the last pink glow of day." If we want the reader to get the same impression as we do from an object, we must make him or her see the object as we do. A student who found St. Paul's Basilica "impressive" wisely left that word out of his description, impressing his reader instead with this concrete view:

The light from the stained glass windows pours into the darkness of the cathedral, as if the sun itself were at the end of that dark tunnel.

(For a more detailed discussion of how to avoid vague language and other word choice errors, see pages 173–78.)

Arranging Descriptive Details

Description, then, like narration, presents the writer with the problem of selecting concrete details to support a thesis. Moreover, in description as in narration, the writer must order the selected details effectively. However, the logic behind the ordering of details in description differs from the logic behind narrative order. Because description is basically timeless, the writer of description cannot rely on chronology—order in time—to arrange his details. Rather, she must arrange them spatially, deciding what part of a scene or object to describe first and in which direction to move from there.

Let us look back at Auden's description of Brueghel's painting to see how alternative arrangements of the details included might affect the reader. Here, written out in essay form, are Auden's supporting details:

> In the painting *Icarus*, Auden writes, "everything turns away . . . from the disaster." The ploughman, though he "may have heard the splash" and "cry" made by Icarus as he fell, does not consider it important to himself. The sun shines as it must "on the white legs" of the drowning boy. And the "expensive, delicate ship"—despite what it has "seen"—sails "calmly on" to its destination.

In this version, which follows Auden's ordering of details, the first focus is broad: "everything turns away. . . ." Then the focus narrows in, first on the ploughman, then on the sun, then on Icarus's legs, and finally on the ship, sailing, in our imagination, out of the picture. This order, from broad to narrow focus, starts with a sense of the whole, which helps the reader to appreciate the smaller details that follow. Turning second to the ploughman, third to the sun, and fourth to Icarus's legs gives an appropriate insignificance (in view of the poet's thesis) to the drowning boy. And the ship's sailing beyond the boundaries of painting and poem—imaginatively at least—seems a suitable detail with which to conclude the description.

Let us look now at the same details arranged in a different order:

> In the painting *Icarus*, the white legs of the drowning boy slip into the water as the sun shines as it must. The "expensive, delicate ship"—despite what it has "seen"—sails "calmly on" to its destination. "Everything," writes Auden, "turns away . . . from the disaster." The ploughman, though he "may have heard the splash" and the "cry" Icarus made as he fell, does not consider it important to himself.

Here, the reader is asked to focus first on Icarus's legs—something he would never do in looking at Brueghel's painting (indeed, in the painting it is difficult to find the legs unless one knows where to look). Next the reader's eye is drawn to the sun, and next to the ship, sailing out of the picture. Then the reader is called back to the picture to take in the broad view. And finally, he is asked to narrow his focus again, this time on the ploughman. Clearly, this order is altogether less satisfactory than that of the original.

In description, the student writer must make conscious decisions about the ordering of details. Focus can move from broad to narrow or from narrow to broad, but rarely should it skip back and forth between broad and narrow views. The most important detail might come first or it might be saved for last, but generally it should not be buried in the middle among less important details. If the writer is describing a room or building, he must decide if he is on the inside or the outside; or if he wants to describe both inside and outside, he must move in an orderly and logical way from one position to the other. Students deciding how to order descriptive details should position themselves, actually or imaginatively, in one spot in relation to the object they are describing and should ask themselves questions such as these:

- What do I notice first?
- Which way are my eyes (or ears, and so forth) drawn next?
- If I need to change position to complete my view, in which direction do I move?

If the writer chooses according to what is effective for himself, it will likely be effective for the reader.

Advantages That the Foreign Student Has in Writing Description

Despite the difficulties of selection and arrangement of details and despite the demands of descriptive vocabulary, description can be a most effective pattern in the hands of the foreign student writer. Often, students living out of their culture recall people, places, and things from their own culture in a new, sharp way and see things in their new surroundings with fresh eyes. The following essays were written by foreign students in response to an assignment to describe a person, place, or object so as to evoke—call forth—a feeling or idea. These essays each describe a place. Two of the essays are about places the students remembered from their own countries. The third is about a place discovered in the students' new life abroad. All are successful descriptions because the features described are united by a single thesis.

Example A

A Part of the Ancient City, Kyoto

To reach the temple, one ascends the gentle slope, walks on the old cobblestones. A hundred stores stand by the wayside. They sell Japanese traditional crafts: native costumes which we call kimono; handicrafts such as wood carvings, folding fans, and paper works of dolls and wallets; Oriental china. Merchants still wear the clothes of a few centuries ago and sell old-style goods busily. It seems that this area has not changed since it prospered as a market in the Middle Ages.

Leaving the shops behind, at the head of the slope, one stands before Kiyomizu Temple, which in daytime is crowded with people on pilgrimage. Since this temple was built, pilgrims from all over Japan have visited here. It was crowded every day a few centuries ago, and it still is even now.

In the night, however, it is very quiet and peaceful. The temple keeps the silence of old days. In daytime and nighttime the temple and the town retain almost the same appearance and atmosphere they had in the old days, except that the wall of the temple has cracked slightly and the color of the building has faded.

Looking beyond these little reminders, one is still able to see in Kyoto the ancient world.

Example B

Doha Souk

I was raised in Doha, the capital of Qatar, within a stone's throw of the "souk." Souk in Arabic means marketplace, and it is the heart of my city. When I used to be sent to the souk in the mornings to fetch milk for my family, I would wander through it in wonder. It seemed that this market had every possible item one could think of.

I used to love going to the souk in the morning, for at that time of day the air was still cool and clear, giving everything a sparkling, fresh look in the sun. Everybody was saying hello to each other as they made their way.

The dairy stand was in the center of the souk and to reach it I would pass by many different shops and stalls. There were pottery and kitchen goods merchants over here and a stand where sweets were sold over there. I hurried past these, but when I came to the rug merchants, I had to stop and stare. There were so many different rugs of such different textures and colors, all gorgeous and intricate, that I felt I had to touch them. Sometimes I did, and then the merchants would chase me away. Then I would pass to the leather merchants and admire their beautiful craft work. The leather crafters had designed their leathers a hundred different ways, sometimes cutting hair, sometimes leaving color on the skin, sometimes not. Their stalls were always covered by dark awnings casting a dimness over the leather, and this mixed with the rich, heavy smell of the leather to give me a shiver of mystery.

Finally, arriving at the dairy stall, I used to ask the owners for a liter of milk and then, as they went to the large wooden barrels with a huge dipper to get the milk, I would squat down and reach under the stand for the baby lamb or goat that was always there. As I stroked the unimaginably soft hair, I could smell the warm little body and the fresh milk splashing into the barrel.

As I walked home, I felt full of the smells and sights and sounds of the souk, and felt the fullness of the life within the marketplace. It is a feeling I still remember to this day.

Example C

Terminal

My train passes suddenly into darkness; I am in a long, long tunnel. I have lost the sunlight, and the train just keeps running to the depth of the tunnel. It is so dark that I actually feel fear. However, I remind myself that I am sitting on a commuter coach in a crowd of people who do this everyday. I try not to shiver.

When the train arrives at Grand Central Station, I am bewildered by the atmosphere. The station is huge and dim, with only a few lights on the dusty ceiling to relieve the darkness. In addition, contrary to my expectation, there is no poster, no decoration, but only dust and soot.

The passengers rush out of the train onto the platform, then face straight to the exit. Nobody converses; nobody laughs. All just walk at a rapid pace, carefully watching their barely visible footsteps. In the light of dust-covered fluorescent lamps, their down-turned faces look ghostly.

In the stuffy station, there seems to be little air. There is, of course, no window in this deep underground. I hardly breathe as I step off the train. When I finally turn to leave, I too go at a trot for the dimly lit exit sign, as if I too want to escape from the darkness and back into life.

Summary

To write description adequately, the student must select details to support his or her thesis, being careful to omit irrelevant details. Details should be concrete and specific. The student should avoid overuse of abstractions or vague modifiers. Moreover, details must be arranged spatially in a logical order.

Exercises

For Consideration

Exercise 1.   Choose one of the model descriptions you just read. Read it carefully. Write its thesis in one sentence. What details in the essay support the thesis? Are there any irrelevant details? Can you suggest any details that might make the thesis stronger?

Exercise 2.   Below are two versions—a first draft and a revision—of a student's description of her father. For each version of the essay, write the theme in one sentence and list all the details the writer has included. Are there sufficient concrete details to support the thesis of each version? Explain. How has the revision (Version B) improved upon the original? Can you make any suggestions for further changes?

A.   Description of My Father

My father is a person who is sure of himself and very optimistic. With constancy, dedication, and positivism he gets almost everything he wants. He never gives up when he finds adversity; quite the opposite, he tries even harder than before until he achieves his objectives.

His wrinkles and his white hair announce the maturity and security that the years have given to him.

As a father he is lovely. In his eyes is reflected his kindness. He is always ready to help no matter what problems you have. He is always prepared to advise you and to give you the courage to go on.

Now he is seventy-nine years old and he is still working. He has to be doing something because he needs to feel that he is helpful. In spite of his age, he is an active man. He likes to change and to know different things. He hates the monotony of life, of always being in the same place and seeing the same people everyday.

B.

My Busy Father

My father is almost eighty, but he doesn't seem to know it. Despite his age, he still works; he has to be doing something every moment to be helpful.

The wrinkles on his face are always shifting as his expression changes. He is a very active man. He is always moving from one place to another. If he is forced to sit for a few minutes, he gestures with his hands or moves his head this way and that looking about the room. The white hair on his head is the only thing about him that is still.

When he visited me in America, my father found a new way to work. Because he didn't have anything else to do, he decided to be the house-wife in our apartment. It was very funny to see my father, wearing an impeccable suit, cooking, washing the dishes, sweeping the floor, and thinking all the time that he was doing everything as well as my mother does it in our home in Venezuela—while really the house was a disaster.

Exercise 3. In the following essays, two students describe Christmas, a holiday they experienced for the first time. Which essay does a better job of making the reader feel the way he felt about the holiday? Why? Are there any irrelevant details in either essay? Identify them.

A.

Christmas Day

Last year, when I was living with the Chapman family in England, Christmas came. In England, the most important day of the year is Christmas Day. On Christmas Day, people give presents to their family and friends and have a big family dinner.

The Chapman's house looked really beautiful. The day before Christmas, Mr. Chapman and his sons had worked all day putting up holly and colored paper ornaments over the doors and pictures. They put a big Christmas tree just inside the front door and hung colored electric lights along the branches. Everything looked gay and exciting.

The Chapman's cousins were staying with them, and the house was full of children. Before bedtime on Christmas Eve, all the children called up the chimney to Father Christmas and told him what they wanted, then hung up their stockings at the foot of their beds. Mrs. Chapman told them, "If you are good children, Father Christmas will fill them with presents." The children went to bed smiling.

For Christmas dinner, there was a big turkey and Christmas pudding. The table was loaded with dishes. In the afternoon, everyone watched the Queen on television. Then the older people rested while the younger ones played games with the children.

Christmas Day in England is a family day. It is a day to enjoy at home, a day when home is special.

B.

Christmas

In the United States, the Americans are mostly Christian, either Catholic or Protestant. Therefore, during the Christmas period, Americans really have an enjoyable time. There are many days off from school—almost a week from Christmas Eve until New Year. Christmas in this country is very impressive.

Last week, I went to a Christmas party. It was very nice. There was a really big Christmas tree in the room where the party was held. We had refreshments. The party was very nice. I talked with many Americans, both students and nonstudents. I was the only foreigner there. I learned that Christmas is the day that Christ was born. Christmas is celebrated on December 25th each year, and a day before that is called Christmas Eve. What Americans do on Christmas Day is to make a party. Usually, family members get together in the evening and have dinner together. Sometimes, the members of a family have some activities or a conversation together after not seeing each other for a whole year. When midnight comes, they go together to church. Mass lasts for about an hour.

When the morning of December 25th comes, people give Christmas presents to each other—father and mother to their children and children to their parents. Generally, people send Christmas greeting cards to each other. That causes delays in the mail as I have heard on television. That is the one thing I don't like about Christmas!

Exercise 4. Read the following essays. Are they successful or unsuccessful? Why? What suggestions can you make to improve them?

A.

The Beauty of Nature

I remember the first day I came to the university. The first thing that caught my interest was that the campus was situated in a natural setting. In fact, I could look out my dorm window and see the ocean. It was beautiful.

There were many lovely trees all around on the green grass. There were birds in the sky. They were very beautiful. There was a pleasant atmosphere. It was a beautiful day.

Different aspects of nature caught my eye as I surveyed the campus. The natural environment created a sensation of relaxation. The beauty of nature gave me a wonderful feeling.

The university is very attractive. It makes me feel good to be in such an attractive natural setting.

B.

Familiar Landscape

The sea breeze was coming through the window of the fourth floor in Todd Hall. The cool wind traveled through the dormitory. Through the window I could see the ocean sparkling under the bright sun. A flock of seagulls was flying over the small waves; others were playing on the beach. The grass and the leaves of trees in front of my dorm were trembling in the breeze. It was a perfect summer day.

The sparkling seascape held my eyes and made me feel comfortable. I was very confused at that time because that was my first day at the university. Everywhere around me was strange. This view of sea and sky and sand was the first thing I found familiar.

After this I started to walk around the school. Especially near my dormitory I found many glittering landscapes and seascapes that reminded me of the scenery in the countryside around my hometown in Japan. Sometimes, looking at the wide, sunlit sky or at the endless sea, I could forget I was in a strange new city and imagine myself at home.

Exercise 5.   In the essay that follows, a student describes her room. What problems do you see in the essay? What suggestions can you make to improve it?

My Room

I used to live in a room which I think is interesting enough to write about. It is a large room with huge windows.

When you walk in, the first thing which catches your eye is a big, brown monkey hanging on the wall. On the left side wall you will see many kinds of posters and signs.

My bed is in the left corner of the room, and right beyond the bed is my turntable, placed on a book shelf. My desk is right beside the window.

Instead of a chair, I have big pillows around the room. I have about ten plants hanging from the ceiling. My perfume collection is on my mirror table on the right side of my bed. I have a nice carpet covering the floor. It's an old carpet. My grandfather gave it to my mother when I was born.

I can say I have a warm room and the color combination makes your eyes travel from point to point.

My friends love my room. My mother thinks it's a zoo and my father thinks it's a good place to get lost. But they never disagree with me about my room because it's always clean.

For Composition

Exercise 6.   Make an informal outline for your own description of a place—a street, room, building, outdoor scene—that you remember well from your hometown or that you have discovered in your new surroundings. Write in one sentence the main feeling the place gives you (thesis). Then list as many details as possible about the place that give you this feeling. Draw on your senses to capture how the place looks, sounds, feels, smells. Try not to include details that do not support your theme.

Exercise 7.   Using the outline you assembled for Exercise 6, write a descriptive essay of two to five paragraphs about the place you have chosen.

Exercise 8.   Write a descriptive essay about the customs associated with a holiday in your own culture. For your thesis, focus on the main feeling the holiday is supposed to give people or on the meaning of the holiday. In writing about the holiday's customs, include only the details that give people this feeling or convey this meaning, that is, that support the thesis.

Exercise 9.   Write a one- or a two-paragraph description of one of the following:
  • a piece of apparatus that you use in one of your courses

  • an instructor (from the present or past) whom you found to be unusual
Give special attention to ordering details logically and effectively.

Chapter 5

Illustration

Most of us are well acquainted with illustration from the literature that is most familiar to us. For example, religious literature provides many moral tales in which events and characters are important not mainly for themselves, but because they point to some truth, some moral. Fables—animal stories, such as the tales of the Greek Aesop—are illustrations: in one well-known fable by Aesop, a tortoise challenges a hare to a race; when the tortoise beats the lazy hare, it illustrates the moral that a slow but steady effort will succeed over a hurried but inconsistent one.

Illustration is one of the most common patterns for paragraphs and essays. Whenever a writer says "for instance" or "for example" (as I did in the second sentence of this chapter) and proceeds to support with specific detail a point he has made, he is writing an illustration. The description of *Icarus* in W. H. Auden's poem "Musée des Beaux Arts" (Chapter 4) is, in fact, treated as an illustration of the idea that the old masters understood that life continues despite others' tragedies (indeed, Auden writes, "In Brueghel's *Icarus*, for instance . . .").

Sometimes an illustration is treated in an extended way, as with the description of *Icarus*. Sometimes several examples are listed to illustrate one idea, as in the first paragraph of this chapter. Such short illustrations are used by Auden in the first half of his poem. Tragedy, he tells us, takes place while others eat, open windows, walk along; while children ice skate and dogs act like dogs.

Both brief and extended illustrations can be effective tools in making a thesis clear and convincing. If we say readers appreciate concrete details more than they do abstract ones, we are clearer if we give examples of concrete and abstract details: *shooting* versus *violence*, or *continuing a card game* versus *remaining unaffected*. If, as in the first paragraph, we say that a fable is an illustration, we show what we mean more clearly by summarizing an actual fable and pointing to the moral it illustrates. If we say that with effort and skill a foreigner can become fluent in a new language, we are more likely to convince our readers if we give the example of Joseph Conrad, a Pole who learned English as a youth and became a great English novelist.

Balancing Thesis and Supporting Details

The dangers in writing illustrations are basically those we have seen in narration and description. On the one hand, the writer may spend so much time stating and explaining the abstract idea he wishes to illustrate that his essay becomes dull and uninteresting to the reader. On the other hand, the writer may become so involved in the details—irrelevant as well as relevant—of his story that he confuses the reader and fails to make clear the abstract idea he wishes to express. (For examples of these errors, see the two poorly written versions of the Morris piece on page 13.)

The essay that follows treats a powerful subject. However, the writer fails to communicate his theme powerfully to his reader. Let us see why:

Unbearable Situation

A lack of freedom and goods can create a situation of great hardship. This is the situation in Saigon in these days. In Saigon there is much poverty and scarcity of the commodities that make life pleasant and enjoyable. The lack of freedom and commodities are hardships on the people. These circumstances are very difficult to live with.

For example, commodities like foodstuffs are not easy to get in Saigon. People eat poorly. And there are few opportunities for the consumption of special foods.

Entertainment, too, is scarce and uninteresting. And people do not even enjoy each other's company. Worse still, people are obsessed with the lack of freedom in Vietnam. That is why there are lots of people trying to escape from my country.

All these examples show clearly why I say the situation in Saigon at present is one of extreme hardship.

In this essay, the stating of the thesis is given too much space. The writer devotes the full five sentences of the first paragraph to stating the theme—in abstract and repetitive terms—and then states it again in roughly the same terms in the final paragraph. The middle paragraph is crowded with examples, but none of them are concrete or specific. Although the essay is "unified," the thesis is not well supported because the examples are so vague. The next version shows much improvement:

The Sadness of Saigon

Life in Saigon, the city in which I was born and lived until a year ago, is hard these days. The lack of freedom and commodities makes the people sad and tired of life.

For example, food in Saigon is very expensive and precious. Meat and rice are rare. Generally, one family (about six persons) can buy two or three pounds of meat each year. Rice is very, very precious—like gold. The restaurants that served Vietnamese delicacies and such specialties as beefsteak, fried chicken, and French food are empty or closed.

Facilities in the town seem like nothing: there are no movies, no television, no shows. Popular music such as Beatle songs or traditional songs of Vietnam are not played now in Saigon. Instead a kind of music composed by the government, very dull and dry, is played on Saigon radio.

People do not crowd the streets on the weekends. There are no student couples walking side-by-side, hand-in-hand on Catinal Boulevard on Saturday afternoon. Imprisonment and death obsess the people of Saigon. That is why so many people are trying to escape from Vietnam.

I escaped from Vietnam last year. Now I am trying to rebuild my life and help my family to leave Vietnam if possible. If I succeed, I will be very happy, and I will try to disconnect myself from the old hard time which follows me always.

In this essay, the thesis is stated in two sentences at the beginning of the essay. And even here phrases such as "make the people sad and tired of life" are more concrete than anything in the first paragraph of the previous version. The writer follows with numerous concrete and specific examples the reader can appreciate: the family's ration of "two or three pounds of meat each year," rice "very, very precious—like gold," "Vietnamese delicacies," "beefsteak, fried chicken, and French food," "Beatle songs," "government music," "student couples walking side-by-side, hand-in-hand," and so forth. These are images the reader is familiar with and they help to convince him or her of the writer's theme.

Finally, the last paragraph, while it returns to the thesis, does not merely repeat the first paragraph as does the final paragraph of the essay above. Rather, it develops the thesis, that life in Saigon is hard, by applying it to the writer's own life, thereby giving it deeper, more personal significance.

Summary

Illustration, then, presents the writer with the same problem that we have seen in our discussions of narrative and description—that is, selecting concrete details that clearly support a thesis. In addition, the writer must decide whether an illustration is to be brief or extended and whether to support his thesis with one or several different examples. Above all, in illustration the writer must work to achieve an effective balance between the statement of the thesis and the examples he or she uses to support it.

Exercises

For Consideration

Exercise 1.   Read the essay below and answer the following questions:
   a.   What is the thesis of the essay? Is it stated clearly enough? Underline the sentence(s) in which the writer states the thesis. Are there any problems with the way in which he states it?
   b.   List the examples the writer uses to support his thesis. Are the writer's examples concrete and specific enough to convince the reader of his thesis?
   c.   Has the writer included any irrelevant details? List them.
   d.   Is the balance between thesis and examples effective here? Explain.

Science and Its Application Are Advantageous to Society

Science is the theoretical explanation of natural phenomena. Application of science, or engineering, is the use of scientific knowledge to the benefit of mankind though sometimes it has been used to mankind's detriment. Engineering is a quite recent field which came into being in the sixteenth century. Science is a rapidly increasing field and new branches appear rapidly, but there are three main areas: physics, chemistry, and biology.

Engineering—the application of scientific principals—is responsible for the high technology of present times. Engineering is responsible for the creation of most of the commodities that are taken for granted at present. The vast majority of comforts available to modern man derive from efforts in engineering.

For example, electricity, which runs most of our household equipment, owes its present form to the application of electrical science first discovered in the Middle Ages. Electricity is responsible for the development of telecommunications. Telecommunications has greatly influenced the expansion of cities. Engineering has developed telecommunications to such an extent that at present the possibilities for global communications are practically limitless.

Engineering is also responsible for the development of different forms of ground, air, and sea transportation. Ground and sea transportation have developed greatly within the past couple of centuries while the one to develop fastest has been the latest form, air transportation. The development of the different forms of transportation have helped the development of the remotest parts of countries and have helped to transport people and equipment to distant areas.

From this it can be seen that engineering has given man comforts that he enjoys today.

Exercise 2.   In the following essay, a student illustrates a proverb with a story of her own experience. Is the thesis clearly explained? Does the illustration support the thesis? Has the writer provided enough detail to make the reader feel as she does? Are there any irrelevant details? Can you suggest details which might make the illustration stronger?

No Pains, No Gains

The expression "no pains, no gains" has great meaning for me. I know personally that to reach a special goal we have to try hard.

Always, one of the great goals in my life was to attend a university. But in my country it is hard to get accepted at a university. When I was in high school, I learned how high were the requirements for university admission, so I knew I had to study hard to get good grades.

All through high school I used to think only about my books, my lessons, and my grades. My classmates thought that I was becoming sick from studying so hard, but I didn't think about anything except being accepted at a university. When I finished high school, I had about three months' time to study for the big university exam. So I continued to study all day, every day. Sometimes I didn't have time to eat lunch or dinner. My mother used to bring my lunch into my room. The time flew on those days.

Finally, the day of the exam came, and I went to have the biggest test of my life. I was so nervous that I shook. It took me three hours to finish the exam. At the end, I was exhausted.

Two months later I received a paper that made all my pain worthwhile. I had been accepted at the university. Out of about 300,000 students that had participated in that exam, I was in the first 3,000 students accepted.

Exercise 3. In the following essay, a student tells a traditional tale from his country. What is the moral that the tale illustrates? Is it stated in the essay? Would the essay be improved if the writer stated the moral at the beginning? Why or why not?

An Old Iranian Story

A farmer had three lazy sons. They didn't help him in the field. The farmer was very sad. One day he felt he would die very soon. He called his sons to his deathbed and told them: "I have a treasure for you; it is hidden somewhere in the field." The farmer died very soon after.

The sons remembered what their father had said about the treasure, so they went into the garden and began to work very hard, digging everywhere. They didn't find any treasure, but they planted their crops in the earth they had turned and that year they had a very good harvest and earned a lot of money by selling their crops. They were happy and thanked God and their father. In fact, they found the treasure by working hard in the field.

Exercise 4. In the essay that follows, a student describes her feeling of surprise on returning to her own country after being away. She focuses on one characteristic of her city and gives several examples to illustrate it. Make an informal outline of the essay; write the thesis in one sentence and then list all the examples that the writer uses to illustrate it.

Reverse Culture Shock

Sometimes, when one returns to one's own country after having been away, one may feel shocked by what one encounters.

This summer, when I went back to Japan after two years' absence, I was amazed at how different it felt to be back in the city. The view of Tokyo through the window of a train had not changed that much although there did seem to be a few more skyscrapers. But when I walked on the streets in the center of Tokyo, I felt confused by the crowds of rushing people. People walked so fast that they seemed not to care about others.

For example, crossing a street after a red light turned green, some people pushed the others in front of them because they wanted to cross the street as fast as they could. In Los Angeles—even in the downtown—I had never experienced this behavior. There, people walked at their own pace. On the subway, the same thing happened. People pushed other people aside in order to get to their train on time.

During the time I stayed in Tokyo, I became afraid of going out any place by myself. The crowds made the roads seem very narrow. Everything looked small except for the crowds of people. I felt as if there was no place for me on the sidewalks.

I have heard that many students who had studied in other countries for many years and come back to Japan had gotten this same shock. Many went back to the countries where they had studied because they could not stand the pushing crowds, busy-ness, and narrow streets of Japan's capital.

For Composition

Exercise 5.   Suggest several possible examples to illustrate the following ideas:
a. The university is a friendly/an impersonal place.
b. The menu at the student cafeteria is/is not nutritionally sound.
c. Hard work does not always add up to a good grade.
   or
   Laziness does not always result in a poor grade.

Exercise 6.   Write a two- to four-paragraph essay on *one* of the following:
a. Retell in your own words a traditional tale from your own culture that illustrates a moral. Be sure the moral is clear to the reader.
b. Choose a proverb from your own language and translate it into English. Then illustrate it with an original story, perhaps something from your own experience.

Exercise 7.   Write an essay to illustrate the following thesis:

Attending an American university can cause a foreign student to feel culture shock.

Illustrate the thesis with either
a. several brief examples or
b. one extended example.

Be sure you include enough specific supporting details to convince your reader of your thesis. Do *not* include irrelevant details.

Chapter 6

Definition

In college writing, the student frequently may need to define, or give the meaning of, terms. Thus, he or she will need practice in writing definitions. We are all familiar with dictionary definitions, so it might be helpful to analyze a typical one. Let us look at a brief dictionary definition of the term "college":

> College: a school of higher learning that grants a bachelor's degree

Parts of the Definition

There are three parts that make up this simple definition:
1. The *term* (*college*)
2. The larger *class* to which it belongs (*school*)
3. the *differentia/ae* or distinctive quality or qualities that make it different from other members of the same class (*of higher learning; that grants a bachelor's degree*).

We might draw a diagram of term, class, and differentia for the word "college" as shown in Figure 6-1.

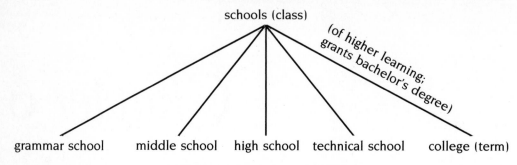

***Figure* 6-1** Parts of the Definition

Of course, in a dictionary definition, additional information is generally provided: spelling (and variations), pronunciation, syllabication, part-of-speech label (*n.* for noun, *v.* for verb, and so forth), additional forms (plural, past tense, and so on), etymology or word origin, and sometimes, examples of usage. (See, for example, the labeled parts of the sample definition on page 169). Most often, however, all the writer will need to define a word adequately are the basic parts of what is called the *classical definition*— that is, term, class, and differentia.

Definition Length

Frequently, the writer can define a term parenthetically. A *parenthetical definition* is inserted directly into the sentence in which the new term first occurs, set off by commas, dashes, or parentheses, as in the first sentence of this chapter and the following examples:

> Mr. Smith teaches English composition—essay writing—to the international students.

> We had a lunch of ground meat wrapped in tortillas, flat corncakes baked on a griddle.

(Note that with commas and dashes, only one is needed when the definition closes the sentence, whereas two are required when the sentence continues after the definition.) Sometimes a simple *synonym* (a word with the same meaning as the term being defined) will be sufficient:

> The essay was vague, that is, unclear.

Parenthetical definitions are appropriate where a definition is simple, short, and possibly already familiar to the reader. When a definition is more complex or when it is vital to the reader's understanding of an essay, it may require a full sentence or several sentences, as in the following example:

> When I first left Hong Kong, the thing I most regretted leaving behind was my wok. The wok is a large cooking pot that fits directly over a flame and can be used for many different cooking procedures. The wok can be

used for stir frying and deep fat frying, for steaming or braising—even for boiling.

Sometimes a definition will occupy a whole paragraph or several paragraphs. Indeed, it may even be the subject of an entire essay. This is especially true of definitions of terms that are abstract or complex and, thus, difficult to define. A definition of *democracy*, for example, or of *totalitarianism* might be the subject of an entire essay of many, many pages—indeed, of an entire book. Such *extended definitions* are often developed with examples that help make abstract meanings clear. If the examples are concrete and well chosen, definitions can be highly entertaining as well as informative essays. In the following essay, a student defines a term—*bubator*—from his language, Turkish:

Bubator

A *bubator* is a person who studies all day and all night, studying more than he has to. Although studying can be useful, this term has a negative connotation, for if somebody has to study all the time, it may mean that he can't rely on his intelligence. Also, bubators are often very one-sided people; a book is their friend, hobby, and Saturday night date. Studying is the purpose of the bubator's life, and it makes him happy. But it makes it difficult for him to adapt to "real" life, and nobody except other bubators likes him.

One might imagine a conversation between two bubators to go something like this:

"Hi! Could you solve Problem 2 on page 44, section C, part 3?" asks the first bubator.

"You have to use Table X from Chapter 5, section Y, part Z," says the second bubator. "Goodbye."

Actually, a bubator's conversation is about as interesting as listening to a banging drum. The drum has only one tone, while bubators have only one interest in life—studying.

Bubator is a slang word in Turkish, and it is used mostly in young people's conversation. The word is made up of two parts: the root *bubat*, meaning "to study" and the suffix *or*, which makes it a noun. Originally, its meaning was merely "one who studies." But gradually it came to have its present meaning, perhaps because those who never studied wanted to look down on those who studied at all.

Unfortunately, many Turkish young people don't study as much as they should because they don't want to be called *bubators*. As a result, those who are not intelligent enough to pass their courses without studying often find themselves in big trouble.

The writer of the above essay has used several means to define his term. He has given its *classical definition*: announced the *term* (*bubator*), identified the *class* to which the term belongs (*one who studies*), and provided the *differentiae* (*too much, possibly because he cannot rely on his own intelligence*) that separate the term from other members of the same class. He has also given a concrete *example* of the term in the little dialogue between two bubators. He has provided a brief *etymology*—word origin—of his term, breaking it down into root and suffix. He has even used comparison in his likening of the banging of a drum to a bubator's conversation. The writer has made it possible for the reader to have a very good idea of the meaning of *bubator*. And he has done something more. He has entertained the reader with his exaggerated, imaginary conversation between two bubators and with his concrete comparison to the drum, and he has provided a little social commentary along the way.

Avoiding Common Errors in Definition

In writing definitions, the student must be careful to be clear and accurate. One of the most common flaws in defining is the *circular definition*, in which the term being defined is itself used (often in altered form) in the definition, for example:

Circular Definition

To *define* a word is to give its definition.
A *circular definition* is a definition that goes in a circle.

A circular definition will probably not make clear the meaning of the word being defined. One can correct this flaw by changing the term used in the definition so that it is not the same as the term being defined:

Revised

To *define* a word is to identify its class and differentia, the qualities that make it distinct from other members of the same class.
To *define* a word is to give its meaning.

Student writers should also be careful to avoid definitions that are either too broad or too narrow. Definitions that are too broad can refer to other terms as well as to the term being defined, for example:

Too Broad

An orange is a citrus fruit.

It is true that an orange is a citrus fruit, but so is a lemon, a lime, and a grapefruit. In order to limit the definition so that it pertains to *orange* only, the writer must narrow the differentiae:

Revised

An orange is a round citrus fruit with an orange rind and a generally sweet pulp.

Definitions that are too narrow are those in which the class or differentia is so limiting that they cannot refer to all types of the term being defined, for example:

Too Limited

An orange is a round citrus fruit with an orange rind, a sweet pulp, and pits, used to make juice.

Since not all oranges have pits or are used to make juice, it would be better to leave out the last qualifiers or to rewrite as follows:

Revised

An orange is a round citrus fruit with an orange rind and generally sweet pulp, that may have pits, and is sometimes used to make juice.

Examples of Definition

In the following essays, student writers have defined terms from their own languages using tools of definition discussed in this chapter: classical definition (class + differentia), concrete examples of usage, etymology. The essays are also noteworthy for their engaging *tone*, in one case sentimental and heart-felt, in the other, humorous. Indeed, we can see from these essays that a definition can inform without being dull.

Jahaagi

"Jahaagi, how is it going?" said the old man to his friend as they passed one another on their way to the field.

"Everything is fine, Jahaagi," said the other in return.

As a young girl growing up in the Fiji Islands I always thought that "Jahaagi" was a strange thing to say to someone. We children would laugh because this word sounded like the Hindustani slang word for "fat" (*jahag*). Then one day my grandmother sat us down under a shady tree and told us the history of *jahaagi*.

In the 1870's the British brought indentured laborers from India to work in the tropical climate of Fiji. My ancestors and others from all parts of India came by boat in the hope of finding a better life. Almost every state in India has a separate language. There are many dialects even within the same language. And out of necessity a new language, Fiji Hindi, developed, mixing Hindi, Punjabi, Urdu, Tamil, Fijian, and even English.

The language of origin of *jahaagi* is not known. It is a term which was born on those voyages. *Jahaagi*, which literally means "passengers on the boat," is now a greeting of friendship among the Indians of Fiji. And it is a reminder that even though our origins varied, the boats that we came on blended us together and began to remove almost all of the old cultural barriers and prejudices that existed between cultures in India. There is no caste system left in my country, and the hatred between the Hindus and Moslems of India is something we only read about. Moreover, no one is starving or in extreme poverty in Fiji. And all of these things came about perhaps as the need to work together and survive became stronger than the differences that had kept the people apart.

Now when I heard the word *jahaagi*, I remember how these simple sailing vessels acted as the melting pot that made a new people of the "passengers on the boats."

Mabui

Mabui, in the Japanese language, is an adjective which means "beautiful," "cute," or "pretty" when used of young women. This word is usually used by young people, and it is considered slang. Assume that a pair of friends, Tomoya and Yosh, get in a train, and they see a beautiful girl there. Their conversation might be as follows:

Tomoya: Hey! Look at the girl with the long hair, standing near the door. Isn't she *mabui*?

Yosh: Which one? That lady with the brown paper bag?

Tomoya: Are you crazy? The one with the paper bag is an old woman. Look at the one behind her, the one with the high boots and the beige coat. She's *mabui*.

Yosh: Oh, yeah! She is definitely *mabui*. Also, she has a great sense for clothes. If she were my girlfriend, I don't think I'd let her get on a train without me.

A *mabui* girl, thus, is not only good looking and well dressed, but one whom a young man might want as his girlfriend. For obvious reasons, this word is frequently used by male high school or college students.

Although the word is generally used in a good spirit, it is not always received in that way. Consider, if a woman is called *mabui*, how she might feel. If she is a woman who goes to discotheques or is always out with boyfriends, she may be glad to hear that she is *mabui*. But if she is a conservative woman who does not like drinking or going to discotheques, then she may feel insulted, or she may judge the speaker to be rude. Therefore, one must use the term *mabui* only among friends—or very quietly!

The word *mabui* originates from the word *mabushii*, which means "bright, shining, dazzling." Therefore, *mabui* originally meant "glittering beauty." But now we use it only of beautiful, splendid women. Such is the working of young men's minds!

Summary

As we have seen, definitions come in various sizes depending on the complexity of the term defined and on the centrality of the term to the writer's thesis. All definitions, however, should include the *term* being defined, the class to which it belongs, and the *differentiae* that separate it from other members of the class. Students should avoid circular definitions and definitions that are either too broadly or too narrowly construed. In addition, students should bear in mind that a well-written definition may entertain as well as inform the reader.

Exercises

For Consideration

Exercise 1. For each of the essays above ("Jahaagi" and "Mabui"), briefly identify the following items:

a. term

b. class

c. differentia/ae

d. etymology

Exercise 2. Using a dictionary when necessary, write classic definitions for the following terms. Then, for each definition, underline <u>class</u> with a single line and <u>differentia/ae</u> with a double line.

> Example: An orange is a <u>round citrus</u> <u>fruit</u> <u>with an orange rind and a generally sweet pulp.</u>

a. hamburger   f. passport

b. ice cream   g. ~~immigrate~~

c. university   h. instruct

d. dormitory   i. literate

e. freshman   j. bilingual

Exercise 3. Using a dictionary, write a simple etymology (word origin or history) for each word in the list above. (Note: Etymologies are generally located after inflectional forms or at the end of the definition. Language of origin is indicated by abbreviations, the key to which is generally given along with other introductory material at the beginning of the dictionary. Ask your instructor for help if you cannot find the etymologies in the dictionary you are using.) Choose one of the words on the list and write a paragraph commenting on how well its etymology fits its current usage.

Exercise 4. The following student essay attempts to define "mariache," a Mexican-Spanish word. However, it is not as successful an essay as the examples found earlier in this chapter.

First, read the essay and identify within it the *term, class,* and *differentia* as indicated by the student writer. Then analyze why the essay is not a complete success. In making your analysis, try to answer the following questions:

a. Does the writer provide an etymology? The word *mariache* may derive from the French word for marriage; could this etymology have been pertinent?

b. The writer gives two different meanings of *mariache*, one in the first paragraph, the other in the second paragraph. Does he successfully relate the first meaning to the second?

c. The third and fourth paragraphs do not contribute as much as they might to the definition. How might they be improved? Would they be better off deleted?

d. Are any concrete examples offered to illustrate either meaning? Can you think of other examples that might have made the definition clearer or more interesting?

Mariache

A *mariache* is a group of people who play a kind of Mexican music. *Mariache* music is happy music that almost always starts with a loud cry of a man. Mariache music is often played at celebrations, such as weddings, in Mexico. Mariaches can be formed of from six to twelve persons. Of course, the larger the number of persons, the better the mariache sounds. The instruments they play are guitars, violins, and trumpets. A medium-size mariache may have four guitars, three violins, and two trumpets.

The word *mariache* can also be used in the same way as the English words *shy* or *timid*. For example, if a boy is afraid to talk to a girl, one might say, "Come on; don't be mariache."

Sometimes this word is used incorrectly to name the Mexican dances. I have heard more than once the expression, "Let's dance a mariache." This is wrong because the mariache is the one who plays so that others can dance. Each Mexican dance is named differently.

This word is very commonly used at parties or during drinking. In fact, when I hear this word, the first thing that comes to my mind is drinking.

Exercise 5. Choose a word in your language with an interesting etymology. Briefly define the term and relate the meaning to the etymology in an essay of two or three paragraphs.

Exercise 6. Choose a word in your language that has no exact equivalent in English. Define the word in a complete essay, including classic definition, examples, and etymology (if pertinent), making your essay at once informative and entertaining. (Students who have difficulty coming up with appropriate topics for this exercise or the two that follow it might try thinking in terms of particular foods, dances, types of music, or particular customs, all of which vary widely from one culture to another.)

Exercise 7. Think of an English word you have learned that has no exact equivalent in your language. Define the word in a complete essay, including classic definition, examples, and etymology (if pertinent). Write your definition to inform readers from your own country about the particular word and, if possible, about an aspect of American culture revealed by the word.

Exercise 8. Think of an English word that has made its way into your native language. How is the word used in your country? Is it used differently in the United States? Write an essay comparing these usages and making a social commentary on the reasons for their similarities or differences.

Chapter 7

Analysis

Analysis means the breaking up of a whole into its parts, generally to examine the parts and see how they relate to one another and to the whole. When we identify different types of something, compare one thing to another, try to determine the causes of a phenomenon, or outline the steps needed to achieve a goal, we are analyzing—breaking into parts for the purpose of examining.

The separate names for these different kinds of analysis are *classification*, *subdivision*, *comparison and contrast*, *cause and effect*, and *process*. As noted about essays in general (see page 5), analytical essays commonly use more than one rhetorical pattern. A subdivision essay, for example, may employ classification, comparison and contrast, illustration, or any other combination of patterns, although subdivision will predominate.

The rules for writing analyses are similar to those for writing narratives and descriptions. There is, however, one important distinction. Whereas the thesis of a narrative or description may be either explicit or implicit, the greater complexity of analysis generally requires an explicit thesis to be stated early in the essay.

Classification

As you may recall from the discussion of definition, when we classify an object, we identify the larger group or class to which it belongs. Thus, we may classify *college* in the larger group *schools*, or we may classify *orange* in the larger class *fruits*. In this kind of essay, the basic classification constitutes the thesis:

> An orange is a fruit.
> France is a democracy.

Establishing and Testing for Criteria

In order to classify an object as a member of a class or larger group, we must establish the criteria—the determining characteristics—by which all members of the class are recognized. For instance, *schools* are institutions for instruction and learning: these are the criteria that determine whether or not an institution is a school. Since colleges are institutions of instruction and learning, they are schools. Thus, there are two steps in the process of classification: (1) establishing the criteria by which members of the group are recognized, and (2) confirming that a particular object meets these criteria.

In the following essay, a student writer classifies his college library as inadequate (his thesis). In order to do this, he must establish the criteria by which a college library is determined to be adequate, and then show with concrete examples that his library does not meet these criteria. Let us look at his essay.

Empty Space

When I first saw our college library from the outside, it was so tall and massive I thought it held a million volumes or more. Ah! I thought, this is a real library!

However, after entering and having a look around, I was surprised and disappointed. The building was full of unused offices and empty spaces. The shelves were barely half-filled. The card catalogue lacked many titles I could have used in my course work.

Not only was there a small number of books, there were also not enough periodicals to satisfy all the interests of our college's students. For instance, there are many foreign students from several different countries at our college, but the college library doesn't carry more than three or four foreign newspapers. When we Turkish students asked a librarian if the library could take a subscription to a Turkish newspaper, the librarian said that the library's budget was all used up and that no new subscriptions could be ordered until the end of the school year.

Guides to the periodicals are incomplete, making it hard for students to find articles on subjects of interest to them. Many current periodicals— as well as books—are missing. I have heard that people steal newspapers and other items from the library easily. And I can believe that.

The library has plenty of space to sit for reading and working. But most of that space is empty. Maybe this is because there is not enough in the library for students to read or work on!

Natural Versus Mechanical Analysis

One of the best qualities of this analysis is that it seems natural, not mechanical or stiff as the term *analysis* might imply. The writer does not set out a list of criteria for a good college library and then take them up one by one in outline form. The criteria are there, but they are a natural part of the essay. We might ourselves "outline" the essay as follows:

Thesis: the library at our college is not an adequate college library.

1. Criteria for an adequate college library:
   a. large number of books college students might wish to use for course work
   b. periodicals to meet interests of students
   c. complete periodicals guides
   d. availability of library materials
   e. utilization of library space
2. Characteristics of our college library:
   a. books far fewer than space would allow; many titles missing from card catalogue
   b. very few foreign periodicals despite large foreign student body
   c. incomplete periodicals guides
   d. books and current periodicals missing; library materials are easy to steal
   e. much empty space, unused offices, empty shelves, lack of students in reading and working areas.

Indeed, the student writer may have planned his essay with this kind of outline. However, if he had written it in just this way, his essay might have sounded artificial and uninteresting, as does the version that follows.

Our College Library

A good college library should have many books. It should have periodicals to meet the interests of the students at the college. It should have complete periodicals guides. Its materials should be available to students. And, finally, its space should be fully utilized.

Our college library does not meet these criteria. Much of its space is empty. Books occupy only about half the available shelf space. Despite the college's large foreign student population, the library carries only three or four newspapers from foreign countries. Guidebooks to periodicals are incomplete, and the library is missing current periodicals and other materials as well. Much of the library's space is empty or unused. For all these reasons, it seems to me that our college library is inadequate.

This second version is also a classification analysis. Like the first version, it establishes the criteria by which a college library may be judged to be adequate and then shows how a particular library fails in these criteria (and, thus, cannot be classified as an adequate college library). But the second version is dry and mechanical, too much like an outline. It lacks the specific details, the sentence variety, the transitions, and the tight organization that make the first version a pleasure to read. Such an essay may be adequate for a particular course or professor. Indeed, when time is limited, as in an in-class exam, or where information is more important than style, as in some kinds of reports, a mechanical analysis may be appropriate. But the student who wishes to write well should remember that, although an analytical essay is an analysis, it is also an essay.

Organizing a Classification Analysis

In writing classification analyses, the writer has several organizational options. He or she can start by establishing the characteristics shared by all elements of a class and proceed to show how the object being classified also shares these characteristics. This is the organization followed in the dry, mechanical essay above. However, such organization need not be dry and mechanical. A less usual variation is to start with the characteristics of the object and move to the general characteristics of the class. Alternatively, the writer can devote separate paragraphs or sections of the essay to individual characteristics, listing a characteristic and showing whether or not the object he or she is classifying is endowed with it. (This is the organization followed by the writer of the essay in Exercise 3, below.) Finally, the writer may entirely omit explicit mention of shared characteristics, suggesting them only by what he or she says about the characteristics of the object being classified (as does the writer of "Empty Spaces").

Combining Classification and Subdivision

It is worth noting that classification analysis is often coupled in one essay with subdivision, the pattern we will be discussing in the following section. In such essays, in addition to classifying one or more objects as members of a particular class, the writer identifies all or several of the types or subgroups of the class, perhaps showing characteristics shared by some members but not by others. (An example of an essay combining classification with some elements of subdivision can be found in Exercise 3, below). Some composition handbooks, in fact, treat subdivision and classification as one process, calling it by either one name or the other. We have chosen to treat the twin processes of classification and subdivision separately to make the individual processes clearer to the student writer who wishes to master them.

Exercises

For Consideration

Exercise 1. Draw a line from each of the *objects* in List A to the *class* in List B to which it belongs:

A	B
English	fruit
human being	language
apple	monument
Statue of Liberty	religion
Christianity	animal

Exercise 2. Choose one of the pairs from Exercise 1 and, listing the criteria that all members of the class share, give concrete examples to show that the object is a member of the class.

Example:	fruit (class)	apple
	a. bears seeds	a. has a core with seeds
	b. grows on a plant	b. grows on a tree, replacing blossom
	c. ripens	c. may turn from green to red or yellow, and from tart to sweet
	d. may be edible	d. is my favorite snack

Exercise 3. In the following essay, a student classifies the dining hall at his university as being untrue to its name: the dining hall is not, he maintains a "dining hall" at all. (This is his thesis.) Read the essay and outline it by listing, first, the characteristics of a real dining hall as mentioned by the writer and, second, the failures of this particular dining hall to meet those criteria. (For guidance, refer to the college library analysis on page 57).

Not Fine Dining

To have a meal only once in our dining hall is enough for one to understand that to call it a "dining hall" is a joke. A dining hall should be a place of order, where the diner can enjoy a meal in comfort. Our dining hall is in such disorder that, for instance, when one enters it toward the end of dinner time, it seems like a battlefield. Trays are left all over the tables, the floor is dirtied by foods, glass particles, and even saltshakers and tableware. If one manages to wade through all this to an empty table, by the time he gets there he will have lost his appetite.

Students are not expected to remove their trays from tables when they leave. And by the middle of a meal time, it is usually impossible to find a clean or trayless table. Furthermore, it is not possible to find metal forks and spoons or real glasses. Instead, only plastic tableware and paper cups are available, both inconvenient to use. One can hardly "dine" with such tableware, which is fit only for picnics and meals taken on the run. The atmosphere of the dining hall doesn't fulfill the promise of its name either. A dining hall should be a place of digestion-aiding peace and quiet. Perhaps our dining hall would be more true to its name if music were played during mealtimes. To listen to music would be much better than to listen to screams and noise—which we hear enough of outside the dining hall.

But the food is the worst aspect of the dining hall. While the variety of food is far from being satisfactory, the quality isn't that good either. Maybe the cooks are trying to hypnotize us by serving hamburger and calling it steak. Maybe they figure if they don't cook the rice completely, we won't ask for more. And they're right! One cannot "dine" on food of this quality. Indeed, one can barely eat it.

Is the classification successful? Has the writer established the criteria by which a dining hall is judged to be worthy of the name? Has he provided enough concrete examples to show that his university's dining hall does not meet these criteria? Can you find places where he might have benefited by providing more concrete examples?

Is the essay stiff and mechanical or has the writer been successful in making his essay sound like an essay rather than like an outline? Explain.

For Composition

Exercise 4.   Each major college subject belongs to a particular class: humanities, natural sciences and mathematics, social sciences, language, fine arts, or business. In one or two paragraphs, identify the class to which your major belongs, giving the main characteristics of that class and showing specifically why your major belongs to it.

Exercise 5.   Classify one of your professors or teachers as an adequate or inadequate instructor.

Exercise 6.   Classify your country's form of government. Be sure to provide specific examples to show how the government meets the criteria you establish.

Subdivision

Subdivision is a close relative of classification, but the processes move in opposite directions. In classification, a subject is assigned to a class according to the characteristics it has in common with other members of the class. In subdivision, a class is divided into its various subgroups according to the characteristics that distinguish one member of the class from another. Thus, a subdivision of libraries could divide the class into subgroups such as college libraries, public libraries, technical libraries, and so forth. A subdivision of college dining facilities might list subgroups such as dining halls, snack bars, cafés, and so on. And a subdivision of forms of government might include representative democracies, military dictatorships, authoritarian governments, and monarchies.

In the following essay, a student writer subdivides beginning skiers into three subgroups. His essay is clear and simply organized and it is enlivened by concrete examples drawn from his own experience of each of the three types he identifies.

Starters on the Slopes

As a skiing instructor I learned that beginning skiers can be divided into three basic types depending on their mental point of view. Knowing about these types might help a beginning skier improve his abilities.

The aggressive skier usually seems to have an aggressive temperament off the slopes as well. On the slopes, he is not afraid of height or speed. Such a positive mental attitude is an important factor in skiing, even for expert skiers. When one skis down a steep slope of 25 to 30 degrees, if he wants to keep his skis in control, his center of gravity must be over the balls of his feet, never on or behind his heels. A positive mental attitude permits the skier to keep his center of gravity forward.

One of my students, John, was an aggressive skier. He wasn't afraid of the slopes. When I told him to keep his knees bent and his center of gravity forward, he obeyed without hesitation. He was always eager to try. And as a result, he was always the first to pass to the next step in the course. This kind of person can make faster progress in skiing than others can. But at the same time, such skiers are likely to be reckless at times. As a result, they may lose control and injure themselves.

Passive skiers contrast sharply with aggressive types in that they are afraid of speed and slopes. More women than men seem to belong to this group. As they are afraid, they hold themselves back, throwing their hips to the rear. Often, they fall as a result of their holding back.

Kelly was a typical passive-tempered skier. Because she was always afraid, she kept her whole body stiff as if she was a log. Her fear seemed to pull her body backward. The result was simply that Kelly fell down in the snow again and again. Her tense body could not handle even the little bumps in the slopes.

The most successful beginners are what I call easy-going skiers. They are not scared of slopes, but rather enjoy the snow. Many children belong to this group. In their innocence and simplicity, they seem to forget they have long skis on their feet and are going down a steep slope. Since they are relaxed, they react naturally to bumps in the slope and, thus, keep their balance. In other words, they learn from their own bodies' signals what they must do.

Tom, a five-year old boy, was a good example of the easy-going skier. When I met Tom, he had never skied. Although he didn't listen to my lesson well (most small children do not), he learned by watching what I was doing and then imitating it. In addition, Tom didn't care about falling, and this is essential for improving. Tom went up the slope before I taught him to climb, then simply glided down. How did he learn? It surprised me at first. But I believe, though we adults can't be children, we can learn from them. Like children, adult skiers should be positive mentally, but not reckless. They should not be ashamed—or afraid—of falling. Above all, skiers should follow their bodies' natural inclinations. This simple strategy will change a beginner's ski manipulation dramatically—and make a ski instructor's job a lot easier as well!

In this essay, the writer divides the class *beginning skiers* into three subgroups, showing the main characteristics that distinguish one member of the class from another. The outline for such a subdivision could be very simple, as in the diagram below:

Beginning Skiers

Aggressive	*Passive*	*Easy-going*
brave	afraid	relaxed
positive	hold selves back	positive
reckless	tense	react naturally
(example: John)	(example: Kelly)	(example: Tom)

But the essay goes far beyond an outline. Its concrete details and personal point of view make it clear and readable. And it even treats the reader to a skiing lesson! Again, as in our discussion of classification, we see that analysis can be clear and informative without being stiff and dry. (Note that subdivision is commonly coupled with classification analysis.)

Exercises

For Consideration

Exercise 7. The essay that follows is adapted from an analysis of Washington Square made by a Chilean studying in the United States. Read it carefully and then answer the following questions:

   a. What is the thesis of the essay? Is it implicit or explicit? If explicit, where is it stated?
   b. What are the main subdivisions of the people in Washington Square recognized by the writer?
   c. What characteristics typify each separate group?
   d. Has the writer included sufficient detail to support the thesis?
   e. Is the analysis effectively and clearly organized? Would you recommend any revision of its organization?
   f. Is the essay dry and mechanical or natural and readable? Why?

Dissecting the Square

On Sunday, Washington Square is full of people. At first glance, they might seem to position themselves about the area randomly. Actually, however, each special group gravitates to its own special section of the park as surely as if the sections were marked "_____ Only!"

On one side of the park are families. Black, Hispanic, Oriental, and Italian parents sit on blankets and benches watching their children toss a ball, skip rope, climb, run. That part of the square is full of strollers and baby carriages, tricycles, and mothers burdened with diaper bags stuffed with bottles, toys, and cookies. Some families bring picnic lunches in large coolers and jugs full of iced juice. Others patronize the vendors of ice cream, pretzels, hot dogs, and soda, who congregate in this area busy with hungry children and indulgent parents. The vendors' calls of "Hot pretzels!" and "Get your ice cream here!" mix with the sounds of children's chatter and an occasional infant's cry to make a pleasant music.

All the way across the square is the section of the artists and intellectuals. Here, there is always a painter or two sitting before a canvas, surrounded by his tools: tubes of color, brushes, palette—as well as a thermos of coffee. Sometimes a small crowd gathers to watch the work progress.

Sometimes the artists sit idly gazing before themselves or talk to one another in voices that are always quiet and often serious.

In one corner of the square, beside a secluded entrance where a row of heavy stone benches and tables marked for chess are located, old people gather. They are mostly men dressed in coats that look too warm for the weather. They sit leaning over the tabletops, some engaged in chess games, others in conversation, others just sitting and watching. Here and there an old man lifts to his lips a styrofoam cup filled with steamy tea. Canes tilt at various angles against the sides of tables and hang from tabletops and bench backs. Voices thin with age murmur in accents old as Europe. A slow stillness hangs about the place, perfect for quiet reflection on the late-summer heat, the turning of the leaves, the chance of rain.

In sharpest contrast to this is the heart of the square. Here, boxes blast the latest hard rock hits, while couples dance barefoot, flashing the glitter and color of outrageous clothes, jewels, and make-up. Skaters swirl alone and in groups, often to their own music, piped into their heads by Sony Walkmen. As they move, they eat, drink, smoke, talk, all at once, so that sights and sounds are both a frenzied blur.

Through this maze of varied types, the tourists stroll, wide-eyed, watching, wondering, seeming not to realize that they trespass through sharply defined territories. They are, in fact, a sector in themselves, moving through but never a part of the square.

Exercise 8.   List possible subgroups for each of the following classes:
- a.   The distinct regions of your native country
- b.   The music of your native country
- c.   The religious groups in your native country
- ✓ d.   The political parties or factions in your native country
- e.   The types of programs on American television
- f.   The leisure activities popular among students at your college or university
- g.   The requirements in your chosen major

For Composition

Exercise 9.   Write a subdivision essay on one of the topics above. Aim at writing an essay that is concrete and readable rather than abstract and mechanical.

Exercise 10.   Write an essay subdividing the students or faculty at your college or university into various types. Aim at amusing as well as informing your reader while expressing a point of view.

Exercise 11.   Reread "Dissecting the Square," then plan and write your own essay analyzing the types of people one is likely to find in a particular place. Possibilities might include an American supermarket, a market in your own country, a particular park, museum, sports arena, office, or organization. Have in mind a reader who is unfamiliar with the place and people you are analyzing. Be sure to support your analysis with sufficient concrete details.

Comparison and Contrast

Like classifications and subdivisions, comparison and contrast analyses seek common and distinguishing characteristics. However, it is not necessary when comparing and contrasting to seek out all the subtypes within a class, nor even to treat two members of the same class. Rather, any two objects can be treated together as the writer seeks the similarities and differences between them. Comparisons point to similarities between two objects and contrasts point to differences. Sometimes the processes of comparison and contrast are combined within one essay. Sometimes, as in the following essay, inspired by a professional essay discussed in a later chapter (see page 193), the writer focuses on only one of the processes:

Ba, Fiji

According to Eric Sevareid's "Velva, North Dakota," towns all over the world are losing their individuality as they are influenced by modern technology. However, technological advancements have not changed my hometown, Ba, very much. Most people still make their living at simple farming as they have done for decades.

Ba is surrounded by farmlands; the green fields of sugarcane stretch to the distant mountains. Roosters still wake the farmers daily with their crowing, and the wooden yokes creak as the bullocks march slowly to the fields. The same cane cutters' hymns that were heard in decades past still float on the wind as the cutters pass by on their horses. The smell of burning wood still mixes with the smell of the vegetable curry mothers have always prepared for the family breakfast.

A twenty-cent ride on a bus with no windowpanes still brings people to the market. There, fresh pineapples are still four for a dollar. And for as long as I can remember, sugar has always been eleven cents a pound. A noise comes from every part of the market as each merchant explains why his goods are the best, in familiar phrases handed down through the years.

When I return to Ba in a few years, I don't think that I will be too surprised. There may be more electricity, a few more tar-sealed roads, but the people will continue in the same slow, peaceful way as always—what we call "the South Pacific way."

"Ba, Fiji" focuses on comparisons, on showing that the writer's town is the same now as it was in the past. Only a part of one sentence is devoted to contrast ("more electricity, a few more tar-sealed roads"). It is worth noting that in making her comparisons, the writer mentions almost exclusively the characteristics of the present-day town. The writer indicates their similarity to the characteristics of the town of the past by such words and phrases as *still, always, as they have done, for as long as I can remember,* and *handed down through the years.*

The next essay is a contrast piece. The student writer focuses on the changes that have occurred in his city: the differences between the island of the past and the island of the present.

Sea Changes

My hometown is an island in the Aegean Sea. But though it is surrounded by water, it has not been insulated from the changes brought by modernization.

I will never forget the chicken house my uncle made out of an old room close to our house. I used to sit on a rock and stare at the chickens as if they were strange people and I was trying to understand their language and behavior. Now, where the rock and chickens used to be is a big, well-furnished apartment, which is used as the family's summer condominium. It is not the only one in the town. The backyards full of flowers and vegetables are now cement patios with glass windbreakers surrounding them.

I like to wander through the small paths of the town and admire the architectural style of the few old, surviving houses. There, one might still see a big shade tree in the yard, protecting the table on which the family used to have its traditional Sunday lunch on the hot days of August. Nowadays fans and air-conditioning systems have taken over for the tall trees and meals are taken indoors.

When I was a little boy, I used to wake up every morning from the swoosh of the beach next to my window. But the only thing that wakes me up now is the terrible noise of the powerful engines excavating for a new high-rise building. The little sounds of the tiny animals that still live in the trees, in the grass, under the rocks are now covered by the roaring motors of passing cars. And during the night, when only the owls and the nightingales used to be heard, a popular singer is singing through the loud-speakers of a discotheque.

Even the people have changed. The farmers and fishermen of my island have become businessmen. Farmers have sold their farms to hotel-keepers to get money to build extra rooms or buy an extra television set in order to draw more paying guests. Fishermen have left their boats to corrode on the shore and have opened shops, selling handicrafts and popular art objects. The people used to be kind and friendly people. They would always offer hospitality to strangers. Not anymore. Now the only thing on their minds when they deal with strangers is their money.

Alternating Versus Divided Patterns of Organization

"Sea Changes" is organized on what is sometimes called the *alternating pattern*. The writer looks at one aspect of the island after another, showing how each aspect was in the past and then how it is in the present. Specifically, he focuses first on backyards, contrasting chicken houses and gardens to condominiums and cement patios, then moves on to the contrast between the tree-shaded outdoor dining of the past and the air-conditioned indoor meals of the present, and so on. In each case, we get an alternating pattern: a picture of past conditions contrasted immediately with a picture of the present.

It is also possible to organize comparison and contrast analyses according to a *divided pattern*. In this pattern, one paragraph (or group of paragraphs) treats all aspects of one object, and another paragraph (or paragraph group) treats all aspects of the compared or contrasted object.

The following essay is modeled on the *divided pattern*. It is also distinct from the previous two essays in that it combines the processes of comparison and contrast rather than focusing on either one process or the other.

The Miraflores Neighborhood

Living in Miraflores, a neighborhood in Quito, Ecuador, has always been a pleasure because of its people. I can still remember, when my family moved to this neighborhood fifteen years ago, how quickly I felt a part of it, how everybody seemed to know each other. And, in those days, I remember too how the neighborhood seemed as hospitable as my neighbors. Life in Miraflores was relaxed and tranquil. Traffic was light—very different from how it was in all other parts of the city. The usual sound was the sound of people talking or children playing at school. From the center of town one had a view of the forest. And people's strolling or driving to the forest for a rest—or simply hanging around with friends in the store on the corner— was everyday life in Miraflores.

But commercial growth has changed the life of the Miraflores neighborhood. A tunnel built on its border has increased traffic and traffic noise to the level of other places in the city. Big businesses have replaced the small shops neighbors used to meet in. Large buildings block out the familiar forest view. Now the only thing that makes Miraflores special is the warmth of its people. And I wonder how long this special warmth can survive in what has become just another part of the big city.

The first paragraph of "The Miraflores Neighborhood" describes the neighborhood of the past, as it was 15 years before. The second paragraph describes the same neighborhood as it is in the present. The writer contrasts one set of details (light traffic, human sounds, forest view, meeting places) with the other (heavy traffic, traffic noise, view of buildings, no meeting places). He also notes one similarity: the people in Miraflores are the same at present as they have always been. This comparison opens and closes his essay, giving the concept special importance while at the same time giving his organization added complexity. And this unmechanical but clear organization as well as the writer's own personal voice makes the essay natural and readable.

(For a discussion of one special type of comparison, the *analogy*, see page 182.)

Exercises

For Consideration

Exercise 12. Identify each of the following themes as a comparison, contrast, or combination:
    a. College entrance requirements in the United States are very different from those in my country.

   b.   College students in the United States seem to have many of the same interests as those in my country.

   c.   The university is just like a factory.

   d.   Although the computer has many similarities to the human brain, there are ways in which the two are not alike.

   e.   Though they are both considered Third World nations, the problems of oil-rich Mexico are very different from those of oil-poor Brazil.

Exercise 13. Like "Ba, Fiji," the essay below was inspired by the essay "Velva, North Dakota." However, the student writer of this essay was largely unsuccessful in his attempt to compare his town as it is in the present and as it was several years before. Read the essay and answer the following questions:

   a.   What is the thesis of the essay? Is it clearly stated? Does it focus on comparisons, contrasts, or both?

   b.   How is the essay organized? What would the writer need to do to make the organization logical and effective?

   c.   Has the author provided sufficient concrete details to support his thesis? Where might he have been more or less concrete and specific?

   d.   Despite its many problems, this essay includes several effective details. Underline those details in the essay which you feel are especially effective.

Kabbala: Religious Town

      Like the town in the essay "Velva, North Dakota," my town has changed under the current political regime. It is changing as the President orders. There are no more any complicated religious men who make the people cry because of religion. The idea of the society about these things has changed. The sights and sounds have changed. I can't hear the sounds of the animals in my area. All has changed to the sounds of the new transportation. There are no more people crowding about the men who collect money to help the poor families according to our religion. New technology has replaced the old. The old machines have not made the clothes for a long time. Telephones, television, cars have given the people more time and information about the world. The people have changed. Most people have become businessmen and are very rich. The farmers sell their fields and come to the town to collect more money; they forget about the fields and don't care about education. And that is why my country is very late in technology. The people eat differently. There are frozen foods. Moreover, they dress differently. Most old women still wear black dresses and some of the girls do too. The colorful way of dressing has become very common, and even my grandmother dresses differently. I think my town needs more technology. Though it has begun to change, it doesn't yet reach the level of Velva, North Dakota, that Eric Sevareid describes in his essay.

Exercise 14. Write a brief essay comparing and contrasting one of the following as it is in your country and as you have experienced it in the U.S.:

   a.   television news (or television entertainment programs or commercials)

   b.   student work (or leisure) habits

   c.   customs of greeting (or dining or dating)

Exercise 15.   Compare and contrast one of the following:
   a.   two of your professors
   b.   two of your classmates
   c.   two members of your family
   ✓ d.   two career choices you have considered or are considering

For Composition

Exercise 16.   Write an essay comparing and contrasting either (a) your hometown as it is now and as it was at an earlier time or (b) your hometown and another town or city you have lived in or know well.

Cause and Effect

In the previous section, several student essays compare their hometowns as they were in the past and present. In the essay, "The Miraflores Neighborhood," the writer also suggests causes for the changes he describes: "Commercial growth," he states, "has changed the life of the Miraflores neighborhood." Moreover, the writer wonders whether the physical changes in the neighborhood (heavier traffic, bigger businesses, and so forth) will ultimately cause the people to change as well.

An essay that focuses predominantly on trying to find the *causes* or *reasons* for a particular phenomenon or tries to determine what the *results* of a particular action might be is a cause-and-effect essay. Such essays can identify either causes (why something happens) or effects (what is likely to happen) alone. They can also work in both directions identifying the causes of a phenomenon and then projecting the further effects of that phenomenon. (Indeed, the author of "The Miraflores Neighborhood" does just this. He identifies the *cause*—commercial growth—of the physical changes in his neighborhood; then he projects the effect of those changes—loss of the people's special warmth.)

In the following essay, a student writer gives his reasons for his choice of major, setting out several reasons for his having decided to study architecture:

Building My Future

Ever since I was a kid, I liked building. I had building blocks and used them everyday, building different things and destroying them so I could rebuild them with different shapes. As I grew older, every time I had a piece of paper, I drew a house design, something I still like to do. When I draw, I think of the house I'm planning as my own.

When I decided to study architecture two years ago, it was in part because across the street from our house in Venezuela, an architect had built his own house, and I watched him and thought that it was a wonderful thing. He became my best friend. I could go to him and ask for advice and he taught me how to make small repairs and draw simple designs. I liked the way he lived—being his own boss and creating something out of his own imagination to enjoy. It seemed the way I would like to live.

I think my future would be certain if we were living twenty-five years ago, when building was a major career in undeveloped countries like Venezuela. But even today, I think that it is a good career choice because there is still much need for architects. Old buildings are always being torn down to make new ones and new areas are still being developed, and this will continue for a long time.

I know that finding work as an architect is hard. But I believe that if I want to be an architect badly enough, I can do it. I hope that I will have enough power to finish the major and be one of the best architects in my country. I know that if I can go through with my plans, my financial and spiritual future will rest on a firm foundation.

This essay, like other analyses we have looked at in this chapter, is noteworthy for its concrete detail, its clear but natural organization, and its readability. But what is especially worth noting here is the writer's ascribing his choice of major to not just one but *several* causes:

Cause 1 (Paragraph 1):   Building is part of the writer; he has enjoyed the activity since childhood.

Cause 2 (Paragraph 2):   His experience of watching and learning from an architect building his own home made the writer decide to pursue a career in architecture.

Cause 3 (Paragraph 2):   The writer would like to live the way the architect lives.

Cause 4 (Paragraph 3):   There is a continuing need for architects.

Cause 5 (Paragraph 4):   Despite the difficulties of completing the major and finding work, the financial and spiritual rewards of architecture are great.

Avoiding Oversimplification

A common error in cause-and-effect essays is *oversimplification*: the writer ascribes a phenomenon to one cause when in reality there are several contributing causes. Often there is one *immediate* cause (the cause that immediately precedes the phenomenon and seems to be the main cause of it) as well as several *underlying* causes that may, in fact, be equally or even more important than the immediate one. The writer of "Building My Future," for example, originally began his second paragraph thus: "When I decided to study architecture two years ago, it was because. . . ." He then went on to describe his experience with an architect neighbor. This experience was the *immediate cause* for his decision. But, of course, it was not the only cause; indeed, his love of building and designing had been part of him long before he had this experience. Thus, in revising, he rewrote the first sentence of Paragraph 2 to read, as it now does, ". . . it was in part because. . . ." The revised sentence makes allowances for all the other causes that went into his career choice.

Avoiding False Cause

Another common error in cause-and-effect essays is what is known as *false cause*. Two phenomena may exist or two events may occur one after the other without any cause-and-effect relationship existing between them. Students should be cautious not to mistake correlation for causation. (*Oversimplification* and *false cause* will be discussed in greater detail in Chapter 8.)

Exercises

For Consideration

Exercise 17. In this essay, a student writer gives the reasons for his choice of major. Read the essay and answer the following:

    a. What causes does the writer give for his choice? Has he oversimplified the causes?

    b. How does the essay compare with "Building My Future"?

- Is the organization as clear? Why or why not?

- Is the writing as concrete and detailed? Give examples.

- Is the essay as natural and readable, or does it seem more mechanical? Explain.

My Major

    I chose the field of international business when I heard the university I was planning to attend had this major available. I think this field is a good field for foreign students who would like to return to their country and work for an American company as I plan to do. I think this field fits me because I enjoy traveling and meeting as many people as possible. I feel comfortable around people and besides I like getting paid in dollars instead of *drachmas*. I also found out from some relatives that American companies are looking for people such as me who plan to return to Greece and live there for good.

    I would not be a big risk to the company or maybe not as big as an American who some day wants to go back to the United States. I think these reasons some day will enable me to get a good job in Greece. That's why I chose the field of international business.

Exercise 18. Which of the following causal relationships seem oversimplified?

    a. I chose to major in computer science because I got a personal computer for my birthday and really enjoyed working with it.

    b. I chose to major in nursing because the need for nurses is great in my country, the pay is good, and I have always enjoyed helping those in need.

    c. The Vietnam War was caused by the United States' desire to prevent communism from spreading throughout Southeast Asia.

    d. Mexico's economic crisis in the 1980s was caused by the international decline in the price of oil.

    e. Acquired Immune Deficiency Syndrome (AIDS) is caused by various subtypes of a virus that passes from one body to another by means of body fluids.

    f. Acquired Immune Deficiency Syndrome is caused by homosexuality.

    g. Studying hard will result in an A grade.

Exercise 19.   List the effects of the following real or imagined phenomena:
  a.   Your choice to study in the United States
  b.   Your choice to live in a dorm or off campus
  c.   Your failure of English composition
  d.   Your winning of $1 million in a lottery

For Composition

Exercise 20.   Write a brief essay giving your reasons for choosing your current major. Be as concrete as possible and try to organize your essay in a clear, yet unmechanical way.

Exercise 21.   Write a cause-and-effect essay on one of the following topics:
  a.   The reasons you chose to study at your college or university
  b.   The causes of a particular development or crisis in your country
  c.   The actual or likely consequences of the last change of government in your country, or the likely consequences of an imagined change of government.
✓ d.   The conditions that make Americans behave differently from the people of your country
✓ e.   The reasons women live longer on the average than do men
  f.   The effects of the discovery of the birth control pill

Process

The last type of analysis we will discuss in this chapter is *process* analysis. Process essays outline the *steps* that are necessary to achieve a *goal*. Process is similar to cause and effect in that, if certain steps are followed, a particular phenomenon (the goal) will result. Process differs from cause and effect in that the focus is on the *orderly progression* from one step to another. When a writer explains how a piece of equipment works or how an experiment is conducted or a native dish prepared, or when he traces the steps that occur in a natural phenomenon, such as the birth of a baby or the eruption of a volcano, he is writing a process essay.

In the following essay, a student writes, as in the exercises in the previous section, about his choice of major. Here, however, the focus is on the process used in making that choice rather than on the reasons for the choice.

Choosing My Career

Selecting a vocation and future career has been on my mind for as long as I can remember. From the time that I was a child to the time that I was a senior high school student, I used to think about it. In my last year of high school, when I was going to enter a university and had not yet chosen a future career, I became serious about this important decision.

To select a vocation I had to consider many things. First, I considered my values. The most important value for me was my interest. Since I have always been interested in engineering, the general field of my vocation seemed clear to me. The value next in importance to me was the need of my society. I thought: there is no value in several years of studying if nobody in my country needs workers in the field of my choice. So I eliminated all the fantasy jobs and focused my attention on the practical jobs in the field I loved.

My next step was drawing up a list of possible jobs in engineering such as mechanics, communications, electronics, and computers. Then I had to find information about the jobs which I had on my list, so I checked out several books on various types of engineering from our school library. After studying these, I was still undecided between electronics and computers. Thus, I consulted with various people in these two fields to find out more about the particulars of each job: the financial rewards, the job requirements, and the possibilities for employment. On the basis of these talks, I chose computer engineering as my field and circuit designing as my particular career.

The logical next step was to begin my college education in the field I had chosen in order to make sure that this should be my future career. And now, after several months of study, I am very interested in my major and have decided definitely to complete my education as a circuit designer in computer engineering.

The writer here, like the authors of "Building My Future" and "My Major," tells us what career he has chosen. But that is only by way of illustrating his main focus: the process he used in making his choice. We might outline that process as follows:

Step 1: I considered my most important values.

Step 2: I drew up a list of possible jobs in the field of my interest.

Step 3: I found information on the various jobs on my list and chose two that seemed most appealing.

Step 4: I consulted with people in these two fields to gather specific information about each field.

Step 5: I made my final choice.

Guidelines for Writing Process Essays

The basic guidelines for writing a process essay are:
Include all major steps.

Omit any irrelevant steps.

Arrange steps in a logical and orderly progression.

Had the writer of "Choosing My Career" omitted the fact that he drew up a list of possible jobs, or had he chosen books on the various fields in his list before making the list, or had he added that he joined the chess team after consulting the books he chose, his essay would have been weakened. In addition, as with all other analytical essays, process analyses can be either mechanical and dry or natural and readable. Concrete details, the author's own voice, and an unmechanical structure make this essay enjoyable as well as informative.

Exercises

For Consideration

Exercise 22. The following student essay deals with subject matter that could be rather dry and uninteresting. Yet the writer skillfully manages to keep the essay reasonably enjoyable as well as informative. Read the essay and answer the following questions:

a. What steps does the writer identify in this process essay?

b. Does the essay seem to be complete? Is there enough concrete detail to make the essay clear and readable? Have any irrelevant steps been included?

c. Is the organization logical? Does it appear mechanical? Why or why not?

d. What in particular about the essay keeps it from being dry? Can you think of ways in which the writer could have made the essay even more readable?

How to Kick a Soccer Ball

Although a soccer kick happens quickly, actually, there are many steps that go into making it successful. First, a person must step correctly while his kicking leg approaches the ball. If a right-handed person wants to kick the ball, he must step on his left foot about a foot away but parallel to the ball so that he can use the full strength of his right foot while kicking. A left-handed person steps with his right foot and kicks with his left.

In actually making contact with the ball, the player must decide how he wants the ball to travel before he touches the ball with his foot. If he wants to give spin to the ball, he must make contact with the ball with the area from the tip of his foot to a quarter way back to the heel on either side of the foot. To give inside spin, he must use the inside of his foot; to give outside spin, he must use the outside. In order to make a "confidential" or a straight kick, the player must use either the middle or upper surface of his foot. Or he might choose heel kicking, making contact with the ball with the tip of his heel. This is used mainly to "fake" or fool opponents.

Finally, the player must make contact with a particular part of the ball. Kicking on the ball's lowest part will result in a long kick. The higher on the ball contact is made, the shorter the kick is likely to be.

If the player performs these steps accurately, the ball will go just where and how he wants it to—much to his opponents' grief.

Exercise 23. Identify problems in the following outlines for process essays.

a. Sewing a hem

Step 1: Buy thread to match garment.

Step 2: Thread needle.

Step 3: Knot thread.

Step 4: Stitch edge of hem to garment with in-and-out stitch.

Step 5: Remove pins.

Step 6: Iron new hem.

  b. Cooking a hamburger
    Step 1: Turn oven to broil setting.
    Step 2: Form about one-quarter pound of ground beef into a round patty.
    Step 3: Sprinkle with salt.
    Step 4: Turn patty over and grill on other side.
    Step 5: Check whether rolls and French fries are ready.
    Step 6: Remove hamburger from oven when brown.

For Composition

Exercise 24. Write a brief process essay of two or three paragraphs on one of the following topics:
  a. how to prepare a special dish from your native country
  b. how to perform a dance step, exercise, or particular sport maneuver
  c. the steps involved in seeking university admission in your country
  d. the process involved in performing a customary task in your field of study (for example, an experiment in physics or chemistry, a geological identification, a cost-price analysis)

Exercise 25. Write an essay advising other students on how to be an A or an F student. If you like, give your essay a comic tone. In any case, be sure to be concrete and to develop your advice as an orderly process.

Exercise 26. Write a comic essay on how to be an American. Using your experience of Americans, tell a non-American reader what steps he would have to follow—that is, what style, manners, and customs he would have to adopt—in order to appear to be an American. Alternatively, you may choose to tell an American reader the steps necessary to appear to be a native of your own country.

Exercise 27. Imagine yourself a college advisor counseling an audience of high school seniors from your own country who wish to continue their education in the United States. In an essay of from three to five paragraphs, indicate to these students the steps they should follow in choosing a university to which to apply.

Summary

Analysis is a breaking up of a whole into its component parts for the purpose of examining the relationship of one part to another or to the whole. In writing, analysis can take several forms: classification assigns an object to its class; subdivision separates a class into its subgroups; comparison and contrast shows the similarities and differences between two objects; cause and effect seeks the reasons for or results of a phenomenon; process outlines the steps necessary to complete a goal.

In an analysis, the thesis is of primary importance and it is generally made explicit early in the essay. The student writer should aim at making his analysis clear and logical, but also readable and unmechanical.

Chapter 8

Argument

In all the essay patterns we have discussed so far, the writer's job has been to present a thesis along with sufficient details to support it adequately for the reader. In argument, the writer's job is more formidable. In argument, the writer must try to *persuade* the reader. That is, the writer must try to move the reader to adopt his position on an issue of controversy or, if the reader already shares his opinion, to become more firmly convinced of it. Thus, for an essay to be an argument, the writer himself must take a stand—that is, form an opinion—on a controversial issue, an issue on which opinions differ. Then he must try to convince the reader to share his opinion (1) by stating his opinion clearly, (2) by giving evidence to support his opinion, and (3) by answering the arguments generally made against his opinion.

Many students enjoy writing arguments. Most of us have opinions on the great issues of the day. We want to make our opinions known and to show how strongly we feel about the wrongs and injustices we see about us. But in writing arguments, students sometimes forget that the main purpose of argumentation is not simply to express strong feelings, but to persuade another person to share an opinion. Thus, in argument even more than in other forms of writing, the writer must keep his *audience* in mind (see pages 5–6). He must know who it is he is trying to persuade and he must adapt his argument to that audience.

Some audiences, granted, are easily persuaded. History is full of sad examples of masses of people convinced by the weak and deceiving arguments of unscrupulous leaders tragically gifted with a stirring voice and a shrewd understanding of how to rouse the ugliest of human passions. Indeed, what we say in this chapter may be less important for what students learn about writing arguments than for what they learn about listening to them. For we are all part of the audience of mankind, and it is our responsibility to evaluate critically the emotion-stirring arguments of those who want to persuade us and to determine who makes sense and who just makes noise.

In academic writing, the student must assume an audience of responsible readers. He must direct his argument at an audience that will regard it critically and that will be persuaded not by rabble-rousing rhetoric, but by sound reasoning, solid evidence, fairness, and self-control.

The argument below was written by a student at the time of the Iranian hostage crisis, during which a group of 52 Americans were held captive in the American Embassy in Iran. The writer himself was not an Iranian, but he was nonetheless deeply disturbed by the reactions of Americans to the crisis. In his essay, he argues that the hostage-taking was not unjust, and claims that it should teach the American government to stay out of other nations' affairs. Let us look at his essay:

America Held Hostage

Americans should take what happened in Iran as a lesson for the American government. It shows what happens to people who don't mind their own business. I know this may be a little offensive to you, but try to look at it with logic and not with feelings. When Americans look at the situation in Iran, they use their feelings, which tell them that what is happening is wrong simply because fellow Americans are held hostage. If the Iranians had asked for the Shah peacefully, the United States would have told them to go and (x$*+?x''&!). So they had no choice but to do what they did. Furthermore, the Iranians have every right to ask for the Shah to be returned—the guy is a murderer and a thief. I personally think that the Iranians should have been even more strict—like by starving the hostages. This would have left the United States no time to beat around the bush as it has and the Iranians would have had their Shah back a month ago.

The American government wants the Iranian government to kiss its feet the way the Shah did. Americans must be crazy to expect that the Iranians will continue to be their puppets. They think the world exists only for them. America should let Iran take care of its own problems and stop trying to control the world.

The student author of "America Held Hostage" has some writing skill; he is fluent in English and he writes with style. However, in this argument he forgets that his purpose is to persuade his audience to his point of view. As a result, he writes in such a way that he most likely turns his audience away from his opinion.

The writer's intended audience is Americans. In his third sentence, he even addresses his American readers as *you*, granting that his argument may be offensive to them. But in the course of his essay, he insults Americans and their government several times, using strong and offensive language. The reference to the American government as "people who *don't mind their own business*," the statement that the American government "wants the Iranian government to *kiss its feet*," the suggestion that Americans "must be *crazy*," and that America has been trying to "*control the world*"—all these are examples of "loaded" language, language so weighted on the arguer's side that there is no way to argue against it. Of course, America would be wrong not to mind its own business or to try to control the world or to expect others to kiss its feet; and if Americans are crazy, their opinion is worthless. But few Americans are likely to be persuaded by such language. Similarly, the writer's calling the former Shah (the "guy") a "murderer" and "thief" without offering the least supporting evidence will likely be accepted only by those who either read uncritically or already share this view. The writer should use more restraint in his choice of words—or should supply a great deal more support—if he hopes to convince responsible readers who do not already agree with him.

Style without substance does not necessarily persuade. When the student writes that "If the Iranians had asked for the Shah peacefully, the United States would have told them to go and (x$* + ?x"&!)," the style is arresting. It catches the reader's attention. But the statement itself is questionable and the language vague and unconvincing. Finally, when the writer suggests that the Iranians might better have tried a starvation policy on the hostages, it is unlikely that many American readers will be moved to go along with him. Indeed, such a viewpoint probably would prompt some readers to reject the argument as written by an extremist.

All the writer says may be a true reflection of how he feels. The problem with the essay as argument is that it is unlikely to fulfill the main purpose of argument: It is unlikely to persuade its intended audience to share the opinion it expresses.

Elements of Argument

Of what, then, does a good argument consist? The writer of argument should be sure to include each of the following elements:

1. *Thesis*: The writer should clearly present his main idea, expressing his stand on the issue he is addressing.

2. *Supporting evidence*: The writer should supply statements or data sufficient to persuade the reader of the correctness of his stand.

3. *Recognition of objections*: The writer must show the reader that he is aware of the arguments generally made against his stand.

4. *Answers to objections*: The writer must invalidate the objections he has recognized by showing that they are either false (refutation) or, though true, less significant than his supporting evidence (concession).

The following pages will discuss each of these elements in depth.

Thesis

As with analyses, the *thesis* of an argument is almost always *explicit* and generally stated early in the essay. It is important to remember that the thesis of an argument must *take a stand* on a *controversial issue*. Thus, the thesis

> Some people believe in the freedom of a woman to seek an abortion while others oppose it.

is not a satisfactory argumentative thesis because it does not take a stand. Rather, it merely states two sides of a controversy. Such a thesis is sometimes called a *weaseling thesis* because, like the slender animal it is named after, it slips between two positions. A satisfactory thesis on this topic might be written as follows:

> Despite objections to it, women should be free to seek an abortion.

or

> Women should not be legally permitted to seek an abortion.

Or, if the writer does not support either of these positions, he might still take a stand in this manner:

> Contrary to the views of both prolife and prochoice activists, there is no clearly correct answer to whether or not women should be free to seek abortions.

Similarly, the thesis

> In 1973 the U.S. Congress passed a law giving all women in the U.S. the right to seek an abortion.

is not a satisfactory thesis for an argument because there is no controversy involved. The statement that a law was passed in a certain year is simply a matter of fact.

In addition to taking a stand on an issue of controversy, the thesis of an argument should be *limited* enough to be adequately supported within the scope of the writer's essay. It would be difficult in an essay of three or four paragraphs to write a persuasive argument on theses such as

> War is the natural state of mankind.

or

> The purpose of life is to live in harmony with the universe.

And, indeed, arguments on such broad topics as a woman's right to an abortion, the wisdom of nuclear disarmament, or solar versus nuclear energy would probably require more space—and knowledge—than a brief and unresearched student essay generally allows. The writer will have an easier job persuading his readers if he limits his thesis in accordance with the length of his essay and the evidence he is able to gather to support his argument. For example, in a brief essay a student writer would probably have an easier job defending a narrowed thesis such as

> The decision to abort her baby may have serious emotional consequences for the mother.

or

> No abortion should be performed against the will of the would-be father.

than he would have defending a more broadly construed thesis on this sensitive and complex issue.

Some writers find it helpful in planning an argumentative essay to write out a one-sentence *thesis statement* (see page 96), indicating not only the writer's basic stand but also subordinate information including the major points of supporting evidence and the major objections. Evidence can be expressed in a clause beginning with *because* or *since* or a phrase introduced by *due to* or *given*. Objections can be introduced by *although, even though, despite,* or *in spite of*. For example, the thesis just above could be made into a thesis statement such as the following:

> Even though the fetus grows within the mother's body, no abortion should be performed against the will of the would-be father because the fetus is a part of him as well as the mother, because it is possible for a fetus to develop independently of the mother, and because the father's emotional well-being may be affected if he is unable to keep a life he helped create from being destroyed.

Naturally, a sentence like this would never actually appear in an essay. But writing out a thesis statement may help the writer put his ideas into shape.

Supporting Evidence

The *evidence* in an argument is similar to the supporting details in other essay patterns. The difference is in the rigor with which such evidence must be selected and used. Readers of other kinds of essays are likely to accept the writer's theme or thesis more or less on faith (although carefully selected supporting details will make it more convincing). Readers of argument, on the other hand, may have fundamental doubts about the writer's thesis. They need to be persuaded of its accuracy by a logical structure of precise statements based ultimately on uncontroversial facts. Consider the following argument:

> Abortion should not be legal because it is a crime. We know it is a crime because abortion is nothing but murder. In an abortion, human life is destroyed without a trial. This is murder, and the woman who seeks the abortion and the doctor who performs it are murderers.

The writer of such a paragraph may feel pretty pleased with herself reading it. She's made some strong statements and supported them with other strong statements. However, all the statements in the paragraph are, in themselves, controversial. And all hinge on the reader's acceptance of the highly controversial statement that in an abortion "a human life is destroyed." This is a statement of judgment made by the writer, and she may have a hard time persuading critical readers of the statement's accuracy unless she can back it up at a deeper level with statements that are uncontroversial or, at least, less controversial. For instance, a statement that is not entirely uncontroversial, but is less controversial than the statement above is the following:

> The fetus is similar in many ways to a newborn baby, and newborns are generally regarded as human beings.

Such a statement could be supported, in turn, by facts, such as a description of the appearance, functioning, and capabilities of a fetus as compared to a newborn infant. Or it could be backed up with statistics: figures such as the number of nerves or brain cells in the fetus compared to the number in a newborn baby or the results of experiments measuring reactions of the fetus to outside stimuli. Other supporting statements might take the form of examples, for instance, the human appearance of the hand of the fetus or the fetus's sucking its thumb and hiccuping in the mother's uterus. In addition, the writer might want to support her statement that in an abortion "a human life is destroyed" with voices of authority: recognized experts in various fields who have made considered judgments on the matter and supported them with fact, logic, and experience. In the case of this statement, the writer might seek support from such authorities as physicians and biologists, as well as from psychologists and perhaps philosophers. Depending on her audience, the writer might include the voices of religious leaders as well (though some readers might dismiss such authorities as *biased*— prejudiced in the matter by a prior belief).

None of these statements will prove absolutely that the fetus is a human being in the way that mathematicians prove theorems or scientists prove that a particular vaccine will prevent a particular illness. Positions on controversial issues cannot be proved absolutely (if they could be, the issues would not be controversial). However, by backing up her controversial statements with less controversial statements, as well as with facts, figures, and the judgments of authoritative experts where available, the writer will help ensure that her thesis is well supported and her argument is persuasive.

Recognizing Objections

Even when an argument is supported by strong evidence, many readers are still likely to ask: What about the arguments on the other side? Thus, the writer of an argument cannot simply hide from the other side of an issue, hoping that his readers will not know or wonder about it. The writer must confront the opposition by recognizing the *objections* it is likely to raise. The writer of the argument against abortion, then, must consider the objections that will be raised against her thesis. These might include the following:

1. If abortion is made illegal, many unwanted babies will be born who might then suffer neglect.
2. Making abortion illegal places a heavy financial burden on parents of children born through unplanned pregnancies.
3. Even if abortion is made illegal, people will still seek abortions and the unauthorized abortions available may be dangerous to the mother.
4. Because the fetus cannot survive independently of the mother, it is not human and, therefore, not entitled to human rights.

If the writer does not raise such objections, the reader of her argument might do so herself, giving the writer no opportunity to answer them. The reader's trust in the writer's argument is strengthened by the writer's confronting the arguments of the opposition as squarely as possible.

Answering Objections

Having recognized the objections, the writer must answer them, again supporting controversial statements as much as possible with uncontroversial evidence. There are two ways for the writer to confront an objection against her argument. Either she can *refute* it—prove it false—or she can *concede* it—accept the objection as true while showing that it does not override her argument.

The writer of the argument against abortion would have to consider how best to answer each of the objections she has recognized. Perhaps she will choose to concede the second objection—that making abortion illegal places a heavy financial burden on parents of children born through unplanned pregnancies. She might word her *concession* as follows:

> Of course, some parents whose children are the result of unplanned preg-nancies might encounter a financial burden for which they are unprepared. While this is a hardship, it is of relatively little significance when weighed against the hardship the unborn suffer when deprived of their right to live.

Thus, the writer accepts the objection, but *invalidates* it by suggesting that it is insignif-icant compared to the arguments she is raising against legalized abortion. (She might then back up her statement with whatever concrete supporting evidence she can gather: the aid available to the financially burdened, examples of financially burdened fami-lies who nonetheless manage to lead satisfying and productive lives, the unwillingness of many severely handicapped people to give up their lives despite the everyday hardships they must endure.) Words and expressions that can introduce a concession include the relators *of course, granted, to be sure, it is true, true* (see page 163).

Whichever way she deals with the other objections, she will probably want to *refute*—prove false—the fourth objection because her argument hinges on the reader's acceptance that the fetus is entitled to human rights. She might deal with this objec-tion in the following manner:

> Some deny the humanness of the fetus on the grounds that it cannot sur-vive independently of the mother. However, under present technology, pre-mature infants of twenty-four weeks—within the time limit in which abortion is permitted—have survived. Moreover, in the future, it may be possible for a fetus of any age to be brought to maturity in an artificial womb, out-side the mother's body. And independence is a shaky principle for deter-mining humanness. Newborns and even older infants as well as infirm adults often cannot survive independently of others, and yet are still generally considered humans entitled to all available support necessary to their sur-vival.

Whichever way the writer chooses to answer objections, it is vital that she answer each one recognized in her essay. Only in this way can she convince the reader of her trustworthiness and of the strength of her argument.

Tone in Argument

In addition to all the elements mentioned above, there is one other feature of argument that the student writer must master: tone. We already discussed tone in an earlier chapter (see pages 5–6), and most likely the student has gained some skill in controlling his tone in order to communicate his ideas effectively to his readers. How-ever, even students who are able to control their tone adequately in writing other kinds of essays sometimes lose control when they are arguing. Perhaps they just have a hard time keeping their tempers about issues that anger them. Perhaps they feel, if they yell as loud as they can, they will be persuasive.

This is not the case, as "America Held Hostage" should prove. The written equivalent of yelling and stamping your feet—failure to control tone in argument—may get attention, but it is unlikely to persuade thoughtful readers. It is facts themselves that will persuade, not the writer's anger over them. Showing your emotions in print is generally not an effective way to convince your reader of their validity. Present your thesis clearly, support it with solid evidence, answer objections fairly, and there is a good chance that reasonable readers will come to appreciate and even to share your feelings.

Analysis of an Argument

Let us return to the argument "America Held Hostage." In that essay, the writer does present a thesis (though not as clearly or as tactfully as he might). The thesis is expressed in his first and last sentences:

> What happened in Iran should be a lesson for the American government
> that it should let Iran take care of its own problems.

When it comes to supporting that thesis, however, his essay is woefully weak. He does not give any clear evidence to show that the American government was, indeed, interfering in Iran's affairs. Although he claims that the Iranians "have every right to ask for the Shah to be returned" because the Shah "is a murderer and a thief," he does not support either statement with specific evidence. The student writer tells the reader to try and look at the issue "with logic and not with feelings." But he himself offers little logic, while his angry feelings are clearly evident.

As for the objections likely to be made against his stand, the writer recognizes only two, and he answers these rather casually. First, he concedes that his thesis may be "a little offensive" to his readers. He answers this by suggesting that it would not be offensive if Americans would respond with logic instead of feelings—that the feelings that tell his readers that the hostage taking is wrong are not a valid reason for deploring the hostage taking. The writer recognizes a second objection against his argument when he suggests what would have happened if the Iranians had "asked for the Shah peacefully." The writer attempts to refute this objection by indicating that, had the Iranians made a peaceful request, the United States would not have cooperated. According to the writer, the Iranians "had no choice" but to take the hostages.

Neither objection has been satisfactorily answered by the writer. First, the feelings that tell many Americans it is wrong to hold other Americans (or individuals of whatever nationality) hostage—feelings of justice and respect for human life and safety—will not be automatically accepted as insignificant. As for the second objection, while it *may* be true that the American government would not have honored a "peaceful" request for the Shah's return, the writer has not proven this. He should *qualify* his statement—make it less definite—by writing, "If the Iranians had asked for the Shah peacefully, the United States would *perhaps* have denied their request." It does not necessarily follow that the Iranians "had no choice but to do what they did." The writer cannot know that, and the reader may question him: How do *you* know? Couldn't they have tried negotiations? Might they have used some tool other than human lives to try to get the Shah back?

Furthermore, the reader might raise other objections to the thesis: If the Shah asked for asylum, didn't the United States government have a responsibility to protect him? Isn't the terrorizing of innocent victims always an unjust way to settle international grievances? When an argument leaves the reader unsatisfied that the objections to the writer's thesis have been fully recognized and satisfactorily answered, the reader is unlikely to be persuaded.

Let us look, then, at a "revision" of this essay—an argument that takes the same stand, but argues for it in a more restrained and better reasoned manner.

An Injustice to Win Justice

For forty days now, Iranians have held hostage personnel of the American Embassy in Iran. Americans naturally feel angry about this, and most Americans probably feel it is unjustified. However, what happened in Iran should also be taken as a lesson for the American government that it cannot interfere in the affairs of another nation without some fear of reprisals.

For many years, the United States government supported the Shah in Iran. Such support continued despite the widely known corruption that characterized the Shah's regime. The Shah and members of his family lived in great wealth at the expense of the poor and hungry in Iran. When the people of Iran demonstrated against this, they were brutally killed by the Iranian police and armed forces. In several years of protests, there were thousands of killings and arrests of Iranians suspected of disloyalty. Through all of this, the United States supported the Shah as a friend and ally.

When the new government of Iran came to power, the crimes of the Shah's regime were exposed. Thus, when the Shah fled, the United States might have refused to grant him amnesty. Instead, the U.S. government continued to support the Shah. This support was a further example of the U.S. government's interference in Iran's affairs. It was an interference the Iranians could no longer tolerate. They felt they had to get the Shah back.

Of course, it might be argued that Iran should have sought the Shah's return in some more peaceful way. But the Iranians who took the hostages were not in a mood—or a position—for considered action. They were outraged citizens, furious at the crimes that had been committed against them. Moreover, there is a great likelihood that the United States would not have honored a request for the Shah's return. Although the Iranian government might have tried negotiating or even threatening the U.S. with an oil strike or some other economic weapon, the U.S. is so much more powerful than Iran that it is unlikely that it would have felt obliged to give in to Iran's demands.

Some might also feel that the United States had an obligation to grant the Shah political asylum. Asylum, however, is generally granted to the innocent victims of brutal regimes, not to those who have inflicted brutality on others. War criminals, for example, do not enjoy asylum in the United States, but are extradited to the government representing those against whom their crimes were committed. Certainly, the people of Iran have a right to try the Shah for the crimes they feel he committed against them.

Iranians claim that the Embassy personnel were, in reality, spies. At present, there is no definite proof establishing their guilt or innocence. Of course, if they are innocent, their suffering for the Shah's crimes and for the U.S. government's support of those crimes is an injustice. However, the injustice against the Americans may be the only way for the Iranians to win justice for themselves: justice in trying their own Shah and justice in running their own affairs without the interference of the American government.

Let us look more closely at this argument. The opening sentences announce the issue that the argument will address, giving an indication of where the opposing side is likely to stand ("Americans naturally feel angry about this, and most Americans probably feel it is unjustified"). We might note that the writer here does not belittle such feelings as does the writer of "America Held Hostage." Nor does he insult his audience by telling it to "try to look at [the argument] with logic." The thesis, stated at the end of the first paragraph, is the same as the thesis in "America Held Hostage": "What happened in Iran should . . . be taken as a lesson for the American government that it cannot interfere in the affairs of another nation without some fear of reprisals." Paragraphs 2 and 3 give evidence that the United States was interfering in Iran's affairs despite its knowledge of the injustices of the Shah's regime. The evidence is not extensive: we have only the writer's word that the Shah's regime was corrupt and cruel. But because the writer is restrained yet concrete in describing what went on, the reader likely tends to believe him.

Paragraph 4 recognizes the objections that Iran should have used peaceful means to regain the Shah and that the Shah deserved asylum, and refutes both claims. And Paragraph 5 concedes the objection that it is terrible and unjust for innocent people to suffer, but suggests that the injustice may have been the only way to gain justice. Finally, the last sentence in the essay makes a transition from this concession back to the thesis.

Of course, not all readers would be convinced by this argument. Some would require more fully *documented* evidence (see page 218)—specific citations of authorities and statistics from sources they know and trust. Some would hold such firm beliefs that the hostage taking was wrong (or the Shah deserving of protection, or the United States government justified in its actions) that the writer could never persuade them to the contrary. But a restrained and careful argument will have a better chance of persuading readers who do not already share the writer's opinion than will an angry, careless one.

Organization of the Argumentative Essay

The organization of the essay above is rather unusual in that it ends with a concession. Generally, an argument should finish strong. Objections that must be conceded or weakly refuted should be handled early on, and the end of the essay should resound with the writer's most convincing arguments. The argument on bilingual education to be found in Chapter 19 conforms to this organizational pattern.

Nonetheless, as with most matters of writing, there is no hard and fast rule regarding the organization of arguments. The writer of the essay above felt that the analogy of one injustice to another was his most convincing argument. For this reason, he chose to abandon conventional wisdom and conclude his argument with a concession.

Argumentative Fallacies

In order to maintain reason and restraint, there are several *fallacies* the student writer must avoid. A *fallacy* is a flaw—a mistake—in reasoning or argument. The student writer should be able to recognize the following fallacies:

1. *Overgeneralization*: This is the name given to overstatements that extend the application of a principle more widely than can be demonstrated. Writers of argument should be careful about using terms such as *all, every, everybody, none, always, never, only*, and so forth. In addition, they should be careful in using such nouns and proper nouns as *people, students, old people, Americans, Iranians*, and so on, unless they are qualified by a modifier such as *some* or *many*. Terms such as *all, none, Americans*, and *young people* are absolute—they allow for no exceptions—and they usually make careful readers wary. Does the writer of "America Held Hostage" really know how "Americans look at the situation in Iran" or only how *some* Americans do? Did the Iranians really have "no choice" but to take the hostages? Do they have "every right" to ask for the Shah's return? In writing argument, student writers should be careful of their use of absolutes, restricting their terms where necessary by using such modifiers as *some, many, most* (if justified), *sometimes, often, frequently, rarely*, and so forth.

2. *Begging the question*: This is the name given to the error of construing an argument in such terms that there can be no argument against it. Begging the question can take either of two forms:
   a. The use of *loaded language*—that is, language that is so weighted emotionally against the opposition that there is no argument against it. (If the Shah is a "murderer and a thief" certainly he does not deserve protection.)
   b. *Self-evident* reasoning—that is, reasoning that maintains that an argument is true because an argument is true. This is the kind of reasoning young children sometimes use (to the distress of their parents) when they defend their actions: "Why don't you like green peas?" "Because I don't."

3. *Avoiding the question*: This is the name given to the error of misrepresenting the position of the opposition. The writer of argument should be careful to represent the opposition fairly and accurately. When a writer misrepresents the opposition, he not only falsifies his argument, he also risks losing his reader's trust. Misrepresentation thus renders argument ineffective as well as false. Avoiding the question may take either of two forms:
   a. Setting up a *straw man*—that is, a representation of the opposition that is so exaggerated it is as easy to knock down as a man made out of straw. The writer of "America Held Hostage" writes: "The American government wants the Iranian government to kiss its feet." Of course, if that is what the American government wants, it is unjustified. However, the reader might ask: Is that really what the American government wants?
   b. Arguing *ad hominem*—that is, against the man, by attacking the character of those who oppose the writer's position rather than their arguments. Ameri-

cans who disagree with the writer of "America Held Hostage" are attacked as "crazy" and characterized as thinking "the world exists only for them."

4. *Ignoring alternative possibilities*: This is a general form for three related causal fallacies. The writer of argument must not assume causality without substantiation. The causal errors include:

   a. Either/or reasoning—that is, reasoning that suggests only two alternatives are possible when more actually exist. The writer of "America Held Hostage" states that "had the Iranians . . . asked for the Shah peacefully," the United States would have told them to go and "(x$* + &x!)." To avoid the fallacy, the writer could have written "the United States might" or "possibly would" or even "would likely" instead of the absolute "*would have told.*"

   b. Oversimplified cause (or catchall reasoning)—that is, reasoning that gives only one cause for a phenomenon when many may exist. The writer of "America Held Hostage" assumes that Americans believe that "what is happening in Iran is wrong simply because fellow Americans are held hostage," that Americans care only because Americans are involved. He does not allow for the possibility that some Americans would think that taking hostages of any nationality was wrong, or that some Americans would, in fact, defend the Shah's regime.

   c. False cause (or *post hoc ergo propter hoc* reasoning)—that is, reasoning that suggests a causal relationship between two phenomena that are not, in fact, related. In a later essay on a related topic, another student wrote that the Shah's cancer (of which he subsequently died) was proof of his crimes against Iranians—in other words, that his evil had *caused* the disease. While some readers may believe in this kind of supernatural cause-and-effect relationship, such arguments are not generally persuasive and are best avoided in arguments aimed at an academic audience.

Testing Arguments

To test his arguments, a writer might set up a model of his logic, outlining the *premises* or statements of fact and judgment upon which his argument or *conclusion* is based. There are always two premises involved in such a model, and the writer's conclusion is *deduced* or drawn from those premises.

For example, the writer could have set up a model of one of his arguments as follows:

Premise 1:   If Iranians had asked for the Shah peacefully, the U.S. would have told them to go and (x$* + &!x).

Premise 2:   Iranians had two choices: to ask for the Shah peacefully or to take the Americans hostage.

Conclusion: Iranians had no choice but to take the Americans hostage.

Had the writer done so, he might have seen more clearly the either/or fallacy involved in each of the premises on which his conclusion here is based. Both Premise 1 and

Premise 2 ignore alternative possibilities. If either of the premises in such a model is false, the reader cannot trust in the conclusion based upon them.

Of course, as we granted earlier, an argument may be full of such fallacies yet may still persuade some readers. Generally, such readers will not themselves have learned how to evaluate argument and will be easily swayed by strong, absolute language, misrepresentation of the opposition, and faulty reasoning. False or imprecise claims in advertisements, political campaigns, and even some newspaper editorials and columns often persuade a gullible public to buy a product, vote for a candidate, form an opinion. Knowing the elements of good argument and the fallacies that weaken it should help students not only to write better arguments themselves but also to evaluate more wisely the arguments of others.

Summary

In argument, the writer tries to persuade the reader to take his stand on an issue of controversy. He does this not by expressing his emotions over an issue about which he feels strongly, but by stating his thesis in a reasonable way, presenting convincing evidence to support it, and answering the objections generally raised against it by refutation or concession.

The thesis for an argument must take a stand, and it must be limited enough to be supported within the scope of the writer's essay. The supporting evidence, while not constituting absolute proof, should aim at being uncontroversial. All prominent objections should be recognized and answered, so that the reader will perceive the argument as fair. Finally, the tone of the argument must be controlled: the writer must keep in mind the audience he wishes to persuade and modulate his argument accordingly.

The writer should be careful to avoid several common fallacies in reasoning: arguments that overgeneralize, use loaded or self-evident language, attack opponents rather than their ideas, or ignore alternative possibilities. Arguments can be tested by setting up a model of the two premises upon which a conclusion is based.

Exercises

For Consideration

Exercise 1. Is each of the following a valid thesis for an argumentative essay? Why or why not?

  a. Some people favor construction of the Big Boom Nuclear Power Plant, while others oppose it.

  b. The Big Boom Nuclear Power Plant may endanger our community.

  c. The Big Boom Nuclear Power Plant should be approved by our town board.

  d. The Big Boom Nuclear Power Plant will be completed in 1990.

  e. The Nuclear Regulatory Commission has approved the construction of the Big Boom Nuclear Power Plant.

  f. Despite the difficulties involved, studying abroad for at least one year is preferable to studying only in one's native country.

Exercise 2. Identify by name or error the fallacy or fallacies in each of the following arguments:

 a. Foreign students have difficulty adjusting to American culture.

 b. Writing cannot be taught because it is unteachable.

 c. Maria's English is good because she worked in an American firm in her country.

 d. People who oppose legalized abortion are narrow-minded religious fanatics who are still trying to live in the nineteenth century.

 e. Those who support abortion care only about the feelings of irresponsible women who allow themselves to become pregnant; they do not consider the fetus at all.

 f. Americans do not try to understand foreign cultures.

 g. Students cannot survive on the poison served at our campus cafeteria.

 h. The food in our campus cafeteria should be improved because it is inadequate.

 i. The administration seems to want to raise tuition so high that the only students who will be able to complete their degrees will be the sons and daughters of millionaires.

 j. The disease AIDS is caused by sexual perversion.

Exercise 3. Supply the missing premise or the conclusion for each of the following logical models. Then discuss the validity of each model.

 a. *Premise* 1: Studying for some time in an English-speaking country is the best way to learn English well.

  Premise 2:

  Conclusion: Foreign students should spend some time studying in an English-speaking country.

 b. *Premise* 1:

  Premise 2: The only way to prevent unwanted pregnancy is through legalized abortion.

  Conclusion: Abortion should be legalized.

 c. *Premise* 1: Americans do not live with their elderly parents.

  Premise 2: People who do not live with their elderly parents are heartless.

  Conclusion:

 d. *Premise* 1: Smith was unsure of himself in the debates.

  Premise 2:

  Conclusion: Smith's unsureness cost him the election.

 e. *Premise* 1:

  Premise 2: The Iranians freed the hostages after Reagan took office.

  Conclusion: The Iranians freed the hostages because they were scared of Reagan.

Exercise 4. Read Arguments A and B below and then answer the following questions for each of them:

   a. What is the thesis of the argument? Does it take a stand on an issue of controversy? Is the thesis clear and prominently stated? Is it limited enough in scope to be adequately defined in the space the writer has allowed?

   b. What evidence supports the thesis? Does the evidence consist of uncontroversial facts as well as statements of judgment? What additional evidence (if any) is needed?

   c. What objections to his argument has the writer recognized? Has he answered them adequately? Has he answered them by refutation or by concession?

   d. Are there any objections to the argument that have not been recognized by the writer? What are they?

   e. Is the essay well organized? Have thesis, evidence, objections, and answers been arranged logically and effectively?

   f. Is the tone of the argument sufficiently restrained?

   g. Has the writer avoided fallacies that might weaken his argument or cost him his reader's trust? If so, what fallacies has he committed? How might he have avoided them?

A.
America Ashamed

Comparing some American customs to customs in my country, I feel disappointed. I never thought about that when I was living in my country. One of the American customs which compares badly to how things are done in my country is the way children treat their elderly parents. About 80 percent of them send their old parents to a place where they have to stay for the rest of their lives because they don't want to be bothered with their parents once they are old. These old age homes are prisons with nurses for guards. The only escape from them is dying.

Children know the responsibility parents have for them and the difficulties they go through from the day they are born until they are old enough to stand on their own. They know about the money which the parents spend on their children's education, the time spent in care and all the sacrifices they make for us. Taking all into consideration, children should come to the conclusion that they owe their parents the responsibility of taking care of them when they are old and not able to support themselves. Yet, American citizens, once they get married, only care for their wives and children and neglect their parents entirely. There's a proverb in my language which says, "Hand goes, hand comes." They cared for us when we were children and we should care for them when they are old.

B.
Discrimination in Sri Lankan Universities

The ministry of education in charge of universities in Sri Lanka should have a more diverse outlook in selecting undergraduates. Currently, selection of university undergraduates is based on several factors. Mainly, it is based on a grade obtained in a standardized exam. In addition, selection depends on the caste—or social group—to which the individual belongs and on the area the individual comes from.

Because selection is based on a grade obtained on a standardized exam, many individuals specialized in fields not included on the exam are ignored. For example, one who is exceptionally good in woodcrafting is unable to get into a university because this subject is not included in the general exam. He is only able to get into one of the technical colleges, which are usually of a low standard.

Selection based on the caste one belongs to discriminates against certain minorities. For example, the Sinhalese, who consider themselves the majority caste, can get into a medical school with a QPR of 3.0 while a Tamil needs a QPR of 3.8 to get into the same school. Similarly, people who are in highly populated areas are discriminated against by the regional quota system. This system tends to select an equal number of students from all regions of Sri Lanka without considering the number of students applying from each region, a number which varies considerably. The same quota system exists for selection of students for each field. For example, every year the government allows a certain fixed number of students to enter the field of medicine, but the number of people applying for that field varies. Because of this, many talented students are ignored in years where application to that field is high.

One might say that having a general exam is necessary because Sri Lanka has only a few universities. But this could be solved by building many more universities with money that is now spent in many unnecessary ways. Some argue that, without a quota system to regulate the number of students in each field, there will be an overflow in certain fields which will cause unemployment. But Sri Lanka needs more people in all fields. In fact, presently, Sri Lanka employs people from other countries to meet its needs. The government's defense for selecting the same number of people from every region might be that equal opportunity should be given to everyone and also that people from the less populous regions are not so well educated. But the people from these areas are inefficient and they are an obstacle to others who are well educated.

Without these selection principles for university entrance, the Sri Lankan government could make its educational system fairer to the individual as well as more responsive to the needs of the country.

Exercise 5. Read the essay "Bilingual Education: One Method among Many" (page 234) and evaluate the argument made by its author, answering the questions listed in Exercise 4.

For Composition

Exercise 6. Choose one university policy which you would like to see changed. Then,
   a.   Write a clear thesis stating the change you would like to see.
   b.   List the evidence required to persuade others that the change is necessary.
   c.   List the objections that the other side is likely to raise against your thesis.

Exercise 7. Write a well-reasoned essay arguing for a change in the policy you chose in Exercise 6. Your essay should be written for an audience of students, faculty, and administrators alike. Be sure to do the following:

a. Present your thesis clearly.

b. Support your thesis with evidence which includes uncontroversial facts as well as statements of judgment.

c. Recognize and answer the objections likely to be raised by those who oppose your position.

d. Maintain a controlled tone.

e. Avoid argumentative fallacies.

Exercise 8. Write an argument supporting or opposing one of the following aspects of university policy in your native country:

a. Admissions policy

b. Selection of major subjects

c. Tuition policy

d. Requirements for graduation

e. Academic freedom

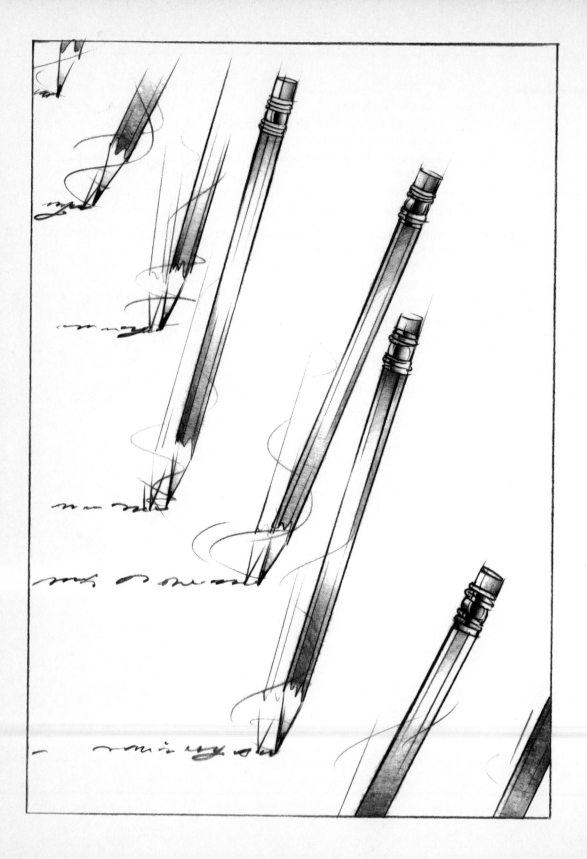

Part Three

Writing
the
Essay

Chapter 9

Getting
Started

A freshman English class received an assignment to write five separate 250-word essays on topics of the students' own choice. On the due date, one student handed in five page-long essays with the following titles:

- Life
- Love
- Religion
- Nature
- Death

The instructor knew even before reading them that these were unlikely to be successful essays.

What is the problem with these titles? They indicate that the student writer's focus is too broad. No one can treat a broad subject such as religion or love—let alone life—in 250 words. The essays were vague and rambling; there was no controlling idea to unify any of them. The student merely threw together as many vague thoughts about his five grand subjects as he needed to fill the word requirement.

Subject, Topic, Thesis

One of the hardest jobs for the student writer is finding a topic on which to write and then developing his theme or thesis. Even when a specific assignment is given—in this text or by an instructor—the student generally must do further work on the assigned subject to find the precise topic he wants to write about and to know what it is he wants to say about that topic (theme or thesis).

Exercise 8 in Chapter 3 of this text, for example, asks students to write about a personal experience that led them to an insight. This assignment obviously has to be narrowed down: the student has to limit himself to a particular experience and define clearly the insight to which it led him. If a student is to compare American customs to the customs of his own country in 500 or 1,000 words, he cannot hope to treat every similarity and difference in all the customs he can think of. Rather, he must limit his topic; perhaps he will write only about differences in mealtime customs or about similarities in dress or in dating. The student who finds himself trying to write about Persian music or Japanese literature or African art—or about freedom or feminism—in a two-page essay had better stop and think again. These are large subjects that require whole books for adequate treatment. No brief essay can possibly treat them meaningfully.

From Subject to Topic

How, then, can a student narrow down a broad *subject* such as religion or Persian music or feminism to a *topic* manageable within a given word limit? One method is by dividing the broad subject into various subcategories. The student who wanted to write a 500-word essay about Persian music, for example, found that he could subdivide the subject as follows:

Persian music
      The musical instruments of Persia
      Persian musical theory
      Forms of Persian music
      Composers of Persian music
      Performers of Persian music
      The origins of Persian music
      Western influences on Persian music

Considering his list, the student decided he wanted to write about the last item, western influence on Persian music. He found that he could further subdivide this into three categories:

Western influences on Persian music
      The influence of Western classical music on Persian music
      The influence of Western popular music on popular music in Iran
      The influence of Western popular music on Iranian youth

He chose to write about the first of these, the influence of Western classical music on Persian music. Since he was aware that such influence had taken many different forms (tours by Western orchestras in Iran, the prominence of Western recordings on Iranian radio, Iranian adaptations of pieces by Western composers, Iranian musicians responsible for the introduction of Western musical traditions into Iranian music, the teaching of Western musical theory in Iran, and so on), he decided to limit himself still further. Choosing to focus on one particular figure, Vaziri, responsible for this phenomenon, the student at last arrived at his real topic:

> Vaziri's contribution to bringing the influence of western classical music to Persian music

From Topic to Thesis

The student now had a topic he could handle in 500 words. But his work was not yet complete. He had narrowed his broad *subject* down to a manageable *topic*: he knew what he wanted to write about. However, he still needed to narrow his *topic* down to a clear *thesis*, to state what it was he wanted to say about the topic.

Whereas a subject or topic can be expressed in a word or phrase (for example, *music* or *Persian music* or *Vaziri's contribution to bringing the influence of Western classical music to Iran*), the thesis can be expressed only in a complete sentence. It may be possible to create a thesis by merely turning the phrase that expresses the topic into a sentence (for instance, *Vaziri helped bring the influence of Western classical music to Iran*). However, the writer will have something more definite to work with if he considers the topic and decides more precisely what he wants to say about it before beginning to write. The more definite the thesis, the more controlled and unified the essay is likely to be. In the case of the essay on Vaziri's contribution, the student writer expressed his thesis as follows:

> By introducing Western instruments and musical ideas into the orchestra he founded in Tehran, Vaziri created a new kind of Persian music.

Core Thesis Versus Thesis Statement

The thesis sentence above is long and complicated, qualifying the main idea (*Vaziri created a new kind of Persian music*) with several subordinate pieces of information (Vaziri founded an orchestra in Tehran and introduced Western instruments and musical ideas into it). The main idea in a thesis is sometimes called the *core thesis*. The combination of core thesis with subordinate material expressed in phrases and subordinate clauses can be called the *thesis statement*. A short, simple thesis may be adequate for planning a short narrative or simple description. For planning a lengthy or complex analysis or argument, however, a long and complex thesis statement is preferable.

A thesis statement like the one above will probably not actually appear in the student's essay. Its purpose is to guide the student in giving the essay shape. The student need not worry about making the thesis statement easy to read, but only about making it accurate. In getting started, the student has to decide *what* he wants his thesis to say. He can decide *how* to say it later.

Deciding on a Thesis

Before he can decide on his thesis, the writer will probably have to do some preliminary writing. The kind of writing he starts with will depend on the kind of essay he is writing.

Taking Notes. If the essay relies on outside sources, the student writer will begin by *taking notes* on the sources he is using. The form of these notes will depend on whether the essay is based on class texts or on sources the student has gathered through library research. If the sources are class texts, the student can generally take notes informally—in the margins of the texts themselves or on separate sheets or index cards. If the sources have been gathered through library research, the student should follow the note-taking method outlined in the unit on the research paper (page 214).

Prewriting. Whether or not outside sources are used, a useful technique for finding a thesis is *prewriting*. This technique is sometimes called *freewriting* or *brainstorming*, and each of these terms should give a good picture of how the technique operates.

In prewriting, the student writer lets his mind—and his pen—run freely. Without worrying about grammar or style—without bothering to look up translations of words he does not know—and without thinking about how one idea connects with another, the student simply writes, continuously, all the ideas that occur to him on his topic. If he wishes, the student can set himself a time limit of 10 or 15 minutes or longer. Or he can simply write until he runs out of ideas, put away his work, and begin again later. When he finishes, the student should find among what he has written ideas from which he can form a thesis.

In addition to providing a thesis (and often a better-defined topic than the one he began with), prewriting should provide the student writer with some of the detail he will need to develop his essay. Of course, much detail will have to be discarded, some will have to be added, and all will have to be shaped and organized before the student actually writes his essay. However, prewriting will give the student a body of ideas with which he can at least begin to work. Indeed, once the student has defined his thesis, he may want to do a more *focused prewriting* with the thesis as his starting point. In this way, he can check whether he has enough specific detail to support the thesis adequately. If he finds he cannot gather sufficient detail, the student may want to revise the thesis to one he can better support.

Summary

One of the fundamental tasks of the essay writer is limiting his topic and developing a thesis. Prewriting can help the student execute both of these tasks.

Exercises

For Consideration

Exercise 1. Identify the following topics as either suitable or unsuitable for a two- or three-page essay:
  a. Ancient architecture
  b. The Temple of Solomon
  c. United States politics
  d. The U.S. electoral process

e. Wok cookery

f. Food in China

g. Writing around the world

h. The Cyrillic alphabet

Exercise 2. Identify each of the following as either a Subject (S), Topic (T), or Thesis (Th):

a. Solar energy

b. How solar energy is used to heat homes

c. There are several types of solar collectors available for home heating.

d. The availability of bilingual textbooks in the U.S.

e. Bilingual education

f. American colleges should require foreign language study.

g. Teaching reading in two languages

h. Rock music video tapes

i. The influence of rock music video tapes on American youth

j. Music video tapes are less popular now than they were when they first began to appear on television.

k. Rock music

l. How to make a rock music video tape in your own home

m. Listening to music is more stimulating than watching a music video.

For Composition

Exercise 3. Divide each of the following subjects into at least two subcategories. Then divide one subcategory into at least three topics. Finally, write a thesis for one of the topics:

a. Abortion

b. Foreign language study

c. Air travel

Exercise 4. Do 10 minutes of prewriting on one of the topics you generated in Exercise 3. When you have finished, see if you have narrowed the topic still further. Can you identify a thesis in your prewriting?

Chapter 10

Organizing
the
Material

The student writer has defined the thesis and has gathered sufficient detail to support it. But it is not yet time to write. First, the writer must organize the material she has gathered: she must discard irrelevant details, add any necessary details, and arrange all in an orderly manner.

How organization is achieved will depend on the length of the essay the student is writing and on the complexity of the topic she is writing about. For shorter, simpler essays, informal planning may be sufficient. For essays of more than 500 words on complex topics, the student will likely want to make a formal, subordinated outline. Both types of planning merit a closer look.

Informal Outlining

Informal outlining can take many forms, but it should always begin with a thesis. Written in one clear, *complete* sentence, the thesis gives the plan control; indeed, it is often called the controlling idea. Once the student writer has formulated her thesis, she has a rationale for including a detail (it is necessary to support the thesis) or for not including it (it is unnecessary or irrelevant).

We have already seen some examples of informal outlines in the exercises in Chapter 2 (among others). In Exercise 3 of that chapter, you are asked to list all the facts and events included in your own autobiographical essay and to write out the thesis of the essay. Then you are asked to eliminate facts and events that do not support the thesis. Finally, you are instructed to use the thesis and the revised list of facts and events to revise your autobiography. Exercise 4 asks you to write one sentence stating how you felt on your first day in the U.S. (the thesis) and to list all the events that made you feel this way (supporting details) before writing an essay based on these materials. Such informal plans are often called *scratch outlines*, and the form they take is generally up to the student's (or the instructor's) discretion. Looking back at an essay in Chapter 1 (page 3), for instance, we can speculate on how the student writer's scratch outline might have looked:

> *Thesis*: My first day in the U.S. was tiring.
>> *Supporting details*: Little sleep night before, got up at 6:00 a.m., two-hour drive to airport, two-hour wait at airport, eight-hour flight, went through immigration, did baggage pick-up, went through customs, answering questions, finding taxi, taxi ride, too tired to eat, fell asleep in my clothes

Possibly, the student included more details in his first scratch outline. He might have told about the long lines for immigration and customs, about how long it took to find a taxi, about the traffic he was stuck in on his way to the hotel. Perhaps he decided later that he didn't need all these details, that he could adequately support his theme with only some of them. The scratch outline is a convenient place for making decisions about eliminating, adding, or combining details. In the outline above, for instance, the student lists immigration, baggage, and customs procedures separately; in his essay, he combines them into one sentence. By writing details out in scratch outline form, the writer sees more clearly how such combinations might be made.

The scratch outline could have taken other forms. It might have been shorter and simpler, with fewer details included as here:

> *Thesis*: I felt tired on my first day in the U.S.
>> *Supporting details*: Early start, long trip, airport procedures, trip to hotel, went right to bed

On the other hand, details could have been written out in full sentences (closer, therefore, to the form of the final essay) as here:

> *Thesis*: My first day in the U.S. was tiring.
>> *Supporting details*: I hardly slept the night before.
>>> My father woke me at 6:00 a.m. (and so forth)

Whatever the form in which the writer lists the details to be included in the scratch outline, it is important that the *thesis* be written out in a complete sentence. Some students try to skip this step and to start their outlines from a *topic*, for example, My *first day in the* U.S. The problem with this is that a topic by itself provides very little control over the details to be included in an essay. Judging from the topic above, anything that happened to the writer on his first day in the U.S.—from calling the airport to check that the plane would be on time to brushing his teeth and putting on his underwear—would be appropriate for inclusion in his essay. The topic provides an insufficient rationale for selecting supporting details. The ideas resulting from it will not be sufficiently controlled or unified. The place for such uncontrolled, disunified thoughts is in prewriting, not in organization.

Once the scratch outline has been written out, the writer can make decisions about how best to order her ideas. First, the writer has to decide where (and in some cases whether or not) to state the thesis. Then, each essay pattern brings with it its own problems for ordering details. For example, narrative is generally organized according to the time at which events occurred, although a later event is occasionally treated before earlier ones (see page 22); description requires spatial ordering that helps the reader move in an orderly and logical way from one feature to another (see page 34); comparison and contrast can be ordered according to either alternating or divided patterns (see page 65). The scratch outline is the place to make decisions about such organizational matters. In the scratch outline, the brief essay on a simple topic begins to take shape.

Formal Outlining

For longer, more complex essays, the scratch outline is rarely sufficient. The large number of ideas in such essays, as well as the need to distinguish between ideas of greater and lesser importance, requires formal outlining. By the time they begin their college English courses, many international students will have had some practice in preparing formal outlines.

Subordinating Symbols

Formal outlining uses a system of progressively indented numerals and letters to create a *subordinated* ordering of ideas—that is, ideas ordered so that some are shown to be of greater importance than others. The symbols used for numbering entries in a formal outline are listed in indented format below, in order of descending importance:
Roman capital numerals (I, II, III, IV, V, VI, . . .)
  Roman capital letters (A, B, C, D, E, F, . . .)
    Arabic numerals (1, 2, 3, 4, 5, 6, . . .)
      Roman lowercase letters (a, b, c, d, e, f, . . .)
Formal outlines can show subordination to degrees even finer than this with systems involving parentheses, decimal points, or other characters. However, for most students' purposes, four degrees of subordination should be sufficient.

Stating the Thesis

As with the scratch outline, the student should begin the formal outline, by stating her thesis. The thesis gives control and unity to the separate parts of the outline. As she plans, the student should look back at her thesis frequently to make sure all parts of the outline are clearly related to it.

Topic Outline Versus Sentence Outline

Having stated her thesis, the student must choose between two kinds of outlines: the *topic outline* and the *sentence outline*.

The Topic Outline. For simpler ideas a *topic outline*, in which subdivisions are expressed in words or phrases, is often sufficient. For example, a student writing about a restaurant in her country organized her essay with the following formal topic outline:
Thesis: Because of its family-style food and service as well as its prices, Chorlaui Hos-

telry is one of the best restaurants in Ecuador for families who want to spend a pleasant day out of the city.

I. Location
  A. Convenient to city
  B. Within a green valley
II. Facilities
  A. Gardens
  B. Sports areas
    1. Tennis courts
    2. Swimming pool
  C. Weekend market
  D. Parking lot
III. History and Decoration
  A. Former ranch
  B. Special features
    1. Exterior
      a. Old chapel
      b. Stone fountain
      c. Main entranceway arch
    2. Interior colonial antiques
IV. Food
  A. Great variety
  B. Special weekend menu
    1. Children's dishes
    2. Ecuadorean specialties
V. Family-style service
VI. Hospitable atmosphere
  A. Andean music
  B. Folk dancing
VII. Prices
  A. Range of prices
  B. Reasonable prices
  C. Special weekend prices

The outline above is fairly extensive for the given topic. Possibly, the student could have written an adequate essay without listing so many subtopics in the outline. Probably, however, her thorough outlining saved her time and trouble in writing the actual essay.

The well-made topic outline helps the student writer to see the shape of an essay based on simple ideas that are relatively easy to handle. The same ideas, however, could be organized in a *sentence outline*, with each item written out in a full sentence. The outline above, for example, could be rewritten as a sentence outline, as follows:

Thesis: Because of its family-style food and service as well as its prices, Chorlaui Hostelry is one of the best restaurants in Ecuador for families who want to spend a pleasant day out of the city.

I. Chorlaui Hostelry is located conveniently for families in Quito, Ecuador.

    A. It is a one-hour drive from Quito.

    B. It is surrounded by a green valley.

II. It offers many family-oriented facilities.

    (and so on)

Such a thorough outline, while likely helpful to the student-writer, is probably not necessary for this topic. For more complex ideas, however, such as those in an argumentative essay or a research paper, the sentence outline is generally preferable. Ideas can be expressed only in complete sentences, and the student dealing with complex ideas does well to write them out before beginning her essay.

    The essay in Chapter 19 (see page 234) is based on the *sentence outline* below. Students can look ahead to see how the organization detailed in the outline shaped the essay.

Bilingual Education: One Method Among Many

    Thesis: Because no one method has been shown conclusively to be superior to others in helping language-minority students learn English and other subject matter, a variety of methods should be used for teaching these students.

I. Since its introduction into U.S. classrooms, transitional bilingual education (TBE) has been the primary method to teach English-deficient language-minority (EDLM) students.

    A. The scope of the program is large.

    B. Although no law mandates its use, it is virtually the only method used in most programs serving EDLM students.

    C. Some urge that TBE be mandated as the only permissible method.

II. Efforts at mandating TBE as the only valid teaching method for EDLM students are not justified by current evidence of its effectiveness.

    A. In the early 1980s, a proposal to turn the recommendation of the Lau Remedies into a federal regulation mandating transitional bilingual education as the only valid teaching method for teaching EDLM students was put forth and later withdrawn after a thorough reviewing process.

    B. In 1985, Education Secretary William Bennett asked Congress to increase spending for alternative methods for teaching EDLM students because of insufficient evidence that TBE was benefiting them.

III. In examining teaching methods for EDLM students, we should eliminate many issues that have little to do with academic achievement.

    A. The difficulty of implementing the program should not cause it to be abandoned.

    B. Critics worried about bilingual education's divisive influence are really talking about maintenance and not transitional programs.

    C. Those who advance bilingual education as a means of fostering cultural diversity lose sight of the real goal of TBE and frighten its opponents.

IV. The question to be asked of any teaching method used for EDLM students should be whether it promotes English proficiency without sacrificing other learning.

    A. Students living in the U.S. need to learn English.

    B. They also need to learn nonlanguage subject matter.

V. Much of the debate has been founded on general impressions.

    A. Many have an opinion, but no evidence to support it.

    B. Historical impressions of immigrants "making it" or getting "slapped for speaking Spanish" may not be applicable.

    C. Some critics refer vaguely to "convincing studies" with no concrete details.

VI. For various reasons, our knowledge about teaching methods for EDLM students is poor.

    A. Studies on such methods may fail due to several complications.

        1. Terminology is complex.

          a. In TBE, students are taught in their native language.

          b. In immersion, students are taught in English by a teacher who can answer questions in their native language.

          c. In ESL, students are taught in immersion classes for half a day and spend the other half in intensive English classes.

        2. Methods are often combined.

        3. No control groups are available for comparison.

        4. Methodology in many studies is flawed.

    B. Results of valid studies are contradictory.

    C. The results of long-term studies are not yet available.

VII. There is insufficient support for any one method to be asserted over others.

    A. Time is needed to obtain more conclusive results.

    B. Meanwhile, a variety of methods should be encouraged.

    The writer of this outline has made an attempt to relate each item in it to her thesis. In her original outline, she used topics in place of the sentences that now constitute the outline's largest subdivisions. Thus, Item I was simply *History* and the next-to-last item (VI in the present outline) was *Studies*. In revising her outline, she realized that these entries did not give her sufficient guidance as to what she wanted to say about the history and study of bilingual education in regard to her thesis. Her first attempt at revision, however, was only partially successful. For *History* she substituted:

    Bilingual education has had a long history in the U.S.

In place of *Studies* she inserted:

    There have been many studies of bilingual education.

In checking the entries against her thesis, she realized that these sentences did not relate clearly to her main idea. Therefore, she revised again, giving the entries their present form.

Combining Formats. An outline may combine topic and sentence formats as well. For example, in the outline above, the student might well have eliminated some of the sentences from item VI.A., as in the example below:

VI. For various reasons, our knowledge about teaching methods for EDLM students is poor.
   A. Studies on such methods may fail due to several complications.
      1. Complex terminology
         a. TBE
         b. Immersion
         c. ESL
      2. Combination of methods
      3. Lack of control groups
      4. Flawed methodology
   B. Results of valid studies are contradictory.
   C. The results of long-term studies are not yet available.

It is essential, however, that each degree of subordination be uniform in its structure. For example, all Roman numerals might be sentences and all capital letters topics, or all Roman numerals might be topics and all capital letters questions. When such order is not maintained and structures are mixed within a single degree of subordination, the outline may be confusing, as in this version of item VI.A.:

VI. For various reasons, our knowledge about teaching methods for EDLM students is poor.
   A. Studies on such methods may fail due to several complications.
      1. Complex terminology
         a. In TBE, students are taught in their native language.
         b. Immersion
         c. ESL
      2. Methods are often combined.
      3. Lack of control groups
      4. Flawed methodology
   B. Contradictory results on studies
   C. Current lack of long-term results

At the very least, such an outline will not be as helpful to the writer as it should be.

Errors in Outline Structure

It is important to note that an outline category cannot be divided into only one subcategory. This version of the topic outline we looked at earlier, for example, is incorrect:

I. Location
   A. Convenient to city
II. Facilities
   A. Gardens
   B. Sports courts
      1. Swimming pool
   C. Weekend market

The problem with this outline is that the various topics are subdivided illogically. Under Topic I ("Location"), for example, only one subtopic ("Convenient to city") has been listed. It is not possible to divide a topic into a single subtopic. Rather, Item A should be eliminated from the outline and the subtopic it enumerates should be included as part of the larger topic, as here:

I. Convenient location

In the same way, item II.B. has been incorrectly subdivided. If there are courts for various sports as well as a swimming pool, these should be listed as two subtopics of an inclusive topic, for example, "Sports areas":

B. Sports areas

   1. Courts

   2. Swimming pool

The rule is as follows: if there is a I, there must be a II; if there is an A, there must be a B; if there is a 1, there must be a 2; and so forth.

The Paragraph Outline. Before ending our discussion of outline types, we might mention one other type: the *paragraph outline*. The paragraph outline is used largely to help a reader understand what he is reading. In a paragraph outline, the reader states in one sentence the main idea of each paragraph or group of related paragraphs in a piece of writing. In this way, she forces herself to consider the precise meaning of the written material. Paragraph outlines are useful in summarizing essays and, thus, in writing research papers based on outside sources. In addition, they may be useful to a student writer interested in checking her own work. If a student writes in one sentence the main idea of each paragraph in her own essay, she can check whether or not the essay as a whole is sufficiently unified and clear.

Changing the Outline

Whatever kind of outline the student writer chooses to make, he should regard it as a *tentative* plan. As he writes, he may find that something placed late in the outline needs to be stated earlier or that his outline omits an essential idea. The original outline for this text, for example, omitted the material on audience and tone included in Chapter 1; the material was added during revision of the manuscript. The outline should serve as a guide for the writer, but it can be changed and should be changed if the writer finds it necessary.

Summary

Planning for an essay can take the form of an informal (scratch) or a formal (subordinated) outline. Longer and more complex essays generally require the latter type. Formal outlines can have either topic or sentence formats or a combination of the two. Sentence outlines are particularly appropriate for research papers and arguments. All outlines should begin with a thesis. An outline must be logically subdivided. It should be regarded as a tentative plan.

Exercises

For Consideration

Exercise 1. What is wrong with the informal (scratch) outline below:
My position within my family

- Father
- Mother
- older brother who is very ambitious
- younger brother who is very lazy
- I

Exercise 2. Look back at the informal outlines you made for Exercises 3 and 4 in Chapter 2 (page 16). Are the outlines adequate? Why or why not? What changes, if any, would you now make in the outlines?

Exercise 3. Insert appropriate ordering symbols (Roman numerals, capital letters, and so on) for each item in the following formal outline:

Course Requirements for English Composition 1

Thesis: The course requirements for English Composition 1 cannot possibly be completed in a single semester.
Length of Semester
Requirements
   Essays
   Other Assignments
      Writing Notebook
      Grammar Exercises
      Quizzes
         Pretest
         Review
         Retest
Time Needed for Requirements

Exercise 4. What is wrong with the formal outline below?

Foreign Language Study in U.S. Public Secondary Schools

I. History of foreign language study in U.S. secondary schools
  A. Previous requirement of three years of foreign language study
    1. Ineffectiveness of three-year course
    2. Generally, the three-year requirement was discarded in the 1970s.

II. Current state of U.S. foreign language study
   A. Elective study in secondary schools
      1. Small enrollments in elective courses
   B. Few school systems require any foreign language study.
   C. Growing interest in foreign language study in the U.S.

For Composition

Exercise 5.   Make an informal (scratch) outline for an essay on the topic:

Why I am happy (or unhappy) at my present university.

Exercise 6.   Write a formal sentence outline on a particular change you would like to see at your college or university. Start by stating your thesis and show at least three degrees of subordination for at least one major subdivision.

Chapter 11

Writing
it Out

Once a student has organized his essay, he is ready to write. Or is he? Many students—as well as many professional writers—have sat down to write . . . and . . . just . . . sat. We sometimes call this "writer's block"; the writer just cannot seem to get started. It is almost as if he or she is *afraid* to write.

The First Draft

Writing should not be so fearsome. The important thing to remember is that a first draft is not a permanent commitment. It can be incomplete or incorrect or over-long or just plain dull. The writer will be able to finish it, correct it, cut it, or brighten it up as he or she revises and makes subsequent drafts.

Some students forget this. They want to create a finished product on the first try, especially if they have waited until the last moment before beginning an assignment. They sit down and fill their sheets with their best penmanship and consider the job done. Without so much as rereading what they have written, they give their essay to the teacher and hope for the best, glad to have it off their hands.

Good writing, as a rule, does not happen this way. Good writing requires rereading and rewriting. It is true that, occasionally, an inspired author writes out what he or she wants to say and gets it perfect the first time. But for most of us, the first time is only the beginning.

So instead of agonizing over that first sentence—or that first word or that title—just begin to write. As you proceed, there will be time to reread what you have written and make it better, time to add that interesting introduction or find that perfect title, time to find a better word for an imprecise one and to check whether *recommend* has one *c* or two. Leave ample margins and skip lines—at least one, maybe two—so that you can make changes or additions later. Write on one side of the paper only. Do not be afraid to cross out. And by all means, if you write longhand, save your best penmanship for your final draft. By the time you have finished revising it, your first draft will probably be a mess.

When a first draft is completed, the student writer should go back over his essay giving special attention to three special features: the introduction, the conclusion, and the title.

The Introduction

Introductions are important. The way in which an essay begins may determine whether or not a reader continues reading it. Some student writers have an instinct for introductions. Their essays always begin with an arresting image, an amusing anecdote, an intriguing quotation. Their introductions catch the attention of the reader and draw him into the essay.

Weak Introductions

Other students do not know how to begin. They chew their pencils trying to get started. Sometimes they start too far back, giving information that is not relevant to their essay's thesis (see, for example, Version A of "The Traffic License," page 24). Or they start to write without knowing what they want to say, hoping that a good idea will come to them as they go along and that the reader will not pay too much attention to the beginning. Their essays often begin with a statement like this:

I am going to write about bilingual education.

This is deadly—and a waste of six words. Its only real purpose is to delay. The writer is marking time while he thinks of something to write. Do not tell your reader what you are going to do. Do it. By all means, write about bilingual education or about Persian music or your college dining hall. But do not tell your reader you are going to do it. If you do it well, making your thesis clear and supporting it from the outset, the reader will know what you are writing about without your having to tell him.

Another introduction that serves only to delay is one such as

Bilingual education is an interesting (or *important* or *vital*) topic.

The reader assumes that the writer would not have chosen to write about a dull or unimportant topic. And how interesting the topic seems to a reader will be determined by what the writer says about it, not by the writer's empty assertion.

On the opposite extreme is the writer who apologizes in advance for his essay's weakness:

Although I don't know much about bilingual education, . . .

If the writer does not know much about his topic, he should not be writing about it. The writer needs to show that he believes in what he writes if he wants the reader to believe in it.

Strong Introductions

How, then, should an essay begin? It should begin with something as concrete and to the point as possible. An essay that starts too broadly or too far back confuses the reader. A good introduction focuses immediately on the precise issue being addressed without wasting time or words. If a student is assigned to write about a personal experience that led to an insight, he wastes time with an introduction such as the following:

Often in life, people have experiences that lead them to new insights about the human condition.

Such an introduction is too broad and unfocused. It fails to give the reader an idea of what the writer is going to say. It is also too obvious to be worth mentioning. Given this same assignment, several student writers began their essays more successfully:

A car is a necessity in the U.S., and I quickly realized this.

I had often heard that Americans were uncaring people, . . .

A year ago Paul was a freshman basketball player on a big scholarship. His life was happy-go-lucky and you knew it everytime you saw him sprinting down the street.

These introductions immediately focus the reader's attention on the particular experience or insight the writer wishes to communicate. None of the three actually states the thesis (indeed, each of the opening premises is overturned in the course of the essay it introduces). But all use specific information to catch the reader's attention and focus it on the issue addressed in the essay.

Some introductions are especially catchy, surprising the reader with an intriguing word, image, or expression:

I guess you could say I am a nomad.

My train passes suddenly into darkness.

On no! I could recognize the smell which was spreading through the airport.

In research papers, a striking fact or example may make for a catchy introduction. A student writing about child abuse began his essay:

A five-year-old is admitted to the hospital. She has never walked and weighs 13 pounds.

A well-chosen quotation can also catch a reader's attention, as in this essay defending bilingual education:

"I speack Spanich because my mother can't speack English. . . . But I promise I won't speack Spanich no more. Am sorry I catch speack Spanich. Hope
I won't do it again." So writes a student thrown into an all-English class to
"sink or swim."

Of course, not every paper needs to have such a catchy opening. Indeed, students
writing academic papers dealing with serious subject matter should be careful not to
be too cute. An essay can begin with the thesis itself or with a straightforward an-
nouncement of the issue to be addressed, as in these examples:

No organ or function of the human body is immune from the ill effects of
smoking.

Computers play a major role in many fields of education.

Analyses of bilingual programs for preschool children show that such programs are beneficial for children's general development.

If, in writing an essay, you cannot find a solid introduction, forget it for a while
and write the rest of the essay. As you write, you may discover an image, fact, or
quotation perfect for your introduction. Or you may come to be better able to focus
your introduction on the issue. You may even find, when you look back, that what you
wrote as the middle of the essay makes a perfectly good beginning!

In any case, do not waste your introduction. Do not spend precious words and
your reader's precious time in aimless rambling. Come to the point without delay, and
your reader will stay with you.

The Conclusion

Finishing an essay may be as difficult as starting it. Writing is a little like being on
an unfamiliar bus; we know we have to get off somewhere, but we're not sure where.

Weak Conclusions

Sometimes student writers stay on too long. They go on writing—repeating themselves, adding facts, overexplaining, summarizing unnecessarily—long after they should
have stopped. As a result, their conclusions weaken rather than strengthen their essays.

We have already seen examples of such conclusions. The poorly written versions
(page 13) of Willie Morris's commuter train passage both go on too long. Morris ended
the passage effectively:

Then, after the pause, I heard the first man say: "Two hearts."

The poorly written versions of this essay, on the other hand, fail to recognize the
power in the writer's concluding with the resumption of the card game. Version I continues:

He didn't even say anything else about the boy. By the way, the man with
the deep voice won that hand.

The writer of this version makes two mistakes. First, he explains the meaning of Morris's final image. The explanation is unnecessary; the meaning is clear without it. The
explanation serves only to weaken the image's chilling effect. Then, in his final sen-

tence, the writer of Version 1 continues with the narrative beyond the point of the story, telling us the unnecessary facts about the outcome of the game. Going on too long is like starting too far back: it confuses or bores the reader.

Version 2 of the Morris passage commits a different kind of error. This version ends with a broad platitude:

> Indeed, observation can lead to understanding.

Not only is this conclusion abstract and unfocused, it is also too obvious to state. Moreover, it is a repetition of this version's first sentence. Morris's conclusion does not need explanation. It does not need additional details. It does not need justification through broad platitudes. It is perfect the way it is. Sometimes, the writer's problem is to recognize a conclusion as a conclusion—and to end there.

Where to Use a Concluding Summary. Of course, a brief summary or explanation may be appropriate in a long essay full of complex arguments or explanations. For example, most of the chapters in this textbook end with a summary of the chapter's main points. But beware of the conclusion that begins "As we have seen" and then merely repeats the words or ideas of a brief essay's introduction. A good ending, as everything else in an essay, should reinforce the thesis. It should not merely *repeat* what has already been stated.

Strong Conclusions

What, then, makes for a good conclusion? A particularly striking idea or example, a revealing quotation, or a question relating to the thesis makes for a satisfying ending, reinforcing the thesis without boring the reader. The student writing about the ill effects of smoking concluded with a striking fact:

> Studies show that respiratory ailments are most acute if smoking is continued during the illness. Discontinuation of the habit usually results in a marked decrease in damage—and sometimes even in total disappearance—of ailment symptoms.

An essay opposing bilingual education concluded by quoting former U.S. president Theodore Roosevelt:

> "Any man who comes here must adopt the institutions of the United States, and therefore he must adopt the language which is now the native tongue of our people."

A third student, writing about the safety of the DC-10 concluded with a question:

> The time of madness and anxiety has passed and people fly in DC-10s as if nothing ever happened. But there is a question that has never been answered, and it is a question we should all ask ourselves before flying: Are our skies really safe?

Completing a Circle. Among the most satisfying conclusions are those that complete a "circle"—linking the end of an essay to its beginning. Again, mere repetition is not desirable. But bringing to conclusion an idea raised at the beginning of an essay or closing with an image or quotation that makes a faint echo can be very effective. The student author of "A Revealing Train Ride" (page 21) begins his essay:

> Before I came to the United States, I had often heard that Americans were uncaring people. As the crowds pushed past me on my first day in New York, I was convinced my friends had been right.

He concludes:

> Perhaps I had better wait and see before judging the Americans, I thought.

This technique can also be effective in longer, impersonal essays. We have already looked at this introduction to a research argument promoting bilingual education:

> "I speack Spanich because my mother can't speack English. . . . But I promise I won't speack Spanich no more. Am sorry I catch speack Spanich. Hope I won't do it again." So writes a student thrown into a class with all English-speaking students to "sink or swim."

The student writer returns to this image in her effective conclusion:

> When the student makes his promise not to "speack Spanich no more," it must be remembered that many of the children thrown into the same classes with English-speaking students to "sink or swim" may, indeed, sink.

What these introductions and conclusions have in common is a feeling of completeness: the conclusions circle back to the ideas expressed in the introductions, giving the students' essays a definite shape, a feeling of being whole.

In conclusion, perhaps the best formula for beginning and ending an essay is the one given by the Mad Hatter to Alice in Wonderland: "Start at the beginning, and when you come to the end, stop."

The Title

An essay's title is like an advertisement: if it is good, it will draw a reader into the essay. It is also like a signpost: it can point the reader in the right direction, giving him or her a clue to the essay's thesis or a feeling about the essay's tone. In order to do this, a title must be carefully chosen. The writer who leaves his essay untitled or who settles for a weak title throws away an important opportunity.

Narrowing the Title

The student writer should narrow in on his title in much the same way that he focuses in on his theme or thesis. In general, a more specific title is more intriguing as well as more informative than a more general one. Perhaps the broadest and least helpful titles are those that merely reflect a topic assignment. Little interest or information is provided by titles such as these:

> My First Day in the U.S.
> The Story of My Life
> A Personal Experience

To be more interesting and informative, a title needs to reflect the thesis, or at least a narrowed topic, rather than the broad terms of an assignment. The student writing about his tiring first day in the U.S., for instance, might have titled his essay "A Tiring

Journey" or "A Long First Day" or even (playing with the title of a famous American drama) "Long Day's Journey." Two other essays we have looked at recalling students' first days in the U.S. bore the titles "The Broken Pickle Jar" and "Culture Shock"—each, surely, more intriguing and informative than "My First Day in the U.S." Students writing autobiographies came up with titles such as "Wandering," "New Challenges," "One More Chance," and "Search for Peace"—all vast improvements over the broad and uninteresting "My Life." And though the assignment to write about a personal experience led to many essays with that bland title, it also led to such intriguing titles as "Never Again," "A Lucky Escape," "Last Farewell," "Home Feelings," "The Nightmare I Survived," and "What a Day!"

Impersonal essays can also have better and worse titles. It is hard to imagine anyone's titling an essay "Research Paper," but student writers frequently settle for titles broader than necessary. Several students writing about bilingual education started with the subject itself as their title, grandly heading their essays "Bilingual Education," as if they could cover every aspect of that large subject in 5 or 10 pages. After revision, several essays that started out with this same broad title bore the following different, narrower, more informative titles:

> No Government Funds for Bilingual Education
> The Need for Bilingual Education in Public Schools
> Bilingual Education: Help for Foreign Students in the United States
> Bilingual Education: Should It Be Continued?
> Why Juan Can't Read

Actually, two of the examples above bear the same *title*: "Bilingual Education." They have been made distinctive, though, by the student writers' inclusion of distinctive *subtitles*, in one case a statement reflecting the thesis ("Help for Foreign Students . . ."), in the other case a question raising an issue ("Should It Be Continued?"). Especially in a long essay on a broad topic, a subtitle may be a handy way to reflect the thesis and intrigue the reader without making the topic seem narrower than it is and without making the title overlong and unwieldy.

Playing on Words. Attention-grabbing questions and "turns" or "plays" on familiar phrases can make a title particularly intriguing. The student writing about the safety of DC-10s titled his research paper "Are Our Skies Safe?" and made his readers wonder about the answer. A student writing about integrating public schools by busing students across school district lines titled his essay "To Bus or Not to Bus?" playing on the familiar Shakespearean quotation. The title "Why Juan Can't Read" plays on the title of a popular essay concerned with the teaching of reading, "Why Johnny Can't Read," putting the issue into a bilingual context.

Title Length

All things being equal, short titles are generally more effective than longer ones. A student writing about soccer player Johann Cruyff titled his essay "Superstar." Such a title may not be fully informative, but it does get the reader's attention. Sometimes a single word can make for a very suggestive title, as in the student's description of Grand Central Station, in which the word chosen for the title—"Terminal"—is on one level a simple name for the last station at which a train stops, but on another level suggestive of an illness ending in death—a suggestion that fits well with the writer's impression of his subject.

Narrowing a title does not necessarily mean adding words. The six words in the broad title "My First Day in the U.S." have been cut to four in "The Broken Pickle Jar," three in "Long Day's Journey," and two in "Culture Shock." Sometimes more words will make a title more specific; sometimes fewer words that have been chosen more precisely can do the job better.

There are no hard and fast rules about a title's length or structure. Sometimes a long title is necessary. Occasionally a longer title is more effective than a shorter one. Although most titles are phrases (that is, not complete sentences), on occasion a complete sentence makes for an effective title. One student, for example, gave to his personal experience essay the title "It Feels Good to Help." Generally, however, if a shorter title can do the job, it is better than a longer one; if a phrase says what you want to say, it is better than a complete sentence.

Misleading Titles

Above all, student writers should beware of misleading titles—titles that suggest an essay is about a topic that it does not discuss or discusses only peripherally. A student writing about child abuse titled his research paper "Child Abuse and Its Causes." In the paper itself, however, the causes of child abuse were discussed only in the last paragraph of the essay and then only as an unanswered question that might bear further investigation. Most of the essay dealt with how doctors, family members, friends, and acquaintances could recognize cases of child abuse. Such a misleading title confuses the reader. The reader keeps looking for the information promised in the title and may consider all the other information—however well put together—beside the point. In revising, the student writer changed his title to "Signs of Child Abuse." Now his title truly reflected his topic and the reader would not be disappointed by a false advertisement.

Summary

The first version of an essay should be treated as tentative, as a rough draft. The student writer should not worry unnecessarily about how to begin nor waste time making a first draft look good. After the first draft is completed, the writer can give special attention to three important essay features: introduction, conclusion, and title. Because the title and introduction should draw the reader into the essay and the conclusion should leave a lasting impression, the writer needs to make these features relevant and intriguing.

Exercises

For Consideration

Exercise 1.   Which of the following introductions seems most likely and least likely to interest a reader? Why?
   a.   Abortion is an extremely important topic in our world today.
   b.   Every twenty seconds a baby is aborted in the United States.
   c.   Abortion has become quite frequent in the United States.

Exercise 2. Which of the following conclusions seems most likely and least likely to satisfy a reader? Why?
  a. Thus, as we have seen, abortion is a vital topic in today's world.
  b. In conclusion, it seems clear that although some abortions may be necessary, they are too readily performed in the United States.
  c. In the time it has taken you to read this essay, sixty, perhaps more, babies have been aborted in the United States. Isn't that too many?

Exercise 3. Which title seems most and least likely to attract a reader? Why?
  a. Abortions in the U.S.
  b. Too Many Abortions
  c. There Are Too Many Abortions Performed in the U.S.
  d. A National Tragedy

Exercise 4. The excerpts below are from brief student essays. In each, the title, introduction, and conclusion have been included. Read each excerpt. What strengths and weaknesses can you identify? What suggestions can you make for improvement?

A.
Iranian Music

There are many kinds of music all over the world. Every country has a special music and music almost always expresses the culture of the country.
....
There are many local songs in Iran. Each is accompanied by particular local dances. The clothes for these dances are very beautiful.

B.
Music

Iranian music has a long history. In very old Iranian books, there are many stories about musicians who could make people happy and sad at the same time.
....
Modern Iranian music is more or less like Western music, and it is very sad, which is popular with teenagers. And there is nothing more important to write about it.

C.
The Concrete Desert

My home city, Tokyo, has changed a great deal since I was a small boy. And with her, her children have changed.
....
Nature has vanished from the metropolis of Tokyo, and its vanishing has changed the children's way of playing. I wonder how children who have never known nature will grow up. Before we find out, adults who have known the greatness of nature had better do something to bring it back to the concrete desert.

D.

My University

"It's the worst place in the U.S.!" That was the reaction of Bob and Howard, two American students, when I told them that I would be a student at Crumb College.

....

At last Bob said, "Listen. You could have gone to another college, couldn't you?" I said yes, and then he asked: "Why didn't you?"

E.

Humanism

I am going to write about humanism. Humanism is a philosophy that sees man as more important than anything else—even God.

....

In conclusion, as we can see, humanism views man as more important than God.

Exercise 5. Look through this text and find sample essays to illustrate each of the following:
  a. An effective title
  b. An ineffective title
  c. An effective introduction
  d. An ineffective introduction
  e. An effective conclusion
  f. An ineffective conclusion
(Note: Do not choose examples used as illustrations in this chapter.)

Exercise 6. Exchange an essay your class is currently working on with a fellow student. Focus on the essay's title, introduction, and conclusion. Are they effective? Why or why not? What suggestions can you make for improvement?

For Composition

Exercise 7. Referring to your outline for Exercise 5 in Chapter 10 (page 108), write three or four possible titles, including one which you know is poor, for your essay on the topic "Why I am happy/unhappy at my present university." Which one is best? Why? What makes the poor title bad?

Exercise 8. Look back at the autobiographical essay you revised for Exercise 3 in Chapter 2. If the essay has a title, explain why the present title is effective or ineffective. Then give the essay a new title, making it as effective as possible.

Exercise 9. Look back at the essay you wrote for Exercise 5 in Chapter 2 (page 16). First, rewrite the beginning and end to make them as effective as possible. Then try to find an effective title for the revised essay.

Chapter 12

Revising

The first draft is complete. Having narrowed down your topic and found your thesis, you have written your essay from intriguing introduction to satisfying conclusion and headed it all with a carefully chosen title. At last, you sigh, the essay's ready to hand in.

Not so fast! A first draft is only a beginning. Before an essay is ready to be handed in, it should be reread, rethought, and rewritten. It will need cutting, additions, corrections, changes. This process is known as *revision*.

The Writer as Critic

Revision is perhaps the hardest task of the student writer. In revision, the writer must step back from his work and look at it not with his own eyes, but with the eyes of a reader. He must ask himself how successful his essay is—and he must be a tough critic. It is not easy to cross out words, lines, and paragraphs that have just been completed; it is not easy to admit that a word found after a long search is not really right; it is not easy to check all the "little" details—spelling, word form, punctuation, capitalization. But it must be done. The essay is not finished until it is revised at least to the satisfaction of the student writer's own "inner critic." The tougher the critic inside the writer, the better the essay will be.

Of course, in a writing class, revisions of a student's work may also be suggested by an outside critic—the course instructor. The red ink or pencil marks on a student's final draft will indicate revisions his inner critic missed. But in other courses there will be no second chance. The student will hand in only one draft of a paper, the final draft. And his grade will depend in part on his inner critic's success in revising. Thus, learning to write really involves mastering two processes: a creative process and a critical process. The writer as creator invents and organizes. The writer as critic looks at the creator's work as objectively as possible and decides what is and what is not successful. Then the creator goes to work again, reinventing, reorganizing. And again the critic passes judgment, and so on until the inner critic is satisfied.

It is difficult for the writer to divide himself in this way. Often, a writer identifies so closely with his words and thoughts that it is hard for him to separate himself from them, to view them objectively. The hardest task may be cutting. A writer may become so attached to what he has written that discarding some of it may seem like discarding a part of himself. For some students, the process is even more painful when an instructor acts as critic. The instructor's red marks on his essay and the red lines through his precious words and sentences may hurt so deeply that the student refuses to believe they are valid. In order to develop his writing skills, the student should try to overcome these feelings. The student writer should remember that virtually all writers revise, that there is no shame in revision, that it is the final draft that matters, not the steps leading up to it.

Several Stages

Revision can come in several stages. Some revision takes place immediately, during the writing of the first draft. Some revision takes place after the first draft, or a subsequent draft, is completed. Often, it is a good idea for the writer to let time pass between completing a draft and revising it. This enables him to return to the draft "fresh," to look at it with perhaps a little more objectivity and distance than would otherwise be possible. Indeed, the writer who leaves enough time before revising may find himself staring at a particularly confusing passage and wondering, "Did I really write that?"

Taking Time

Perhaps the most important element in successful revision is the student writer's willingness to take the time to make his essay right. A writer should never hesitate to make a necessary change just because it will spoil his essay's appearance. After revision, a first draft should virtually never be clean enough to be handed in as is but will need to be rewritten or typed in final form. Nowadays, some writers use word processors to prepare first drafts, largely because it is easier to make revisions on a word processor than on a typed or handwritten draft. The time spent in learning word processing and in typing a rough draft on a word processor can be more than made up for by the ease of revision. In addition, many software packages include features such as spelling checkers that actually do some of the revising *for* the writer as he is writing.

Longhand or typewritten revisions take longer than those made on a word processor. However, the writer can save time by following the advice given in the previous chapter. In writing your first draft, plan ahead to make changes: provide room for corrections and additions by leaving ample margins, double-space the pages, and do not write on the back of any of the sheets. Do not fuss over neatness and perfect penmanship. Remember that no one but you needs to see the rough draft. Even if you write in pencil, cross out rather than erase deletions. It saves time and enables you to change back to an earlier version if you later decide it is a better one. Consistently using the same size (8½ by 11-inch) paper for first drafts will help give a rough word count when a word limit is specified.

Deciding What Needs Revision

The first job in revising a completed draft is deciding where to begin: do only minor details need reworking, or is a major restructuring or even rethinking called for? The student writer must be honest with himself and thorough in checking the following points for possible changes:

1. *Theme or Thesis*: Is it clear? limited enough? (See pages 94–96.)

2. *Supporting Details*: Are they relevant? necessary? concrete? sufficient? (See pages 12–14.)

3. *Organization*: Are the various parts of the essay arranged logically according to some principle of order? Is the introduction interesting and the conclusion satisfying? (See pages 101, 110–14.)

4. *Transition*: Are there clear markers between sentences and paragraphs to show how one sentence or paragraph relates to another? (See pages 160–65.)

5. *Paragraphs*: Are paragraphs unified? complete? Are topic sentences (implicit or explicit) apparent? Are the ideas or sentences within each paragraph logically arranged? (See pages 130–41.)

6. *Sentences*: Are sentences complete? concise? varied in structure? Is the main idea of each sentence expressed in the main clause? (See pages 147–57.)

7. *Word Usage*: Are words precise? Have they been checked for their connotations as well as denotations? for their level of usage? Are they concrete and specific enough? (See pages 167–83.)

8. *Grammar and Conventions*: Is word form correct? Are sentences correctly punctuated? Are sentences unified in tense, number, person, form, structure, and so on? (See pages 262–96.) Are capitalization, italics, abbreviations, numbers and figures, word division, and article usage conventional? (See pages 299–312.)

9. *Spelling*: Is spelling correct?

Depending on the kind of essay the student is writing, he may also need to check other matters as well:

1. For a *summary*, the accuracy, brevity, and completeness of his restatement of the original's ideas, see pages 192–98.

2. For an *argument*, the presence of adequate evidence and the raising and answering of objections to his thesis, see pages 79–81.

3. For a *research paper*, the accuracy of quotations and adequacy and form of documentation, see pages 218–27.

4. For an *essay question*, the relevance of his answer to the question asked, see pages 251–55.

As the writer becomes more experienced, he may not need to think in terms of separate elements of an essay. He may be able to identify a problem in, say, paragraph unity or transition or punctuation without thinking about these special labels or categories. For now, however, the student writer will likely find it helpful to think in terms of the categories listed above, considering separately the various points for revision. When he has gone through the entire list, rereading and revising his essay several times for the various problems the list identifies, he is ready to hand in the final draft.

Revising After Criticism

In addition to making revisions on their own, in most writing classes and in some classes in other subject areas, students will also have to make such revisions as are indicated by their instructors on marked drafts. Sometimes an instructor will ask to see a rough draft and mark it for revision before actually grading it. Sometimes a student will receive two grades: one on the rough draft and one on the revised draft of the same essay. To revise adequately, students must be able to understand and comply with the instructions indicated by their instructors.

Although many instructors use marking systems of their own invention, generally certain standard printer's marks are used to indicate the need for a number of common revisions. Familiarity with the symbols in Figure 12-1 will help the student to revise efficiently.

The Final Draft

Your instructor will probably establish his or her own guidelines for the appearance of your final draft. Sometimes these are quite specific, indicating the exact number of lines to be skipped between the written or typed lines of the essay, whether or not a cover sheet is to be included, the form of the heading (assignment, title, name, class, date, and so forth), and even the color ink to be used, the type of paper, the manner in which the essay is to be folded for handing in. Follow the instructor's guidelines carefully. If you are unsure what a specific instruction means, ask for clarification.

General Guidelines

When no specific instructions are given, the student can follow the guidelines below:
- Use 8 ½- by 11-inch lined white paper for handwritten final drafts or 8 ½- by 11-inch white medium- or heavy-weight typing paper for typed final drafts.
- Write or type on one side only of each sheet of paper. (Note: Some instructors insist on typed drafts.) If you are writing on looseleaf paper, make sure to use the front side of each sheet (with holes at left).
- Use blue or black ink only.
- Leave 1-inch margins at top, bottom, right, and left of all sheets.
- Write or type on every other line only.
- Indent the first line of every paragraph 1-inch for written or five spaces for typed drafts.
- Include a separate cover sheet stating your title and name as well as class, instructor's name, and date (and any other material requested).

Figure 12-1   Revision Abbreviations

∧	add	ℋ coh	paragraph coherence lacking
ℓ	delete	ℋ dev	paragraph development lacking
✓	good		
//	faulty parallel	ℋ unity	paragraph unity unity lacking
abbrev	faulty abbreviation	org	faulty organization
agr	faulty agreement	P	punctuation error
awk	awkward	pl	plural form needed
case	wrong pronoun case	poss	possessive error
cap	capitalization required	pred	faulty predication
colloq	colloquialism	ref	faulty pronoun reference
dang	dangling modifier	rep	unnecessary or awkward repetition
D	inappropriate diction		
div	faulty word division	run-on	run-on sentence
frag	sentence fragment	S	sentence structure error
id	faulty use of idiom	sing	singular form needed
ital	underline	sp	spelling error
lc	lower case required (do not capitalize)	sub	faulty subordination
		T	tense error
logic	faulty logic	tone	inappropriate tone
mm	misplaced modifier	trans	weak transition
num	wrong form for number	vb	wrong verb form
ℋ	begin new paragraph here	wdy	wordy
noℋ	do not begin new paragraph here	ww	wrong word

- Repeat your title on the first page of your essay.
- Number all pages after the first (first pages are unnumbered) with Arabic numerals (2, 3, 4, and so on). The page number can be placed either in the center of the page or in the upper right-hand corner.
- Correct errors neatly, using an eraser for ink or white-out for typed drafts. The proofreader's marks in Figure 12-2 can be used *sparingly* to indicate certain changes.

Figure 12-2   Some Proofreader's Marks

Cross out unnecessary letters with a slash (/):

    instruc/ktor

Substitute a letter above the slash:

        c
    instru/ktor

Cross out unnecessary words or phrases with a single line and a deletion mark ( ):

    the ̶o̶t̶h̶e̶r̶ instructors

Add a letter or words with a caret (∧) below the line:

        other
    the ∧ instructors

Add a space between words or letters with a slash and a space mark (#):

            #
    the other/instructors

Insert a comma:

    the other instructors∧who

Insert a period:

    the other instructors⊙

Close up space with a bow above and below:

    the ot‿her instructors

Transpose letters or words:

    the instructors other

Indicate a paragraph break by inserting the paragraph symbol (¶) to the left of the first letter of the new paragraph:

> Fortunately, she was only one of the instructors.¶The other instructors

Indicate a new paragraph that you neglected to indent by inserting a paragraph symbol in the left margin:

> ¶ The other instructors

Indicate that an indented line should not begin a new paragraph by drawing a line from the conclusion of one sentence to the beginning of the next and writing "no ¶" in the left margin:

> *No* ¶ The other instructors were human.
> One of them, for example, postponed an exam

Again, a final draft should be neat. If you find yourself making numerous proofreader's marks on a single page of your final copy, it will probably be necessary to redo the page to avoid a sloppy appearance. The research paper reprinted in Chapter 19 presents a good example of a typed final draft.

Summary

Revision requires that the writer review his essay with the eye of a reader. It can occur in several stages and it requires time. The beginning writer should revise several times, looking for various kinds of problems. Some revision takes place after outside criticism. Familiarity with common proofreader's marks can make such revision more efficient. Final drafts should be neatly drawn up in accordance with specific guidelines.

Exercises

For Consideration

Exercise 1. Revise the following brief essay as indicated by the editing marks:

> When a student finishes writing ∧essay, his real
>
> work <u>had</u> just begun. Before he hands his essay in for   T
>
> grading ∧he needs to revise it. He <u>not only</u> needs to   P, mm
>
> check spelling, punctuation, <u>C</u>apitalization, etc.∧but   /c, P

also content and organization. He may have to revise

his thessis or find additional maerail to suport it. ¶He   *sp*

may have to eliminate unecdessary material. ¶Even after

[an essay is handed in, a student may have more work to   *//, T*

do]. His Pofessor may suggest ⌒revisions additional⌒ in   *lc*

red marks in the margins and empty spaces of his pa-

per. [sometimes minor changes only will be necessary,   *cap, mm*

sometimes major changes will be called for.] Sometimes   *run-on*

a paper be so full of red marns, the student wonder if   *T, agr*

the teacher cut himself shaving and bled all over his   *ref*

composition.

no ¶ ↪However, the student should not be discouraged.

Even shakespeare has to revise!   *cap, T*

For Composition

Exercise 2. Read the student essay that follows. Mark errors with appropriate editing marks. Then write a paragraph or two explaining what revisions need to be made to make the essay more effective.

"Autobiography"

This essay will talk about my life. It is difficult for me to talk about my life, but I'll try to right what I still remembered about my life. I was born in Amman the Capital of Jordan on 1961, at that time my family were on vacation in Jordan. My Parents were very happy when I born, because I am the 1st boy between my sisters. After that my family goes back to my country Qatar, it is in saudi arabia. However, when I was 6 years old I went to school, I was very intelligent, I used to take A or B. I remember that all the people liked me, because I am very freindly with them, especially I grew up in a religious country, also in a religious house, my parents used to teach me how to respect people, how to respect my self, and how to make freinds. Actually when I finish the high school 2 years ago, I was responsible for my family, because I working in the bank to help my father, at the same time I was studying In the College.

However, I studied in Qatar university one semester then the ministry of education over there gave me a Scholarship to the united state.

I came to Smith City in 11-1-86, I studied at the Intensive Language institute during 4 mos., then I studies for the Summer at scu. I am now Freshmen student, and my major is Mechanical Engineering, and I hope to do well in this semester.

Exercise 3.   Look back at one of your early rough drafts that you believe needs more than minor revision. Mark errors with appropriate editing marks. Then write a paragraph explaining the more fundamental revisions that have to be made.

Exercise 4.   Revise the essay you analyzed in Exercise 3.

Exercise 5.   Exchange rough drafts of one of your essays with a fellow student. Read his or her essay carefully. Mark errors with appropriate editing marks. Then write a paragraph or two explaining how the essay needs to be revised to make it more effective.

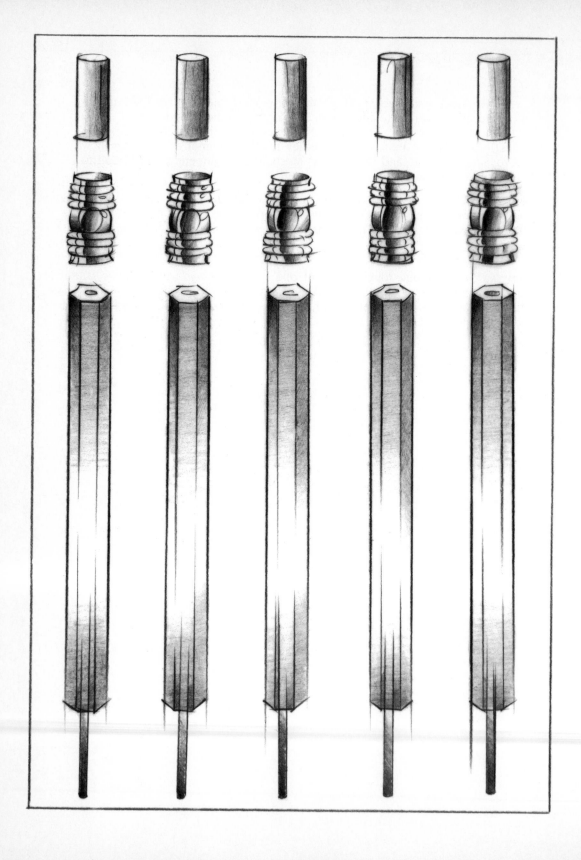

Part Four

Units
of the
Essay

Chapter 13

Paragraphs

Up to now, we have been looking at the essay as a whole. In this section, we will turn to the units that make up the essay. We will move from larger to smaller units: from *paragraphs*, to *sentences*, to *words*. We will also look at *transitions*, at the way one thought in an essay is linked to another.

In books, dissertations, and master's theses, units or chapters generally make up the largest subdivisions. In most college essays, however, the largest subdivision is the *paragraph*, a group of statements closely related by a central idea. Just as the parts in this book headed "The Essay," "Patterns for Essays," "Writing the Essay," "Units of the Essay," and so forth help the reader recognize where one subtopic leaves off and another begins, so paragraphs subdivide an essay's material to help the reader recognize shifts in thought, approach, or attitude.

Of course, all statements in an essay must relate to the overall thesis. However, individual paragraphs relate to an essay's thesis in different ways. The physical appearance of paragraphs on a page helps the reader to recognize these differences. In a well-written essay, the reader perceives shifts from one way of relating to another without paragraph markings. But the markings make the reader's job easier by giving him or her a physical sign of the shifts. In academic writing, paragraphs are usually marked by indention—by starting a line a few letters to the right of the left-hand margin.

Paragraphing, however, is not merely a question of indenting a line every now and then for appearance's sake. The student must determine where it is best to start a new paragraph—that is, why a new paragraph ought to begin at one particular sentence and not at another. To be sure, paragraphing is more a matter of style than science, of better and worse choices rather than wrong and right ones. However, there are certain principles the student can master that will guide him or her in making sound choices about where new paragraphs ought to begin.

To make paragraphs that will help his or her reader, the student must learn to write in unified, complete units of thought that are logically developed. He or she must also provide, where necessary, a clear signpost to the main idea of each thought unit. To do this, the student must master paragraph unity, order, and completeness, and he or she must learn to make use of the theme sentence.

Paragraph Unity

Just as all parts of an essay must be related to the essay as a whole, so all parts of a paragraph must be related to the whole paragraph. The paragraph is a unit of thought within an essay, consisting of sentences related to a central idea that is narrower than the theme or thesis. As a rule, we do not talk in orderly paragraphs. We start to express one idea, then think of something else, and come back to finish our first idea (if we do at all!) later on. In essay writing we must be clearer. If we confuse someone to whom we are talking, he can ask for an explanation; if we confuse a reader, he is lost.

Let us look at the following essay and see how well the student writer has handled paragraphing:

My City

I live in a small city within a big forest in a narrow valley near the beach in the north of Iran, where there is always rain and too much fog and humidity. Most of the people who live there are friends. They have much association with each other because there is not much entertainment; specifically there are just four cinemas, one park, two or three night clubs, and a few good restaurants and hotels.

The city is very quiet. Nothing exciting happens there. Eighty-five percent of people who live there are educated. Everything which one wants is fresh and ready, like milk, every kind of vegetable, meat, etc. In summertime the city gets crowded because of the beach, but it doesn't become overcrowded; at the beginning of fall, it gets quiet again.

There are no traffic jams, no air pollution. The weather in my city is terrific, always like spring, not hot, not cold. Everywhere it is green with many flowers all around. There are also many rivers around the city which are good for fishing. My family has lived there for eight years. Maybe one of the reasons that I love my city is that my parents are there. There is nothing except the beach that is exciting or interesting for a person of my age. However, I love it and I hope I will go back there forever to be near my wonderful parents and friends.

Reading such an essay is like entering a maze full of false entryways and closed doors. The essay starts to take the reader in one direction, stops suddenly, and starts again someplace else entirely without any clear path for the reader to follow. Even a quick glimpse at the topics covered by each paragraph reveals the essay's confusion:

Paragraph 1
  Sentence 1: Location of city
  Sentence 2: Bad weather in area
  Sentence 3: Closeness of people
  Sentence 4: Lack of entertainment
Paragraph 2
  Sentence 1: Quietness of city
  Sentence 2: Education of people
  Sentence 3: Availability of fresh food
  Sentence 4: Summertime crowds and fall quiet
Paragraph 3
  Sentence 1: Freedom from traffic and pollution problems
  Sentence 2: Good weather of city
  Sentence 3: Natural beauty of city
  Sentence 4: Availability of fresh fish from rivers
  Sentence 5: Length of family residence in city
  Sentence 6: Parents' presence in city as one reason writer loves it
  Sentence 7: Lack of anything else to interest writer there
  Sentence 8: Love of city for sake of parents and friends

Why should a reader bother fighting her way through such confusion! Even if she manages to struggle through the bad weather, friendliness, and lack of entertainment covered in Paragraph 1, when she comes to Paragraph 2 and finds in the first three sentences material about the city's quietness, the education of the people, and the availability of fresh foods, she is likely to despair. If she bothers to keep reading and gets to the second sentence in Paragraph 3—"The weather in my city is terrific"—and remembers the bad weather described in the first sentence in Paragraph 1, she will almost certainly give up. There is no clear path through such an essay. The reader is lost inside it. The fastest way out is simply to stop reading.

This is a shame because the student who wrote this essay had an interesting point to make and sufficient concrete details to support it. The problem in the essay is the total lack of paragraph unity. There are no clear units of thought to help the reader grasp the essay's theme. Rather, thoughts come and go and come again without any sense of unity, development, or completion. Let us look again at this essay, revised to make its paragraphs unified:

My City

The city I come from is a beach town in the north of Iran. Except for 1
the beach, it would appear that there is nothing in it to interest a person
of my age. It is a quiet town without many places for entertainment. In the
whole town there are just four cinemas, one park, two or three night clubs,
and a few good restaurants and hotels. Nothing exciting ever happens in
my town.

However, the town does have its appealing aspects. The weather in my 2
city—unlike the weather in the rest of the humid, foggy, and rainy North—
is terrific—always like spring, not hot, not cold. Everywhere it is green with

many flowers all around. Everything which one wants is fresh and available: fresh milk and meat, every kind of vegetable. In addition, the many rivers around the city are good for fishing. Although the beach draws crowds in the summer, the city never becomes overcrowded. As a result, there are no traffic jams and no air pollution.

In addition to the town's natural beauty, the charm of the people makes   **3** it an appealing place. Most of the people who live in my town are friends. Perhaps because there is not much entertainment, the people associate a great deal with one another. In addition, most of the people are well educated and interesting.

My family has lived in this city for eight years, and one reason I love   **4** my city is that my parents are there. Some people might think that because there is nothing exciting in my city, I would want to leave. However, I love my city and hope I will go back there forever to be near the beauty of the beach and my wonderful parents and friends.

There is, perhaps, nothing startling about this revised essay. But it is clear and readable. The reader can make her way through the essay, following from one unit of thought—from one paragraph—to another. In Paragraph 1, all sentences are related to the idea that the writer's town is quiet. In Paragraph 2, all sentences relate to the town's pleasant natural aspects. Paragraph 3 covers the charm of the people of the town, and all its sentences relate to that idea. Finally, in Paragraph 4, the writer expresses her theme: despite the quiet, the writer loves her city for its beauty and for the presence of her parents and friends. If Paragraph 1 had introduced the idea of good or bad weather or Paragraph 2 had dealt with the people's education as well as with natural beauty, the paragraphs would have lost their unity—and confusion would have resulted. In Chapter 2 of this text, we discussed how an essay should include no details irrelevant to the essay. In just the same way, a paragraph must include no details irrelevant to the paragraph.

Theme Sentence

In Chapter 2, we also discussed how the *thesis* unifies an essay. In a paragraph there is also a unifier, which we will call the *theme sentence.* Just as the thesis expresses the main idea of an essay, so the theme sentence expresses the main idea of a paragraph. Many texts call the theme sentence by another name: the *topic sentence.* However, *theme sentence* suggests more clearly the function of this sentence to state an idea rather than merely to announce a topic.)

Let us look back at the revised essay we have just analyzed and see if there is a theme sentence for each of its paragraphs. In Paragraph 1, the second sentence is the theme sentence: "Except for the beach, . . . there is nothing in it to interest a person of my age." In Paragraph 2, the theme sentence comes first: "However, the town does have its appealing aspects." The theme sentence is also first in Paragraph 3: "In addition to the town's natural beauty, the charm of the people makes it an appealing place." And in Paragraph 4, the theme sentence comes at the end: "However, I love my city and hope I will go back there forever to be near the beauty of the beach and my wonderful parents and friends."

As we can see in these examples, the theme sentence is the most general statement of the main idea of a paragraph; all other statements in the paragraph must relate to it. In Paragraph 2, the general statement about "appealing aspects" is followed by several specific examples: good weather, greenery and flowers, fresh food, lack of traffic and pollution. In Paragraph 4, specific details about the writer's parents' residence in the city and the idea that some people might think she would want to leave are followed by the general statement that she wants to return to her city because of its beauty and the presence of family and friends.

In revising an essay, it may be a good idea for the beginning writer to underline the theme sentence of each paragraph to make sure that

    a.   All other sentences in the paragraph relate to it (that is, there are no irrelevant details), and

    b.   There is no other equally general statement in the paragraph (that is, there is only one main idea).

For practice, the student might try this with the revised version of the essay we have just looked at.

As in an essay where the thesis can be implicit—that is, suggested rather than stated explicitly (see page 11)—so in a paragraph, the theme sentence may be omitted as long as the main idea is made clear by the existing sentences in the paragraph. Paragraph 3, for example, might have been written as follows:

> Most of the people who live in my town are friends. Perhaps because there is not much entertainment, the people associate a great deal with one another. In addition, most of the people are well educated and interesting.

Here, the main idea of the paragraph, that the charm of the people makes the writer's town a pleasant place, is not stated. However, it can be inferred—deduced—from the details supplied by the writer.

As with the essay, so with the paragraph: the student writer will generally be better off if she makes the theme sentence explicit. If, however, she wishes for variety's sake to omit a theme sentence from a paragraph occasionally, she should make sure that the main idea of the paragraph is clear without it. (The beginning writer can check this by writing out a theme sentence on a separate sheet of paper for any paragraph that does not have an explicit one. If she cannot express the main idea of the paragraph in one sentence, the paragraph probably needs revision.)

Paragraph Order

Another way to achieve variety is by varying the placement of the theme sentence within the paragraph. As we saw above, the theme sentence can appear anywhere within a paragraph. In the revised version of "My City," the theme sentence appears in various paragraphs as the first sentence (Paragraphs 2 and 3), the last sentence (Paragraph 4), and a sentence in the middle (Paragraph 1). Each of these positions has its own rationale.

Initial Position

The most common order is that of Paragraphs 2 and 3: a theme sentence followed by supporting sentences. This pattern is sometimes called the *direct* pattern. Most sentences you read and, probably, most sentences you write follow this pattern. Readers appreciate the theme sentence in the initial position because it lets them know what to expect. Paragraphs written according to this structure are extremely clear and easy to follow.

It is essential that the student writer master writing paragraphs with the theme sentence in initial position. However, some instructors go so far as to ask their students to write every paragraph according to this plan, insisting that they start each paragraph with a clear theme sentence followed by two to five supporting sentences. Such a strict rule does not necessarily make for good writing. Essays written according to such a plan are likely to sound mechanical rather than natural. The repetition of the same pattern over and over again is likely to bore the reader. And many paragraphs make more sense when the theme sentence appears in a position other than first. (To test this out, you might reread Paragraph 4 of the revised version of "My City," as if it began with the theme sentence instead of concluding with it. Does the paragraph sound better or worse?)

Let us look at writing situations in which alternative positions for the theme sentence might be recommended.

Intermediate Position

There are two writing situations in which it is appropriate to place the theme sentence in an intermediate position. One situation is when certain background material is necessary as a *context* for the theme sentence. In such paragraphs, preceding sentences announce the topic of the paragraph before the *theme sentence* states its main idea. We have already seen an example of this in Paragraph 1 of our revised essay, reprinted below:

> The city I come from is a beach town in the north of Iran. Except for the beach, it would appear that there is nothing in it to interest a person of my age. It is a quiet town without many places for entertainment. In the whole town there are just four cinemas, one park, two or three night clubs, and a few good restaurants and hotels. Nothing exciting ever happens in my town.

In this paragraph, Sentence 1 announces the topic: the student is going to write about the city she comes from. The main idea, that there is nothing in the city to interest a person of her age, is reserved for Sentence 2.

In most paragraphs, there will be only one or perhaps two such sentences preceding the theme sentence. However, in very long or very complex paragraphs, three or more sentences may be necessary to provide the necessary background for the theme sentence.

The second situation in which it is appropriate to place the theme sentence in an intermediate position is when the paragraph contains *limiting* material. Limiting material presents an idea contrary to the main idea of the paragraph—that is, it relates to the theme sentence in a negative way. Although it might seem to be confusing to the reader, presented in the right way, limiting material can actually enhance the strength of the theme. Such material helps convince the reader that the writer is being fair, that he or she has considered both sides of an issue. By triumphing over limitations, the theme is strengthened.

In the essay we have been reviewing, the first paragraph is actually a limiting paragraph: it states objections to the theme of the essay presented in the last paragraph. However, we could rewrite the first paragraph of the essay to include both the limiting material it now contains and the theme itself, as below:

People often wonder why a girl my age would want to live in the city I come from. A beach town in the north of Iran, it is a quiet city where nothing exciting ever happens, and where the places for entertainment are few. Nevertheless, I love my city and want to go back there forever. I love it for the natural beauty of the beach. I love it for the charm of its people. And I love it because my wonderful parents live there.

Here, the first two sentences seem to lead the reader away from the main idea, suggesting that there are reasons the writer might not wish to live in her home city. Then, in Sentence 3, the writer turns around to state the main idea: she loves her city and wants to live there. The final three sentences are used to support this main idea. Such a paragraph structure is sometimes called a *pivoting* structure because of the way in which the writer turns away from the initial direction to state the main idea.

In paragraphs using the pivoting structure, the limiting information is almost always presented first, with the writer pivoting in the direction of the main idea to conclude the paragraph. If the limiting information were reserved for the end of the paragraph, the main idea would likely be weakened, as in the version below:

I love my city, a beach town in the north of Iran; I want to go back there forever. I love it for the natural beauty of the beach. I love it for the charm of its people. And I love it because my wonderful parents live there. However, people often wonder why a girl of my age would want to live in the city I come from. It is a quiet city where nothing exciting ever happens and where the places for entertainment are few.

Here, after a strong beginning, the paragraph trails off into a list of limitations, undercutting the main idea. As a result, the main idea is weakened, and the reader is confused. It is important to get the limitations out of the way early in a paragraph and to finish strong.

Other structures would also be problematical. If, for example, the theme sentence were not followed immediately by supporting sentences, the result might be somewhat weak or confusing:

People often wonder why a girl my age would want to live in the city I come from. A beach town in the north of Iran, it is a quiet city where nothing exciting ever happens, and where the places for entertainment are few. Nonetheless, I love my city and want to go back there forever.

This kind of structure, with the theme sentence pivoting away to close the paragraph, is intriguing. And a writer might sometimes wish to use such a structure for its surprise effect—providing in subsequent paragraphs, of course, details to support the theme sentence. The beginning writer, however, should be careful when using such tricks.

The writer should also be careful about pivoting more than once within a paragraph. Actually, the last paragraph of our revised essay does just this, as we can see below:

My family has lived in this city for eight years and one reason I love my city is that my parents are there. Some people might think that, because there is nothing exciting in my city, I would want to leave. However, I love my city and hope I will go back there forever to be near the beauty of the beach and my wonderful parents and friends.

This paragraph starts with details that support the theme, then turns away for a limiting sentence, and turns back again for the theme sentence that closes the paragraph. Occasionally, such a complex structure works well. However, it may be confusing. In general, you should limit yourself to one directional shift within a paragraph. If you pivot more than once, you should try to make certain that, as often as you pivot, the reader will pivot with you.

Final Position

Of course, as we have just seen, the theme sentence can also occupy the final position in a paragraph. Generally, it is preceded by supporting sentences, although as we saw above, it may be preceded by some limiting sentences as well. A paragraph in which the theme sentence occupies the final position is called a *suspended paragraph*. And, indeed, its effect is one of suspense and often of surprise.

Take, for example, this paragraph that closes a student's research paper on the DC-10:

> Almost two years after the worst crash in U.S. aviation history, the DC-10 is flying again all over the world. A McDonnell Douglas commercial appears on television advertising the DC-10 as a safe plane. However, no statement has yet been made about changes in the plane's design. The time of madness and anxiety have passed and people fly DC-10s as if nothing had ever happened. But there is one question that has never been satisfactorily answered: With the DC-10 in the air, are our skies really safe?

Here, Sentence 1 and even Sentences 2 and 4 have a calming effect on the reader. A note of doubt is introduced in the third sentence. But the theme sentence—in the form of a frightening question—is reserved for the end, where it will have maximum effect. The writer holds the reader in suspense—lulling him with a false sense of calm—and then startles him with the final frightening sentence.

Even when there is no real surprise in the theme sentence, placing it in final position can intrigue the reader. In a sense, the writer is playing a game with the reader, supplying the reader with clues and inviting him to guess their meaning—as in a mystery. This introductory paragraph from a student research paper is a good example:

> A five-year-old is admitted to the hospital. She has never walked and weighs 13 pounds. A six-month-old baby who has kept crying is thrown from a window by his mother, and, when found alive, drowned in the tub. A sixteen-month-old does not come when called, and is pulled by the ear by his father. When the child is admitted to the hospital, it is found that his ear has been partially torn from his head. The list is long and appalling. The atrocities are beyond comprehension. But they do exist and they are increasing. Child abuse is becoming a major public health problem in the United States.

Here, the list of concrete examples—almost too painful to read—clearly adds up to the final theme sentence. But their impact on the reader is enhanced by the structure of the paragraph. Because he is not initially told that the main idea of the paragraph is that child abuse is a major public health problem, the reader must concentrate more intensely on the specific details. As he reads, his mind is constantly working, wondering: What point is the writer trying to make with these horrible details? When the answer is given in the final sentence, the reader, having probably guessed by then what that point would be, feels a sense of satisfaction (despite the grim subject matter) for having solved the mystery.

Of course, the paragraph could have been handled differently. The writer could have started with the theme sentence and followed with the specific examples. But with an initial theme sentence, the reader's concentration on the subsequent examples would likely be lessened. He would no longer be a participant in a game or mystery. His involvement—and probably his interest—in the paragraph would be lowered.

It is worth noting that the paragraphs we have just looked at have been either introductory or concluding paragraphs. These are generally the most appropriate places for paragraphs with theme sentences in final position. In an introductory paragraph, the suspended theme sentence intrigues the reader, drawing him into the essay. In a concluding paragraph, the suspended theme sentence can give a sense of satisfaction or surprise. It can even leave the reader with a "chilling" sensation—a feeling he may retain after he finishes reading.

Used well, the various positions of the theme sentence can enhance paragraph unity. In initial position, the theme sentence establishes the unity of the details to come. In intermediate position, the theme sentence ties the beginning of a paragraph to the end. And in final position, the theme sentence draws together what may seem to be isolated details into a unified whole.

Paragraph Completeness

Of course, in addition to being unified and orderly, paragraphs must also be complete. In order to be complete, paragraphs must convey one main idea and develop it adequately, without introducing a second main idea and without elaborating unnecessarily.

The rules for paragraph completeness are like the rules for essay completeness. Just as an essay must include all details necessary to support the thesis and no irrelevant details, so a complete paragraph must include all sentences necessary to support the theme sentence, but no sentences that are unnecessary or irrelevant.

Paragraph Completeness and Paragraph Length

Although paragraph length is not the same thing as paragraph completeness, length is often a good indicator of completeness. Most fully developed paragraphs contain from three to five well-developed sentences. This average length appeals to a reader's eye as well as to his or her mind. A string of short paragraphs has a choppy look and a confusing effect. Very long paragraphs are tedious—difficult for the reader to look at and think through. Naturally, occasional paragraphs will be shorter or longer than the average. But a long string of very short paragraphs or an essay consisting of one very long paragraph is likely a sign of trouble. Possibly, such paragraphs need only formal revision: grouping together several short paragraphs into one longer one or dividing one long paragraph into several shorter ones. Often, however, unusual paragraph length indicates a more fundamental problem, requiring radical revision.

The String of Short Paragraphs. Let us look, for example, at an essay consisting entirely of one- or, at most, two-sentence paragraphs:

ELS Center

ELS Center is that part of our university where many people come to learn English.

There are many students from different countries and cultures, and you can learn and know many things from these people.

Most of the students are grateful to ELS because they say that it is a good institution.

The teachers are very kind and they try to teach as much as they can and to motivate the students.

The Center has many events for the students, such as parties, shows, etc.

ELS has been in existence for many years and there have been good results with it.

The way that English is taught at ELS is different from the way it is taught at other centers because at ELS learning is accelerated so students can learn the language quickly. This is advantageous to students because they can get into the university sooner, although the students still have many problems sometimes.

I was a student at the ELS Center here and I am thankful to it because the English that I know now I learned there, and I have beautiful memories of my teachers and of my friends.

In this essay, the student is all over the place. She flies from one short paragraph to another, without developing any idea fully and without drawing any ideas together. The essay consists of eight paragraphs—and only nine sentences! Immediately, this should tell us something is wrong.

Formal revision—regrouping of short paragraphs into longer ones—is not the answer here. The ideas expressed in the separate paragraphs are not sufficiently unified to form a coherent essay. The only remedy is a radical revision. The student needs to focus on a clear theme and to develop paragraphs that support it with relevant concrete details.

It is worth noting that the paragraphs in the student's original handwritten essay *looked* pretty good. If one did not actually read it, the large chunks of writing formed by her sentence-long paragraphs made it look like a legitimate essay. Indeed, the student's large handwriting may have fooled her into thinking she had written real paragraphs. Students who write longhand rather than type must be especially careful about paragraph length. Large handwriting can make short paragraphs look substantial. In the original ELS Center essay, for example, the student's paragraphs are all at least three lines long and many are longer, even though most consist of only a single sentence. For paragraph completeness, however, it is the adequate development of a thought rather than length to the eye that matters. If your writing is large, counting sentences—or even words—per paragraph may be helpful until you get used to writing complete paragraphs. Typing an essay might also help you see your paragraphs as they really are.

Overlong Paragraphs. At the opposite extreme from students who write consistently short paragraphs are those who write essays containing overlong paragraphs or even one long unbroken paragraph. Sometimes such essays need only formal revision: the student merely needs to mark as paragraphs the divisions in thought that already exist in the contents of the essay. Sometimes, however, one-paragraph essays betray more fundamental problems, as below:

One Aspect of Life at My University

One of the most important advantages of being a student is that you can have more friends than you've ever had before, and the easiest way that you can do so is by living in the dorm, where most of the students live during regular semesters. Sometimes they have parties, mostly on Friday nights, and you can enjoy yourself. But sometimes they do these things too much, and that's why I got tired of living in the dorm. I don't know when they get time to study. Of course, I agree that it is nice to have parties and to enjoy oneself. But the main idea for all of us who are here is to study. These days the only thing that you don't see at the dorms is studying, and when they aren't having a party, students play pool or go to their rooms and turn their tape recorders up as much as they can. Once I thought it was an earthquake when the guy who lived next to my room turned his tape recorder on! But, despite these things, living in the dorm is one of the best experiences that I've ever had.

Faced with such an essay, the reader wants to say, "Whoa! Wait a minute!" The writer has jumped on his horse and galloped away, dragging the poor reader exhaustedly behind him. The reader cannot hope to keep up with the pace the writer's mind sets in charging from one thought to another.

In this essay, major revision is necessary. As in the essay with one-sentence paragraphs, so in this one-paragraph essay, the writer has not defined his thesis. His ideas tumble out, undeveloped, unsubordinated, unconnected. The writer expects the reader to organize his thoughts for him. More likely, the reader will simply stop reading. An adequate revision of this essay would require that the writer define his thesis and reorganize his thoughts. Theme sentences should be identified and paragraphs constructed to support them.

Useful Paragraphs of Unusual Length. Occasional short and long paragraphs are not only all right, but useful. Variety of paragraph length makes an essay less tedious for the reader. A short paragraph can highlight an arresting detail, or it can make a sharp transition between parts of an essay, as in the examples below:

This is the picture of child abuse in the U.S. today. What can be done about it?

So said the publicity; then a short four years later came the crash.

An occasional long paragraph (see, for example, the commuter train passage from Willie Morris's *North Toward Home,* page 11) may be necessary to develop a complex idea adequately. Different disciplines may favor paragraphs of unusual length. Journalism, for example, favors shorter than average-length paragraphs. Technical and medical writing, on the other hand, has a tendency toward paragraphs of greater than normal length.

Padded Paragraphs. Moreover, average length does not ensure paragraph completeness. "Padded" paragraphs, fleshed out with unnecessary words, repeated ideas, or irrelevant details, may be incomplete despite their conforming to the three- to five-sentence average length. Ideas thrown together without development may be broken up into neat paragraph-size parcels without genuinely constituting complete paragraphs.

Guidelines for Paragraph Length. Nonetheless, essays consisting of odd-length paragraphs bear special scrutiny. To reiterate:
- A string of short paragraphs may need formal revision through the combination of several short paragraphs into one longer one or radical revision through additional explanatory and/or supporting sentences.
- Very long paragraphs may need formal division into several shorter paragraphs or radical revision through reorganization into unified paragraphs grouping theme sentences with related explanatory and/or supporting material.

The Art of Paragraphing

A student in my first composition class wrote deadly compositions. Every one of them had exactly three paragraphs and the pattern was always the same: an introductory paragraph stating the thesis, a middle paragraph developing it briefly, a closing paragraph restating it. When I asked him why he wrote all his essays exactly like this, he explained that his high school teacher had said this was proper essay form.

It is not. Paragraphing is more than a matter of neat-sized chunks of writing. It cannot be laid out on the same plan for every essay by every student on every topic. It is not a matter of science, and there is room for differences of opinion and judgment about where paragraph breaks should occur. The important thing to remember about paragraphing is that the only formula for doing it well consists of arranging thoughts in unified, orderly, and complete units.

Summary

The paragraph is the largest subdivision in most college essays. A paragraph is a unit of thought consisting of sentences related to a central theme that is narrower than the thesis. Each paragraph in an essay relates to the thesis in a different way.

Paragraphs must be unified. The theme sentence expresses the main idea of the paragraph. It may be implicit or explicit. Explicit theme sentences may occur in initial, intermediate, or final position, the order depending on which structure is most effective for the contents of the paragraph. Paragraphs must also be complete—that is, they must be developed adequately with relevant supporting detail. Although paragraph length is not an absolute indicator of completeness, paragraphs should generally approach an average of from three to five sentences. Paragraphs that deviate widely from this average should be scrutinized carefully.

Exercises

For Consideration

Exercise 1.   Read the following essay. Are the paragraphs well unified? Mark the theme sentence for every paragraph that has one. For any paragraph that does not have a theme sentence, write one in the margin.

Identify theme sentences by position as initial, intermediate, final, or implicit. What is the reason for the position of each theme sentence in the essay? Has the writer chosen the best position for the theme sentence of each paragraph?

TV Networks in the United States

One of the hundreds of things which surprise us who come from Indochina to the United States is the television network system here. Television stations seem to be available everywhere. Besides ABC, NBC, and CBS, the Public Broadcasting System is counted as a fourth main TV network in the United States. These networks surprise us because they are rich with programs and are the biggest networks in terms of their distribution around the world.   1

Each TV network has its own independent programs in addition to network programs. These programs run constantly twenty-four hours a day. By watching various networks, it is possible for one to see the big events in every field, such as movies, education, entertainment, or news events occurring around the world.   2

Commercial advertising on network television reaches to the top of excitement for my family. My wife has become a good customer for every kind of cosmetic or food and all outlets for discount shopping. My children are loyal customers of toys and of breakfast cereal advertised by Bruce Jenner.   3

The news shown every evening is attractive to me. My wife sometimes complains that I am not available to help with anything between 6:30 and 8:00 p.m. every night. However, she must consider that the news shown on the networks every night is the most important part of network programming. By watching it, we can know about every major event occurring locally or abroad. News comes from everywhere—from inside the United States itself as well as from inside Communist countries on the other side of the world.   4

My family enjoys watching TV programs of every variety. We depend on them. From them, we learn about this country which we are living in as "second" natives. Besides, U.S. television programs help us to understand English better and better.   5

Exercise 2. Look at the above essay and at the theme sentences you identified for each paragraph. Proceeding paragraph by paragraph, determine whether each paragraph in the essay is sufficiently unified and well developed. Are there sentences in any paragraph that are irrelevant to its theme sentence or unnecessary for its support? Do each of the paragraphs provide sufficient supporting details and/or explanation to develop the paragraph adequately? Identify any problems in paragraph unity or completeness.

Exercise 3. Look at one of your early essays.
a. Are the paragraphs unified? Are they complete? Why or why not?
b. Underline the theme sentence of each paragraph. For any paragraph for which there is no theme sentence, write one in the margin.
c. Identify each theme sentence by its position as initial, intermediate, final, or implicit. Is the position you have chosen for each theme sentence the best for that paragraph? Explain.
d. Can you suggest any changes that would improve particular paragraphs? Can you suggest deletions that might enhance paragraph unity or additions that might make poorly developed paragraphs more complete? Are paragraph markers properly placed? If not, where should new paragraphs begin?

Exercise 4. The two essays below each consist of strings of short paragraphs. Read each essay and decide whether it needs formal revision only or more radical revision. If only formal revision is needed, identify the paragraphs that should be combined to form longer ones. If more radical revision is necessary, identify what is needed to make the short paragraphs complete.

A Live Concert

1   When I was in New York with my sister two months ago, we had the opportunity to go to Madison Square Garden and see my favorite rock group, Aerosmith.

2   As it was the first time I had gone to a show like that, I felt very happy and surprised. I never imagined a coliseum could have such order or that it could hold fifty thousand people.

3   We entered the Garden by the main door, walked into the first room, where they were still selling tickets, and then crossed through the lobby. Some people were taken away because they were carrying drugs or alcohol or guns.

4   After going up three escalators, we stepped onto our floor and then found our seats.

5   It was outrageous: the whole place was crowded, noisy, and covered with clouds of cigarette smoke mixed with marijuana.

6   The lights went out; the whole crowd began to scream and whistle; the stage was covered with a big black curtain. Then the curtain was raised and the group began to play. What a feeling! I was living it, well called a "live" concert. As each song was played, all the people become happier until even a policeman behind us was dancing! Some of the songs were chorused by the crowd. Can you imagine a thousand people singing?

Then they suddenly finished playing. The lights went on and then off. 7
In the darkness, all the people lit up a match or a lighter.

That was wonderful, like a clear sky seen from a very high mountain. 8
That lasted for a few minutes, and then the group came out and began to
play their best song. It sounded extremely good. What a sound!

Then it was all over. The thing that surprised me was how all the peo- 9
ple went out so fast and orderly.

I loved it and I promised myself to come back again. 10

Easter

Easter is a special holy day for Christians around the world. Different 1
people have different customs for celebrating Easter. We Armenians in Iran
celebrate Easter forty days after New Year's Day. The celebration starts with
a special dinner and a church ceremony on the following day, and it ends
with the visiting of relatives and friends.

The dinner party is usually given by the oldest member of the family. 2
But, of course, everybody who is invited has to do his part of the job.

The dinner table is full of a variety of foods, fruits, sweets, and drinks. 3

Before we start dinner, one of the young members of the family prays 4
with a loud voice, and everybody prays with him or her. Then it's time for
a toast with red wine and, finally, dinner.

Different games and funny jokes and stories follow dinner. 5

The next morning is church day. Everybody dresses up and goes to the 6
church for a special ceremony. The churches are always filled with people
because there are only six Christian churches in Tehran.

A cake with a cross on it and painted eggs in a basket are the symbols 7
of Easter.

I miss these days so much. 8

Exercise 4. The two essays below each consist of one long paragraph. Read each
essay and decide whether it needs formal revision only or more radical revision. If
formal revision only is needed, divide the essay into groups of sentences to form
complete paragraphs. If more radical revision is necessary, explain what is needed
to make the paragraphs unified, orderly, and complete.

Fire Alarm

(1) After eighteen hours flying, I was in New York, tired and headachy.
(2) It took three hours to get to the university. (3) Fortunately, my cousin
was here, and when I entered the dorm, I went to her room. (4) All her
friends came to her room to visit me, but I was so tired that I slept and
everybody left the room. (5) I was just going to sleep when suddenly I
heard a kind of voice which was telling me "fire"?!!! (6) I was so scared, I
jumped out of the bed and I tried to find the emergency door. (7) After a
few minutes, I found that and I tried to go out of the building as soon as
possible. (8) I was running and running very fast. (9) I thought if I went
slowly I would burn. (10) When I went out of the building, I couldn't see
anybody outside. (11) I was the first person who was out of the building.

(12) I had my nightdress on. (13) I was almost freezing. (14) After ten minutes, I saw students coming out one by one, very calmly, and some of them with their pillow and blanket. (15) By luck, my cousin found me and she gave me something to cover myself with. (16) I asked her why nobody cared and why everybody was late coming. (17) She told me there was no fire; some drunken boys had pulled the fire alarm to have fun. (18) What fun? (19) It was not my first and last time to experience a fire alarm. (20) Every week, two or three times, some nights four times, we have them. (21) It has been very harmful to me. (22) Every time I have an exam there seems to be a fire alarm the night before. (23) It is destroying my mind. (24) I hope the security people at our university care about it seriously because a fire alarm at four o'clock in the morning in the middle of winter on a snowy night is no joke.

Indians in Venezuela

(1) In my country there are many Indians. (2) They are faced with significant problems. (3) First, as a group of Indians with its own language and culture, each tribe wants to keep its traditions and preserve some of its native customs. (4) The adults want their children to be proud of being Indians as well as to survive in the outside world. (5) The young people want to enter the modern world which they see on TV and in movies. (6) Like everyone else, they are anxious to get a good education and a good job. (7) However, the Indians see little prospect for success and become frustrated because they usually go to inferior schools and often can't adjust to life in the city. (8) In addition, many feel that they are discriminated against by other people. (9) They have lost much of their self-confidence and pride, and they must acknowledge this fact in order to get rid of their problems.

For Composition

Exercise 5. Choose from Exercise 3 or 4 one essay which you felt needed radical revision. Rewrite the essay, concentrating on forming paragraphs that are unified, orderly, and complete. If particular paragraphs are poorly developed due to a lack of supporting or explanatory detail, feel free to invent material in order to develop them adequately.

Exercise 6. Exchange with a classmate an essay you are presently working on for English composition class. Write a criticism of the essay, focusing on how effectively paragraph divisions have been made. Are paragraphs sufficiently unified, orderly, and complete? If not, make specific suggestions on how paragraphs in the essay ought to be revised.

Exercise 7.   Reread one of your early essays and answer the following questions:
   a. What length are most of the paragraphs?
   b. Would any short paragraphs be better off regrouped into one longer one?
   c. Would any long paragraphs be better off divided into several shorter ones?
   d. Would formal revision of paragraphs be adequate or is more radical revision called for?

e. If paragraphs are of average length, are you certain that they are neither "padded" to make them longer nor artifically divided into "neat chunks" of writing?

f. Are there any short or long paragraphs that you feel are justified in having an unusual length? Explain.

g. Revise the essay you have analyzed, concentrating on making its paragraphs as unified, orderly, and complete as possible.

Chapter 14

Sentences

We now turn to sentences, the units that make up paragraphs. The sentence is the smallest unit of composition capable of expressing a complete thought. There are, of course, smaller units of composition—words and groups of words such as

- Woman,
- American woman,
- An American woman with a briefcase,
- Speaking to an American woman with a briefcase,
- Although I was speaking to an American woman with a briefcase.

But these smaller units do not express *complete thoughts*. It is for this reason that, as Chapter 2 states, a thesis can be expressed only in a complete sentence: only a sentence (or an independent clause that can be punctuated as a sentence) is capable of expressing a complete idea.

Since sentences express ideas, a writer's sentences must be clear in order for his or her ideas to be clear. To achieve clarity, the writer must learn to compose unified, well-structured, and complete sentences. Indeed, what we have said about writing paragraphs is true also about writing sentences: the writer's aims are unity, sound structure, and completeness.

In this text, sentence unity and completeness are covered in the unit on grammar (see page 262). We consider them matters of grammar because they are governed by definite rules determining what constitutes a complete sentence and what unifies parts of a sentence with the whole. To some degree, of course, rules also determine the structure of English sentences. For example, the words in the sentence

> The girl felt bad.

could not be rearranged as

> Girl the bad felt.

Many matters of sentence structure, however, are not governed by definite rules. There is no rule, for example, to determine whether

> She felt bad, and she cried.

is preferable to

> She cried because she felt bad.

or

> Feeling bad, she cried.

It is a matter of judgment. Nonetheless, such matters of sentence structure can be crucial to sentence clarity.

Of course, we do not generally talk in perfectly structured sentences; indeed, often we do not talk in sentences at all. Take, for example, this reelection campaign statement by U.S. president Ronald Reagan, responding to a question about postponing defense expenditures:

> Now we have been doing this and we have, we ourselves, with all of the talk about defense spending as being the source of added funds for reducing the deficit, and I've seen the terms used many times in the media, that record defense spending.

In speech, such nonsentences pass by quickly, and the listener has to be pretty quick to catch them. What the average listener probably comes away with is an impression that he does not quite understand the ideas being expressed. Actually, such fuzziness may be the speaker's intention. If a politician has to say something that is not going to please everybody, he might want to keep it fuzzy.

In composition, such fuzziness will not work. The reader is at leisure to look over what the writer has said and consider the clarity of the writer's ideas. If the writing does not seem clear, the reader blames the writer, not himself. The writer, therefore, usually wants to construct the clearest possible sentences—especially if he is writing an essay for a college course. To do so, he must not only learn the rules governing sentence unity and completeness, but also develop judgment about sound sentence structure.

Some student writers do not consider the various possibilities of sentence structure when they write essays. They are content to write a series of complete sentences all structured in more or less the same way, as in this excerpt from a student's autobiography:

> My name is Fatemah Shadlou. I was born in 1960 in Tehran, Iran. My family is fairly well off. My physical characteristics are brown hair, brown eyes, and a fair complexion. I am neither too short nor too tall; I am almost medium height.
>
> My language is Persian, and I started to learn English in elementary school. I started elementary school at six years old. I spent about six years of my life in elementary school. That was a great time for me. I had fun with school friends in that child world. It seemed free of any bad thing.

In this passage, every sentence follows the same general pattern:

$$\textit{Subject} \quad + \quad \textit{Predicate}$$

My name	is
I	was born
My physical characteristics	are

The foreign student fresh out of an introductory English as a second language program may be particularly prone to writing sentences like these because they are easy to write and because ESL exercises and model compositions generally consist of them. A good college essay, however, should not sound like an ESL exercise.

The most obvious problem with an essay consisting of such sentences is that it is boring: the reader is lulled to sleep with the repetition of the pattern I *was, my characteristics are,* I *am, My language is,* I *started, it was,* and so forth. But in addition to this tedium, the essay also suffers from a lack of clarity. Because the sentences are expressed as if each thought were isolated from any other thought—and just as important as every other thought—the ideas do not seem related to one another. The reader is left to himself to make the connections between and to determine the relative weights of ideas. Only by altering the pattern here and there can the sentences be made to express clearly such connections and weights. For example, the second paragraph of the preceding passage might be revised as follows:

> Starting at six years old, I spent about six years of my life at elementary school. That was a great time for me because I always had fun with school friends in that child world, which seemed free of any bad thing.

There is no definite rule to determine just how the sentences should be written. Every change in sentence structure potentially alters the way the reader perceives the relationship between and the relative importance of one idea and another. Sentence meaning depends not only on the words in a sentence, but on just how those words are put together.

Variety

Many composition texts instruct the student to vary sentence structure. This is good advice as far as it goes. The question remaining, however, is how. The truth is, although variety within an essay is one sign that sentence structure is sound, the writer does not achieve sound sentence structure merely by setting out to write varied sentences. What the student writer should try to develop is a knowledge of the various structures available to him or her and a sense of the effects of those structures on meaning.

Position of the Main Idea

At its most basic, sentence structure depends on the position of the main idea within the sentence. The main idea (sometimes called the *core idea*) is the most important part of a sentence. It consists of one or more independent clauses (coordinate conjunction or no conjunction + subject + verb; see page 263).

Loose Versus Periodic Sentences. When the main idea is stated first, followed by additional information, we have what is called a *loose* sentence:

> Foreign students must put in extra hours on their term papers because English is not their native language.

When additional information is expressed before the main idea is stated, we have what is called a *periodic* sentence:

> Because English is not their native language, foreign students must put in extra hours on their term papers.

Although most sentences in a given essay will probably be loose, writers must have command of the periodic sentence. Like the suspended paragraph (see page 137), the periodic sentence has a climactic effect: where the loose sentence trails off into details, the periodic sentence rounds off an idea, giving a sense of satisfaction, of tying up loose ends.

Of course, if every sentence in an essay were periodic, the effect—with one climax coming after another—would likely be somewhat overwhelming, as in the example below:

> Because English is not their native language, foreign students must put in extra hours on term papers. Having found books and articles on their subject, they must read in a language they are not fully comfortable with. Having done the research and written the first draft and revision, they must still check the language for proper use of vocabulary, idiom, etc. Although writing research papers is difficult for all students, it is harder for foreigners.

As with the loose structure, when the periodic structure becomes repetitious, it grows tedious. That is why variety is so important. Coming amid several loose sentences, a single periodic sentence can give special emphasis to a point a writer wishes to highlight.

In writing periodic sentences, the student writer must make certain that his or her meaning justifies the emphatic structure. The periodic sentence

> Because English is not their native language, when writing term papers, foreign students must put in extra hours.

might be appropriate in a paragraph focusing on the extra burdens carried by foreign students. In a paragraph concentrating on foreign students' need for intensive English classes, the loose structure

> Foreign students must put in extra hours when writing term papers because English is not their native language.

might be more appropriate.

The Balanced Sentence. In addition to loose and periodic sentences, there is a third type of sentence useful to the writer: the *balanced* sentence. Balanced sentences consist of pairs of matched elements, such as those in the sentences below:

> Foreign students may have difficulty reading their textbooks; they may have trouble writing their term papers.
>
> Foreign students may have difficulty both in reading their textbooks and in writing their term papers.

Such sentences, with their use of repeated words and grammatical structures, can have a striking effect upon the reader. Indeed, they figure in many of our most memorable quotations:

> If nominated, I will not run; if elected, I will not serve.
>
> Ask not what your country can do for you—ask what you can do for your country.

This repetitive structure would be tedious if overused; but used judiciously, it makes for an effective change from the more common loose and periodic sentence structures.

Some balanced sentences tend to give equal weight to each of the matched elements in a pair. Because of this, they are especially useful in paragraphs of comparison and contrast or subdivision. In writing such sentences, students should try to make certain that the elements in the pair are actually of equal weight. A sentence such as

> Foreign students may have difficulty both in reading their textbooks and in coping with all the necessary routines of their everyday lives.

would make more sense expressed in a different way:

> Foreign students may have difficulty reading their textbooks. Indeed, they may have difficulty coping with all the necessary routines of their everyday lives.

To improve their ability to write balanced sentences, students should become familiar with certain words and phrases, such as

> and; but; or; nor; both . . . and; either . . . or; neither . . . nor; whether . . . or; not . . . but; not only . . . but also; more (less) than;

and punctuation marks including the comma, semicolon, and colon.

Series. A related structure is the series of three or more matched elements. A series, like a balanced sentence, may consist of equal elements, as in this example:

> Foreign students may have difficulty in reading textbooks, writing term papers, and taking exams.

However, when the elements in a series are not equal, such sentences tend to put special emphasis on the final item in the series. And student writers must be careful that the item appearing in that emphatic position justifies the emphasis placed on it. For example, look at these sentences:

> Foreign students may have difficulty in talking to roommates, writing term papers, and even in reading their textbooks.
>
> Foreign students may have difficulty in reading textbooks, writing term papers, and even in talking to roommates.

It is easy to see that the second version of this sentence makes more sense than does the first. (*Note*: Punctuation of items in a series is covered in Chapter 21.)

Sentence Length

Unvarying sentence length can be an indication of inadequately varied sentence structure. Students who tend to write strings of short, choppy sentences should look for ways to combine some of their ideas into longer sentences. There is nothing wrong with the short sentence, per se (indeed, some writers, Ernest Hemingway for instance, are praised for their masterful use of short, simple sentences). And a short sentence amid long ones can have great impact on the reader. However, most students will find that longer sentences can express many of their ideas more precisely than short ones can.

Student writers should not vary sentence length or structure randomly, merely for the sake of variety. Rather, they should try to use the various structures available to them to achieve precision in expressing their ideas. If a student tends to write strings of loose sentences, or short choppy sentences, or long periodic sentences, he or she should consider whether or not some of the ideas might be expressed more clearly in sentences of a different sort.

Subordination

Before a writer can decide where to place subordinate ideas, he or she must determine that some of the ideas *are* subordinate—that is, of less importance than others. As we know, the main idea, the most important part of a sentence, is expressed in one or more main or independent clauses. But generally, there are modifiers and/or additional pieces of information that need to be conveyed to the reader. If these are also expressed in independent clauses as separate sentences, the result is confusion: a string of similarly structured sentences giving equal weight to all pieces of information. Such writing is sometimes called *primer* English because it sounds like the simple and repetitive writing used in textbooks from which schoolchildren learn to read:

John completed his term paper. Then he handed it in. Then he went out and celebrated. He had a good time. Then he came home. Then he remembered he had another term paper to write.

The key to avoiding *primer* English is *subordination*. With subordination, points of lesser importance are expressed in stuctures of lesser weight, leaving main or independent clauses for the most important points in a sentence, as here.

Having finished his term paper, John handed it in. Going out to celebrate, he had a good time until he came home and remembered he had another term paper to write.

Subordinating Structures

There are numerous grammatical structures that can be used to express subordinate information.

Subordinate Clauses

when he had completed his term paper

Phrases

having completed his term paper

Absolute Phrases

the term paper completed

Modifiers

completed quickly

Appositives

the assignment, *a completed term paper*

The names of the various structures are not essential. But the structures themselves are. The more structures a writer masters, the more tools he or she will have. With these tools, subordination need never become mechanical or repetitive. The writer can decide just how important each piece of information in a sentence is and just how weighty a construction he or she wants to allow for it. All the samples above, for instance, subordinate the idea of the student's completion of his term paper. Each of these subordinate constructions allows for something else to be the main idea—to be more important than the completion of the paper. We should be able to perceive the difference between sentences with no subordination, such as

José completed his term paper and he handed it in.

or

José completed his term paper and handed it in.

and a sentence with subordination, such as

> *Having completed his term paper, José handed it in.*

The versions with no subordination give equal importance to José's completion of the paper and his handing it in. The version with subordination, on the other hand, makes José's handing the paper in more important than his completion of it.

Just which form of subordination a student uses is less important than his decision to subordinate a particular idea. However, each variation in sentence structure, no matter how small, changes the meaning, focus, or feel. For example, the absolute *the term paper completed* makes less of the actual process of writing the term paper than does either

> *having completed his term paper*

or

> *when he had completed his term paper.*

Again, it is important to remember that subordinate structures are not necessary in every sentence. An essay consisting entirely of sentences employing subordinate structures might sound fussy or overly complex. Students should, however, use subordination where it is appropriate.

Economy

In an essay, irrelevant ideas confuse the reader by obscuring the thesis. In a sentence, unnecessary words confuse the reader by obscuring the main idea. That is why economy is so important. Every word saved is one less obstacle for the reader. What reader would willingly struggle through a sentence such as this one from a student's research paper:

> From the available information, it would seem that, despite some indicative research findings to the contrary, the campaign against television programming of a violent nature as a contributor to the increase in aggressive and violent behavior has experienced no success in the establishment of a direct and definitive relationship between the promotion of such violent and aggressive attitudes in children and TV watching as it is at the present time.

How much easier the reader's job would be if the writer had simply—and directly—said what she meant:

> Despite some contradictory evidence, campaigners against televised violence have not yet established a definite relationship between violence on television and aggressive attitudes in children.

Omitting Needless Words

In writing, as in all art, the dictum "Less is more" applies. The fewer the words, the less time a reader must spend reading them and the more time he or she will have to consider those that are genuinely important. By this, we do not mean that shorter sentences are preferable to longer ones. Naturally, some ideas require longer sentences than others do. But where the same idea can be expressed with equal precision in either more or fewer words, fewer is better. Essayist E. B. White recalls an English professor who began one class each semester with the instruction: "Omit needless words." The professor himself saved so much time by omitting needless words that, to use class time fully, he simply repeated all his instructions three times:

> Omit needless words. Omit needless words. Omit needless words.

Advice this good bears repetition.

Omitting Words Through Subordination. We have already looked at some of the ways in which needless words can be omitted. Subordination, for example, in addition to being useful for its own sake, has the added advantage of cutting out unnecessary words. The sentences

> John completed his term paper. Then he handed it in.

are *wordy*—unnecessarily repetitive. A revision employing subordination

> Completing his term paper, John handed it in.

cuts out needless words as a result of subordinating one idea to another.

Simplifying Wordy Constructions. In addition, students should learn to avoid constructions that add unnecessary words to their sentences. Wordy phrases such as *the fact that, there is/there are, the nature of,* and so on may add weight without substance. Often, they can be simplified to advantage. Take, for example, this sentence:

> Another problem is the fact that there are some instances in which foreign students may experience difficulties in comprehension in instructional situations.

By omitting phrases such as *the fact that, there are,* and *instances in which,* and by simplifying the phrases *experience difficulties in comprehension* and *instructional situations,* the sentence becomes more direct:

> Another problem is that foreign students do not always understand their instructors.

Similarly, *passive sentences* often benefit by revision. The passive sentence

> Too much work is assigned by my English professor.

is stronger in the active voice:

> My English professor assigns too much work.

Passive voice shifts emphasis from the performer to the receiver of an action. Indeed, with the passive voice, it is not even necessary to identify an action's performer, as here:

> Too much work is assigned in my English class.

Thus, the passive is appropriate when the performer of an action is unknown, understood, or relatively unimportant or when naming the performer might seem discourteous. For example, in the sentence

> The letter was delivered to the wrong address.

the performer is understood to be some sort of delivery person. Very likely, his or her precise identity is unknown. Moreover, it is unimportant; the *letter* is the center of attention. Finally, putting the sentence in the active voice,

> The delivery person delivered the package to the wrong address.

would place blame directly on the delivery person—an unnecessary rudeness.

Such sentences, however, are the exception. Generally, the performer of an action is known and important and should appear as the subject of the sentence. Compare, for example, the following sentence pairs:

> Children are made more aggressive by television violence. (passive)
> Television violence makes children more aggressive. (active)

> The agreement was signed in the Oval Office. (passive)
> The president signed the agreement in the Oval Office. (active)

Each time you use the passive, ask yourself why you are using it. Unless there is a reason for de-emphasizing the performer, active is preferable to passive voice.

There is a place for all the constructions used above. However, if a writer commonly employs such phrases, the result will be tiresome. The writer of wordy prose forces the reader to plow through needless clutter to get to his meaning. Most readers will not go to the trouble.

In revising your essays, watch out for wordiness. One sign of wordy prose is reliance on the verb *to be* in all its forms. Sentences that use a form of *to be* as the main verb generally rely on nouns rather than verbs to express meaning. Since verbs are the only words capable of communicating action in English, a weak verb may weaken a whole sentence. In the essay "The Traffic License" (page 25), the student author wrote of his having failed his driving test:

> It was quite a shock and a surprise for both my mother and me.

It may have been. But the wordy sentence fails to communicate that shock to the reader. Changing the verb and eliminating unnecessary words improves the sentence significantly:

> The failure shocked us.

If most of your sentences employ a form of *to be* as the main verb, look for ways to revise. Compare the strengths of the following sentence pairs:

> Her grade *was* dependent upon this one exam.
> Her grade *depended* upon this one exam.

> My parents *were influential* in my decision about which college I should attend.
> My parents *influenced* my decision about which college I should attend.

Eliminating needless words. In addition to all the ways mentioned above of shortening and strengthening sentences, much can be achieved by cutting down on phrases employing abstract words and by eliminating redundancies. Discussion of this, however, belongs more properly to the final chapter in this unit.

Summary

The sentence is the smallest unit capable of expressing a complete thought. As with paragraphs, the writer must aim at making sentences unified, well-structured, and complete. Sentence unity and completeness are governed by definite rules in English. Sentence structure is often a matter of judgment rather than rules.

The student should aim at writing sentences that are varied in structure, with subordinate elements occurring in various constructions and in various positions within the sentence. In loose sentences, subordinate material follows the main idea; in periodic sentences, it precedes it. Balanced sentences consist of matched pairs. Unvaried sentence structure or length bears scrutiny. Finally, to achieve economy, students should omit from their sentences any unnecessary words.

Exercises

For Consideration

Exercise 1. In each of the following sentences, underline the <u>main clause</u> once and the <u>subordinate material</u> twice. Discuss the relative importance of the underlined parts of each sentence.

Example: <u>The airplane,</u> <u>a DC-10,</u> <u>was waiting at the airport.</u>

a. Climbing aboard the airplane, John felt suddenly nervous.
b. Feeling suddenly nervous, John climbed aboard the airplane.
c. Suddenly nervous, John climbed aboard the airplane.
d. John climbed aboard the airplane and felt suddenly nervous.
e. When he climbed aboard the airplane, John felt nervous suddenly.

Exercise 2. Identify each sentence as loose (L), periodic (P), or balanced (B). Discuss the effect of structure on meaning for sentences a–e and f–j.
a. The professor is neither fair nor sympathetic.
b. Although she is fair, the professor is not sympathetic.
c. The professor is fair, although she is not sympathetic.
d. The professor is fair; she is not, however, sympathetic.
e. The professor is fair, but she is not sympathetic.
f. Either I pass this exam, or I fail the course.

g. If I don't pass this exam, I will fail the course.

h. I will fail the course if I don't pass this exam.

i. Since September I have not had a day off.

j. I have not had a day off since September.

For Composition

Exercise 3. Rewrite the loose sentences below as periodic sentences. Then choose one rewritten sentence and explain the effect of the change you have made on the meaning of the sentence.

> Example: The takeoff was delayed when snow began to fall.
>   When snow began to fall, the takeoff was delayed.

a. Sam chose to major in chemistry because he wanted to go to medical school.

b. Paul met his wife while he was studying in England.

c. I did poorly on the last math exam although I studied hard.

d. My roommate generally does well on his exams even though he doesn't study.

e. Foreign students should see the international student advisor if they have a problem at the university.

f. You can find material on English as a second language under the subject heading *Education, Bilingual*.

g. I could tell she had an accent without even hearing her speak.

h. The students have to write a 10-page term paper for their English class.

Exercise 4. Combine the following sentence pairs by subordinating one sentence in the pair to the other in any way possible.

> Example: Snow began to fall. The takeoff was delayed.
>   The takeoff was delayed when snow began to fall.

a. Carlos is a Peruvian student. He is a business major.

b. Carlos is very outgoing. He enjoys being with people.

c. He likes to travel. It enables him to meet new friends.

d. He will get his degree this June. Then he wants to work for an airline.

e. Kim is a Korean. He works very hard.

f. He had a cold. He decided to go to class anyway.

g. He put on two coats, a hat, and a scarf. Then he went to class.

h. The class had been canceled. Kim felt a little warm and very disappointed.

Exercise 5. Rewrite the following passage of primer English, using sentence variety, subordination, and economy to improve its style.

> John is a student from India. He left for the United States yesterday morning. He went by plane. It was a long trip. The plane landed at the airport. John got off the plane. Then he went to collect his bags. He went through customs. Then he found a taxi. And he took the taxi into the city. He checked in at a hotel. Then he had dinner. He finished at midnight. He got to sleep early the next morning. That was a long day.

Exercise 6. Underline word groups containing needless words. Then rewrite the underlined passages more economically.

In recent times, there have been several instances in which the fact that my roommate is of American nationality has been of help to me. For example, one day there was a meeting between another student of American nationality and myself. There was an argument between us two. However, the fact that I have been involved in an interrelationship with my roommate proved a helpful aid to me and the final result was that there was an understanding reached between the two of us.

In addition, my knowledge of the urban environment in which I find myself currently in residence has also experienced improvement through the fact that I have had the help of my roommate. The nature of the city is better understood by me due to the fact that its customary ways and means of living have been explained to me by her. And there is also much sharing of wearing apparel, reading materials, and edible items between her and myself. Indeed, the only aspect of the relationship between me and my roommate which is to some extent a troublesome matter as far as I am concerned is the fact that there is American music being blasted loudly by her at times ranging from early morning to the latest hours of the night. There is a wishful desire on my part for this one item not to be shared by her quite so freely—or at such a high level of volume.

Exercise 7. Exchange with a classmate an essay you are presently writing for English composition class. Criticize the essay, focusing on sentence structure. Are the sentences adequately varied in structure? Are sentence elements appropriately subordinated? Are sentences economical or do they include unnecessary words? Cite specific examples to support your criticisms and indicate specific revisions the student should make to improve sentence structure.

Exercise 8. Look through the essays you have written up to now and choose one that suffers from weak sentence structure (for example, primer English, lack of subordination, wordiness). Revise sentence structure in the essay, concentrating on appropriate variety, subordination, and economy.

Chapter 15

Transitions

Sentences and paragraphs are the large units of the essay. Transitions are what connect these units one to the other. They move the reader from one thought to another thought by indicating how two thoughts are related. Thus, transitions make an essay flow by helping the reader follow the writer's line of thinking.

Transitional devices may indicate either continuity or change. Writers can either continue a thought from one sentence or paragraph to the next, or change from one pattern of thought to another.

Indicating Continuity

There are several transitional devices that indicate continuity of thought to the reader.

Repetition and Implied Repetition

Writers can repeat a word or phrase used in the previous sentence or paragraph.

The only people affected by the course curriculum *are students.* But *students are the only people* who aren't given a choice in the matter.

Or they can prompt the reader to supply a word or phrase used in the previous sentence or paragraph:

A few students asked that grammar be included. A few [students] wanted only writing assignments. One [student] even hoped the curriculum would consist of conversation practice.

Personal Pronouns

Writers may substitute a personal pronoun for a noun or proper noun used in the previous sentence or paragraph.

One student said *he* didn't mind if all the class did was grammar. But then *he* admitted *he* was transferring to a different school.

Demonstrative Pronouns and Adjectives

Writers may substitute *this, that, these,* or *those,* either alone or in conjunction with a noun, for material used in a previous sentence or paragraph.

A few students decided they themselves should draw up the curriculum. *These students* soon learned *this* was not a possibility, however.

Indicating Change

Expressions of continuity are fairly simple to understand. The transitional expressions that indicate change, however, are more complex because the relationships they express are more complex. When a writer changes from one thought or pattern of thought to another, these expressions show just how the new thought is related to the previous one. For example, take the following pair of thoughts:

The sun is shining. It is cold.

We can, of course, write these thoughts just as they appear above, with no relator between them. On the other hand, we can add a word or expression to relate them:

The sun is shining. *And* it is cold.

In these sentences, *and* ties the thoughts together more closely.

But is *and* the word that best expresses the relationship between these two ideas? *And* is a word of addition. It says to the reader that the writer is *adding* another thought to the previous one. And, of course, fundamentally, addition is the relationship between any two sentences; any second thought represents an addition to a previous one.

Another relator, however, might better express the precise relationship between these two thoughts, as here:

The sun is shining. B*ut* it is cold.

But is a word of contrast. It indicates that the second thought is contrary to what we might have expected given the previous thought. If the sun is shining, we might expect it to be warm (though this is certainly not always the case, especially in January). *Cold* contrasts with the *shining sun.*

In addition to *but*, other expressions of contrast could be used to indicate the precise relationship between these two thoughts. *However* and *nevertheless* are two common conjunctive adverbs that express contrast just as the coordinate conjunction *but* expresses contrast:

The sun is shining. However, it is cold.

The sun is shining. Nevertheless, it is cold.

And any of these expressions can be used between two paragraphs as well as between two sentences:

The sun was shining. It lit the sky and the light fell on the leaves of the trees and on the windows of the buildings. It was so sunny, it almost hurt my eyes to look up.

But it was cold. So I pulled my coat more tightly around myself as I walked along the street.

Here, *but* indicates the contrast of the idea expressed in the second paragraph to the idea expressed in the whole of the first paragraph.

Addition and contrast are two of the most common relationships writers need to indicate to their readers. There are many others. In the last paragraph of the extract above, for example, the writer has used the coordinate conjunction *so* to express *result.* The second idea is a result of the first idea. Again, the writer could have used *and* (and in some writing situations he or she might legitimately choose to use *and* between two such sentences), but the word *so* more precisely indicates the cause-and-effect relationship between the two sentences.

A chart may help you keep straight all the expressions that indicate different transitional relationships. In Table 15-1, each relationship is followed by the various words and combinations of words (coordinate conjunctions and conjunctive adverbs) that express the relationship. These words are followed by a model sentence pair illustrating the relationship. The blank between the sentences in the pair accommodates most of the relators listed. (Note, however, the exceptions listed in table footnote *a.*)

The coordinate conjunctions and conjunctive adverbs in the table can all relate two complete sentences to one another or two paragraphs to one another. They can also relate two parts of one sentence to one another. Thus, they are different from subordinate conjunctions and prepositions, which can relate ideas only within a single sentence and not between one sentence or paragraph and another. (Punctuation of clauses containing conjunctive adverbs is discussed on pages 264–65, 271–72.)

In addition to the relators listed in Table 15-1, the ordinal numbers (*first, second, third,* and so on) are sometimes used as transitional devices. There is nothing wrong

Table 15-1
Indicators of Change

| Relationship | Relators[a] | | Model Sentences |
	Coordinate Conjunctions	Conjunctive Adverbs	
Addition	and, nor[a]	also, in addition, additionally, moreover, further, furthermore, too, besides[a]	It is cold. _____ it is windy.
Contrast	but, yet	however, nonetheless, nevertheless, on the other hand[a]	It is sunny. _____ it is cold.
Result	so	thus, therefore, as a result, accordingly, hence	It was cold. _____ I wore my coat.
Reason	for		I wore my coat. _____ it was cold.
Similarity		likewise, similarly, in the same way	Today it is warm. _____, yesterday it was warm.
Example		for example, for instance, to illustrate	The weather this time of year is pretty bad. _____, yesterday it was cloudy, today it is raining, and tomorrow we are supposed to get snow.
Emphasis		indeed, in fact, as a matter of fact, truly, yes,[a] no[a]	The weather this time of year is pretty bad. _____, I haven't seen the sun once this month.
Emphasis by contradiction		instead, rather, on the contrary	The weather was not good. _____, it was bad.
Explanation (restatement)		that is, in other words, that is to say, to put it differently, more simply, in short	On the afternoon of our picnic, the atmospheric conditions were disastrous. _____, the weather was terrible.
Concession		of course, to be sure, granted, it is true, true	The bad weather on the day of our picnic was a real disappointment. _____, it is not necessarily a good idea to schedule a picnic in February.
Alternative	or	otherwise	The weather had better be good for our next picnic. _____ it will probably be our last picnic.
Summary		in conclusion, to summarize, all in all	_____, although good weather doesn't necessarily make a good picnic, it certainly helps.

Table 15-1 (*Continued*)

| | Relators[a] | | |
Relationship	Coordinate Conjunctions	Conjunctive Adverbs	Model Sentences
Time or place		then, now, after, afterward, later, subsequently, before, earlier, formerly, hitherto, at the same time, simultaneously, until now, so far, here, there, elsewhere,	(various)
Change of viewpoint or topic[b]		anyway, anyhow, in any event	So much for our picnic! _____, we had several other activities planned for the semester.

[a]Several of the relators will not work in particular pairs of sentences. Their use is limited as follows:

Nor is used only to indicate the addition of one negative thought to another negative thought. (E.g., It was not cold. *Nor* was it windy.) Note that in sentences or clauses beginning with *nor*, normal subject–verb order is reversed.

Besides is used only when giving an additional reason for some phenomenon. (E.g., I didn't want to go outside. It was cold. *Besides* it was windy.)

On the other hand is used to indicate a balancing of two ideas of equal or near equal importance. (E.g., She would like to go to the movies. *On the other hand*, she still has a lot of homework to do.)

Yes is used only with affirmative sentences. (E.g., The weather here is good. *Yes*, it is as good weather as I have ever experienced.)

No is used only with negative sentences. (E.g., The weather here isn't good. *No*, we haven't had a good day all year.)

[b]When used to indicate a change of topic, *anyway, anyhow,* and *in any event* make loose connections and are therefore to be avoided in unified, formal essays.

with such usage where it is appropriate—say, in listing the steps in a process or the events in a series, or in assigning rank order. However, students should take care not to enumerate falsely, as in the example that follows:

> The weather was terrible for our picnic. First, it was cold. Second, it was raining on and off. Third, the wind was so strong most of our food blew away before we could eat it.

The enumeration here makes sense neither in terms of chronology (in all probability it was cold, rainy, and windy all at the same time rather than one after the other) nor in terms of importance (coldness, for example, is not necessarily either better or worse than windiness for a picnic).

It is especially important for you to take care in your use of transitional expressions. Until you become fully comfortable with formal writing in English, you should check your use of these expressions carefully. Faulty use of transition can confuse or mislead the reader. It is better to omit transition than to use it incorrectly.

Furthermore, remember that not every sentence should be introduced by a transitional expression. Overuse of these expressions will tend to make an essay monotonous sounding and tedious to read. A real essay should by no means sound like the exercises that follow this chapter. There should be more variety in the sentence patterns.

Summary

Transition connects one thought or group of thoughts to another, either by showing continuity or change. Continuity may be indicated by the use of repetition or implied repetition, personal pronouns, demonstrative pronouns or adjectives. Change may be indicated by any of a number of relators or transitional expressions, each of which expresses a specific relationship between two thoughts or ideas.

Exercises

Exercise 1. Circle the conjunctive adverb that best expresses the relationship between clauses or sentences in the following essay.

A university student should come to class. *Thus/Moreover*, he should hand in assignments on time. *However/In fact*, some students at this university do not seem to know this. *For example/Instead*, one student came to class on the first day of the term, filled out a class card, and never returned. *However/Similarly*, another student, who has never attended a particular class, came only to the final exam.

It is difficult for teachers to plan a program of work around such an ever-changing group of students. *Otherwise/Consequently*, many teachers become frustrated. *However/Indeed*, some professors become so frustrated that they resort to such strange behavior as throwing darts at their record books, making funny faces at students, and taking jobs with insurance companies. Some teachers suffer "teacher burnout"; *that is/for example*, they feel growing despair and purposelessness about their profession.

Such teachers are usually advised to get away for a term or two; *otherwise/however*, it is feared they might go crazy. Of course, on a teacher's salary, suffering teachers generally don't go to Miami, Honolulu, or the Riviera for their restoration; *moreover/rather*, they spend their vacations taking courses which they neither attend regularly nor complete on time.

Exercise 2. Circle the conjunctive adverb that best expresses the relationship between clauses or sentences in the following essay:

I like my English teacher. *Moreover/In fact*, she is my favorite teacher this semester. *Nevertheless/Instead*, one thing I don't like about my English teacher is that she is a "task master"; *in other words/in addition*, she requires us to do a lot of work. *As a result/For example*, this week we have to read three chapters in our text, write a summary, and study for a quiz. *Nonetheless/Likewise*, last week we had to read two chapters, write an analysis, and do several exercises. *Of course/As a result,* I have to do several hours of English homework every night. *Granted/In fact,* I am learning a lot of English. But I wish I had time to do a few other things—go out once in a while, take a shower, eat.

Exercise 3. Fill in appropriate transitional expressions to link one thought to another. Add commas after conjunctive adverbs.

Variable April

In the Northeast, the weather in April is very variable; _____ it may change greatly from day to day and from week to week. _____ April's weather is probably the most changeable weather of the whole year. _____ the first week of this April began with a heat wave and ended with a snow storm. _____ the second week was warm through Friday and then freezing on the weekend.

_____ dressing for a day in April is not easy. _____ it is quite difficult to choose one's clothes for an April day. _____ one can manage. One can dress in layers, with light clothes underneath and heavier ones on top. ___ one can listen to the weather report before dressing for the day. _____ it would be a lot easier if April would simply make up her mind.

Exercise 4. Supply appropriate transitional expressions. Add commas after conjunctive adverbs.

At present, foreigners make up an important part of American university student bodies. _____ foreign students are in the majority at a number of smaller institutions of higher education. At one campus, _____, the number of one country's students alone outnumbers American and other non-American students combined. _____ foreign student performance is an important determination of American collegiate quality.

Up to now, universities have been free to manage their own foreign student populations. _____ university irresponsibility in this matter has prompted proposals that government take a hand in monitoring the enrollment and progress of foreign students in the United States. _____ some propose that the government itself establish the standards that must be met by all students, foreign as well as American, in order for a university to maintain its accreditation. _____ standards for attendance, completion of course requirements, and general comportment might someday no longer be established by university administrations. _____ government would set such standards. Numerous authorities support such a plan.

Many, _____, argue against government interference. The detractors argue that university autonomy is a cornerstone of academic freedom. ___ they feel that the university must be free to exercise its own judgment in administrative matters if it is to remain free in academic matters. _____ they maintain that many American universities need substantial foreign student enrollments. The decline of the birth rate from the early 1960s on has seriously depressed American student enrollments to the point that some institutions must be assured of continuing foreign student enrollments. ___ some institutions might be forced to shut down altogether.

Chapter 16

Words

At last we come to the smallest meaningful units of the essay: words. Words are the basic building blocks of composition, and choosing words well is fundamental to good writing. A writer's meaning depends ultimately upon precisely which words he or she chooses to use.

This is unfortunate for the writer of English as a second language. Whereas grammar, sentence structure, and paragraph structure can, to some extent, be learned in large lumps from a textbook, it takes years of listening and especially of reading to build up a vocabulary that will provide just the word needed at a given moment.

Take, for example, the word *write*. Thinking in your own language for a moment, translate *write* and list all the words in your native vocabulary that mean roughly the same thing. Probably, you can come up with several words, each with a slightly different meaning, each appropriate in a different situation. The same is true of English, which, as a result of its varied historical development, is especially rich in *synonyms*—words that have the same meaning—and words that are similar in meaning to one another. The list of English words that could be substituted for *write*, for example, includes the following:

author	scribble
compose	scrawl
copy	transcribe
pen	set down
print	take down

But, probably as in your own language, we could not substitute any of these words in every situation. For, although these words might be called *synonyms*, no one of them is exactly equivalent to another. Each has its own particular meaning and feel. Each one would be appropriate in certain situations and not in others. For example, note the difference between the following sentences, each using a synonym of *write*:

The student *composed* an essay for his English class.

The student *scribbled* an essay for his English class.

If we are acquainted with the italicized words in these sentences, we have higher expectations of the *composed* essay than of the *scribbled* one. Or compare

He *took down* her number on a notebook page.

with

He *scrawled* her number on a notebook page.

Familiarity with the terms used here will give the reader a very different impression of the scrawler from that of his more careful parallel. As we can see, the precise meaning and feel of a sentence depends on just which synonyms one chooses.

Probably the greatest problem for the student writing in a foreign language is his limited vocabulary. Perhaps the student has never heard or seen the words *compose* or *scribble* or the words *author* or *pen* used as verbs. Perhaps he has heard or seen them, but not often enough to remember them when they might prove useful. A limited vocabulary limits word choice options: the student writer with a limited vocabulary is stuck with *write* where *pen* or *print* or *scribble* might be more appropriate.

Building Vocabulary

What can the foreign student do to widen his word choice possibilities? Listening to English speakers—in class, on television, in conversation with schoolmates—is, obviously, a big help, but it is not the whole answer. For one thing, it is difficult to focus on and remember new words heard in passing. For another, much of what the student hears may be colloquial—informal—and therefore not suited to the tone required in college essays. Rather, it is reading, wide and careful, that the student must count on to provide the ample vocabulary necessary for precise writing. The student must spend time reading books, magazines, and newspapers in order to develop a vocabulary that will raise the level of his essays to that of the native writer. This takes time and effort. But there is no way around it. To write well, the foreign student must read.

How the student reads is also important. The student cannot adequately develop his vocabulary by rushing past all new words as he meets them. To build an ample writing vocabulary, he needs to understand new words precisely, and to be able to use them. For reading comprehension, understanding a word by its context—by the words surrounding it—is a handy timesaver. For vocabulary building, however, the dictionary is a necessity.

For writing college essays, the foreign student needs more than the handy foreign language/English dictionary he was probably armed with when he arrived in this country. The foreign student must become familiar with standard English dictionaries as well. While his foreign language/English dictionary can give him a translation for a word in a hurry, standard English dictionaries will provide additional important information about a new word: precise meaning and alternative meanings, level of diction, connotations, examples of usage, etymology (word origin)—all of which are important for precise word choice.

Probably, the student will be required to own a standard college dictionary for his composition class. He should keep a list of the words he looks up, noting for each its translation, definition, and examples of usage (the sentence in which he first saw the word or a sentence of his own).

Familiarity with the parts of a dictionary entry and with certain standard symbols will make looking up new words less painful. Take this entry for one of the definitions of the verb *pen*:

> **pen** \\'pen\vt penned; penned; penning; pens [ME *pennen*, fr. *penne* pen]: WRITE: **a:** to record in writing in proper form ⟨a minute was *penned* that the corporation might pay . . . the cost—Cromption & Royton Chronicle⟩ **b:** to compose and commit to paper ⟨~a letter⟩ ⟨the best novel he ever *penned*⟩ **c:** to write with a pen ⟨Salesman A ~s angular letters—H. O. Teltscher⟩

The student learns from this entry that
- *pen* is spelled p-e-n;
- *pen* is a one-syllable word and cannot, therefore, be divided;
- *pen* can be used as a verb (as well as a noun meaning "a writing instrument");
- *pen* is a transitive verb (it requires an object);
- *pen* has regular forms for past tense, past and present participles, and third person singular;
- *pen* derives from the Middle English word *penne*, meaning "pen";
- *pen* in the meanings listed belongs to the middle level of diction (otherwise, the meanings would be preceded by a label such as *colloq.* or *slang*)
- more information can be found under the entry for the synonym *write*.

Most important, the student learns that the meaning of *pen* is "to record in writing in proper form" and sees examples of *pen* in actual use. The combination of definitions and examples of usage indicates not only the denotation—the direct meaning—of the word, but also its connotations—the associations suggested by it. From the definition and examples of usage here, we learn that *pen* is associated with "proper form," that it might be used to refer to the minutes of a corporation, the composing of a letter, or the writing of a good novel.

Compare the entry for *scribble*:

scribble \'skribəl\vb scribbled; scribbled; scribbling . . . \scribbles [ME *scriblen*, fr. ML *scribillare*, fr. L *scribere* to write . . .] vt: **1:** to write hastily or carelessly without regard to legibility, correctness, or considered thought, ⟨had to ~ the very first ideas that tinkled in his head—Earle Birney⟩ ⟨just enough time to ~ their own name—H. A. Smith⟩ . . .

Here, definition and examples of usage indicate very different connotations: haste, carelessness, sloppiness, impulsiveness. The student who comes across *pen* or *scribble* in his reading and wants to add these words to his writing vocabulary must learn the connotations the words carry as well as their denotations. While context might give the student clues to connotations; the dictionary offers fuller and more precise information and a way of checking up on guesses.

Level of Diction

One of the difficult lessons for the foreign student is that the language she hears around her may not be appropriate for her essays. As she grapples with a new language, the student may find it hard or impossible to distinguish between words that are appropriate for college compositions and those that are for conversation only. When even professors talk about *guys* and *kids* or describe things they approve of as *fabulous* or *incredible*, it may be unclear to the student why her English instructor keeps circling these words in her essays as inappropriate.

It is important to remember that even educated speakers use colloquial language in conversation, but that such use does not make a colloquial term suitable for college writing. In college essays, the student writer should strive to achieve a *middle level of diction*, in between the colloquial English of street conversation and the highly formal English of official documents. This middle level of English, sometimes called *edited* English, is the language used in serious journals and high quality nonfiction, including the textbooks and other reading material normally assigned in most college courses. Such sources talk about *men* or *people*, not *guys*, about *students* or *children*, not *kids*.

Understanding Diction Labels

Again, the dictionary sets the standard by which students can determine whether or not a word belongs to the middle level of English. If a word is included in the dictionary, but labeled as *slang* (as *kid* is slang for *child*) or *colloquial* or *informal* (as *guy* is for *man*), that word generally will not be appropriate in a college essay. Labels such as *archaic* or *obs* (obsolete), meaning that a word is no longer in use, or *dial* (dialectal) or *regional*, meaning that a word is used only in a particular area or kind of speech, also indicate that a word is generally not suitable for college writing. If a word or a specific meaning does not appear in a standard unabridged dictionary at all, chances are, again, that the word is inappropriate. The absence of the word from the dictionary indicates that the word has not become an accepted part of standard English—at least not yet. The student should generally avoid such *neologisms* or newly coined words. For example, although people all around her may be saying that the war between Iraq and Iran has *impacted* oil prices, the student should avoid this newly coined verb and choose a standard form, either *has had an impact on* or *has affected* or *influenced*.

Avoiding Jargon

Also to be avoided—or at least used judiciously—in college essays is *jargon*, the specialized or technical language of various fields, such as sociology, psychology, medicine, and so forth. In a research paper on child abuse, one student, a capable writer, slipped into jargon:

> The family structure model focuses on interrelationships within the familial nucleus that sometimes evolve into an abuse syndrome.

This sentence sounds pretty fancy, but it is full of unnecessarily technical terms: *structure, model, interrelationships, familial nucleus, abuse syndrome*. Of course, in a paper for a psychology course, some of this language might be acceptable and even inescapable. But much of the writer's thought can be stated more simply:

> One way of looking at child abuse focuses on family relationships that may lead to it.

Generally, student writers should avoid writing psychologese—or sociologese or computerese or medicalese or bureaucratese—and instead write good plain English. Calling wounded and dead soldiers by the euphemism *inoperative battle personnel* or a lie by the euphemism *disinformation* is a trick of politicians to avoid speaking directly about unpopular or repugnant policies. Although it sounds fancy, such language is not worthy of imitation. (See pages 179–80 for a discussion of the term "euphemism.")

Avoiding Fancy Language

Indeed, the student should generally avoid all kinds of fancy language. Just as a child should not be a *kid* in a college essay, so he or she should generally not be a *juvenile*; a *man* should not be a *guy*, but there is no reason in ordinary circumstances to make him an *individual, human being*, or *mortal* (although any of these terms might be appropriate in a particular situation). The middle level of diction is just that—right between the colloquial and the formal, between casual and fancy terminology.

Occasional Uses

Of course, a writer occasionally may want to use a colloquial or even a slang word in a composition. Perhaps she wishes to strike an informal tone, become intimate with the reader—or shock him. Perhaps, if she is a student, she wants to talk to her classmates in terms she knows they will understand. If a writer knows what she is doing, an occasional nonstandard term may prove useful. Similarly, a formal word may sometimes be needed to express a writer's meaning precisely. Technical subject matter, for example, often requires technical language. In general, however, the middle level is the level of choice; it will appeal to the greatest number of educated readers without confusing or offending anyone.

A student begins an essay about her hobby as follows:

> Sport is my bag. It really turns me on.

The result is silly. The inappropriate use of the slang terms *bag* and *turn on*—especially juxtaposed with the formal-sounding singular form *sport*—makes the essay awkward and comical where the student wants it to sound natural and fluent. The foreign student's ear may not be sensitive enough to such awkwardness. He may not be able to rely on how his writing sounds to tell him if his tone is consistently modulated. Of course, over time, he can develop his ear by reading the right kind of writing. Until he does, however, the dictionary must be his guide.

Concreteness and Specificity

Students in my class were assigned to write an essay describing a scene from either their hometown or their new surroundings. Two students described weekend scenes, one set in Central Park, the other in a square in the student's Turkish hometown. Let us compare their essays:

Central Park

I am usually in New York every two weeks for a visit to my uncle there. Once it was Sunday and my uncle asked me if I would be interested in a trip to Central Park, as he said it might be interesting to me. So we went to Central Park. When we got there, there were many people of different colors and languages. But they had one thing in common; they were enjoying themselves and forgetting about their own problems.

There was a great deal of activity. Some were participating in sports, some were having conversations, some were just resting. And the interesting thing about it was that nobody was bothering anybody because they were having too much fun to think about bothering.

At night we had to go back home because my uncle said that after dark it was dangerous to walk in the park. So we left. But I had a wonderful day in Central Park.

A Sunday Afternoon on Konuralp Street

After a long, silent morning, children begin playing hopscotch, marbles, or cowboy games. After a while, older boys start gathering in front of Settat the Tailor's and Sam's Grocery Shop, which sit next to each other, and on the other sides of the square, where Dalyan and Konuralp Streets intersect, in front of another grocery shop, which changes owners almost every year. In front of Sam's Grocery, boys eat sunflower seeds, drink sodas, play backgammon, and chat excitedly, mostly about soccer: the teams they'll form for the next match, the plays they'll make better, the goals they'll score.

As the time passes and everyone gathers, there comes the biggest time of all: time to play soccer. Time for excitement, for burning off energy and showing off skills; time to taste playing their favorite sport. The boys separate into teams; they find four big rocks to make two goals facing each other on the road. From then on, only passersby and cars can interrupt their match.

Sometimes the owners of the cars parked on the street complain, shout, or threaten the players not to hit their cars with the ball. More often, however, those who live on the street enjoy watching from windows or front doors, or even joining the game. Some volunteer to referee or to reward the winning team with cold drinks all around.

They play and play and play until the sky darkens and the parents of the players begin calling their sons back home for dinner. As the match ends, so does the competition; curses shouted earlier are forgotten. The only thing that won't be forgotten are those vivid, exciting, joyful hours of playing soccer on Sunday afternoons on Konuralp Street.

Which scene do you see more clearly? Which seems more exciting, more alive? Which do you feel more a part of?

If you rely on the writer's description alone, it will certainly be the scene of Sunday afternoon soccer games on Konuralp Street. The writer's description is so vivid, so full of life, the reader can almost see it, almost feel himself there. From the boys eating sunflower seeds and chatting excitedly to the car owners threatening the boys not to hit their cars with the soccer ball, the essay is full of vivid detail that makes the scene seem real.

Not so with the essay describing Central Park. If you have been there yourself, you may, of course, have your own mental pictures of the scene: you may be able to *make* vivid pictures out of such general ideas as people's being of different colors or having different languages, of their "enjoying themselves" and "participating in sports." But the writer has not drawn a clear picture. And the reader who does not know Central Park before reading the essay will hardly know it any better after reading it.

What qualities make the Konuralp Street essay more vivid than the essay about Central Park? A quick glance reveals that both writers organize paragraphs adequately, write complete sentences, and use language correctly and without awkwardness. However, a closer look reveals a crucial difference: the language of "A Sunday Afternoon on Konuralp Street" is generally concrete and specific (sunflower seeds, sodas, backgammon, soccer), whereas the language of "Central Park" tends to be abstract and general (colors, languages, activity, sports).

Let us take a closer look at these qualities and at how they affect the reader.

Concrete Versus Abstract Language

Concrete is the stuff sidewalks are made of. It is solid and can be experienced physically. You can see it with your eyes and feel it with your feet and with your hands. Concrete language is the same: solid, physical. If you can perceive an image with your senses—if you can see, hear, feel, smell, or taste it—it is concrete.

Abstract language is the opposite; it cannot be perceived by the senses. Abstractions are the *ideas* behind physical things, concepts without any practical existence. *Sunflower seeds* and *sodas* are concrete; *edibles* are abstract. *Backgammon* and *soccer* are concrete; *activities* is an abstraction.

Concrete terms such as *sunflower seeds* and *sodas* generally make a stronger and more lasting impression on readers than do abstractions such as *edibles* and *activities*. This is because people tend to appreciate more fully the images they perceive with their senses. If we have eaten sunflower seeds before, we can remember the way they looked, smelled, and tasted, the way they felt in our mouths. Even if we have not eaten them, we have probably eaten something enough like them to imagine what they are like. If we have played backgammon or watched it being played, we can remember the shape and design of the board, the appearance of players seated on each side of it, rolling the dice, and pushing the pieces across. Generally, our appreciation of such sensually perceived or concrete images will be stronger than our appreciation of abstract ideas such as *edibles* or *activities*, which we cannot clearly see or taste or smell or hear or feel.

The language of children is powerful precisely because it is concrete. When a child says another child bit his arm, took his ball, or hit him with a truck, it makes more of an impression than when an adult calls the other child *aggressive*. As we mature in our use of language, our speech and writing frequently become peppered with abstractions. We take them as a sign of sophistication in our thinking, speaking, and writing. And they are useful, often indispensable, in communicating ideas quickly and efficiently, and in helping us to generalize and analyze, especially when shared sensory experience is lacking. However, when the balance tips too far in the direction of the abstract, meaning becomes vague and weak. When a writer says "There was a great deal of activity," his meaning is less vivid—less clear and strong—than it would have been if he had written: "People walked, jogged, and raced along." Note that concreteness does not necessarily add words to the sentence. The abstract "There was a great deal of activity" requires seven words; the concrete "People walked, jogged, and raced along" uses only six. By favoring concrete words over abstract ones, the writer can add power to his writing without adding weight.

Even—and perhaps especially—good student writers may overuse abstractions in writing college essays. Serious subjects may seem to lend themselves to technical-sounding abstract terminology. But the writer should resist the urge to write in *collegese*. To make his writing clearer and stronger, the student should identify abstractions in his writing and, unless he has a good reason for using them, try to replace them with concrete verbs, nouns, and modifiers.

Concrete Versus Abstract Verbs. The verb is often thought of as the most important part of speech in English. Indeed, it is the only part of speech that can form a sentence by itself:

Write!

Moreover, verbs are the most vibrant parts of sentences. They are the only words that act—-that go, talk, walk, run, race.

Yet, in college essays, students often avoid all such vibrant, active verbs and choose in their place verbs that do not act: *be* (and its forms), *seem, exist, appear*. Indeed, in the Central Park essay, more than half of the verbs consist of a form of *be*, alone or with a participle:

I *am* usually in New York. . . .
Once it *was* Sunday. . . .
. . . if I *would be* interested in a trip. . . .

In the entire essay, only 6 other verbs (*ask, say, go, get, have, leave*) are used in a total of only 9 instances, compared to 13 uses of the verb *be*.

Compare this to the use of verbs in "A Sunday Afternoon on Konuralp Street." In this essay *to be* appears only 3 times, all in the last paragraph. And there are 27 other verbs in the rest of the essay, including many that are vividly concrete: *eat, drink, play, chat, pass, come, separate, find, interrupt, complain, shout, threaten, darken*. Indeed, even inanimate objects *act* in this essay as shops "sit" next to each other, streets "intersect," and a grocery "changes" owners. The result is that, although both writers wish to show activity, only the Konuralp Street essay feels active.

The trick here is not just to look for colorful or fancy verbs. If the student had written

> I usually migrate to New York every two weeks for a sojourn with my uncle who resides there. Once Sunday descended upon us and my uncle inquired whether I would relish a trip to Central Park as he said it might stimulate me.

the reader would probably wonder what the writer was drinking when he wrote his essay. Rather than fanciness, the writer should aim for precision in verb choice and for the elimination of abstract words. In effect, the writer's task in choosing verbs is largely the same as in writing economical sentences: he must cut out the fat. To do this, the writer should do the following.

1. Look for concrete verbs that precisely express his meaning:

play ball rather than *participate in sports*

2. Limit his use of the verb *be* by avoiding
   a. the passive voice:

Central Park would interest me rather than *I would be interested in Central Park*

   b. participial phrases:

People participated rather than *People were participating*

   c. *there is/ there are* constructions:

People walked rather than *There was a great deal of walking*

3. Favor simple verbs over longer verb-plus-noun combinations:

complain rather than *make a complaint, converse* (or *talk* or *chat*) rather than *have a conversation*

The only time the student should not try to cut out words by substituting a verb for a verb plus a noun is when the verb is an invented, technical-sounding one made by adding *-ize* to an adjective (for example, *Finalize, personalize*). Although such verbs do save words, they are more abstract than *make final, make personal,* or *make concrete*. These and verbs made out of nouns such as *impact* and *interface* are popular now perhaps because they sound high tech. However, the simpler, standard forms are actually more concrete and, at least for the present, preferred.

Concrete Versus Abstract Nouns. By now we should have a clear idea of what is meant by concrete nouns: *sunflower seeds* rather than *edibles*, a *soccer game* rather than an *activity*. It remains to point out some of the more commonly used abstract nouns that students should watch for in their writing. Words to be aware of in college essays include:

aspect, basis, case, character, circumstance, element, facet, fact, factor, field, instance, nature, phenomenon, quality, relationship, and so on.

Of course, such words have their place in writing. But when nearly every sentence is stuffed with them, when a student finds himself writing

There are numerous facets of the factors that serve as the basis for this phenomenon.

it is time to get out the red pencil.

Students should watch out for combinations of nouns where a single noun would suffice:

I want a job in *business* rather than *the business field*.

There was another *hijacking* rather than *hijack situation*.

The delay was caused by a *storm* rather than *storm conditions*.

Jargon from many sources (television, technology, government, advertising) has accustomed our ears to the longer, deader forms—to *storm conditions* instead of *storms*, *health fields* instead of *health*, to *terrorism incidents*, *child abuse cases*, and *lifestyles* instead of *lives*. But the shorter forms are stronger: Our picture of a *storm* is clearer than our picture of *storm conditions*; our imagination of *child abuse* is more intense than our imagination of a *child abuse case*; *She leads a simple life* makes more of an impression (and more sense) than does *She leads a simple lifestyle*. The added terms make the ideas fuzzier, more abstract, less real.

Similarly, nouns added to adjectives are often unnecessary. *Round shape* is no rounder than *round* by itself. And the same can be said for other such constructions: lazy manner, shy nature, red color, smooth texture, short height.

Students should get used to spotting abstract nouns in their writing and should eliminate those that serve no purpose.

Concrete Versus Abstract Modifiers. Spoken English is generally full of *plaudits*: a book is "great," a TV program "excellent," a movie "terrific," a rock video "awesome." It is also full of *slurs*: a course is "awful," a professor "terrible," a roommate "bad news." The problem with such modifiers is that they are vague. They tell a listener how we feel about something or someone—that we either like or dislike him or it—but they do not explain why. Some modifiers are not even clearly positive or negative. If someone says, for example, that his trip to California was "incredible" or "unbelievable," it is unclear even whether he means very good or very bad.

Vague modifiers sometimes suffice in conversation: a student may decide not to take a course a friend describes as "gruesome" or not to eat at a diner his roommate says is "gross." But even in conversation many of us have at some time wished to gag a critic for whom every recording is "great," every restaurant "lousy," or every movie "really excellent."

In writing, we must be doubly careful to avoid vague modifiers. What is a reader to make of a paragraph like the following?

I will never forget the great time I had on my last vacation. I went on a wonderful trip to Disney World. Disney World is really terrific, perhaps the greatest place for a vacation in the entire United States. The rides, shows, restaurants, and films are all marvelous. And the weather is unreal.

The first step in revising such an essay is getting rid of the vague modifiers. Often, no modifier is preferable to a vague one. Sometimes, a meaningful substitute can be found. When the writer says Disney World is "really terrific," he should decide what he means and substitute appropriately. Is it exciting? restful? fun? designed for leisure or for children? Does it offer a pastime perfect for every visitor? "Terrific"—even "really terrific"—does not tell us. (For a discussion of avoiding vague modifiers in description, see pages 33–34).

In addition to vague modifiers, the writer should also avoid unnecessary modifiers. Redundant modifiers, such as those in the phrases *green grass*, *blue sky*, or *happy smile*, are unnecessary; the reader assumes them without being told. If the grass is brown, the sky yellow, or the smile forced or phony, the modifier is worth mentioning. But the *green* in *green grass* adds nothing and should be omitted.

Other modifiers frequently linked with certain nouns become weak from overuse. Rarely do readers consider the modifier *vital* in the overused phrase *vital role*, *true* in the phrase *true professional*, or *utmost* in *utmost importance*. Confronting such a phrase in his writing, the student should generally look for another modifier or let the noun stand by itself.

Special kinds of modifiers called intensifiers (for example, *really*, *very*, *quite*) and qualifiers (*rather*, *pretty*, *fairly*) should not be overused. There is virtually never a need to call something *really amazing*; to call something *amazing*—capable of affecting one with surprise or wonder—says as much as can be said. The writer for whom everything is *very* something (It's a *very* boring movie; He is *very* dishonest; That is *very* ugly) becomes tiresome *very* fast.

Finally, there are our own habits to consider. If you tend to call every experience *interesting* or every person *nice*, think about eliminating *interesting* or *nice* from your writing for a while. Deprived of the crutch you lean on whenever you need a modifier, you might just come up with something new, fresh, and precise.

Specific Versus General Language

Up to now, we have been talking about words as if they are either absolutely abstract or concrete. Actually, there are degrees of concreteness and abstraction. *Soda* is concrete; so is *soft drink*. But *soft drink* is a little less specific than *soda*. And we could proceed into greater generality still with the terms *beverage*, *liquid*, *substance*, and *thing*. When a writer chooses a word, he has to decide just how specific he want it to be.

The writer of "A Sunday Afternoon on Konuralp Street," for example, mentions *Sam's Grocery Shop* as the place in front of which boys gather to eat, drink, play, and chat. Had he been less specific, calling it "a grocery shop" or "a shop" or even "a building" or "a place," he would have lost that familiar, neighborhood, folksy feeling that works so well in his essay. Other specific details in the essay have a similar effect: *Settat the Tailor's*, *Dalyan and Konuralp Streets*, *sunflower seeds*, *sodas*, *backgammon*, *soccer*.

Of course, the specific names of the shops and streets and the specification of what the boys eat, drink, play, and discuss are not entirely necessary. But they make the scene jump to life for the reader. The student might have written more generally:

> After a while, people start gathering in front of two buildings, and, on the other side of the square, where the streets intersect, in front of a third building. In front of one of these buildings boys eat snacks, drink beverages, play games, and talk.

This description is equally accurate. But it is less vivid than the more specific original.

On the other hand, it is possible to be *too* specific. If the writer had substituted actual brand names for the word *sodas*—for example,

> boys eat sunflower seeds, drink Pepsis, Cokes, Tabs, and Seven-Ups

—the effect would be a little silly, making the reader focus too closely on the brands and detracting from the writer's main idea of leisure enjoyment. Associations the writer never intended might be called up for the reader: competition between soft drink manufacturers, for example, or caffeinated versus noncaffeine soft drinks. The trick, then, is to be as specific as you can be without being so specific that you divert attention from the theme.

Connotation

We have already hinted at how *connotation* helps determine word choice. *Connotations* are the associations a word carries beyond its explicit meaning (its *denotation*). In the previous section, for example, we said that the writer of the Konuralp Street essay would not want to substitute particular brand names for the more general term *sodas*. Connotations of the word *sodas* include refreshment, fun, leisure, and youth, all appropriate to the theme of "A Sunday Afternoon on Konuralp Street." Connotations of the brand names Coke, Pepsi, and Seven-Up, on the other hand, include as well some associations that are inappropriate, such as competition between manufacturers and, perhaps, the debate over caffeine. The writer must be sure that the connotations of the words he or she uses are not at odds with the intended meaning.

Perhaps the clearest way to see how connotations affect meaning is to look at two versions of the same brief description. In each version, different words are used to describe the same characteristics. Note how the substitution of one word for another in the descriptions below changes our perception of the person described:

Version 1

Ed is slender and tall. He dresses casually in a unique style. His hair has a natural look.

Version 2

Ed is skinny and overgrown. He dresses carelessly in an odd manner. His hair is uncombed.

Certainly, Ed would prefer the description in the first version to that of the second. This is because *slender, tall, casually, unique, style,* and *natural* are all words with positive connotations, whereas *skinny, overgrown, carelessly, odd,* and *uncombed* all have negative connotations. Meaning, thus, varies according to the connotations words carry.

Connotations can be positive, negative, or neutral. We might categorize, for example, the many words meaning *heavy* or *overweight* as follows:

Neutral	Positive	Negative
heavy, heavy-set,	plump, robust,	fat, overweight,
large, stocky,	fully packed, round,	oversized, hulking,
stout	buxom, sturdily built,	unwieldy
	portly, well-fed, ample	

If we want to make a heavy person seem attractive to the reader, we can choose a word with positive connotations, such as *robust* (associated with health), *round* (with its associations with perfection), or *sturdily built* (associated with both strength and soundness of structure). If we want to make the person seem unattractive, we can choose instead to call the person *overweight, oversized,* or *over-stuffed* (all connoting excess), *unwieldy* (with its connotations of discomfort), or fat.

We should note that the connotations of words may vary with time. With today's emphasis on slenderness, even words like *stout, buxom,* and *portly* may have negative connotations. Also, particular connotations may be positive in certain contexts and negative in others. The word *plump,* for example, has positive connotations when associated with a baby, a piece of fruit, or, perhaps, a young child. But associated with, say, a grown man, it would almost always be negative.

Of course, the foreign student is at a disadvantage here because he may not know many synonyms for *heavy.* He might, of course, look for synonyms in a *thesaurus*—a dictionary of synonyms. But this can be dangerous because the student may be unaware of the connotations of the words he finds there. For example, the foreign student might be unaware that the word *buxom* is appropriate only to women or that *plump* has connotations of youthfulness and ripeness that would not flatter a mature man. The dictionary may help in checking up on such points, but not always.

What the foreign student can do, however, is be aware that connotations affect meaning and be sensitive to the connotations of the words he chooses. If he is describing a dog that growls at him every day from behind a fence, sensitivity to connotation will tell him not to call it a *pup* in a description. Probably, he will call it a *dog,* but as his vocabulary widens, he may become adept enough to substitute a synonym such as *mutt* or *mongrel.* If he wants to describe a girlfriend of shorter than average size, sensitivity to connotations will likely tell him to call her *petite* (French words often have positive connotations in English) rather than *shrimpy.*

The consequences of insensitivity to connotations can be devastating to an essay. One student, describing a favorite restaurant, explained how each table was provided with a dish of peanuts from which diners could munch, casually throwing the nutshells on the floor. She wrote: "This gives a warm, friendly, atmosphere, reminiscent of a stable." We know what she intended, but the unfortunate choice of the word *stable* brings up connotations not at all compatible with dining out. Maybe an *old-time country store* would have been a better choice.

One special case of choosing words according to connotation is called *euphemism.* As briefly mentioned earlier, *euphemism* is the substitution of a weaker or less negative word for a word the writer fears may be offensive. Calling an overweight man *stout* or *portly* is euphemistic. So is describing a pestering child as *inquisitive* or a stubborn person as *strong-willed.* Often, people describe death in euphemistic terms, saying someone *passed away* or *passed on* rather than *died.* In using the vaguer term, the speaker hopes to spare the listener's feelings—or his own.

The problem with euphemism in writing is that it weakens meaning by making it vague. Indeed, sometimes a euphemism is so vague that we are unsure what the writer actually means: a student writing that her grandmother was "no longer with us," had me wondering whether the old woman had died or simply moved away.

Euphemism can also be a way of lying. Politicians and government officials use— and abuse—euphemism to make proposals that might be unpopular if stated in direct terms, couching controversial policies in what is often called *bureaucratese* (see page 171). Calling an *invasion* an *incursion* is a euphemism that blurs the actual event. Calling a *tax* a *revenue enhancer* does not make it any less costly to the taxpayer.

Student writers should be wary of euphemism. They should try to convey their meaning honestly and directly without fuzzing it up with blurry vocabulary. On the other hand, students should not confuse exaggeration with honesty. If a writer calls someone a thief or a murderer, he should be able to present evidence of criminal action. It is also important to remember that some terms commonly used to describe certain subjects are controversial. What for one person is a *freedom fighter* may for another be a *counterrevolutionary* and for still another a *terrorist*. The student writing about a controversial subject should be especially sensitive to connotations and wary about choosing terms that he or she cannot back up with solid supporting evidence.

With connotation, as with level of diction and specificity, the important thing to remember is that there are no perfect synonyms: each word carries its own set of associations that alters meaning and makes it appropriate in some contexts, inappropriate in others. As much as possible, the student writer must be aware of these associations and choose his or her words accordingly.

Figurative Language

"Figurative language is the icing on the cake." This sentence is an example of the aspect of word choice we will discuss in this section: figurative language. When we represent something in a way that is not literal—not actual—we are using *figurative language*. The reader knows that figurative language is not *icing* and that an essay is not a *cake*; what the sentence means is that figurative language is something additional, something optional, something that is not necessary but that makes a good essay better, just as icing makes a good cake better.

Metaphors and Similes

There are two basic figures: metaphors and similes. The figure "icing on the cake" is used above as a *metaphor*, equating *figurative language* and *cake* in order to make an *implicit* comparison between them. Similes make comparisons *explicit* by using the words *like* or *as*. We could turn the opening metaphor into a simile, as here: "Figurative language is *like* the icing on a cake." In general, metaphors make a stronger impression than do similes; saying something *is* something else makes a stronger comparison than saying something is *like* something else. But similes can be powerful as well.

Clichés. Although *icing on the cake* is a figure, it is not an especially good one. This is because *icing on the cake* is a *cliché*—an expression that has been used so often, it is worn out. When a figure becomes a cliché, the reader does not focus on it as he would on a new figure he has never seen or heard, and he may not even consider the comparison the writer is trying to make. When someone first wrote or said that something was the "icing on the cake," the impression made by the figure no doubt was strong, and the reader or listener was forced to consider the concrete comparison being made. But by the hundredth time a person comes across this expression, it is so familiar that he or she does not need to think about the figure in concrete terms, to think about how *icing* relates to *cake*. The reader or listener grasps the abstract meaning immediately and deals with the figure in abstract terms only. Clichéd metaphors are sometimes called *dead metaphors* because they call up no concrete associations. Indeed, the writer might as well have said: "Figurative language is something optional that makes a good essay better."

To take another example, if a native speaker of English reads that someone "eats like a pig," the expression is such a cliché, she does not see the funny image the comparison is intended to call up. She understands the abstract concept: that the subject eats sloppily and eats a lot. But the strength of the comparison—the mental picture of a pig eating—is lost. The same is true for all clichés: similes such as "quick as a bunny" or "neat as a pin" and metaphors such as being "turned on" or "gumming things up" are so worn out, they have lost their impact.

This is a problem for the foreign student. Often, the foreign student spends considerable time collecting clichés, in part because they are amusing in themselves, in part because they make his English sound more "native." An expression that is *as old as the hills* to a native speaker may sound fresh and appealing to a nonnative hearing it for the first time. Even similes and metaphors that are close translations of clichés from the foreign student's own language may sound new in English: the novelty of the language makes the familiar comparison novel.

Moreover, the foreign student does not always know which of his native expressions are clichés in English. When he translates a simile or metaphor, he may not know whether the result is a worn-out figure or a fresh one. Although some translations result in striking new comparisons, often a cliché in one language translates into another as a cliché.

There is even some danger that a simile or metaphor invented by the foreign writer may turn out to be a cliché. However, generally this is not the case. If we allow our own imaginations full play, letting them run through all the comparisons that might possibly clarify an idea, we are individual enough that more often we will hit on something new than on something used before.

Guidelines for Choosing Figures

Freshness. Of course, thinking of new comparisons requires effort. But the effort is worthwhile because of the impact a new figure can carry. A new figure arrests the reader's mind; it makes the reader consider the comparison the writer is trying to make. If we say "eats like a pig," "quick as a bunny," or "neat as a pin," we make little more impression than if we had said "eats a lot," "very quick," or "very neat." But if we say someone eats like a *vacuum cleaner* or like a *steam shovel* or that someone is quick as a *computer* or neat as an *attaché case*, we surprise the reader; we catch his attention, and force him to consider the comparison concretely. To have such impact, a figure must be fresh.

Appropriateness. Freshness alone is not enough, however. The associations called up by the figure must suit the object it is helping to describe. We would not want to describe a tidy homemaker as "neat as a attaché case"; perhaps neat as a "starched apron" or as a "folded napkin" would suit her. We would not describe a running deer as "quick as a computer," though the comparison would work well in reference to a mathematician who solves problems rapidly or a brainy student who does homework assignments with great speed. With figurative language, as with language in general, the writer must be sure that the associations of each word he or she chooses are appropriate to the context in which it is used.

Generalness. In addition to freshness and appropriateness, figures must be generally understood. If I write that someone is "as neat as my mother," almost no one will appreciate the comparison. The figures a writer uses must be accessible to his or her readers.

Logical Combinations. Another thing to be wary of in using figurative language is what is called the *mixed metaphor*. Most often, mixed metaphors result from the writer's accidentally combining two or more dead metaphors without considering their individual associations, as in:

The angry child *exploded* and *stormed* out the door.

If the reader should focus on the comparisons made in such a mixed metaphor, the result can be devastatingly silly. For example, how does one "keep the lid on runaway inflation" as some politicians have promised to do?

Overusing Figures

A long list of varied similes can have a similarly comical effect. A student dressing a description of his girlfriend in high romantic style wrote in one paragraph that she had "a voice like music," walked "like a young deer in the forest," was "active as a bee," and cried tears "like rivers" when saddened; in short, he concluded, she was his "queen." By itself, any one of these clichés would probably be harmless. Listed one after another, they were—much to the student writer's disappointment—hilarious.

Indeed, even with fresh figures, overuse should be avoided. When we ask the reader to make too many comparisons in too short a space, we run the risk of confusing him. Instead of the aptness of one well-chosen comparison, he focuses on the writer's artfulness, his sleight-of-hand. He may stop being impressed by the magic of our comparisons and start trying to figure out how the trick is done. After a while, too much of a good thing may grow tiresome.

The Analogy

This warning sometimes applies to a special figure that bears mention here: the *analogy* or *extended metaphor*. In an *analogy*, several aspects of two dissimilar objects are compared for the purpose of illuminating the writer's ideas about one of the objects. Returning to the figure with which we opened this section, we could extend the comparison as follows:

> Figurative language is the icing on the cake of composition. Like icing, it is not essential, but though it does not alter the basic substance, it has the power to make it special. As with icing, however, figurative language requires careful handling: used sparingly, it makes a sweet impression; spread too thickly, on the other hand, it is not just sweetening, but sickening.

Like any figure, analogies can be overdone or awkward (indeed, the one above may be both!). Used judiciously, however, analogies may clarify a complex concept for the reader in a memorable way, as in an essay we looked at in an earlier chapter, in which a student writer compared his mother to her car—"a white Fiat: compact, tough, and efficient."

Cognates and False Cognates

From the airy heights of figurative language, we must come back to earth to discuss one final word choice problem particular to foreign students. This is the problem of *false cognates*. *Cognates* are words having a common origin and similar meaning: the German *mädchen* and the English *maiden* for example, or the French *mariage* and English *marriage*. Between certain languages and English, there are many cognates, especially among recently coined, technical terms. However, whether or not they have common roots, sometimes words in two languages look alike, but have different meanings. These are *false cognates*.

False cognates are a problem because they may fool foreign students into choosing an English word with a meaning very different from what they intended. As a new speaker of Spanish, for example, I tried to explain to acquaintances in Mexico how I felt when I could not say what I meant in my new language—*embarrassed* was the word I would have used in English. So I translated: I was *embarasada*. Only later did I find out that *embarasada* did not mean "embarrassed," as I had assumed, but "pregnant." I had been inadvertently (and quite falsely) telling people all over Mexico that I was going to have a baby!

The foreign student should become aware of words that are commonly mistaken for cognates of English words. Moreover, he should not translate words from his own language into English by sound or appearance alone, but should check that the meanings of similar words are the same. The use of a false cognate can be confusing or misleading and is at the least a nuisance to the reader. Some Spanish-speaking students, for example, misled by the meaning of the Spanish word *actualmente* ("now"), use *actually* in essays when they should use *at present* or *now*. Unlike the meaning of the Spanish word, the primary meaning of *actually* in English is *really* or *in reality*. The misuse of such a word may be confusing to readers—including professors—unfamiliar with the native language of the writer.

A related problem is the invention of English words by analogy. It is tempting, when nine words can be translated from one language to another by using the same principle—say, changing a *cion*-ending to a *tion*-ending—to translate a tenth word according to the same principle. However, the resulting word may not be an actual word in English. There is a *dirección* and an *introducción* in Spanish, a *direction* and an *introduction* in English. But although there is a *traducción* in Spanish, there is no English *traduction*. The word is made-up.

It is a convenience when the vocabulary of your native language overlaps with that of English. However, such convenience warrants special caution. As in all matters of word choice, the student writer should often resort to the dictionary.

Summary

Words are the smallest meaningful units of composition; they are the basic building blocks of the essay. They are also a special problem for the foreign student who cannot master the meanings and usages of all the words he might need for precise word choice merely by reading a textbook. To build his vocabulary, the foreign student should read widely, using a dictionary to check the meanings of words he does not know. He should also keep a vocabulary list and review new entries frequently.

Although many words in English have similar meanings, there are no perfect synonyms. Generally, the writer has several alternative words among which he must choose by weighing several considerations. As a rule, the writer should choose words that belong to the middle level of diction; generally, he should favor concrete and specific words over abstract and general ones. In addition, he should be sure that the connotations of the words he chooses are appropriate to his subject.

Figurative language uses comparisons to make concepts clearer. Although it is difficult to find figures that are fresh, appropriate, and generally understood, well-chosen figures can be a striking and memorable feature of writing.

Finally, the foreign student must beware of false cognates.

Exercises

For Consideration

Exercise 1. Choose one of the following words: *talk, walk, run.* Look it up in a thesaurus of English words. Choose from the thesaurus five synonyms for the word you have chosen. Try to choose examples that you believe express shades of meaning different from one another.

Using an unabridged dictionary to help you, note briefly the precise meaning of each of the five synonyms. Then use each synonym in a separate sentence appropriate to the associations the word carries.

Example: *eat*: to consume (food)
- feed: to eat; often derogatory in reference to people
- devour: to eat up with greediness, like a beast
- crunch: to chew noisily
- munch: to chew noisily, with enjoyment
- nibble: to eat in small bits

Three times a day, the students *feed* on plates full of indescribable glop at the cafeteria.

The hungry man *devoured* the meat without looking up.

When my roommate *crunches* on her pencil, I generally leave the room.

The children *munched* chocolate bars and giggled among themselves.

The fish *nibbled* at their food and then swam to the bottom of the bowl.

Exercise 2. Look up the words below in an unabridged dictionary. Then answer the questions following each word.

a. *foreigner*
  1) To what part of speech does the word belong?
  2) Does it have regular forms? What are they?
  3) What is the syllabication of the word (that is, What are the word's syllables)?
  4) Are any synonyms listed for the word?
  5) Do any of the meanings listed for the word belong to a level of diction other than the middle level?

b. *translate*
  1) To what part of speech does the word belong?
  2) What is the origin (historical derivation) of the word? (Give both the language from which the word came into English and its original meaning.)
  3) What is the primary meaning of the word now?
  4) Are there other meanings? Give at least one other.
  5) Does the entry indicate any cross-references under which the student might look for additional information?

c. awesome
  1) To what part of speech does the word belong?
  2) What is its pronunciation?
  3) What meanings are listed for the word?
  4) Does the entry indicate any cross-references under which the student might look for additional information?
  5) What examples of usage are provided for the word?

Exercise 3. Look through the preceding unit and find three words that were new to you when you first encountered them here. Write them as you might on a list of new vocabulary words. For each of the three words, give the following:

a. The part of speech to which the word belongs

b. The translation of the word in your own language

c. A dictionary definition of the word as it is used in this chapter

d. The sentence in which you first encountered the word

e. A sentence of your own, using the new word in a way that reveals its meaning.

Example:
coin v. [translation]: to invent (a word or phrase)

"Between certain languages and English there are many cognates—especially among recently coined, technical terms. . . ."

As a speaker of Spanish as a second language, I often *coin* words without intending to!

Exercise 4. In the passage below, some words are too formal and some too informal for a college essay. Read the passage, underlining those words that you suspect may not belong to the middle level of diction. (You can check the words you believe to be too informal in the dictionary to see whether your suspicions about them are confirmed; formal words, however, will not bear indicative labels.)

At our university there are loads of international students domiciled in the dormitories. Many of these kids have unbelievable problems regarding their diurnal existence. Fortunately, the international student advisor at our university, Mr. John Kendall, is a swell guy. He is hip to student needs and really digs how to rap with those for whom English is a secondary language. What a trip it is to have such a personage at our institution.

Exercise 5. Rewrite the passage in Exercise 4 substituting for the words you underlined appropriate words belonging to the middle level of diction.

Exercise 6. In the following passage, underline all abstract terms. Then rewrite the passage, substituting appropriate concrete terms for the abstractions.

I am occasionally in the center of my home city before business hours. The city is very different at that time. There is very little activity on the streets or sidewalks. Because of this, sounds and sights that might ordinarily go unnoticed are more evident. As I experience these unaccustomed sights and sounds, I have a very special feeling.

Exercise 7. Turn back to the two versions of the essay "The Traffic License" (pages 24–26). In the second version of the essay, the writer has substituted concrete terminology for several of the abstractions used in the first version. Look at the abstractions from the first version listed below, then identify the concrete passages that the writer has substituted for them in the second version.

a. I was showing signs of nervousness.

b. The expression on our faces was unforgettable.

    c.   It was a day in one of these authoritarian places where anxieties run high.

    d.   My mother was most affected.

Exercise 8.   For each of the following abstract sentences, write at least one concrete sentence that gives the same idea:

    Example: The town is depressed.
       The ragged lawns in the town are littered with trash, and paint is peeling from the houses, exposing raw wood.

    a.   English composition is a very demanding course.

    b.   The people of my country are very warm.

    c.   There is much ugliness in the city.

    d.   The beauty of the view from my window affects me deeply.

    e.   Wearing tight clothes can create a condition of discomfort.

Exercise 9.   Make word ladders for each of the terms listed, moving in at least five steps for nouns and three steps for verbs from general terms to increasingly specific ones.

    Example: place ⟩ building ⟩ library ⟩ college library ⟩ Fox Memorial Library.

(Note: In word ladders each item must be equivalent to the one preceding it; the name given for each item, however, is more specific than the preceding name. Compare the word ladders below:

Incorrect

    place ⟩ Asia ⟩ Turkey ⟩ Istanbul ⟩ Konuralp Street

Correct

    place ⟩ thoroughfare ⟩ street ⟩ Turkish Street ⟩ Konuralp Street.)

    a.   activity

    b.   material

    c.   creature

    d.   feeling

    e.   place

    f.   move

    g.   do

Exercise 10.   Read the essays "The Beauty of Nature" and "Familiar Landscape" (page 39). Underline words that are concrete, specific, and precise. Circle words that are abstract, general, vague, or unnecessary. Then substitute more concrete and precise words for the words you have circled.

Exercise 11.   In the three passages below, one is the first verse of a poem, "Richard Cory," by the poet Edwin Arlington Robinson, and the other two are variations of the original verse. Read all three verses, noting how particular words have been varied. What is the effect of particular changes on connotation? Is there any effect on denotation? Which of the verses seems the most positive? the most negative? the most neutral? Why? Which do you think is Robinson's original poem?

A.
When Richard Cory into town would come,
We other passers-by would look at him;
Of more than average means and style in sum,
He shaved close, and he kept his figure trim.

B.
When Richard Cory down the street would go,
We folk to gawk at him would never fail.
He was a rich man's son from top to toe,
And beardless, and as skinny as a rail.

C.
Whenever Richard Cory went down town,
We people on the pavement looked at him:
He was a gentleman from sole to crown,
Clean favored, and imperially slim.

For Composition

Exercise 12. Using the thesaurus and dictionary to help you, find synonyms for the neutral terms underlined to change the connotation of each sentence, making it first more positive and then more negative.
  a.   The *food* at our dining hall is *plain*.
  b.   The *large woman hurried* by.
  c.   The *young boy spoke* about his vacation.

Exercise 13. Write a brief description (three or four sentences) describing someone you know. Make the language in the passage as neutral as possible. Then write two alternative versions of the passage, changing key terms to make the passage first as positive and then as negative as possible.

Exercise 14. Think of five similes or metaphors that are clichés in your own language. Translate them, then try to find fresh figures for each of them in English. Finally, use each fresh figure in an appropriate English sentence.

   Example:
   Cliché: white as snow
   fresh figure: white as fresh milk
   The baby's blanket was as white as fresh milk.

Exercise 15. Find fresh similes or metaphors to complete each of the following sentences appropriately. Remember to use figurative, not literal, images to complete each sentence.
  a.   The old woman's flesh was as soft as _____.
  b.   The young boy's cheek was as soft as _____.
  c.   The sand was as soft as _____.
  d.   The leftover meat was as dry as _____.
  e.   The desert air was as dry as _____.
  f.   The old man's throat was as dry as _____.
  g.   The noonday sun was a _____.
  h.   The math exam was a _____.
  i.   Our English instructor is a _____.
  j.   For me, the United States is a _____.

Exercise 16. Write an extended metaphor or analogy making one of the following comparisons:

   a. An airport to a military installation

   b. A university to a machine of some sort

   c. A professor to a prison warden

   d. A dormitory building to a zoo

   e. A foreign student to a newborn baby

   f. The way you or someone else thinks or works to a computer

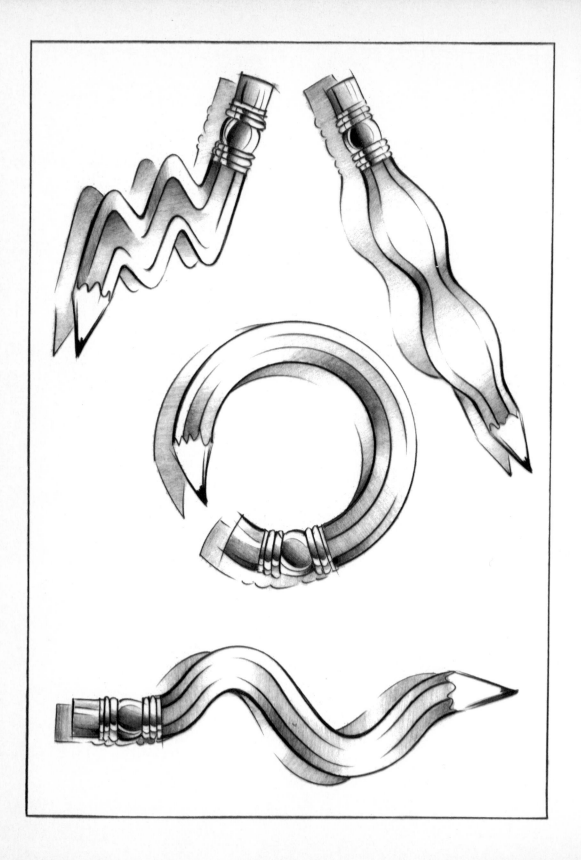

Part Five

Special Forms

Chapter 17

The Summary

Some of what students write in college courses derives from their own knowledge, but much of college writing is based on the ideas and opinions of others. A *summary* is a brief restatement in one's own words of the main ideas of another person's writing or speech. Whenever students present ideas they have found in another text, they are summarizing them. Sometimes, instructors may ask students to write a formal summary of an entire essay, report, chapter, or other text. This chapter provides the guidelines for writing such a summary.

Summary writing, however, is not important only in and of itself. Indeed, its primary importance for college students may lie in its being a fundamental step in two of the tasks most frequently assigned them: writing research papers and answering essay questions. Of course, research papers and essay questions generally require more than summary alone: the writer must analyze and integrate the ideas found in various sources as support for his or her own thesis. However, all such analysis and integration starts with sound summary. The guidelines set forth in this chapter should help the student not only to write sound summaries, but also to apply summarizing techniques to the writing of research papers and essay questions.

In writing a summary, the student should have several aims in mind:

1. *Accuracy*: The summary must correctly reflect the ideas of the original piece of writing. The summary must *not* include any ideas or examples not found in the original. Furthermore, it must *not* include comments on or evaluations of the original *unless specifically requested* and identified as such.

2. *Brevity*: The summary is a *brief* restatement. Therefore, it must either generalize or eliminate many *minor* details and examples. (Note that, in this respect, summary writing is different from essay writing in general.)

3. *Completeness*: A formal summary must include all *major* ideas of the material being summarized. (However, it is important to note that it is not always necessary or desirable to make a formal summary of a source cited in a research paper or essay question. For more on using material from an outside source selectively, see pages 254–55).

4. *Use of the summarizer's own words*: The summary must not *plagiarize* the original (see page 224). The summarizer should rely chiefly on his or her own words to express the ideas of the original writing. Where the summarizer needs to borrow a sentence, phrase, or even *a particularly appropriate word* exactly from the original, he or she must use quotation punctuation to indicate the borrowing.

5. *Logical organization and transition*: In summarizing, the ideas of the original must be arranged in an order that is logical for the summary, which may or may not follow the original order. Transitions (see Chapter 15) must be supplied to guide the reader from one part of the summary to another.

6. *Clarity*: Of course, the summary must be clear. It must not be so general in its restatement of the ideas of the original that they remain vague. The basic ideas of the original should be evident from the summary itself (although some readers might still want to consult the original to achieve a more thorough understanding).

Let us look at an essay by a professional writer and see how two students have summarized it. The essay, "Velva, North Dakota," may be reminiscent of some of the essays in previous chapters of this text (indeed, it inspired some of them). In it, the author, Eric Sevareid, contrasts his hometown, Velva, as it was in his boyhood and as it is now and suggests the causes behind the changes he sees.

Velva, North Dakota

My home town has changed in these thirty years of the American story. It is changing now, will go on changing as America changes. Its biography, I suspect, would read much the same as that of all other home towns. Depression and war and prosperity have all left their marks; modern science, modern tastes, manners, philosophies, fears and ambitions have touched my town as indelibly[1] as they have touched New York or Panama City.

Sights have changed: there is a new precision about street and home, a clearing away of chicken yards, cow barns, pigeon-crested cupolas,[2] weed lots and coulees,[3] the dim and secret adult-free rendezvous[4] of boys. An

[1] permanently
[2] dome-like roof
[3] small, intermittent streams
[4] meeting places

intricate metal "jungle gym"[5] is a common backyard sight, the sack swing[6] uncommon. There are wide expanses of clear windows designed to let in the parlor light, fewer ornamental windows of colored glass designed to keep it out. Attic and screen porch are slowly vanishing and lovely shades of pastel[7] are painted upon new houses, tints that once would have embarrassed farmer and merchant alike.

Sounds have changed: I heard not once the clopping of a horse's hoof, nor the mourn of a coyote. I heard instead the shriek of brakes, the heavy throbbing of the once-a-day Braniff airliner into Minot, the shattering sirens born of war, the honk of a diesel locomotive which surely cannot call to faraway places the heart of a wakeful boy like the old steam whistle in the night. You can walk down the streets of my town now and hear from open windows the intimate voices of the Washington commentators in casual converse on the great affairs of state; but you cannot hear on Sunday morning the singing in Norwegian of the Lutheran hymns: the old country seems now part of a world left long behind and the old-country accents grow fainter in the speech of my Velva neighbors.

The people have not changed, but the *kinds* of people have changed: there is no longer an official, certified town drunk, no longer a "Crazy John," spitting his worst epithet,[8] "rotten chicken legs," as you hurriedly passed him by. People so sick are now sent to places of proper care. No longer is there an official town joker, like the druggist MacKnight, who would spot a customer in the front of the store, have him called to the phone, then slip to the phone behind the prescription case, and imitate the man's wife to perfection with orders to bring home more bread and sausage and Cream of Wheat.[9] No longer anyone like the early attorney, J. L. Lee who sent fabulous dispatches to that fabulous tabloid,[10] the Chicago *Blade*, such as his story of the wild man captured on the prairie and chained to the wall in the drugstore basement. (This, surely, was Velva's first notoriety; inquiries came from anthropologists all over the world.)

No, the "characters" are vanishing in Velva, just as they are vanishing in our cities, in business, in politics. The "well-rounded, socially integrated" personality that the progressive schoolteachers are so obsessed with is increasing rapidly, and I am not at all sure that this is good. Maybe we need more personalities with knobs and handles and rugged lumps of individuality. They may not make life more smooth; more interesting they surely make it.

They eat differently in Velva now; there are frozen fruits and seafood and exotic delicacies we only read about in novels in those meat-and-potato days. They dress differently. The hard white collars of the businessmen are gone with the shiny alpaca coats. There are comfortable tweeds now, and casual blazers with a touch in their colors of California, which seems so close in time and distance.

[5] climbing bars
[6] swing made from bag
[7] soft color such as pink, sky blue, etc.
[8] abusive name
[9] breakfast cereal
[10] sensationalistic newspaper

It is distance and time that have changed the most and worked the deepest changes in Velva's life. The telephone, the car, the smooth highway, radio and television are consolidating[11] the entities[12] of our country. The county seat of Towner now seems no closer than the state capital of Bismarck; the voices and concerns of Presidents, French premiers and Moroccan pashas are no farther away than the portable radio on Aunt Jessey's kitchen table. The national news magazines are stacked each week in Harold Anderson's drugstore beside the new soda fountain, and the excellent *Minot Daily News* smells hot from the press each afternoon.

Sevareid's essay is nearly 700 words in length. It is full of specific details. The summary below, by a student writer, is just over 150 words, a reduction of more than 75 percent. To achieve this reduction, the writer has eliminated many details of the original and expressed the original's major ideas largely in his own words and with his own logical organization and transition. Throughout, however, he has been careful to be accurate and clear in reflecting the ideas of the original essay.

Summary of "Velva, North Dakota"

In his essay, "Velva, North Dakota," Eric Sevareid describes the changes in his hometown. As Sevareid writes, transportation and information systems have been modernized, making separate cities closer than they were before. Specifically, the development of cars, airplanes, highway systems, news broadcasting, telephones, and newspapers have made the distances smaller between different places.

As a result of this, Velva has lost its distinctive features and become like other cities. Both the traditional rural atmosphere of Velva and the citizens' typical lifestyle have changed. Modern homes and streets have replaced country-style ones. Sounds of mechanical vehicles and electronic media have replaced natural sounds. The people wear up-to-date fashions instead of their traditional conservative clothes, and they eat "exotic" foods from farway places rather than only meat and potatoes. In addition, people have become more uniform in accent and behavior. In Sevareid's opinion, towns may need more "personalities" to make life interesting.

We might focus on several features of this summary. Perhaps the most striking is the student's rearrangement of Sevareid's ideas. Sevareid's essay consists of seven paragraphs; the student's summary, of two. Sevareid concludes his essay with the causes behind Velva's changes; the student introduces this idea in his first paragraph. Sevareid discusses changes in sights, sounds, kinds of people, foods, and dress in that order; the student's summary reorders the final three, focusing last on the changes in the kinds of people. (This reordering may help give back to this last idea some of the importance it loses in being reduced from two long paragraphs in the original essay to two sentences in the summary.)

Another striking feature of the summary is its brevity. The student has kept his summary brief, not by omitting any major ideas but by substituting general terms for many of Sevareid's specific details. For example, Sevareid's second paragraph begins

[11] bringing together
[12] independent existences

with a generalization and then lists many specific details (the "clopping of a horse's hoof," the "mourn of a coyote," the "shriek of brakes,") to support it. The student summarizes in one generalizing sentence: "Sounds of mechanical vehicles and electronic media have replaced natural sounds." While presenting Sevareid's ideas accurately, the student has nonetheless managed to use his own words. Where he has borrowed from the original ("exotic," "well-rounded, socially integrated"), he has used quotation punctuation.

Finally, we might look at the references to the original essay and its author. There are three such references in the summary, each of which acknowledges Sevareid as the source of the idea it introduces:

In his essay, "Velva, North Dakota," Eric Sevareid says . . .

As Sevareid writes . . .

In Sevareid's opinion . . .

Textual acknowledgments like these are not always necessary in a summary, and indeed, it is sometimes preferable to omit them for the sake of brevity. But such acknowledgments are useful in writing essays that cite material from other sources, and the student writer should be familiar with them before he or she tackles research papers or essay questions. (For a more detailed discussion of acknowledgments, see page 218).

Of course, it would be possible to summarize Sevareid's essay in many other ways, depending on the writer's purpose. The length of the summary could be cut still further, or it could be increased. The organization could be made to follow Sevareid's more closely. Different terms could be substituted for the quotations used by the student. However, the summary we have just looked at is well done and more than adequate.

Let us turn now to look at a poor and inadequate summary of the same essay, again written by a student:

Summary

Velva has changed and is changing like everything has to change with time. And time has made it change in some good and some bad ways. Sometimes time is our worst enemy.

Velva has changed from wood to concrete and metal. Modern designs and colors can be seen.

Pollution is noticed, also. New machines are destroying the place as in all the world, creating more waste and making our senses tired.

People have changed, of course. Restricted persons can be noticed now, as the natural kind of life has disappeared. Today people have become like robots because they are not free, for example, in New York, the great bee-hive.

The "characters" have changed as in all places: politics, business, etc. The people think only about their own lives. They don't bother with anything else.

Synthetic fabrics and frozen foods are now all around; new fashions can be noticed.

Everything changes with time; everything gets old and has to be changed. Modern times are coming, and we have to accustom ourselves to these changes.

This so-called summary is a disaster. It has broken most of the rules of good summarizing. First, it is not accurate. The student writer has missed the main idea of Sevareid's essay: that Velva is becoming more like other places—less individual—because of the new closeness achieved by modern media and transportation. Instead, he has substituted his own idea: that Velva is becoming generally worse because of modernization. The student adds his own material to the original to support this idea, introducing "pollution," people as "robots" who are "not free," and who "think only about their own lives." He has made his own personal comments (clichés, at that): "Sometimes time is our worst enemy," "Everything changes with time." His language is imprecise—"Time has made it [what?] change in some good and bad ways"—and thus, vague. Finally, he has stuck slavishly to the original's organization, and the result is seven too-short paragraphs that do not hang together.

How, then, do you go about writing a good summary? The first step is to *read* and *reread* the original essay carefully, making sure you understand its main ideas. Next, *write the thesis* of the essay in one clear sentence. If time allows, you might *outline the essay by paragraphs*, writing one sentence to express the main idea of each paragraph or group of related paragraphs in the original. In making this paragraph outline, use your own words as much as possible, inserting quotation punctuation whenever you borrow sentences, phrases, or particularly appropriate words exactly from the original. Then *write your own sentence or topic outline* to establish the order you will follow in your summary, again using your own words where you can. Remember that you do not have to follow the order of the original. *Check your outline against the original* essay to be sure that it includes enough specific information to write a summary that is clear and complete, but not so much as to be overdetailed or overlong. Finally, *write the summary*, being sure to *link one idea to another with appropriate transitions*. When you have finished, *check it against the original* to make sure your summary fulfills all the requirements of good summary writing:

- Accuracy
- Brevity
- Completeness
- Use of your own words
- Logical order and transition
- Clarity

Summary

A summary is a brief restatement in one's own words of the ideas in another author's speech or writing. Writers achieve accuracy in a summary by restricting themselves to expressing the ideas of the original author; they achieve brevity by eliminating or generalizing specific details. Although for research papers or essay questions the writer may summarize only a part of another author's work, a formal summary should include all major ideas.

In writing a summary, the student should use his own words as much as possible, using quotation punctuation when he must borrow words exactly from the original. The order of ideas should be logical for the summary and may or may not correspond to the original organization; new transitions should be supplied to relate one part of the summary to another. The basic ideas of the original should be clear from the summary alone.

Exercises

Exercise 1. Read Eric Sevareid's "Velva, North Dakota." Then do the following:
a. Write the *thesis* of Sevareid's essay in one sentence.
b. Make a *paragraph outline* of the essay, expressing in one sentence, and in *your own words*, the main idea of each paragraph or group of closely related paragraphs in the original. (Note: One pair of paragraphs in the essay can definitely be treated as a unit.)
c. Make a *sentence outline* to show how you would organize your own summary of the essay. You do not have to follow Sevareid's organization.

Exercise 2. Read the following summaries of Eric Sevareid's "Velva, North Dakota." Using the materials you prepared for Exercise 1, evaluate how well each of the summaries satisfies the requirements for good summary writing set forth in this chapter. Support your evaluations with specific examples from the summaries as well as from Sevareid's original essay.

A.
Summary of "Velva, North Dakota"

Eric Sevareid's hometown of Velva has changed in these thirty years of the American story. The ups and downs of modern times have all left their marks.

Sights are different. There is now precision in the way houses and roads look.

Sounds are different, too. There isn't the "clopping of a horse's hoof" now or the "mourn of a coyote." Instead there is the "shriek of brakes" and the "heavy throbbing of the once-a-day Braniff airliner," and "the shattering sirens born of war."

The people are the same, but the kinds of people are different. There is now no "official, certified town drunk," no "Crazy John," and no "official town joker."

The "characters" are vanishing in Velva. The people are all becoming empty and materialistic. All they care about is making money. And this will probably lead to a decline in morality.

The people have better food and clothes in Velva now, and this makes their lives more pleasant.

Distance and time have changed Velva most. Telephones, cars, and smooth highways make life nicer. There is a new soda fountain in the town.

B.
Sevareid's "Velva, North Dakota"

According to Eric Sevareid's essay, Velva, North Dakota, is a town which has changed as a result of the new activities of modern technology and the "philosophies, fears and ambitions" of the people's new way of thinking.

Velva has been influenced by the consequences that "depression and war and prosperity" have had on the entire world.

Nearly everything in this town has changed, from sounds to fashions in dress and eating. The sounds have changed from the noises of animals to the noises that engines of modern vehicles make. New houses have functional windows instead of the ornamental ones of years ago. Neither the way of eating nor of dressing is the same as those of the past. One finds now frozen meals and fancy fare imported from elsewhere instead of home-based foods. And the people wear clothes with a modern "touch" and the "colors of California," rather than their traditional clothes.

Sevareid writes that even though the "people have not changed . . . , the kinds of people have changed." There are no longer individuals such as the "certified town drunk" or the crazy name caller who used to be part of the town. About this, Sevareid expresses his doubts, saying:

> Maybe we need more personalities with knobs and handles and rugged lumps of individuality. They may not make life more smooth; more interesting they surely make it.

The new technological advances have played the most important role in Velva's change. In this town, as in most other towns nowadays, one can be present at distant events with the help of the radio and TV, or go to distant places just by taking a plane or a car.

Exercise 3. Read the essay "Alienation and Affection" by Crauford D. Goodwin and Michael Nacht. Then do the tasks that follow the essay.

Alienation and Affection: Undergraduate Liberal Arts Education

It was striking—indeed almost startling—that throughout our conversations [with Brazilians who had studied in U.S. colleges and universities] we did not meet a *single* person who expressed regret at having studied in the United States. We thought these to be genuinely positive reactions, not merely offered to please two visitors from American academe.[1] Only one person could even recall having heard expressions of disillusionment or dislike from another Brazilian. It was that much more surprising, therefore, that we encountered very little support for Brazilians pursuing undergraduate study in the United States.

Some of the opposition had a protectionist ring: "We have perfectly good undergraduate colleges; why send students away?" Others offered their judgments based upon the best use of scarce resources: "We can only afford to send a few students abroad; they should be at the graduate level." And, of course, most of the people with whom we spoke had indeed gained graduate degrees in the United States and might, therefore, be expected to harbor[2] some bias in this direction. Coincidentally, we heard undergraduate study abroad criticized several times before we had an opportunity to meet and talk over the phenomenon with those who had experienced it.

[1] academic community
[2] hold a thought or feeling

But the most powerful arguments against undergraduate education out-side Brazil were not on these utilitarian grounds. Rather they revolved around an ill-defined phenomenon which we heard discussed more than any other during our conversations: "alienation."[3] The critical argument ran approximately as follows: Brazil, like all developing countries, requires a strong and committed middle class to achieve viable democratic institutions, social progress, and sustained economic development. The commitment to achieve these goals can come only from those who are immersed in their own culture during their impressionable and formative undergraduate years. Undergraduate study abroad, especially in such an environment as that of the United States, leads to "cultural absorption" and alienation from the home-land upon return. Not only would these undergraduate alumni not "know Brazil," we were told; they were likely to be repelled by it and unable ever again to come to grips[4] with many aspects of Brazilian society. One critic of undergraduate study abroad offered the following observation: "If someone without well-established roots in his society is sent aboard to study, he comes back rootless without a sense of where he truly belongs." Another commentator put it to us that "maturity" should be a prerequisite for study abroad. A mature graduate student could easily distinguish between the admirable features of American higher education (dedication, dependence upon logical reasoning, discipline by competition, and an overall "sense of reality") and the irrelevant distractions (fraternities, frenetic social life, semi-professional athletics). Young undergraduates faced with a strange culture as well as the normal academic rigors were likely to adopt the former and in the worst cases neglect the latter. On returning home these graduates were likely to feel serious disorientation,[5] and even loathing, toward family, friends, cultural norms, and political and economic institutions. They would have to make a secondary adjustment to reverse culture-shock,[6] which was often worse than the primary adjustment which they had endured in the United States. Others would never recover from the experience and might degenerate into cynicism[7] and near schizophrenia[8]—little use to their native country or to the one which had given them their college education.

It was fortunate that we heard the arguments against undergraduate study made so forcefully before we heard, and could test, the response. The reaction from those who had lived through undergraduate years aboard was almost as complex as the critique. In general all conceded that alienation or at least significant frustration was indeed a problem; for one, this was solved by a few months of adjustment. For another, it dictated a life-style of vacations in the United States and dependence on American cultural exports. For a third, it had led to a rootless life, moving back and forth between Brazil and the United States like a human yoyo,[9] feeling uneasy

---

[3] state of being or feeling different or separate
[4] to deal satisfactorily with
[5] uncertainty within a situation
[6] feeling of alienation from one's native culture
[7] disbelief in idea that man may be motivated by unselfishness or honesty
[8] psychological disturbance characterized by withdrawal from reality
[9] toy that moves up and down on a string

and frustrated in the former and guilty in the latter for not contributing to the development of the homeland.

But those who had really experienced the American college life were able to provide illustrations of "benefits" which, they thought, justified the "costs" of alienation. One member of a privileged Brazilian industrial family who after an American preparatory school took an undergraduate degree in the United States spoke of the profound effect this experience had had upon his entire life-style and behavior. In contrast to his peer group[10] in Brazil, which he claimed pursued a jet-set hedonistic[11] existence, he had been trained to take a responsible interest in the circumstances around him and to think, read, and discuss. While the conversations of his Brazilian friends centered on fast cars and local scandal, he found his main interest to be in the economic and political problems of the nation and broader concerns about world affairs. His American training made him "forward-looking" in contrast to the search for instant gratification[12] of his locally educated cohorts.[13] Moreover, his U.S. experience gave him a "standard for local appraisal." He now found himself invariably judging Brazil by American criteria which he thought was neither unfair nor unfortunate. He saw contemporary Brazil passing through a "renovation in values." For what the country would become the United States could be the model. But for this to happen it was necessary for there to be an ample number of sophisticated interpreters. He was convinced that only as an undergraduate did one have the time and the real incentive[14] to learn the foreign language and culture—to "get into American life." This individual was quick to accept the notion of alienation from his Brazilian environment as a consequence of his American experience. To this condition he added an acquired difficulty in understanding and sympathizing with some parts of his native environment, and the need to respond to charges of "selling out to the imperialists." On the positive side, however, he stressed the ease of doing business with Americans. Not only were there his former school and college chums as points of contact for commercial interactions, but with accentless English and total acculturation[15] he felt fully "comfortable" with American business partners and they with him. He emphasized that "culture permeates[16] business life" and cited for contrast the difficulties he encountered in doing business with the Japanese. To the extent that such interactions were a source of capital, technology, and markets, in his view, his undergraduate education was an excellent investment for both Brazil and the United States. . . .

In sum, it must be emphasized that relatively small numbers of Brazilians pursue undergraduate studies in the United States, and many of these are from affluent[17] backgrounds. Our dominant impression from

[10] group of those of equal standing
[11] characterized by devotion to pleasure
[12] fulfillment of desires
[13] associates
[14] motivation; something that causes one to make an effort
[15] adjustment to a different culture
[16] penetrates every part of
[17] wealthy

interviewing several such individuals is that this experience can produce a pronounced cultural affinity toward the United States which holds the promise of being translated subsequently into bilateral[18] commercial and investment ties as well as into a valuable comparative perspective on local conditions.

a.   Write the *thesis* of the essay in one sentence.

b.   Make a *paragraph outline*, writing one sentence to express the meaning of each paragraph or group of related paragraphs in the essay. (Remember to use your own words as much as possible, using quotation punctuation to indicate the direct borrowing of any sentence, phrase, or particularly appropriate word from the original.)

c.   Make a *sentence* or *topic outline* to show how you would organize your own summary of the essay. (Remember, you do not have to follow the organization of the original.)

Exercise 4.   Write a summary of the essay you outlined in Exercise 3. Try to fulfill all the requirements for a good summary detailed in this chapter.

[18] two-sided

Chapter 18

The Research Paper

The outside sources used in writing summaries or answering essay questions are generally assigned. In writing a research paper, on the other hand, the students are generally required to find their own materials. Moreover, because they are not using assigned texts, they must acknowledge their sources more precisely than they would be required to do in other forms of writing. Because of these requirements, writing research papers calls for knowledge of two special techniques: how to *gather information* from other sources and how to *document*—that is, acknowledge the sources used.

These special techniques may seem complex to the beginning writer: so many resources to learn about, so many ideas to digest, so many rules to remember. But mastering them is worth the effort. Knowledge of the techniques of information gathering and documentation is fundamental not only to the writing of research papers but also to other special forms of academic writing, including master's theses and doctoral dissertations. Moreover, the techniques involved in writing research papers can be adapted to the writing of many kinds of reports required in various disciplines.

In this chapter, we shall look at the processes of information gathering and documentation and see how they have been applied in the writing of an actual research paper.

Gathering Information

The university or college library may appear formidable to students new to it, especially when the language and cultural environment they are working in are still new. It may at first seem impossible to find the sources needed for a paper on a particular topic among all the volumes housed in the university library. A simple plan of action, however, will make the task manageable.

Before beginning to do any research, the student should have a clear idea of his topic, and perhaps even some idea of his thesis. Having a topic that is narrowly and clearly defined will save the student much time in the library. Once the student has a clear idea of his topic, he can begin looking for library materials—most often, books and articles—relevant to it.

Finding Books

Most students will be familiar with the way in which books are shelved in their library. The books are kept on shelves—or stacks—which in many libraries are open to students: students can enter and select their own books. Sometimes, however, the stacks are closed: students must request particular books, which are then delivered to them by library staff members.

Before looking in the stacks, however, the student must gather the titles of books he thinks might be useful to him. To find these titles, he will use several tools: the card catalogue (or an online catalogue), bibliographies, and as research progresses, references in other books and articles.

The Card Catalogue. All books housed in a particular library are listed in the library's *card catalogue*—several cabinets of index card-size file drawers filled with cards arranged in alphabetical order. For each book in the library, the card catalogue has at least three separate cards: a *title card*, alphabetized according to the first important word in the title—that is, not *a, an, the*; an *author card*, alphabetized according to the author's or editor's *last* name; and a *subject card*, alphabetized, like the title card, according to the first important word. There are additional author cards for books with more than one author and additional subject cards for books *cross-listed* under several different subject headings.

The Subject Card: Students who already know of a particular book or writer concerned with the subject they are working on will naturally look in the card catalogue for the relevant title or author card. Generally, however, for research on a term paper topic, the most important cards are *subject cards*. These cards list, under a given subject heading, all the books the library has on that particular subject. Thus, to find books on a given subject, the student looks at all the cards filed under an appropriate subject heading. (Note that the cards may be alphabetized together or alphabetized separately from author and title cards.)

Let us say, for example, a student wishes to write a research paper on the topic, "Should U.S. public schools be required to make bilingual programs available to students for whom English is a second language?" He looks in the card catalogue under the subject heading *Education, Bilingual*. Among others on this subject, he finds the card in Figure 18-1, which looks as if it might be relevant to his topic.

Figure 18-1 A Card Catalogue Entry

```
              EDUCATION, BILINGUAL—UNITED STATES.
LC
3731    Ramirez, Arnulfo G., 1943—
R28         Bilingualism through schooling:
1985    cross cultural education for minority and majority
        students / Arnulfo G. Ramirez. — Albany: State Uni-
        versity of New York Press, c1985
            xiii, 275 p. : ill. ; 24 cm.
            Bibliography: p. 246—267.
            Includes indexes.
            ISBN 0-87395-891-8
            1. Education, Bilingual—United
        States.  2. English language—Study and teaching (El-
        ementary)—Foreign speakers.  3. English language—
        Study and teaching—Bilingual method.  4. Children of
        minorities—Education—United States.  I. Title

NA1U                                 NAMMsc      83-24246
```

What does this card tell him? On the top of the card, in all capital letters, is the *subject heading* the student has looked under. Below this is the *author* and *title* of a book on this subject. The number in the upper left-hand corner of the card is the book's *call number*. This number is the main information needed to locate the book in the library.

The Online Card Catalogue: In addition to the standard file cabinet card catalogue, many libraries now have an *online* card catalogue available for student use. The online catalogue is a computerized system accessed through terminals generally located near the reference desk. Like the standard catalogue, the online catalogue includes at least three entries for each book it lists: author, title, and subject. Again, the student looking for books on a particular research topic will probably want to search by subject first. To do this, he will enter the appropriate code for a subject search and the subject heading he is interested in. Systems vary, but the subject entry in Figure 18-2 is typical of what the computer terminal will show.

Figure 18-2 An Online Card Catalogue Entry By Subject

```
018 MAIN LIBRARY          - GEAC LIBRARY SYSTEM -        *SUBJECT SEARCH

                                              matches  48  citations
                                              (All in this library)
Ref# Author                        Title                              Date
 25  Ramirez, Arnulfo G., 1943->   Bilingualism through schooling :   1985
 26  Ramirez, Manuel, 1937—        Spanish-English bilingual education> 1970
 27  Reyes, Vinicio H.             Bicultural-bilingual education for > 1978
 28  Rodriguez Munguia, Juan Ch>   Supervision of bilingual programs /> 1978
 29  Stein, Colman B.              Sink or swim :                     1986
 30  Streiff, Paul Robert.         Development of guidelines for condu> 1978
 31  Thomas, Carol H.              Bilingual special education resourc> 1982
 32  Thonis, Eleanor.             Literacy for America's Spanish spea> 1976
 33  Ulibarri, Horacio.            Interpretive studies on bilingual e> 1978
 34  United States. Bureau of I>   Bilingual education for American In> 1978
 35  Valadez, Concepcion M.        Basic skills in urban schools :    1979
 36  Valle, Manuel del.            Law and bilingual education :      1978

Type a number to see associated information -OR-
  IND - see list of headings            FOR - move forward in this list
  BAC - move backward in this list      CAT - begin a new search

Enter number or code: FOR                        Then press SEND
```

***Figure* 18-3**   An Online Card Catalogue Entry by Author

```
018 MAIN LIBRARY              - GEAC LIBRARY SYSTEM -      *AUTHOR SEARCH

  AUTHOR:  Ramirez, Arnulfo G., 1943-
  TITLE:   Bilingualism through schooling :
  IMPRINT: Albany : State University of New York Press, c1985.
  PHYSICAL FEATURES: xiii, 275 p. : ill. ; 24 cm.
  NOTES:   Includes indexes. * Bibliography: p. 246-267.
  SUBJECTS: Education, Bilingual -- United States. * English language -- Study
            and teaching (Elementary) -- Foreign speakers. * English language --
            Study and teaching -- Bilingual method. * Children of minorities --
            Education -- United States.
  LC CARD: 83024246
  ISBN:    0873958918 * 0873958926 (pbk.)
  CATALOGING SOURCE NUMBER:    Call no.: LC 3731 R28 1985




  BRF - see locations and call numbers    IND - see list of headings
  CAT - begin a new search                PRI - print record


Enter code                                          Then press SEND
```

If the student wishes to obtain more information (such as the call number) for a particular title included in the subject entry, he uses the code that accompanies that title to find the more complete entry for it. The full entry for *Bilingualism Through Schooling* (Ramirez), for example, appears in Figure 18-3.

All materials will not necessarily be included in both traditional and online catalogues. At present, many libraries are in the process of changing to the online system. New materials may be included only in the online catalogue; older materials may not be catalogued online at all. For help in using the catalogues in your particular library, ask a reference librarian.

Finding Appropriate Subject Headings. Sometimes a student will have difficulty finding the appropriate subject headings for his topic. If so, he can generally consult *Library of Congress Subject Headings*, a two-volume guide to the categories used in the card catalogue. Most college libraries will have this guide available either near the card catalogue itself or in the reference section.

This guide lists various subject headings alphabetically. Under each of these entries are listed alternative headings accompanied by symbols indicating whether a particular heading is or is not used in the card catalogue. The symbols the student should be familiar with include the following:

- *see* means that the heading under which the student is looking is not used in the card catalogue. He should look instead under the alternative heading(s) listed.

- *sa* (see also) means that the heading under which the student is looking is listed in the card catalogue and that material may also be found under a related heading or headings.

- *x* means that a heading is not used in the card catalogue.

- *xx* means that a heading is used and is related to the heading under which it is listed.

- — indicates that the heading is used as a subdivision of the heading under which it is listed.

Looking at an actual entry will make this clearer. For example, if a student looks in the guide under the heading *Bilingual education*, He finds the following:

> Bilingual education
> >   see Education, Bilingual.

Understanding from this that *Bilingual education* is not a heading used in the card catalogue, he checks in the guide under *Education, Bilingual* and finds the following:

> Education, Bilingual
> > sa   Language and languages—Study and teaching—Bilingual method
> > x   Bilingual Education
> > xx   Bilingualism
> >   Intercultural education
> >   Minorities—Education
> > —   Law and legislation
> > xx   Educational law and legislation

This entry indicates that
1. *Education, Bilingual* and *Language and languages—Study and teaching—bilingual method* are headings used in the card catalogue.
2. Related headings to be found in the catalogue include *Bilingualism, Intercultural education*, and *Minorities—Education*. (Note: a symbol is used only once in an entry and pertains to all headings listed below it.
3. *Bilingual Education* is not a heading used in the catalogue.
4. *Law and legislation* is a subdivision under which material may be found by looking under *Education, bilingual—Law and legislation*.
5. *Educational law and legislation* is another related subject heading used in the catalogue.

By using *Library of Congress Subject Headings*, the student will generally be able to find the exact subject headings under which titles related to his topic are filed in the card catalogue.

In addition, special cards within the card catalogue itself may indicate *cross-indexing*—that is, alternative subject headings under which titles on a particular topic are listed. As with *Library of Congress Subject Headings*, a *see* reference in the card catalogue lists a heading not included in the catalogue and gives the alternative heading under which material on that topic is filed. For example, a student looking for materials under the heading *Bilingual Education* will find a cross-indexing card indicating the following:

> Bilingual Education
> >   see
> Education, Bilingual.

This means that *Bilingual Education* is not a heading used in the catalogue. The student should look under *Education, Bilingual* instead. A *see also* reference indicates that materials may be found under both headings listed. For example, a student looking for materials under the heading *Education, Bilingual* will find a cross-indexing card indicating the following:

Education, Bilingual
   see also
English Language—Study and teaching—bilingual method.

This means that the student can look for materials under both *Education, Bilingual* and *English Language—Study and teaching—bilingual method.*

    Subject cards themselves may list additional subject headings under which a particular book is cross-listed. For example, the subject card for Ramirez's *Bilingualism Through Schooling* lists the other subject headings under which this book has been filed:

1. Education, Bilingual—United States
2. English Language—Study and teaching—foreign speakers
3. English Language—Study and teaching—bilingual method
4. Children of minorities—Education—United States

(Additional subject headings are generally listed on all cards for a given book; if headings are not listed on the subject card, however, the student can check the book's author card—sometimes called the *main entry*.) In the online catalogue, the full entry for a given title will include all subject headings under which that title is listed. Such entries may give the student clues to alternative subject headings under which he may not otherwise have considered looking.

    Listing Book Titles: As the student goes through the titles under a particular subject heading in the card catalogue, he should jot down on individual 3- by 5-inch file cards the author (last name first) and title of each book he thinks might be useful to him. In addition, he should note the call number in the upper left-hand corner, as shown in Figure 18-4. If there is more than one edition of a book and the student needs a particular one, he should note the number and year of that edition as well.

    In this way, if a particular book is not immediately available, the student has a record of how to locate the book elsewhere. Thus, the student can check if the book is available at the reserve desk or if it has been borrowed by another student or

Figure **18-4**   Tentative Bibliography Card: A Book

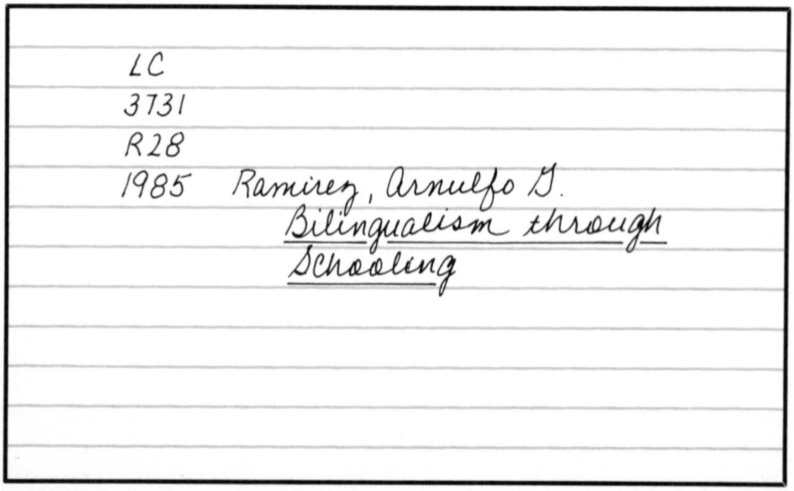

```
LC
3731
R28
1985   Ramirez, Arnulfo D.
            Bilingualism through
            Schooling
```

professor, in which case he can fill out a request slip for the book. (Each library has its own systems for reserve books and book requests. The student unfamiliar with his library's reserve and request systems and unable to locate books listed in the card catalogue should check with a librarian.) If the book is not on reserve and not checked out to another borrower, the student may want to wait and look for the book at a later date. If it still fails to turn up, the student can have the book *traced*— that is, searched for by the library staff. All these procedures require that the student have title and author as well as call number available. In addition, by systematically listing on file cards the titles of books at which he wishes to look, the student will have a head start on preparing both the bibliography cards he will use in taking notes (page 215) and his list of works cited (see page 219).

Bibliographies: Beyond the card catalogue, titles of books (and sometimes of articles) can be found in numerous specialized *bibliographies*—compilations of book titles— on various subjects. The listing below includes bibliographies dealing with disciplines in which international students frequently major.
Business:
    Lorna Daniells, *Business Information Sources* (1976)
Science and Technology:
    H. Robert Malinowsky and Jeanne M. Richardson, *Science and Engineering Literature* (1980)
    Saul Turner, *A Brief Guide to Sources of Scientific and Technical Information* (1980)
Medicine and Health:
    L. T. Morton and S. Godbolt, *Information Sources in the Medical Sciences* (1984)
    Fred W. Roper and Joanne Boorkman, *Introduction to Reference Sources in the Health Sciences* (1984)
Education:
    Dorothea M. Berry, *A Bibliographic Guide to Educational Research* (1980)
    Marda Woodbury, *A Guide to Sources of Educational Information* (1982)
Specialized bibliographies themselves may be listed in the card catalogue on special subject cards, as in Figure 18-5.

Bibliographies of Bibliographies: In addition, there are even *bibliographies of bibliographies*—reference books that list bibliographies that have been compiled on a variety of subjects. The most complete of these is the *Bibliographic Index: A Cumulative Bibliography of Bibliographies* (Laurel Cooley, 1937–present). This multivolume source includes

Figure 18-5 A Sample Card Catalogue Entry, Specialized Bibliography

```
              EDUCATION, BILINGUAL—BIBLIOGRAPHY.
REF     Bilingual education: U.S. Compiled by the staff of
Z           the Educational Reference Center, Commonwealth of
5811        Massachusetts Department of Education and pre-
A94x        pared for publication by the Project Intrex Model
NO.1        Library staff at M.I.T. Reading, Mass., Addison-
            Wesley Publishing Co., 1972.
            1 sheet. 28cm. (A-W library pathfinder[s]: Educa-
        tion, ED 1)
            Pathfinder.
        1. Education, bilingual—Bibl. I. Massachusetts. Edu-
        cational Reference Center. II. Series.
```

references to bibliographies published either as separate books or as parts of books, pamphlets, or periodicals. Other important guides to bibliographies include:

Eugene P. Sheehy, *Guide to Reference Books* (1976, with supplements for 1980 and 1982).

A. J. Walford, *Walford's Guide to Reference Material.* For generalities, arts, and literature (1986); for science and technology (Vol. 1, 1980; Vol. 2, 1982).

Select Bibliographies: Beyond such bibliographies, as the student examines the sources he has already gathered, he may find select bibliographies listing additional sources on his topic. The complete card catalogue entry for a given book will indicate whether or not the book includes a bibliography.

References in Other Books and Articles: Finally, even in books and articles that do not include actual bibliographies, there may be references to other sources on a particular topic. An author may mention a title that looks relevant to a student's topic, or he may mention the name of another author who has published material on the topic. In such cases, the student can consult the title or author cards in the card catalogue for further information on books available in his library.

Acquiring Books from Other Libraries: For students who wish to go beyond the books available in their own library, the *National Union Catalogue* lists all the books held by the Library of Congress as well as some held by other libraries. There is also a computer catalogue, the OCLC, which lists materials available at certain other libraries throughout the country and is generally available to librarians at most large institutional libraries. The *National Union Catalogue* should be available for student use at campus libraries. If the student needs books unavailable at his own campus library and if he has time to wait, he can often arrange to borrow books from other libraries through *interlibrary loan.* (A reference librarian can help the student unfamiliar with the procedure for making such a request.)

In addition, bookseller's bibliographies, including *Books in Print, Paperback Books in Print,* and the *Cumulative Book Index,* may be helpful in supplying recent titles to a student who has only an author's name as a reference. These sources will also tell the student whether or not a book is still in print (and therefore available for purchase).

Finding Articles

Much of a college student's research, especially in fields where it is important to have the most recent information available, will involve not books, but articles in various kinds of periodicals or journals: popular and scholarly magazines and newspapers. Periodicals are publications that are issued at regular intervals—daily, weekly, monthly, and so on. And because regular bibliographies cannot keep up with all the different articles published in the most recent months and years, the contents of periodicals are catalogued in special periodicals' *indexes.*

Finding Articles in Popular Magazines: The Readers' Guide. For beginning college students, the most frequently used index is the *Readers' Guide to Periodical Literature.* Each volume of this guide lists by subject and by author the articles published in most popular U.S. magazines each year (running from March of one year through February of the following year). Thus, there is a volume for March 1983 through February 1984, one for March 1984 through February 1985, and so forth. In addition, there are individual *fascicles*—small paperbound installments—for each month in the current year up to the present. Thus, the *Readers' Guide* is able to offer up-to-date information on the material available on a given topic in many American magazines of general interest.

As in the case of the card catalogue, it is the subject entries that are likely to be of most use to the student researcher, although author entries may be useful if a student knows the name of a particular writer who has written frequently on his topic or if he has a reference to an article written in a particular year by a particular author. Again, as with card catalogue subject cards, the student may have to do some hunting to find the precise heading under which material on his topic is listed.

A student researching bilingual education, for example, looking in the 1980–81 volume of the *Readers' Guide* under that subject heading, would find the cross-reference:

> Bilingual Education
>   see
> Education, Bilingual.

(We might note that, starting with the monthly fascicles for 1986, articles on this subject have been listed under the heading *Bilingual Education*. The student should always be aware in using an index that cataloguing procedures may change over the course of time.) Looking under the heading *Education, Bilingual*, he finds a listing such as that shown in Figure 18-6. Examining one of the entries more closely, we find that it includes the information displayed in Figure 18-7.

Figure 18-6   A Sample Listing in the *Readers' Guide*

EDUCATION, Bilingual
Anyone for Urdu? N. B. Freeman. Nat R 32:1186 O 3 '80
Battle in any language. A. Schardt and others. il Newsweek
    96:93–4 D 15 '80
Battle over bilingualism. il Time 116:64–5 S 8 '80
Bilingual education and the Hispanic challenge [excerpt from the
    1979 Annual report of the Carnegie Corporation of New York]
    A. Pifer. Educ Digest 46:12–15 N '80
Bilingual vocational education [Federally funded projects] J.
    Glickman. Am Educ 16:39 Jl '80
Chalk up one for the English tongue [decision excusing Fairfax
    County, Va. from bilingual instruction] il U.S. News 90:8 Ja
    12 '81
Education Department unveils proposed rules to govern bilingual
    programs. Phi Delta Kappan 62:150 O '80
English, si Spanish no [Department of Education program] G.
    Easterbrook. Wash M 12:37–44 D '80
Going back to Hollister: conflict in bilingual/bicultural education
    [firing of teacher J. Hoover in Calif.] M. Myers. Phi Delta
    Kappan 62:189–92 N '80
How $7.5 million became $1 billion: the biography of a Federal
    program. il Fortune 102:84 S 22 '80
Innovations in bilingual/multicultural curriculum development
    [Hispanic children served by Head Start] S. Arenas. il Child
    Today 9:17–21 My/Je '80
Language issue. Commonweal 107:356–7 Je 20 '80
Meddling in bilingual teaching [Department of Education regula-
    tions] M. Stone. U.S. News 89:84 S 22 '80
Of bilingualism and common ties [Department of Education regu-
    lations] J. J. Kilpatrick. il Nations Bus 68:17 O '80
One nation, one language for all [poll response] Nations Bus
    68:76 D '80
Our language barriers. H. E. Catto, Jr. for Newsweek 96:25 D 1
    '80
Pay for your own tongue [interview by A. McNicoll] S. I. Hayak-
    awa. por Macleans 93:12 Jl 21 '80

Figure **18-7** A *Readers' Guide* Entry

Battle in any language. A. Schardt and others. il Newsweek
96:93–4 D 15 '80

The entry may also give other information, such as an indication that an article is illustrated (il) or includes a map, and so forth. The student will probably need to use the keys both to the abbreviations of periodical names and to the other abbreviations used in entries in order to understand references adequately. These keys can be found at the beginning of each volume, following a brief preface.

Where to start: In using the *Readers' Guide* (or any index of the same sort), the student should start with the year or years most pertinent to his topic. If, for example, he is researching a recent historical event, he should naturally start with the year in which the event occurred and work forward to later volumes that might include references to material on his subject. Other topics, too, may have a historical focal point that will make a convenient starting place for a student's research. A student writing about the safety of the DC-10 airplane, for example, found most of his references in the *Readers' Guide* for 1979, the year in which the plane was grounded by the Federal Aviation Administration. Similarly, a student writing about the career of former football superstar Johan Cruyff relied heavily on articles indexed in the *Readers' Guide* for 1974, the year in which Cruyff joined the Barcelona football team and led it to a world's championship.

For topics in which the most recent information is desirable, students should start with the latest fascicles and work backward through earlier volumes. A student researching recent improvements in computer technology, for example, should probably start with the most recent fascicle available and work back as far as necessary. A student writing about developments in bilingual education would likewise probably begin with the latest available material, working backward through the years to complete his research.

Finding Articles in Newspapers.

The New York Times Index: In addition to the *Readers' Guide*, certain newspaper indexes may be useful. The most widely available is the *New York Times Index* (1913 to the present). This is a subject index to the *New York Times*. Volumes are published yearly, with the previous year covered in quarterlies and the current year in looseleaf monthly fascicles. The *New York Times Index* is especially helpful in that, in addition to citations, it provides *abstracts*—brief summaries—of the articles it cites. For example, if a student looks in the 1984 volume of the index under bilingual education, he finds the following:

BILINGUAL Education. See also
      Education, F 26, Ap 26, Ag 19, D 16.

Looking under the subject heading *Education* for an article published on February 26, 1984, the first of the dates listed in the citation, the student finds the abstract shown in Figure 18-8. The citation following the abstract indicates the length of the article (M for moderate length; S for short; L for long) and precisely where in the paper the article may be found: Section IV, Page 17, Column 1. Note that the date in the citation does not include the year; the student must remember to record it from the volume he is using.

Figure 18-8   A *New York Times Index* Entry

Article by Barbara Mujica, Associate Professor of Spanish at
Georgetown University, contends that it is not role of school
system to teach lessons in languages other than English; says
purpose of bilingual education should be to teach English to
non-English-speaking students so they will be able to function
in regular classes (M), F 26,IV,17:1

Indexes to Other Newspapers: In addition to the *New York Times Index*, indexes for several other major U.S. newspapers may be found at institutional libraries. These may include indexes for the *Christian Science Monitor*, the *Los Angeles Times*, the *Washington Post*, the *Chicago Tribune*, the *Wall Street Journal*, and the *London Times*. Along with the *New York Times*, the first three papers above are indexed in computerized form in the ROM *Catalogue*.

Finding Articles in Scholarly Journals: Although the *Readers' Guide* and *New York Times Index* will be sufficient for certain research projects, some projects will require material from more scholarly periodicals. If this is the case, the student might consult the *International Index to Periodicals* (1907–1965) or its more recent version, the *Social Sciences and Humanities Index* (1965–1974), now divided into the *Social Science Index* and the *Humanities Index* (both 1974 to the present). Finally, for material on a particular subject, the student may wish to consult one of many specialized indexes or abstracting services. Citations indexes include references to sources in which material on particular topics may be found. Abstract indexes include, in addition to source references, brief abstracts of the articles to which they refer. Indexes in subject areas most often pursued by international students include the *Business Index* and the *Business Periodicals Index*, the *Applied Science and Technology Index* and the *General Science Index*, the *Education Index* and the *Current Index to Journals in Education* (CIJF), the *Engineering Index*, and the *Index Medicus*.

Computerized Indexes: Many indexes are available online as databases for computerized searches. In addition, some indexes, such as ERIC (*Resources in Education*), may provide access to source materials themselves through a document delivery service.

Listing and Obtaining Periodicals. As with book titles, the student should list the titles of articles he is interested in looking at on individual 3- by 5-inch file cards. In addition to the title of the article if it is given, the student should note the author's name (last name first) if it is indicated, the name of the journal, and the date on which the article was published, as well as the volume and issue number where relevant. As with books, the call number of the journal in which the article appeared should be indicated in the upper left-hand corner, as in Figure 18-9. Call numbers for periodicals will generally be listed either in a computerized printout or in a special periodicals' card catalogue in your library's periodical room.

Recent issues of periodicals are generally shelved in the periodical room of the library. Back issues are usually available in bound volumes in special stacks or on microfilm. A periodicals librarian can help you locate the issues you are interested in obtaining and get started in using the microfilm reader if necessary.

As with books, if particular periodicals or issues are unavailable at your library, they may be requested through interlibrary loan. The *Union List of Serials in Libraries in the United States and Canada* may be helpful, especially if the needed source is not very recent. For information on library holdings of more recent periodicals, microfiche or computerized listings may be available for the libraries of a particular region.

Occasionally, a student may come across citations to newspapers unavailable through interlibrary loan. If he needs to follow them up, he may use either of two procedures.

Figure 18-9   Tentative Bibliography Card: An Article

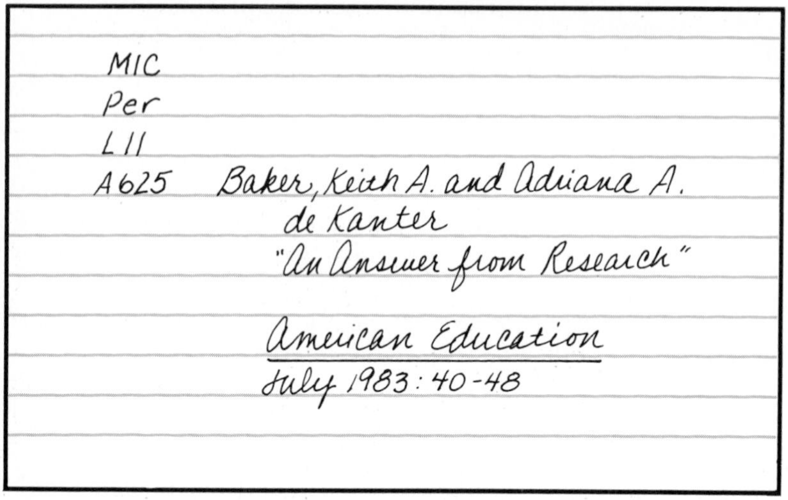

```
     MIC
     Per
     L II
     A625    Baker, Keith A. and Adriana A.
                de Kanter
                "An Answer from Research"

                American Education
                July 1983: 40-48
```

If he is near a major city, there may be a special newspaper library—for example, the New York Public Library Annex in New York City—which retains back issues of many American and some foreign newspapers. Otherwise, he can try requesting offprints from the particular newspaper or the main library located in the city in which the newspaper is published. There may be a fee for such offprints when they are available.

Taking Notes

Some students, especially those who have not done research before, tend to be very inventive in their note-taking technique. When I began my academic career, I did all my note-taking on legal pads, filling each from top to bottom with as many notes on a particular source as I could squeeze in. When it came time to put my research together into a meaningful term paper, I began by cutting my long yellow sheets of notes into strips and blocks of various sizes and laying them in untidy piles according to subtopics. Many lost and skipped-over notes later, I gave up this not very successful process.

Although some successful scholars may take notes in their own eccentric ways (on the backs of envelopes, on bookcovers, in their heads), probably the most dependable method involves using two different sets of index cards: a set of 3- by 5-inch cards for bibliography and a set of 4- by 6-inch or larger cards for notes.

Bibliography Cards. If the student has followed the advice in this chapter for listing titles of books and articles, by the time he begins to take notes, he will already have a stack of partly completed bibliography cards. For each book or article on which he intends to take notes, the student completes the card by adding all relevant publication data in proper bibliographic form (see page 219), as in Figures 18-10 and 18-11. The call number of the book or the journal in which the article is found is noted, generally, in the upper left-hand corner. Below it is the author's name, listed with the last name first for alphabetizing purposes. Title and publication information follow. If the student wishes, he can insert an annotation—a comment on the source's main idea or focus—in brackets at the bottom of the card.

Figure 18-10   Bibliography Card for a Book

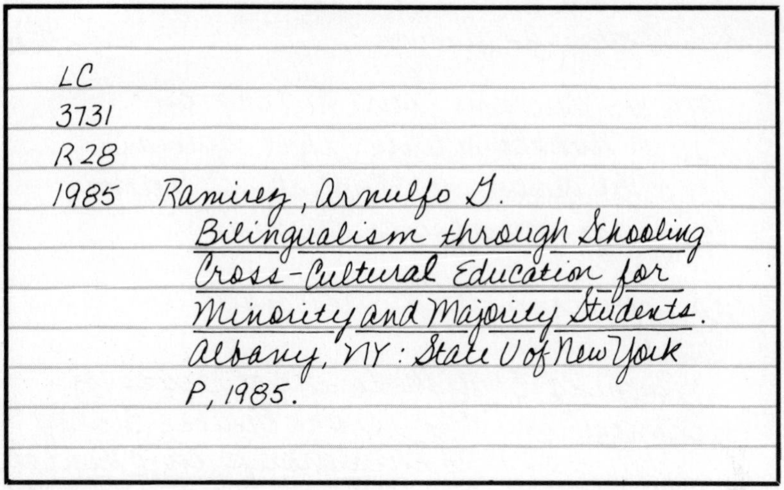

> LC
> 3731
> R 28
> 1985   Ramirez, Arnulfo G.
> Bilingualism through Schooling
> Cross-Cultural Education for
> Minority and Majority Students.
> Albany, NY: State U of New York
> P, 1985.

Figure 18-11   Bibliography Card for an Article

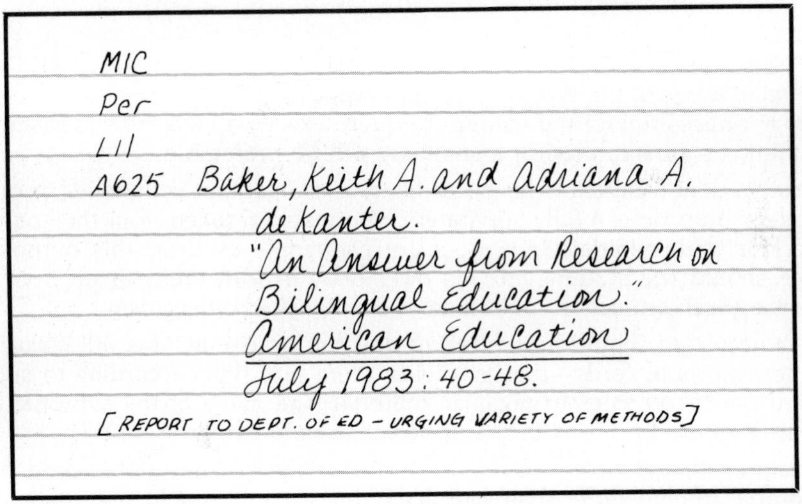

> MIC
> Per
> L11
> A625   Baker, Keith A. and Adriana A.
> de Kanter.
> "An Answer from Research on
> Bilingual Education."
> American Education
> July 1983: 40-48.
> [REPORT TO DEPT. OF ED – URGING VARIETY OF METHODS]

Note Cards: Now the student is ready to begin to take notes. For this, he uses one of his larger file cards. On each note card, in the upper left-hand corner, the student briefly indicates the source of the material. Generally, all that is needed is the author's last name and a page reference. In cases where two authors share the same last name, a first name or initial is necessary. And where two or more books or articles are by the same author, a short title (the first one or two meaningful words) should be added. Following the brief source reference, the student takes his notes. Figure 18-12 illustrates a typical notecard.

Figure 18-12   A Note Card

Baker & de Kanter, "An Answer"   History

  1974 U.S. Supreme Court ruling on
Lau vs Nichols required that special
help be given to "English - deficient
language - minority students."

No specific method prescribed.
Court Stated:
  "Teaching English to the students of
Chinese ancestry is one choice. Giving
instructions to this group in Chinese
is another. There may be others." 40

[AL: SO NO NECESSITY FOR LAU REMEDIES TO LIMIT TO TBE]

Several features of the typical note card bear notice:

1. It is not necessary for the student to quote exactly all material he wishes to use. Sometimes a paraphrase or a summary will be preferable.

2. If the student includes in his notes his own evaluations, comments, or questions, these should be carefully separated from material taken from the source itself. Brackets and/or initials [A.L: . . .] are commonly used for this purpose. In no case should the student mix his own ideas in with ideas taken from another source. (Such a practice could lead to unintentional plagiarism.)

3. Each note card should be limited to one subtopic only. This will make it easier to sort out note cards—that is, divide them into piles according to subtopic—when the time comes to organize material. The name of the subtopic the card deals with can be noted in the upper right-hand corner.

4. No notes should be taken on the backs of cards. When notes on a particular subtopic require more than one card, the student should use a second card, indicating that it is a continuation of a previous card, as here:

    Baker & de Kanter, "An Answer" cont'd.

    Additional cards may be stapled to the first card, if desired.

5. Page numbers should be indicated for all material used. There is no definite rule on where to indicate them; on the card in Figure 18-12, the page number is indicated to the far right, after all the material found on that page. When a quotation runs over more than one page of a source, the student should indicate in his notes where the first page ends and the next begins, as in Figure 18-13.

***Figure* 18-13**   Indicating a Page Break for a Quotation

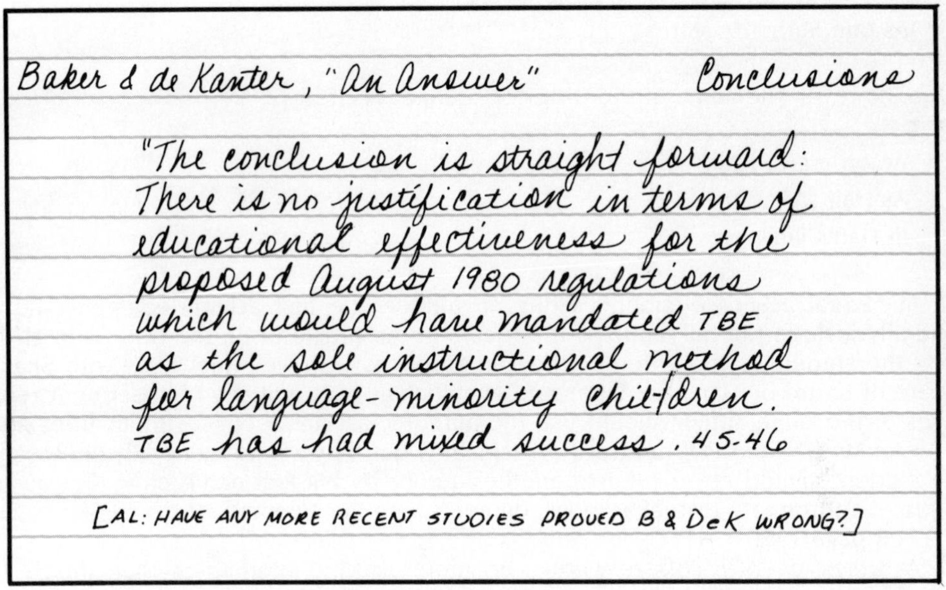

Baker & de Kanter, "An Answer"   Conclusions

"The conclusion is straight forward:
There is no justification in terms of
educational effectiveness for the
proposed August 1980 regulations
which would have mandated TBE
as the sole instructional method
for language-minority children.
TBE has had mixed success. 45-46

[AL: HAVE ANY MORE RECENT STUDIES PROVED B & DeK WRONG?]

This way, if in writing his paper the student uses only a part of the quotation, he will know precisely on what page the quoted material appeared.

Documentation

Having gathered his material and organized his note cards according to a well-developed outline, the student turns to writing up his research. In writing research papers, in addition to following all the other principles of good essay writing, the student needs to know how to *document* his material—that is, how to acknowledge explicitly the sources he uses in writing his essay.

Documentation is important for three reasons. First, documentation provides support for a writer's essay by demonstrating that material used in the essay derives from respected outside authorities. Second, documentation makes it possible for readers interested in a particular idea or position to investigate it further by examining the cited source or sources. And finally, documentation prevents the writer from being accused of *plagiarism*—of stealing another writer's words or ideas—by giving credit to the sources the writer has used in composing his essay.

Informal Documentation

In some kinds of writing using outside sources, it is sufficient for the writer to document informally, as is the practice in popular magazine articles and newspaper editorials and columns. In *informal documentation*, the writer uses only a *textual acknowledgment*, as mentioned in Chapter 17, to indicate that he is borrowing an idea, fact, or quotation from another source. Sometimes, references identify sources vaguely:

> According to experts, . . .
>
> In the opinion of government sources, . . .
>
> As one authority states, . . .

Often, however, the name of the writer or speaker is cited:

> According to Hall, . . .
>
> As Hall writes, . . .
>
> In Hall's view, . . .

In textual acknowledgments citing an author, the first acknowledgment should generally include the full name as it appears in the article or on the title page of the book the student is citing from. (When an author is very well known, as with Shakespeare or Sartre or Marx, the last name is sufficient even initially.) Subsequent references to the same author should use the author's last name only, without titles such as *Mr.* or *Ms.* (*Dr.* and *Prof.* are used occasionally, but they are not generally necessary). The student should never refer to another author by his first name only. (For an example of appropriate textual acknowledgments, see the summary of "Velva, North Dakota" on page 195).

At times, even in college writing, no more specific information than this is required. Students writing in-class exams, for example, may be expected to refer in their answers to the sources they have used, giving an author's last name or a short title only (for example, "As Sevareid writes . . ."; "In 'Velva, North Dakota' . . .") but not expected to give exact page references, dates, or other information about the sources.

Formal Documentation

Textual references are also used in the research paper. However, the research paper, like its cousins, the master's thesis and doctoral dissertation, demands more formal documentation—documentation which adds to textual references more precise information about the sources used.

The information required and the format for presenting it may vary from discipline to discipline, and even from instructor to instructor. Here, we follow the guidelines indicated by the MLA *Handbook for Writers of Research Papers*, 2nd ed. (New York: MLA, 1984), the standard *style sheet* for courses in the humanities. Other disciplines, however, use other style sheets. For courses in the social and physical sciences, for example, the guidelines commonly followed are those set forth in the *Chicago Manual of Style*, 13th ed. (Chicago: University of Chicago Press, 1982). Some instructors may ask students to follow the format required by the editorial staff of a particular journal or group of journals. The student will have to adhere to the specific requirements of his course instructor in writing papers for various courses. If he is in doubt about the format to use on a specific paper, he should ask his instructor for clarification.

Although the MLA guidelines indicated below might not conform to those a particular student will need to follow in all or even most of his college research papers, practice working with one set of guidelines should make it easier to follow the different guidelines used in other courses.

List of Works Cited. Most of the information required in formal documentation is generally included in a list headed *Works Cited* (or sometimes, *Bibliography*, if the list includes books and articles only). For the most part, the student can find all the information he must include on the list of works cited on the *title and copyright pages of books*, and along with other editorial information on the *title page of journals*.

Required Information. The information to be included is indicated below in the order in which it should appear in each entry (items in parentheses are required only for sources for which they are relevant).

A. For a book:

1. Author's name exactly as indicated on title page but with last name first (for purposes of alphabetizing) followed by a comma:

Ramirez, Arnulfo G.

Corporate authors (commissions, councils, and so on) are cited by their title:

United States Commission on Human Rights. A *Better Chance to Learn* . . .

(If no author is indicated, begin with the title.)

(2. Title of part of book—for instance, introduction, chapter title, essay title)
3. Full title of book exactly as indicated on title page, underlined and capitalized correctly
(4. Name of editor and/or translator)
(5. Edition used)
(6. Number of volumes)
(7. Name of series)
8. Place of publication, name of publisher, and date of publication (all of which may incorporate standard abbreviations)
(9. Page numbers, if only a part of a book is cited)

B. For a journal article:

1. Author's name exactly as indicated at beginning or end of article but with last name first, as above
2. Full title of the article (including *a, an* or *the*), capitalized correctly and in quotation marks
3. Name of the periodical as it appears on the title page (but excluding *a, an,* or *the*), underlined and capitalized correctly
(4. Series number or name)
(5. Volume number)
6. Date of publication, including year only for entries with volume numbers; month and year for monthlies; day, month, and year for dailies and weeklies, as in the examples below:

Harvard Education Review 47 (1977) (journal with volume numbers)
American Education July 1983 (monthly journal)
Time 8 Sept. 1980 (weekly journal)

7. Page numbers for the entire article, indicating inclusive numbers appropriately for articles printed on consecutive pages. For articles not printed on consecutive pages, indicate the first page and add a plus sign: 32–42+

Format The material in the list of works cited must be presented according to a standard format specifying how to order, punctuate, and space the items included in each entry. The basic MLA format is diagramed below:

Format for a book

Last Name, First Name. *Title*. Place: Publisher, year.

Format for an article

Last Name, First Name. "Title of Article." *Periodical* Month year: page numbers.

The student should note several features of the above diagrams. The first line of each entry begins at the left margin. Subsequent lines are indented five spaces. The author's name, printed last name first in alphabetical order, is followed by a period and two spaces. The title, appropriately underlined or in quotation marks (see pp. 280, 302), is similarly followed by a period and two spaces.

Publication information follows. For a book, the place of publication is followed by a colon and one space. Then comes the name of the publisher (standard short forms, indicated in the MLA *Handbook*, are acceptable), followed by a comma and one space, and the year in which the book was published. For an article, the name of the periodical (underlined) is followed by the date of publication. This is followed by a colon and one space, introducing the numbers of the pages on which the article is printed. The examples below show a book and an article listed according to this format:

A book

Ramirez, Arnulfo G. *Bilingualism Through Schooling: Cross-Cultural Education for Minority and Majority Students*. Albany: State U of New York P, 1985.

An article

Bethell, Tom. "Against Bilingual Education." *Harper's* Feb. 1979: 30–33.

Variations. There are variations on this format for indicating multiple or anonymous authors, volume numbers, editions, and so on, and for acknowledging such diverse sources as computer software, speeches, lectures, films, television programs, legal references, and dissertations. Naturally, the guidelines here cannot cover all the situations a student writer may encounter in documentation. For specific guidelines on how to handle most variations, the student will need to consult the MLA *Handbook*. A few of the most common variations, however, are illustrated below:

An article with a multiple author

Baker, K., and A. A. de Kanter. "An Answer from Research on Bilingual Education." *American Education* July 1983: 40–48.

An anonymous book or article

"Battle over Bilingualism." *Time* 8 Sept. 1980: 64–65.
Forum. Rosslyn, Virginia. National Clearinghouse for Bilingual Education, 1982.

Two or more books or articles by the same person

Solórzano, Lucia. "A Second Look at Bilingual Education." U.S. *News and World Report* 11 June 1984: 78.
———. "Educating the Melting Pot." U.S. *News and World Report* 31 March 1986: 20–21.

A book that contains an edition number

Lewis, E. Glyn. *Bilingualism and Bilingual Education*: A *Comparative Study*. 2nd ed. Albuquerque: U of New Mexico P, 1980.

A volume in a series

Cordasco, Francesco. *Bilingual Education in American Schools*: A *Guide to Information Sources*. Education Information Guide Series 3. Detroit: Gale Research, 1979.

A book with more than one volume

Andersson, Theodore, and Mildred Boyer. *Bilingual Schooling in the United States*: *History, Rationale, Implications, and Planning*. 2 vols. Austin: Southwest Educational Development Laboratory, 1970.

A reprinted book

Andersson, Theodore, and Mildred Boyer. *Bilingual Schooling in the United States*: *History, Rationale, Implications, and Planning*. 2 vols. 1970. Detroit: Blaine Ethridge Books, 1976.

A preface, introduction, foreword, or afterword

Cordasco, Francesco. New Foreward. *Bilingual Schooling in the United States*: *History, Rationale, Implications, and Planning* by Theodore Andersson and Mildred Boyer. Austin: Southwest Educational Development Laboratory, 1970. iii–vi.

An article in an anthology

Reisner, Elizabeth R. "The Availability of Bilingual-Education Teachers." *Bilingual Education*: A *Reappraisal of Federal Policy*, Ed. Keith A. Baker and Adriana A. de Kanter. Lexington: Lexington Books–Heath, 1983. 175–203.

An article in a reference work (omit place and publisher if the work is a standard one, and omit volume and page numbers if the entries are arranged alphabetically)

"Bilingual Education." *Academic American Encyclopedia*. Danbury: Grolier, 1986.

An article in a periodical published less frequently than once a month (include volume only for periodicals paginated continuously throughout a year, and include volume and issue for periodicals in which issues are paged individually)

> Teitelbaum, Herbert, and Richard J. Heiler. "Bilingual Education: The Legal Mandate." *Harvard Educational Review* 47 (1977): 138–70.

An article in a newspaper in which an edition is specified

> "Report Urges Aid for Bilingual Education." *New York Times* 22 June 1980, late city ed., sec. 1:39.

An editorial or letter

> "Bilingual Danger." Editorial. *New York Times* 22 Nov. 1976, sec. 1:24.
> Parssinen, Jon. Letter. *Chronicle of Higher Education* 21 May 1979: 18.

Material from an information service

> Paulston, Christina Bratt. *Recent Developments in Research on Bilingual Education in the United States*. Bilingual Education Paper Series 6.2. Los Angeles: California State U, 1984. ERIC ED 258 458.

An example of an actual list of works cited is appended to the research paper in Chapter 10.

Source citations. The list of works cited is the beginning of documentation. However, it gives only a general indication of the works a student uses in putting together a research paper. Documentation requires more. It requires that the student indicate for each particular borrowing of another writer's words or ideas the precise source, including page number, of the original. These indications are called *citations*.

Parenthetical documentation: Formerly, citations generally took the form of footnotes or endnotes, and some instructors may still ask that this format be used for writing a particular paper. Nowadays, however, *parenthetical documentation* is standard in research papers. In parenthetical documentation, the citation of the source of a particular point or quotation is inserted directly into the text, within parentheses, as in the following example:

> The language-minority child confronting a new culture at school "inevitably encounters a culture shock" (Andersson and Boyer 43).

As in the above example, in papers including a list of works cited, generally all that is needed to acknowledge a particular point or quotation is the last name of the author of the original source and the page number on which the particular information can be found. The reader can find more complete information about the source by consulting the list of works cited. Indeed, if the name of the author of a source appears in the text itself, the page numbers alone are sufficient documentation; there is no reason to repeat the author's name:

> According to Baker and de Kanter, "TBE has had mixed success" (46).

Of course, if two or more books or articles on the list of works cited are by the same author, more information is needed in either the textual or the parenthetical acknowledgment. Generally, a shortened version of the title of the particular work is given in addition to the author's last name:

> The results of a recent study show that "TBE has had mixed success" (Baker and de Kanter, "An Answer" 46).

And if a book or article is anonymous, a shortened version of the title is substituted for the author's name:

> Another argument is that "grandfather often never really learned English in the melting-pot school" ("Battle" 65).

Finally, to acknowledge more than one source for a particular idea, include the multiple references in parentheses, separated by semicolons:

> It is important to remember that no specific program was prescribed (Baker and de Kanter 40; Birman and Ginsburg xi).

Alternative Formats: In addition, the MLA *Handbook* briefly explains certain alternative formats such as the *author-date system* used in the social and physical sciences, the *number system, footnotes and endnotes,* and *documentation notes* used in papers lacking a list of works cited (for an example, see Chapter 2, Exercise IB). For the purposes of this text, however, the student need be familiar only with the format combining a list of works cited with parenthetical citations.

Plagiarism

Before looking at an actual research paper, we need to say a word—a dirty word—PLAGIARISM. Plagiarism is *stealing.* It is the stealing of the words or ideas of another writer and representing them as one's own.

Sometimes plagiarism is intentional: a student who lacks confidence in his own writing or who has not allowed himself adequate time to do his own work copies an essay out of a book or from a friend and represents it as his own. Of course, this is wrong. And the students who do it know it is wrong.

But sometimes plagiarism is unintentional. The student fails to acknowledge that an idea derives from another source, or he acknowledges the source but fails to use quotation punctuation when he borrows the words of the source. Even though the student may not be aware of his error, this, too, is plagiarism. And the punishment for *either* kind of plagiarism—unintentional as well as intentional—may be severe, ranging from failure on a particular paper, to failure in the course for which it was written, to expulsion from a program or institution. Whether a student steals deliberately or by accident, plagiarism is a crime.

Unintentional plagiarism happens in a variety of ways, all of them preventable. The student writer should take note of the following cautions:

1. In taking notes on outside sources, the student should be careful to use quotation punctuation whenever he borrows a passage, sentence, phrase, or apt

(precisely appropriate) word from another writer. This is especially important for the student whose native language is not English and who may have difficulty finding his own words to express another writer's ideas. As has already been stated, even in note-taking, it is a good idea for the student to use his own words as much as possible; but when he cannot find another way to express the ideas of his source, he *must* indicate that he is borrowing the words as well as the ideas of that source through quotation punctuation (see pages 274–79).

2. In taking notes on outside sources, the student writer should be careful to set off his own ideas with brackets and/or initials (see page 216). In this way, the student will know that all other ideas reflected in his notes are the ideas of other writers and must be acknowledged as such.

3. In writing up his research, the student should take care
   a. to transfer quoted material from his notes to his essay *as quotations*, with quotation punctuation for every passage, sentence, phrase, or apt word borrowed exactly from the original
   b. to acknowledge not only exact borrowings of another writer's words, but also borrowings of another writer's ideas, even when they are expressed in the student's own words. (For each idea borrowed from another source, the student must indicate the borrowing with a textual or parenthetical note or with some other form of formal documentation.)

Common Knowledge

Of course, certain ideas are what we call *common knowledge*. That Columbus discovered the New World, that the Soviet Union is a communist state, that Saudi Arabia is rich in oil, that computers are very important in modern industry: all these are *facts* that are widely known and belong not to any one writer, but to us all. Such facts need no documentation. But if a student gives the current cost per barrel or barrel per day output of Saudi oil, or explains the difference between Soviet, Chinese, and classic communism, or if he suggests that Columbus did *not* discover the New World, he will probably need to document the sources for his facts or ideas. What is considered common knowledge and what needs documentation will change somewhat as a student advances in his particular field and addresses a more and more specialized audience. However, where there is any doubt about whether or not a particular fact or idea needs documentation, it is better for the student to document than to run the risk of plagiarism.

Summary and Paraphrase versus Plagiarism

One of the great difficulties for the foreign student in writing up research is using his own words to express another author's ideas. We have already discussed this problem in relation to the summary. To reiterate, in a summary the student should *use his own words as much as possible*. If he must borrow a sentence, phrase, or apt word, he must use quotation punctuation to indicate the borrowing.

Similarly, in research papers, although quotations are useful, by and large the writing should be the student's own. Using the techniques of summarizing and *paraphrasing*—summarizing sentence by sentence—the student should try to put the ideas he finds from outside sources into his own words, acknowledging the sources as indicated above. Where he does use the exact words of his sources, he must indicate this with quotation punctuation.

Let us look at a passage with which we are familiar—the first paragraph of Sevareid's "Velva, North Dakota"—and see how it might be summarized or paraphrased to avoid plagiarism, and also how plagiarism might occur. We will assume that each version of the passage below has been incorporated into a different research paper. We will also assume that each paper includes a list of works cited giving complete bibliographic information for Sevareid's essay as indicated below the original passage.

Original Passage

My home town has changed in these thirty years of the American story. It is changing now, will go on changing as America changes. Its biography, I suspect, would read much the same as that of all other home towns. Depression and war and prosperity have all left their marks; modern science, modern tastes, manners, philosophies, fears and ambitions have touched my town as indelibly as they have touched New York or Panama City.

(From Eric Sevareid. "Velva, North Dakota," in *This Is Eric Sevareid*. New York: McGraw-Hill, 1964. 281.)

Version A

According to Eric Sevareid, in recent years his hometown has altered much as the rest of America—and, indeed, the world—as it has been "touched" by modern events and phenomena (281).

In this *summary* of the original paragraph, the writer avoids plagiarism in several ways. First, for the most part he uses his own words to express Sevareid's ideas. He puts in quotation marks the one apt word he borrows—"touched." Finally, by combining the textual reference to Sevareid and the parenthetical page reference with more complete publication information in a list of works cited, he provides adequate documentation for the borrowed ideas.

Version B

Velva, North Dakota has changed in recent times, is still changing, and will continue to change as all of America is changing. Recent events and phenomena—"depression and war and prosperity"—as well as modern trends in attitude and technology have affected Velva as permanently as they have affected the big cities of the United States and elsewhere (Sevareid 281).

This *paraphrase* follows the original paragraph more closely, but the writer still avoids plagiarism by using his own words for the most part, by quoting the borrowed phrase, "depression and war and prosperity," and by acknowledging his source through parenthetical documentation combined with a list of works cited.

Version C

The American town has changed in recent years. Modern wars, fluctuations in the economy, and modern technology and attitudes have altered each American town as permanently as they have altered New York and cities outside the United States.

This is *plagiarized*. Despite substantial changes to the language and despite the writer's having included Sevareid's essay in his list of works cited, the writer's failure to acknowledge specifically that this idea was borrowed from Sevareid's essay constitutes plagiarism.

Version D

Velva, North Dakota, has changed in these thirty years of American history. It is still changing and will continue to change as America changes. Its story would read like those of other towns. Depression, war, and prosperity, modern science, tastes, manners, philosophies, fears and ambitions have left the same indelible "marks" on Velva that they have on New York or Panama City (Sevareid 281).

This is also *plagiarized*. Here, the writer acknowledges the borrowed idea, but fails to indicate his substantial borrowing of Sevareid's language. Among the phrases that the writer would have to rewrite in his own words or put in quotation marks are "has changed in these thirty years," "as America changes," "reads," "depression, war, and prosperity, modern science, tastes, manners, philosophies, fears and ambitions," and "indelible."

Version E

According to Eric Sevareid, his hometown has altered in these thirty years of American history. Its story reads like the stories of other towns in America and beyond. Such phenomena as depression, war, and prosperity, modern technology, beliefs, and fears have touched his hometown as they have New York or Panama City (281).

This, too, is plagiarized. Although the writer acknowledges the borrowed idea and alters some of Sevareid's language, there are still too many echoes of the original passage. The phrase "in these thirty years," as well as the apt words "reads" and "touched" should be rewritten or put in quotation marks. (Note that "reads" would have to be changed to "would read" if the writer chose to quote rather than to rewrite.)

Overdocumentation

Not everything in a research paper needs to be documented. Papers in which every sentence or half-sentence is interrupted by a parenthetical citation are awkward to read, as well as tedious to write. To avoid overdocumentation, the student writer can follow these two principles:

- Avoid merely stringing together either quotations or ideas borrowed from other writers. Integrate material from outside sources into your research paper along with (yet distinguished from) your own explanation, analyses, assessments, applications, and arguments (where appropriate). In this way, you will avoid a "cut-and-paste" effect, the appearance that you created your paper by cutting up the work of others and pasting it together again in a different order.

- Where possible, use textual references to indicate that several sentences or even paragraphs derive from a single source. In this way, one parenthetical citation at the end of the passage can take the place of multiple citations of the same source. Again, if there is any doubt that omitting a citation might mislead the reader into thinking borrowed material is your own, the citation should be included.

Using Foreign Language Sources

Occasionally, a foreign student may wish to use sources in languages other than English in writing a research paper. If her instructor permits this, the student should clarify with him how such material should be handled. The most common procedure is to include exact quotations in the original language along with accurate English translations. In advanced work in which knowledge of a particular second language is assumed (for example, German for those specializing in medicine, or French for those specializing in fine art) a translation may not be considered necessary. However, the student should check with her instructor before omitting translations.

Summary

Writing research papers requires two special skills: gathering information and documenting sources. Students must learn to use their campus library to find books and articles on the topic they choose to write about. References to books can be found in the library card catalogue or an online catalogue, in bibliographies, and in references in other books or articles. Periodicals references can be found in various periodicals indexes.

Research papers require formal documentation. Currently, one standard documentation format combines brief parenthetical references with full publication information included in a list of works cited. Specific guidelines must be followed regarding the order of information, punctuation, and spelling in individual entries.

The student must take special care not to plagiarize. He or she must cite the source of any borrowed sentence, phrase, apt word, or idea from another source.

Exercises

For Consideration

Exercise 1.   Fill in the following for each item below.

   a. A card catalogue entry (Figure 18-14):

Figure 18-14   Exercise la

```
                    Abortion and social justice.

HQ       Hilgers, Thomas W
767.5         Abortion and social justice.
U5            Edited by Thomas W. Hilgers and Dennis J. Horan.
H54           New York, Sheed & Ward [c1972]
              xxv, 328 p. illus. 22 cm.

              Includes bibliographical references.

              1. Abortion—United States—Addresses, essays,
         lectures. 2. Abortion, Therapeutic—Addresses, es-
         says, lectures. I. Horan, Dennis J., joint au-
         thor. II. Title.
      HQ767.5.U5H54               301
                     NUAL          72-6690
         ISBN  0-8362-0541-3  A5-901095  A  720085  MARC
```

title:

edition:

author:

subject:

call no.:

subjects under which the book is cross listed:

b. A *Reader's Guide* entry (Figure 18-15)

Figure 18-15   Exercise lb

Abortion in America: ABC's of a raging battle. T. Gest. il *U S News World Rep* 94:47–9 Ja 24 '83

title:

author:

date:

periodical:

value:

pages:

c. Entries from the *New York Times Index* for 1985:

dates on which articles can be found on the education of foreign students (Figure 18-16):

Figure 18-16   Exercise 1c, Topic

FOREIGN Students. See also Basketball, Ja 20. Colls, Ap 5, Je 16, Ag 18,25, D 12,27. Data Processing, Ag 17,24. Educ, My 26, Je 16. English Language, Mr 10. Med, O 10, N 11

Entry for a specific date (Figure 18-17):

Figure 18-17 Exercise 1c, Specific Date

EDUCATION and Schools-Cont
education, including instruction of Latin (Our Towns column)
(M), Je 16,I,38:3
  Article on efforts to open educational opportunities for 'financially deserving and academically promising students' from developing countries to study in US; photo (M), Je 16,IV,22:3

topic:

author:

date:

length:

section:

page:

column:

Exercise 2. Figure 18-18 is an excerpt from the *Library of Congress Subject Headings*. Using the information in the excerpt, answer the following:

Figure 18-18 Exercise 2

Abortion *(Indirect)   Birth control, HQ767-767.7; Medical jurisprudence, RA1067; Obstetrical operations, RG734; Obstetrics, RG648)*
  sa Abortifacients
      Menstrual regulation
  x   Feticide
      Pregnancy termination
      Termination of pregnancy
  xx Birth control
      Fetal death
      Infanticide
      Obstetrics
      Pregnancy, Unwanted
  —Complications and sequelae
  —Government policy *(Indirect)*
  ——Citizen participation
        sa Pro-choice movement
            Pro-life movement
  —Law and legislation   *(Indirect)*
        xx Offenses against the person
            Sex and law
  —Moral and ethical aspects   *(HQ767.3)*
        sa Pro-choice movement
            Pro-life movement
  —Religious aspects
        sa Fetal propitiatory rites
            Pro-choice movement
            Pro-life movement
  ——Baptists, [Catholic Church, etc.]
  ——Buddhism, [Christianity, etc.]
Abortion, Septic
    x   Septic abortion
    xx Infection
        Pregnancy, Complications of
Abortion, Spontaneous
    See Miscarriage

    a. Under which of these subject headings is material filed in the card cata-
       logue?

       1) Abortion

       2) Termination of pregnancy

       3) Infanticide

       4) Abortion—religious aspects

       5) Pro-choice movement

       6) Abortion, Septic

       7) Pregnancy, Complications of

       8) Abortion, Spontaneous

    b. If a student wants to find material on *pregnancy termination*, under what card
       catalogue subject headings might he or she look?

    c. If a student wants to find the appropriate subject headings for material on
       spontaneous abortion, under what subject heading in *Library of Congress Subject*
       Headings should he or she look?

Exercise 3.   The student passages below are from research papers utilizing material from the essay "Velva, North Dakota." Assume that each passage is accompanied
by a list of works cited including the following entry:

    Eric Sevareid, "Velva, North Dakota," in *This Is Eric Sevareid.* New York: McGraw-
       Hill, 1964. 281–83.

Are the passages adequately documented? Have the students avoided plagiarism?
Why or why not?

A.   Modern transportation and communications devices such as telephones, electronic media, cars, and highways have brought the separate
entities of the United States closer to one another, changing small towns
across America profoundly.

B.   According to Eric, the changes in distance and time have worked the
deepest changes in the town of Velva, North Dakota, as such modern phenomena as the telephone, cars, electronic media, and smooth highways have
consolidated the entities of the United States (283).

C.   Modern technology is responsible for the changes in Velva, North Dakota, and other small towns. According to Sevareid, Velva's most profound
changes are a result of the alterations in "distance and time" brought about
by such technological phenomena as the telephone, electronic media devices, the car, and the "smooth" highway, all of which are helping to bring
together the separate "entities" of the United States (283).

For Composition

Exercise 4.   Write one or two paragraphs summarizing the ideas expressed in the
selection "Alienation and Affection" at the end of Chapter 17. Treat the excerpt as
you would treat sources in a research paper combining parenthetical documentation
with a list of works cited. Be sure to include at least

a. one textual acknowledgment,

b. one parenthetical acknowledgment,

c. one quotation.

Exercise 5.   Using your college library's card catalogue and the *Readers' Guide* only, assemble a working bibliography on three- by five-inch index cards on one of the following topics:

a. Foreign student enrollments at American colleges and universities since 1970

b. The Iranian student experience in U.S. colleges and universities, 1976–1981

c. The Iranian hostage crisis of 1979–1981

d. Foreign language study in U.S. public secondary schools, 1975 to the present

e. Job opportunities in a field of your choice

f. Criticism of children's television programming in the U.S.

g. Bilingual education in the U.S.

h. A particular problem or event in your native country

Exercise 6.   Choose one of the topics above as the subject of a research paper. Then prepare a research paper on it, following the steps listed below. (Be sure to save all your work to show your instructor.)

a. Make a working bibliography, using all library resources applicable to your topic (card catalogue, *Readers' Guide*, *New York Times Index*, specialized indexes and bibliographies).

b. Take notes on your topic from the sources you have gathered.

c. Formulate your thesis (in one sentence).

d. Write a working outline for your paper.

e. Organize your notes (according to subsections of your outline).

f. Write your first draft, documenting thoroughly.

g. Revise your paper.

Chapter 19

A Sample Research Paper

The sample essay below represents an adequate research paper for a class in English composition. It is not, by any means, the final word on the controversial issue it discusses. Rather, it is one student's view on one issue of bilingual education. The student's research is not exhaustive; for the most part, her sources are general and popular rather than scholarly (although she has made some attempt to include scholarly materials among the works she cites). Her reasoning, while generally adequate, is not flawless. The purpose of this sample is not to advance any position in the ongoing bilingual controversy, but rather to show the form and content of a typical, adequate college paper.

Materials related to the writing of this paper are included in several other chapters of the text. The thesis statement and outline on which the paper was based can be found in the chapter on planning the essay (page 103). Sample bibliography and note cards used in the preparation of the essay are reproduced in Chapter 18.

Adam Lowman

Professor Brown

ESL 101

November 5, 1986

Bilingual Education: One Method Among Many

Since its introduction into U.S. classrooms in
the mid–1970s, transitional bilingual education has
been the main method used to teach English–deficient
language–minority (EDLM) students––students whose
primary language is not English and whose command of
English is not adequate to understand instruction in
that language. In transitional bilingual education
(TBE) students are taught in their primary language,
with instruction in the second language gradually
introduced as the student gains proficiency in it.

There is no U.S. law requiring schools to use
this method (Baker and de Kanter, ''Federal Policy''
33). A 1980 Carter administration proposal to
mandate TBE as the only valid teaching method for
EDLM students was withdrawn in 1981 (Birman and
Ginsburg xiv)–perhaps significantly, soon after the
beginning of Ronald Reagan's first term of office.
However, despite this, TBE has remained ''virtually
the only allowable instructional method to be used

with language—minority children'' (Baker and de
Kanter, ''Federal Policy'' 33). Moreover, many TBE
supporters continue to urge legislation to insure
that it be the only method permitted in U.S.
classrooms.

In fall of 1984 Reagan administration Education
Secretary William Bennett issued a statement
charging that ''after $1.7 billion of federal
funding [for bilingual education], we have no
evidence that the children whom we sought to help
. . . have benefited'' (qtd. in Solórzano,
''Educating'' 20). The following year Bennett asked
that Congress apportion a greater percentage of
bilingual expenditures for alternative methods (qtd.
in ''The Language'' A30). He urged that ''greater
flexibility'' be allowed schools in deciding how
they teach English—deficient students (qtd. in
''Studies'' 767). This paper will examine the debate
over TBE and its alternatives to see whether there
is justification, in terms of its effectiveness in
promoting English proficiency and academic
achievement, for asserting TBE as the sole method to
be used in teaching language—minority youngsters. As
I hope to show, at least at present, such
justification seems to be lacking.

In examining the debate, it is necessary first
to eliminate from it many arguments that have little
to do with how well children learn. These arguments
are expounded by critics on both sides of the
bilingual issue.

Many who oppose bilingual education claim that
satisfactory implementation of the program is not
possible. Critics cite the large—3.6 million by some
accounts—and increasing number of eligible
participants (Schardt 93). Many note that the number
of qualified bilingual teachers falls short of the
need for them—perhaps by as many as 13,000
nationwide (Birman and Ginsburg xvii). Costs, as
specified earlier, are cited as a further constraint
on effectiveness (Birman and Ginsburg xvii). But
assessing the feasibility of a program is secondary
to assessing its worth. If bilingual education is
not worthwhile, the question of feasibility is
insignificant. If the program is worthy, the means
for implementing it should be fostered to whatever
extent possible.

More extreme opponents claim that bilingual
education threatens to divide the nation. James J.
Kilpatrick predicts possibly ''calamitous
consequences'' to national unity, citing the

''melancholy experience'' of Canada and Belgium to support his fears (17) and Tom Bethell goes so far as to suggest that the American government must be ''afflicted with a death wish'' for it to encourage the program (30). These critics, however, are generally responding not to transitional bilingual education such as the Lau Remedies prescribe, but to <u>maintenance</u> bilingual programs that have in some cases been substituted for them—in which students continue to be taught in their native language even after learning English (Schardt 94; Stone 92).

The fear that bilingual education is an attack on the melting-pot, in which ethnic identities become submerged to some degree in order for minority individuals to achieve assimilation in American society (Nicholas 85), is fueled by those who justify bilingual education not for its effectiveness in helping children learn, but as a tool for fostering cultural diversity by preserving the native languages and cultures of various groups of ethnic Americans (Ramírez 19; Andersson A26; Andersson and Boyer 44-45; Schon 191). One critic even seems to favor bilingual education as a way of making up for past prejudice against minority groups such as Mexican-Americans (McWilliams 264).

Assessing the educational effectiveness of bilingual education is made complicated and fuzzy because bilingual education is perceived as a political and cultural issue, not just as an educational one (Schardt 93). When lawyer and Princeton professor Sanford Levinson actually proposes in the <u>Nation</u> that, in light of the use of Spanish language in media and elsewhere, it is ''open to question whether it is legitimate to expect all American citizens to master English'' (263), some opponents are tempted to reject bilingual education out of hand.

However, an extreme view like this should not be allowed to cloud the central issue. U.S. students should be given the greatest possible opportunity to learn English as well as other subject matter. As Neil Postman writes in answer to Levinson:

> There is no ''legitimate question'' about whether Spanish children need to know English. They need to know English so they can make some money, go to college, go to law school, and write articles for the <u>Nation</u>, just like Levinson, the lawyer from Princeton. The only question is how best to achieve this. Some say

through bilingual classes. Some say by immersing
the children in all-English classes. (266)

Though some Spanish-language facilities exist
in America, Hispanics, like others, need English in
order to achieve full economic and political
opportunity (Mujica 9). Although a few voices may
dissent, bilingual education opponents and
supporters alike recognize the need of those living
in the United States to learn English (see, for
example, Katcher 187; and Schon 190). As bilingual
supporter Angelo González writes: ''One needs to
learn English so as to be able to participate in an
English-speaking society'' (62).

The need to learn other subject matter is also
clear. Journalist Lucia Solórzano, for example,
notes Hispanic leaders' emphasis on insuring that
''language-deficient students do not stumble in
other subjects while studying English'' (''Educating''
20). In a report for the U.S. Department of
Education, bilingual program analysts Keith A. Baker
and Adriana A. de Kanter state that the two
questions that must be asked of any program used to
teach language-minority students are whether or not
the program promotes English proficiency and whether

it leads ''to better performance in nonlanguage
subject areas'' (''An Answer'' 41). The question,
then, is whether or not any particular program best
satisfies the students' need to learn English
efficiently without sacrificing other academic
goals.

Many have a ready answer to this question. But
most of the answers are based on vague impressions.
An editorial question in the December 1980 issue of
Nation's Business brought many responses from
readers, most of them urging that bilingual
education be given less emphasis. But their
arguments are typical of many advanced in the
bilingual debate in that none of them offers any
evidence to show that bilingual education helps or
hinders students' academic performance (''One Nation''
76).

Both bilingual opponents and supporters often
hark back to a previous era to support their stand
on the issue. Bilingual opponents frequently
reminisce about the ''good old days,'' when the
early immigrants were spurred to learn by the
''unifying'' factor of a common language (Nicholas
85). A typical comment is voiced by bilingual
opponent Sylvia Katcher: ''It is time for the 'old'

approach of English immersion that served favorably
for the 'old immigrant' to be reinstated'' (187).
But although some immigrants clearly achieved
success under the older system (Keefe A27), we do
not know how many learned English under the old
submersion method. As one writer puts it:
''Grandfather often never really learned English in
the melting-pot school'' (''Battle'' 65). We do not
know either how many immigrants might have been held
back from learning other subjects because of
submersion. And in regard to those who did succeed,
the conditions that fostered success may no longer
exist (''Battle'' 65). Similarly, support for
bilingual education may be founded in part on
recollections of the old days that are no longer
applicable. Richard Rodríguez writes that the debate
among many Hispanics ''comes down to [the] memory of
going to that grammar school where students were
slapped for speaking Spanish'' (63).

Even those who attempt to be more objective and
empirical in their approach to the subject are often
nonspecific in presenting their views. In the debate
over bilingual education, writers on both sides of
the issue frequently make vague references to
''convincing studies'' showing either the success or

failure of bilingual programs, but fail to mention
any particular study or to elaborate on findings
(see, for example, Schon 190—92; and Keefe A27).

There have been studies—many of them—of
programs designed for English-deficient students.
However, reliable authorities believe the results of
research up to the present have been largely
inconclusive. Bilingual supporter Benjamin Demott
questions whether or not anybody knows much about
the effect of bilingualism on learning (266). David
Ramírez, presently conducting several long-term
studies the results of which are to be released in
1989, concurs, saying we know ''very little'' about
how well bilingual education is working (qtd. in
Reed 48).

One reason for the scarcity of conclusive
results is the difficulty of assessing programs for
language-minority students. According to Ramírez,
all studies face ''serious problems'' (qtd. in Reed
48). One of these problems is the confusing
terminology used to label teaching methods. Usually
these are broken down into three subgroups
(excluding submersion): transitional bilingual
education, immersion, and ESL (English as a second
language). In immersion programs, students are

taught in English, but course content is adapted so
that it is understandable to English—deficient
students. Further, as teachers are bilingual,
students are permitted to ask questions in their
native language (Solórzano, ''Educating'' 20; Baker
and de Kanter, ''An Answer'' 41). ESL programs
combine a half—day of submersion in classes which
require relatively little language—use, like math
and music, with a half—day of intensive English study
(Solórzano ''Educating'' 20). These approaches,
however, are often combined, making difficult
accurate comparisons of their effectiveness (Reed
48; Baker and de Kanter ''An Answer'' 42).

Another problem is the methodological one of
the lack of any ''control group'' (Reed 48). Because
the law requires that students in need of bilingual
education get it, students in traditional all—
English classes are not defined as English—deficient
language—minority students (although some
authorities claim that many students eligible for
special programs are not served by them; see, for
example, González 62.)

Indeed, the methodology of many studies has
been called into question by one critic or another.
Of the hundreds of studies reviewed by Baker and de

Kanter, for example, they found only 39 to be
''methodologically valid'' (''An Answer'' 42). (It
is worth noting, however, that Ambert and Meléndez
cite widespread misgivings about the methodology in
the Baker—de Kanter report itself; see pp. 13—14.

Moreover, the results of the ''valid'' studies
are ''mixed and contradictory'' in terms of the
relative effectiveness of the transitional
bilingual, immersion, and ESL methods. In some
studies analyzed by Baker and de Kanter students in
transitional bilingual classes performed better
than, in some on the same level, and in some not as
well as students in other types of programs (''An
Answer'' 42—43). In addition, Baker and de Kanter
found that many studies ''widely cited'' to support the
effectiveness of TBE were not sound (''An Answer'' 43).

It is true that, since Baker and de Kanter
released their findings, other studies have emerged,
and some of these, at least, support the
effectiveness of TBE. Preliminary findings of a
Department of Education study show that Hispanic
students in bilingual programs perform better in
basic skills than those in all—English programs. But
one of the study's researchers says it is too early
''to draw any firm conclusions'' (''Studies'' 767).

The New York Times reports on a recent study by Yale
University psycholinguist Kenji Hakuta suggesting
that children who can use two languages prove
superior to monolingual children in ''cognitive
abilities'' and ''sophistication in the
understanding of language'' (''Bilingual Pupils''
21). But children from other language backgrounds
can be bilingual with or without TBE, and the
results reported in the Times do not indicate
whether bilingual education has made the difference
reported by Hakuta or has been effective in teaching
English to the children studied by him.

Hakuta believes that studies are asking the
''wrong questions''—and should concentrate on
understanding how children learn rather than on
assessing particular programs (qtd. in Reed 49). But
until there is a greater understanding of how
children learn, comparative studies must be relied
on for sound policy decisions.

For this, time is needed. There must be time
for the long—term studies begun recently to show
results, time for students taught in various kinds
of programs to demonstrate how well they have
learned. There is disagreement about how long a
bilingual program must continue in order to be

effective. Some analysts feel one or two years of
bilingual education should be sufficient (Bethell
32). Others say students' best performance does not
reveal itself until the fifth or sixth year of
bilingual education (Ambert and Meléndez 7). In
addition, there must be time to give a meaningful
trial to certain promising methods, such as
immersion, that have as yet received little study,
despite initial positive results (Baker and de
Kanter ''An Answer'' 46).

As a <u>New York Times</u> editorial argues, research
results are inconclusive as to which program—TBE or
immersion—is better. To Secretary Bennett's request
for Congress to allow more spending on alternatives
to TBE, the <u>Times</u> (whose editors have not been
generally sympathetic to Reagan administration
policies) asserts: ''He's right'' (''The Language''
A30). Bennett's call for flexibility in allowing
schools to determine what teaching methods are best
for them is, at the moment at least, justified.
Indeed, as Lucia Solórzano writes, ''there may be no
single solution'' to the problem (''A Second Look''
78). At present, as the <u>Times</u> editorial concludes:
''Variety in instructional methods is the best
policy'' (''The Language'' A30).

Works Cited

Ambert, Alba N., and Sarah E. Meléndez. Bilingual
    Education: A Sourcebook. New York: Garland, 1985.

Andersson, Theodore. ''America's Stake in
    Cultivating Minority Languages.'' Letter. New
    York Times 4 Sept. 1979: A26.

Andersson, Theodore, and Mildred Boyer. Bilingual
    Schooling in the United States: History, Rationale,
    Implications, and Planning. 2 vols. 1970. Detroit:
    Blaine Ethridge, 1976.

Baker, K., and A. A. de Kanter. ''An Answer from
    Research on Bilingual Education.'' American
    Education July 1983: 40–48.

———. ''Federal Policy and the Effectiveness of
    Bilingual Education.'' Baker and de Kanter,
    Bilingual 33–53.

———, eds. Bilingual Education: A Reappraisal of
    Federal Policy. Lexington: Heath-Lexington, 1983.

''Battle over Bilingualism.'' Time 8 Sept. 1980: 64–
    65.

Bethell, Tom. ''Against Bilingual Education.''
    Harper's Feb. 1979: 30–33.

''Bilingual Pupils Said to Have Edge.'' New York
    Times 25 Aug. 1985, sec. 1: 21.

''Bilingualism: A Symposium.'' <u>The Nation</u> 17 March
     1979: 263–66.

Birman, Beatrice F., and Alan L. Ginsburg.
     ''Addressing the Needs of Language–Minority
     Children.'' Introduction. Baker and de Kanter,
     <u>Bilingual</u> ix–xxi.

''The Controversy over Bilingual Education in
     America's Schools.'' <u>New York Times</u> 10 Nov. 1985,
     sec. 12: 1+.

DeMott, Benjamin. ''Bilingualism: A Symposium'' 266.

González, Angelo. ''Biligualism, Pro: The Key to
     Basic Skills.'' ''The Controversy'' 62.

Katcher, Sylvia. ''Bait.'' <u>English Journal</u> Feb.
     1981. Rpt. as ''Yes: Giving Students the Real
     Tools for Success.'' Noll 186–89.

Keefe, Joan. ''An Alternative to Bilingualism.'' <u>New
     York Times</u> 24 Oct. 1985: A27.

Kilpatrick, J. J. ''Of Bilingualism and Common Ties.''
     <u>Nation's Business</u> Oct. 1980: 17.

''The Language Is the Melting Pot.'' Editorial. <u>New
     York Times</u> 27 Sept. 1985: A30.

Levinson, Sanford. ''Bilingualism: A Symposium''
     263–64.

McWilliams, Carey. ''Bilingualism: A Symposium''
     264–66.

Mujica, Barbara. ''Bilingualism's Goal.'' New York
Times 26 Feb. 1984, sec. 4: 17.

Nicholas, Fotine. Z. ''The Pot Melts No More.'' U.S.
News and World Report 23 June 1986: 85.

Noll, James W. ''Should We Abandon Bilingual
Education?'' Taking Sides: Clashing Views on
Controversial Educational Issues. Ed. James W.
Noll. Guilford, CT: Dushkin Publishing Group,
1980.

''One Nation, One Language for All.'' Nation's
Business Dec. 1980: 76.

Postman, Neil. ''Bilingualism: A Symposium'' 266.

Ramírez, Arnulfo G. Bilingualism through Schooling:
Cross-Cultural Education for Minority and Majority
Students. Albany: State U of New York P,
1985.

Reed, Sally. ''What the Research Shows.'' ''The
Controversy'' 48–49.

Rodríguez, Richard. ''Bilingualism: Con.'' ''The
Controversy'' 63.

Schardt, A. ''A Battle in Any Language.'' Newsweek
15 Dec. 1980: 93–94.

Schon, Isabel. ''Rebait.'' English Journal Feb.
1981. Rpt. as ''No: Balanced and Enriched
Bilingualism.'' Noll 190–93.

Solórzano, Lucia. ''Educating the Melting Pot.''
    U.S. News and World Report 31 March 1986: 20–21.
———. ''A Second Look at Bilingual Education.'' U.S.
    News and World Report 11 June 1984: 78.
Stone, M. ''Bring Back the Melting Pot.'' Editorial.
    U.S. News and World Report 5 Dec. 1977: 92.
''Studies on Transitional Bilingual Education Are
    'Inconclusive': Bennet.'' Phi Delta Kappan June
    1986: 767.

Chapter 20

Answering Essay Questions

Compared to writing research papers, answering essay questions is easy. Or is it? Generally, essay questions are part of exams: the student writes the essay in class, in a limited time period, and often with no resources available to verify information. It is important for the student to think—and write—fast. Wasted time may mean an incomplete essay.

However, some students try to write too fast. They glance briefly at the essay question and immediately begin to write. This is a mistake. The most important part of answering an essay question comes before the writing begins: the student must consider the question and plan his or her answer.

Considering the Question

Students must always bear in mind that the question is central. It is not there just as a device for getting the student to write everything he or she knows about the subject being tested. The time the student spends in considering exam questions is not wasted. But a good way to save some precious exam time is by doing some of the considering before the exam begins.

Considering in Advance

Students can help themselves by considering in advance what questions an instructor is likely to ask. If time allows, the student should write out possible questions and answer them as a way of anticipating what is likely to appear on an exam. Of course, it is not likely that the student will stumble on the instructor's exact wording, but the ideas are likely to be close. And even if they aren't, thinking in terms of specific questions can help students put their knowledge into a framework that will better enable them to answer the questions the instructor does ask.

Careful Reading

Before a student can adequately answer an essay question, he or she must understand it clearly. This places a special burden on students for whom English is a second language. The foreign student should read exam questions carefully at least twice. If the instructor provides time for students to ask questions about the exam, the foreign student should take this opportunity to check on any terms about which he or she is uncertain. The student who spends time considering each question on the exam, asking about anything that is unclear, and listening carefully to the instructor's responses will improve his or her chances of answering successfully.

Points of Consideration

When considering the actual essay question at the time of the exam, the student should try to determine several things:
1. What essay pattern or patterns (narrative, description, definition, classification, subdivision, comparison and/or contrast, cause and effect, process, summary, argument) does the question call for?
2. What content is essential to the answer? (What should the thesis be? What details are needed to support it?)
3. What kind of documentation does the essay question require? (none? general references to sources used in class? specific citations including author, title, and page numbers of sources used?)
4. How long should the essay be, and how much time is there to write it?

What Essay Pattern(s) Does the Question Require? Students who only glance at an essay question usually pick up the topic they are supposed to write about. "The instructor wants to see what I know about circuits," the student reasons—or about the nucleus of the atom or respiration or supply-side economics. This is generally not enough. Of course, the instructor does want to see what the student knows about the topic. But he or she also wants to see if the student can construct a clear and pertinent answer to a specific question. If the student is asked to discuss the causes of inflation, and his answer includes examples of inflation or its effects, he is wasting time. The only pertinent information—the only part of the answer that counts—is information about the *causes* of inflation.

It may be helpful, therefore, for the student to determine what essay pattern an essay question calls for. Although the student may know this instinctively without actually identifying the pattern, thinking in terms of specific patterns might help him present the information in a way that is particularly responsive to the question. Certain

key words and phrases—essential elements embedded within the question—can sometimes help the student determine just which pattern or patterns are appropriate:

Pattern	Key words
Narrative	What happened . . . ? What are the principal events in . . . ?
Description	Describe . . . How does _____ look, feel, sound, smell, taste, appear? What does _____ look like?
Illustration	Give an example/examples of . . . Show by specific examples . . . Illustrate . . .
Definition	What is . . . ? What is the meaning of . . . ? How would you define . . . ?
Comparison and/or contrast	What are the similarities/differences . . . ? How are _____ alike/similar/different/dissimilar . . . ? How has _____ changed? How does _____ resemble/differ from _____ ? Compare/contrast . . .
Classification	How would you characterize/classify . . . ? To what group/class does _____ belong? Is _____ a (typical) _____?
Subdivision	What are the types of . . . ? List the kinds/branches/categories/subtypes . . . How many types of _____ are there? What are the chief characteristics/traits/qualities of . . . ?
Cause and Effect	What are the reasons for . . . Why . . . ? What are the causes/effects/results/consequences of . . . ? What caused . . . ? How might _____ have been prevented?
Process	What are the steps . . . ? How . . . ? What method . . . ?
Summary	Briefly restate . . . Restate in your own words . . .
Argument	Do you favor/support/oppose . . . ? What is your stand/position on . . . What is your opinion of . . . ? What should be done about . . . ? Should . . . ?

Sometimes essay questions call for only one pattern; sometimes, several. Determining
the appropriate patterns will help the student plan his or her answer.

What Content Is Essential to Answering the Question? In addition to determining the pattern called for by an essay question, the student must consider the content. Precisely what material does the question ask for? Again, merely determining the topic and starting to write about it will generally not be adequate. Even more than other kinds of writing, the essay exam calls for a clear thesis and relevant supporting detail.

Some students waste time rewriting the instructor's question before beginning to answer it. If this were necessary, the instructor would ask explicitly that students do it. Assume that the instructor can refer to his or her own copy of the question. If there is a choice among questions, the student can indicate which he is answering by noting its number or letter next to his answer.

The surest way of answering an essay question adequately is to remember that the *thesis* is the *answer* to the instructor's question. The question itself is merely a topic written in question form. Students who begin to write without deciding on a thesis may find themselves writing generally about the topic without actually answering the question.

Students can help themselves considerably by stating the thesis in the first paragraph of an essay exam. The essay exam is not the place for an implicit thesis and certainly not the place for holding the reader in suspense in any way. The most direct course is the best course. In addition to stating the thesis, students might use the first paragraph to indicate how the rest of the answer will relate to it.

Because time counts, it is especially important in answering essay questions to omit anything irrelevant. Students should make sure that each part of an answer contributes to supporting the thesis. They should resist the urge to include details merely because they are interesting—or because they would like to impress the instructor by showing how much they know.

The temptation to include too much may be especially strong when a student is asked to give the views of another author or to analyze a particular aspect of a literary work. Rather than limiting himself to the question, the student may try to summarize an entire essay, story, novel, or text. Perhaps the student feels that, if he writes as much as he can about a source, his instructor will know that he read it and give him a good grade. Generally, this is not the case. Unlike summaries, which should include all major ideas from the source being summarized, essay questions call for selectivity: the student must select from an outside source only the material that is needed to answer the question. A student in one of my classes, asked to compare characters in two works by Hemingway, spent most of his exam time writing out plot summaries of the stories. Although it was clear that he had read the assigned works, his failure to answer the question—that is, to analyze the characters—earned him a much lower grade than he might have earned.

Another temptation students must resist is giving their own opinion when it is not asked for. As with summaries (see Chapter 17), when students are directed to present the ideas of another writer, they should not evaluate those ideas unless they are explicitly asked to do so. Nor should they add ideas or examples of their own unless these are called for by the question. A student who is in doubt about whether a particular question calls for him to offer his own opinion or ideas should ask his instructor for clarification. If he is directed to include his own material, he should make certain his essay distinguishes between his own ideas and the ideas of the outside sources he is using.

Let us look at a student response to a question based on Eric Sevareid's essay "Velva, North Dakota." The question is as follows:

In his essay "Velva, North Dakota," Eric Sevareid notes changes in his hometown's sights and sounds, in the kinds of people in the town, and in their manner of eating and dressing. What does Sevareid gives as the reason for these changes? Do the changes affect only Velva or are they more widespread?

Here is the student's answer:

According to Eric Sevareid, Velva, North Dakota, has changed as a result of the shortening of distance between the separate parts of America. Modern transportation and communications devices have made it possible for the events of the world, such as wars and fluctuations in the economy, to "touch" Velva as they could not before. Modern beliefs and practices, reaching Velva through electronic media, have become part of the town.

The effects are not limited to Velva. Sevareid suggests that all towns in America have probably experienced the same changes. Moreover, as Sevareid notes, the modern phenomena that have altered Velva are the same as those that have altered big cities like New York as well as others outside the U.S.

Notice how the student comes right to the point, giving the reasons for the changes mentioned in the question in the first paragraph and discussing the scope of the change Sevareid describes in the second. Now let us look at another student's answer to the same question:

Velva, North Dakota, has changed in many ways in recent years. Changes in sights have included the alteration of the rural scene into a more urban one. The sounds are no longer natural and old-fashioned, but modern sounds of technological devices such as the diesel locomotive, brakes, sirens, and radio broadcasts. There are no more special "characters," as people who don't fit into society are sent to hospitals.

The changes have been caused by the shortening of time and distance between places. Modern technological devices have made life more comfortable and enjoyable. The quality of food and style of dress in particular have been improved along with transportation, entertainment, and the general awareness of international events. All this has made Velva a more attractive place to live in.

In this response, the student wastes much time and space by repeating the instructor's question (in slightly different words), presenting *illustrations* that are not called for in place of *causes* that are, and offering his own opinions and details when only Sevareid's have been requested. Indeed, the only parts of the answer that respond to the instructor's question are the last clause in the first paragraph and the first sentence in the second paragraph. Such brief remarks are not likely to satisfy the instructor. It is not enough for students to show that they have read the materials on which an essay question is based. They must also show that they can compose a relevant answer to it by supplying the information called for by the question.

What Kind of Documentation Does the Essay Require? Once a student knows what information is pertinent, he or she must determine how that information is to be documented. At times, essay questions may be vague about this. If the student has any doubt, he or she should ask the teacher to specify what kind of documentation is necessary.

Often, essay questions call for no documentation. Although students have gathered information from particular textbooks, they are not asked to credit their sources in their answers. The student is supposed to present the information as common knowledge without reference to particular authors or texts.

Sometimes, however, essay questions seek to find out if a student knows the sources for various ideas. Such questions may ask for the views of several authors on a given subject or may ask the student to present the viewpoint of a particular author or work. In such cases, the student should give explicit credit to the sources he or she has used, even if they are class texts. If the examination is given in a closed-book format (that is, with no texts for the student to consult), simple textual acknowledgments, such as those we looked at in Chapters 17 and 18, should suffice. Take another look at the first student response to the essay question above based on Sevareid's "Velva, North Dakota."

An essay for an open-book or take-home exam may require more specific information, such as exact titles, publication information, and page references. If the teacher gives no special instructions, the student can present information in the manner detailed in Chapter 18. Open-book and take-home exams may also encourage exact quotation from cited works. As in summary or research papers, however, the student should use his or her own words as much as possible, quoting only when the words of the source are particularly helpful to an answer.

How Long Should the Essay Be, and How Much Time Is There to Write It? Finally, the student must consider the time allowed and the space required for writing the answer. Sometimes essay length is specified ("Write a brief essay . . ."; "Explain in one or two paragraphs . . ."). Often, however, length is determined by the material necessary to answer the question. The student should try to determine about how much space he or she will need to write the answer and should allocate the time accordingly.

If the time period is one hour and the question can be fully answered in two or three paragraphs, there will be ample time for thorough planning and revising and possibly even for final proofreading to correct minor errors in grammar and spelling. If the question is going to require several pages of response, probably there will be only the briefest time for planning and revision. The student for whom English is a second language will have to determine (and, again, it may be helpful to ask the instructor for guidelines) how much time to spend on improving the English in his or her paper. Rarely is it wise in a timed exam for the student to agonize over every point of grammar or even word choice. For the in-class essay, clarity of expression and accuracy of information are more reasonable aims than is linguistic perfection.

Exams including several questions may indicate the point value assigned to each. Obviously, in such cases, students should allocate their time in accordance with the worth of each question. The student should not spend 50 percent of the allotted time on a question with a 10 percent point value. Conversely, if he or she has written the answer to a question worth half or the entire grade in the first five minutes of an hour-long exam, the student has probably not given that question enough time.

Planning the Essay

Whatever the length of essay required and however much time allotted for writing, the student should allow some time for planning. However, timed, in-class essays are not the place for formal outlining with neatly arranged symbols of subordination. For these essays, an informal, "scratch" outline (see page 99) or perhaps merely a few jotted notes are more appropriate. Basically, the outline should consist of the thesis and main supporting points and should indicate the general organization of the essay. For an essay answering the question above about Sevareid's "Velva, North Dakota," the outline might look like this:

The changes in Velva and other cities and towns are the result of the shortening of distance and time.
- modern transportation/communications
- news and effects of wars, economic matters
- modern beliefs and customs
- same as in other towns
- also cities here and elsewhere

In this outline, the student notes her thesis and the details that support it in roughly the order in which her answer will treat them. Although more complex questions may call for more detailed outlines, for in-class essays the student should keep his or her plan as simple and brief as possible.

Having considered the question carefully and planned the response, the student is ready to write. It is important to remember that answers to essay questions are *essays*. Generally speaking, the rules for writing them are the same as the rules for writing any other essay. And as with any other essay, if time allows, the student should revise.

Summary

An essay question is a question that is to be answered in essay form. Much of the essential work in answering an essay question consists of considering the question and planning the answer. Students should consider in advance the questions an instructor is likely to ask. During the exam, students should take time to read the question carefully, ask about anything that is unclear, and consider several factors: What pattern and content does the question call for? What documentation is necessary? How long should the answer be, and how much time is there to write it? Students should remember that their thesis is the answer to the instructor's question.

In addition to considering the question, the student should generally take time to plan his or her answer in scratch outline form. If time remains after writing, the student should naturally use it to revise.

Exercises

For Consideration

Exercise 1. What essay pattern or patterns do the following essay questions require?

   a. Identify the various branches of engineering and explain what distinguishes each of them.

   b. What reasons did Iranian students give for taking American personnel hostage in 1979?

   c. How has the foreign- to American-student ratio at U.S. colleges and universities changed in the past decade?

   d. Is Saudi Arabia a Third World nation? Explain.

   e. How does a supernova look when it first appears?

   f. Give an example of "holistic" medicine.

   g. What is the meaning of "supply-side economics"?

   h. What should the United States do to decrease the likelihood of terrorist acts against its citizens?

   i. How is the "Heimlich maneuver" performed?

For Composition

Exercise 2. Choose an article or opinion column from a newspaper or magazine. Read the piece carefully. Write five essay questions based on the piece you have chosen. Label each question according to the essay pattern(s) it calls for (for instance, description, cause and effect, classification). Your questions should call for at least five different essay patterns. (*Note:* You do not need to answer the questions.)

Exercise 3. Reread the essay "Velva, North Dakota" (page 193). Then read the essay question and responses that follow here. Assess how well each of the essays responds to the question by answering the following:

   a. Do the responses utilize the essay pattern(s) required by the question?

   b. Do the responses include all material necessary to answer the question? Do they include any irrelevant material?

   c. Do the responses provide the documentation required by the question?

Essay question: Give three examples of the "characters" that have vanished from Velva, North Dakota, according to Eric Sevareid. What reasons does Sevareid give for their disappearance?

A.   Among the "characters" Eric Sevareid notes as no longer existing in his hometown are the "official, certified town drunk," the social misfit "Crazy John," and the "town joker" who liked to impersonate the wives of his customers over the phone and encourage them to make extra purchases. Sevareid gives two reasons for the disappearance of these characters. For one thing, people who are as "sick" as "Crazy John" are now sent to places where they can be cared for properly. For another thing, schools are "obsessed" with creating people who fit well into society, and that does not include types like those that have vanished.

B. The "characters" are disappearing from Velva, North Dakota. There is no one in the town now like the town drunk or Crazy John or the druggist or the early attorney. Fortunately, there are hospitals to which people who say crazy things can be sent for their own good as well as the good of society. There are drawbacks, however. Life without these characters is smoother, but it isn't so interesting. It is just as we can see around us. Everyone dresses alike, talks alike, listens to the same music, goes to the same bars.

The cause of this is surely the media, as the essay says, especially television shows like *Dallas*.

Exercise 4. Reread the essay "Alienation and Affection" by Goodwin and Nacht (page 199). Then answer one or more of the essay questions below. Consider each question carefully and plan your answer before beginning to write. Be sure to label your answer according to the letter of the question you choose.

a. How do the feelings of Brazilians who have studied at American colleges and universities differ concerning their countrymen's pursuit of graduate versus undergraduate studies in the U.S.?

b. What reasons do Brazilians who have studied at American colleges and universities give to support their contention that Brazilians should not pursue their undergraduate education in the U.S.? Which reason is the most powerful, according to the authors? Why do you think they consider this reason the most powerful of those they mention?

c. What do the authors mean by "alienation"? Do the authors concede that such alienation exists among Brazilians who have pursued a U.S. undergraduate education? Illustrate with specific examples mentioned in the essay.

d. What benefits do the authors mention for Brazilians who have pursued a U.S. undergraduate education? Which benefits do you consider most valid? Are there any you consider invalid? Explain.

e. Imagine that you are being interviewed regarding your opinion as to whether or not students from your country should seek an American education. Do you feel an American education would be advantageous or disadvantageous to most such students? Compare benefits and costs, backing up your generalization with specific examples. What is the optimal age at which study abroad should begin? Why?

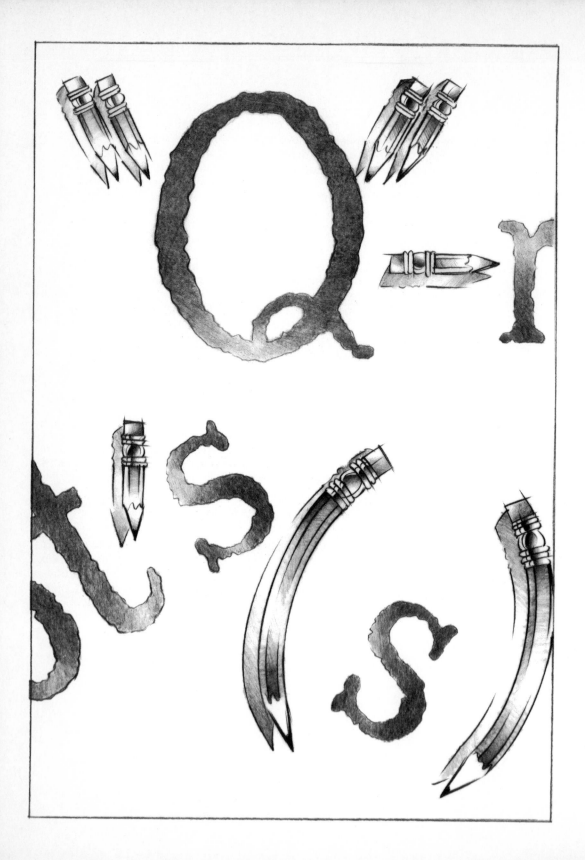

Part Six

Grammatical Conventions

Chapter 21

Punctuation

Sentences and Nonsentences

What Is a Sentence?

One of the most frequent sources of error in English composition by all student writers—whatever their first language—is faulty sentence punctuation. In English, each complete sentence starts with a capital letter and ends with a period (.), question mark (?), or exclamation point (!). The problem is being able to identify a complete sentence. This sounds easy, and often the writer can do it simply by feel. However, this is not always the case. Often, beginning writers feel a period when there is no complete sentence. Or they fail to feel a period when one is called for.

Punctuation, thus, cannot always be handled in this casual way. The student writer needs some rules to support his or her feeling about where a period belongs. Mainly, the writer needs a workable definition of *sentence*.

One popular definition of *sentence* is a complete thought. This is not an easy definition to apply, however. Look at the two following pairs of clauses:

Correct

He feels cold. But it is a warm day.

Incorrect

He feels cold. Although it is a warm day.

The punctuation between the first pair of clauses is possible, but the punctuation between the second pair is not possible. (It should be one sentence: He *feels cold although it is a warm day.*) Yet the thoughts are the same. If the writer uses the "complete thought" definition of *sentence*, he or she might well ask why *but it is warm day* is a complete thought whereas *although it is a warm day* is not.

A more useful definition of *sentence*, therefore, is one that uses grammatical terms—terms that are capable of making a distinction between such words as *but* and *although*. The concepts may appear complicated at first. But once learned, they will make sentence punctuation a regular, mechanical process rather than the mystery it often seems to student writers.

A common grammatical definition of *sentence* is a group of words that includes at least one independent clause. This is a workable definition. However, we still must define *independent clause*. The grammatical definition of *independent clause* is as follows:

An independent clause is a *subject* (s) plus a *verb* (v) preceded by *no joiner* or by a *coordinate joiner*. (Note: Joiners are defined below.)

We might write the definition as a "mathematical" formula:

$$\text{Independent clause} = \left.\begin{array}{c}\text{no joiner}\\\text{or}\\\text{coordinate joiner}\end{array}\right\} + s + v$$

A sentence can, of course, include more than this. But to be a sentence, a group of words must at least fulfill the requirements of this formula. Thus, we have sentences such as those given earlier:

No joiner + s + v

He is cold.

Coordinate joiner + s + v

But it is a warm day.

Of course, the second sentence, *But it is a warm day*, would actually never occur all by itself, without some thought before it such as *He is cold*. But it can be a sentence because it includes at least one group of words that conforms to the grammatical definition of an independent clause.

We must explain here what we mean by *joiners*. Each of the following sentences includes a joiner:

coordinate conjunction
He is cold, *but* it is a warm day.

subordinate conjunction
He is cold *although* it is a warm day.

relative pronoun
He comes from a country *that* has a tropical climate.

As we can see, the joiners include conjunctions as well as relative pronouns. We group these together as joiners because they share the following characteristics:

1.   They are capable of connecting two clauses.

2.   They must occupy the initial position of the clause of which they are a part. Thus, we cannot write, for example: *He is cold, it is a warm day but.* The joiner must occupy the initial position in the clause. (The only exception is that a relative pronoun may be preceded by a preposition: for instance, He comes from a country *in which* the climate is tropical.)

The *coordinate joiners* include the *coordinate conjunctions* (*and, but, or, nor, for, so,* and *yet*) and the *correlative conjunctions* (*both . . . and; not . . . but; not only . . . but also; either . . . or; neither . . . nor*). All other joiners are *subordinate joiners*; that is, the clauses they introduce cannot stand alone as sentences, but are dependent upon the presence of a *main clause*, as in the sentences below:

main clause	+	*subordinate joiner*	+	*s + v*
I am cold		although		it is a warm day.
He comes from a country		that		has a tropical climate.

(Another way of saying this is that a subordinate clause by itself does not equal a sentence.) The *subordinate joiners* include the *subordinate conjunctions* (*although, because, if, when,* and so on) and the *relative pronouns* (*who, which, that,* and so forth).

Students can recognize subordinate joiners as words that share the common characteristics of all joiners but that are neither coordinate nor correlative conjunctions. Thus, the only lists that students need to memorize so they can recognize the various kinds of joiners are those of the seven coordinate conjunctions (*and, but, or, nor, for, so, yet*) and the five correlative conjunction pairs (*both . . . and,* and so forth).

Before closing this discussion, we should look at one last representative pair of clauses:

He is cold. However, it is a warm day.

In *However, it is a warm day,* our subject and verb are not preceded by one of the coordinate joiners. Yet they appear to be preceded by something. To know whether the above punctuation is possible, we must ask if the word *however* is a subordinate joiner. (If it were, the group of words However, it is a warm day could not form a sentence and the above punctuation would be incorrect). The answer is that *however* is not a joiner of any kind. And we know this by remembering that a joiner must occupy the initial position of the clause of which it is a part; it cannot be moved to any other position within the clause. *However,* on the other hand, can be moved to various positions within the clause:

It is, however, a warm day.
It is a warm day, however.

Thus, *however* is an adverb and not a joiner at all. And a subject + a verb preceded by *however* or by any word like it (*conjunctive adverbs* such as *nonetheless, moreover, indeed, thus, then, also,* and so on) is an independent clause and can be punctuated as a sentence. To apply our formula:

no joiner   +   s   + v
However,   it   is a warm day.

Fragments and Run-ons

When a group of words is punctuated as a sentence, but does not fulfill the terms of the definition of *sentence,* we call it a *fragment.* We have already seen examples of fragments such as *Although it is a warm day.* Either a fragment must be rewritten to fulfill the definition (here, by omitting the subordinate conjunction *although* or by changing it to the coordinate conjunction *but*) or it must be attached to the main clause on which it is dependent:

> He feels cold. It is a warm day.
> He feels cold. But it is a warm day.
> He feels cold although it is a warm day.
> Although it is a warm day, he feels cold.

When a group of words is punctuated as a single sentence, but actually contains more than one sentence (that is, subject + verb + subject + verb with no joiner between them), we call it a *run-on.* Run-ons frequently result from the mistaking of conjunctive adverbs (*then, also, however,* and so forth) for joiners, as in the following sentences:

Mistaken conjunctive adverb

> It is a warm day, also it is sunny.
> The sun went down, then it got cold.

Either a run-on must be rewritten to supply a conjunction between the first and second subject–verb combinations:

Replaced with conjunction

> It is a warm day, and it is sunny.

Or it must be rewritten as two separate sentences:

Separated into two sentences

> It is a warm day. Also, it is sunny.
> The sun went down. Then it got cold.

There are, however, exceptions to the rules excluding fragments and run-ons as sentences. Occasionally, for effect, a writer may wish to treat a fragment as a sentence. He or she may do so as long as the reader understands that the fragment is an independent unit of speech. For example, answers to questions may be treated as *independent fragments,* as in the sentences below:

> Was it a warm day? Oh, yes!

Here, *Oh, yes!* includes implicitly the idea *Oh, yes, it was.* Run-ons are also sometimes permissible if they are very short and the elements are close in meaning and grammatical structure:

He got up, he went to class, he came home. It was always the same thing.

Generally, however, it is best for the student writer to avoid fragments and run-ons. The writer should master the rules of writing before he or she begins to bend them for purposes of style.

Combining Clauses, Phrases, and Words

So far, we have been talking about punctuation mainly in terms of what constitutes a sentence. But the student must master the rules for punctuation within as well as between sentences. In order to do so, it is necessary to look again at clauses, phrases, and words.

Punctuation Between Clauses

As we know, there are two types of clauses: *main* (independent) and *subordinate* (dependent). The formula used in this text for each of these types of clauses is given below with examples:

$$\text{Independent clause} = \left.\begin{array}{c}\text{no joiner}\\ \text{or}\\ \text{coordinate joiner}\end{array}\right\} + \text{subject} + \text{verb}$$

	I hate chemistry
but	I like math
however,	I am failing both

$$\text{Dependent clause} = \text{subordinate joiner} + \text{subject} + \text{verb}$$

because	I hate to study

The following shows the options for punctuation between various combinations of independent and dependent clauses.

Independent Clause + Independent Clause The possible ways to join two independent clauses are threefold: (1) insert a period or semicolon between the clauses; (2) insert a comma between the clauses and then add a coordinate conjunction; or (3) when clauses are short and closely related, simply insert a coordinate conjunction between them.

Examples

I hate chemistry. I like math.
I hate chemistry. But I like math.
I hate chemistry. However, I like math.
I hate chemistry; I like math.
I hate chemistry; however, I like math.
I hate chemistry; but I like math.
I hate chemistry, and I hate math.
I hate chemistry and I hate math.

Common errors: The omission of either a conjunction or an appropriate punctuation mark between two independent clauses produces a *fused sentence*:

> I hate chemistry I like math.   (incorrect)

The combination of two independent clauses with a comma only and no coordinate conjunction produces a *comma splice*:

> I hate chemistry, I like math.   (incorrect)
> I hate chemistry, however, I like math.   (incorrect)
> I hate chemistry, also, I like math.   (incorrect)

The fused sentence and the comma splice are two types of run-on sentences.

Independent Clause + Dependent Clause. Generally, joining a dependent clause with an independent clause requires no punctuation. However, in cases where the dependent clause is a nonrestrictive relative clause (see below) or where confusion would result without any punctuation, a comma can be added to separate the two clauses.

Examples

> I like math because it is exact.
> I like math even though I am failing it.
> I like instructors who don't give homework.
> I like my math instructor, who doesn't give homework.
> I hate homework that is difficult, while easy homework I rather enjoy.

(Without the comma, the phrase *difficult while easy* might be confusing.)

Common error: A group of words punctuated as a sentence that does not fulfill the terms of the definition of a sentence is, as mentioned earlier, a *sentence fragment*:

> I like math a lot. Because it is exact.   (incorrect)

Punctuation and the Relative Clause

Students should note that there are two kinds of relative clauses: *restrictive* and *nonrestrictive*. *Restrictive relative clauses* restrict or limit the meaning of a referent:

> The essay *that Jane wrote* won a prize.

In the sentence above, *that Jane wrote* limits the sense of *essay* to a particular essay; it identifies the essay as the one that Jane wrote. *Nonrestrictive relative clauses* give additional information about the referent, but do not limit it:

> Albert Einstein, *who was a scientist*, played a violin.

In this sentence, *who was a scientist* gives additional information about the referent, *Albert Einstein*, but it cannot limit the sense of the referent because it is already limited to one particular individual.

Students should note that restrictive relative clauses are not set off by commas, whereas nonrestrictive relative clauses are. This is important because many clauses can be either restrictive or nonrestrictive, and sentence meaning depends on the presence or absence of commas:

The students who worked hard got an A. (Only some students—those who worked hard—got an A.)

The students, who worked hard, got an A. (All the students worked hard, and all got an A.)

Dependent Clause + Independent Clause. In cases where a dependent clause precedes an independent clause, the only punctuation that can join the clauses is a comma.

Examples

Because it is exact, I like math.

When I understand math, I like it.

Even though I am failing math, I like it.

Incorrect

Because it is exact I like math.

Punctuation Between Phrases and Clauses

The three kinds of phrases that the student should be able to recognize in order to punctuate correctly are *infinitive, participial,* and *prepositional.* A formula and examples for each of these follows:

Infinitive phrase = to + verb (base form) + (optional object, complement, or modifier)

to	pass	this course
to	be	an A-student
to	do	well

Participial phrase = (optional adverb or preposition) + participal + (optional object, complement, or adverb)

	being	a foreign student
while	reading	this chapter
once	written	

Prepositional phrase = preposition + object of preposition

to	the instructor
for	this essay

The illustrations that follow show the punctuation possible between various combinations of phrases and independent clauses.

Infinitive Phrase + Independent Clause. Insert a comma after the infinitive phrase.

Example

To pass this course, the student must study.

Independent Clause + Infinitive Phrase. This structure requires no punctuation after the clause.

Example

The student must study to pass this course.

Participial Phrase + Independent Clause. Add a comma following the participial phrase.

Example

While reading this chapter, I am listening to my stereo.

Independent Clause + Participial Phrase. This structure contains no punctuation between the clause and the phrase.

Example

I am listening to my stereo while reading this chapter.

Prepositional Phrase + Independent Clause. The use of a comma after the prepositional phrase is optional. Insert a comma after the phrase if it will help to clarify the meaning of the sentence.

Example

To this instructor, grammar seems very important.
To this instructor grammar seems very important.
In English, grammar seems very important.

Independent Clause + Prepositional Phrase. No comma is necessary after an independent clause unless the meaning is unclear without one.

Example

Grammar seems very important to this instructor.
I spoke to the instructor, with the text in hand.

(Without the comma, it might appear that the instructor was holding the text.)

In short, punctuation between an independent clause and a phrase modifying it varies depending on the positions of the two units. If the phrase precedes the clause, a comma usually separates the units (although, as just mentioned, it may be omitted after a prepositional phrase if the sense is clear without it). If the clause precedes the phrase, there is generally no punctuation mark between the units (although, again, a comma may be inserted if the meaning would otherwise be unclear).

Punctuation Between Words or Phrases

Two Words or Phrases. There is no punctuation between two words or phrases joined by a coordinate conjunction:

Correct

I like both coffee and tea.
She is poor but proud.

Incorrect

I like both coffee, and tea.
She is poor, but proud.

Items in a Series. There is no punctuation between items in a series of three or more *separated by conjunctions*:

Correct

I like coffee and tea and milk.

Incorrect

I like coffee, and tea, and milk.

Between items in a series listed *without conjunctions*, commas are necessary:

Correct

They serve several beverages on board: coffee, tea, milk, juice, etc.

(Note: *etc.* means "*and* other unspecified items of this class"; thus, students should never write *and etc.* since it is redundant:

Incorrect

They serve several beverages: coffee, tea, milk, and etc.

When the final item in a series follows a conjunction, the comma is optional, but a comma is necessary when meaning would be unclear without it:

Correct

For lunch we had bread, soup, and salad.
For lunch we had bread, soup and salad.
For lunch we had bread, hot soup, and salad.

Incorrect

For lunch we had bread, hot soup and salad.

(In the last example, without the second comma, *hot* seems to modify *salad* as well as *soup*.)

When commas are used *within* individual items in a series, the items themselves are separated from one another by semicolons:

Correct

They serve several beverages: red wine, which costs $10 a bottle and is excellent; white wine, which costs $8 a bottle and is good; and beer, which is free.

Modifiers. When two or more modifiers are *coordinate*—of equal grammatical value—a comma is needed between them:

Correct

He is a responsible, knowledgeable instructor.

Incorrect

He is a responsible knowledgeable instructor.

(The modifiers are coordinate because they both modify *instructor*.)
When one modifier is *subordinate* to another, no comma is used between them:

Correct

He is a knowledgeable English instructor.

Incorrect

He is a knowledgeable, English instructor.

(The modifiers are not coordinate; *English* modifies *instructor*; *knowledgeable* modifies *English instructor*.)
To test whether modifiers are coordinate or not, try switching their order: coordinate modifiers are interchangeable; noncoordinate modifiers are not:

Correct

He is a knowledgeable, responsible instructor.

Incorrect

He is an English, knowledgeable instructor.

Punctuating Parenthetical Elements

Parenthetical elements are words or groups of words that are not integral to the main structure of a sentence; they interrupt the flow of a sentence. They include interjections, appositives, modifiers, conjunctive adverbs, acknowledgments, terms of direct address, nonrestrictive relative clauses, and interpolated comments and questions. When the interpolated material comes at the beginning or end of a sentence, only one comma or dash is needed to separate it from the rest of the sentence:

interjection
Oh, the instructor is a Southerner.

interjection
His accent is difficult for me—*alas.*

conjunctive adverb
In *fact*, he is from Mississippi.

When they occupy a position in the middle of a sentence, parenthetical elements are set off from the rest of the sentence by a pair of commas, dashes, or parentheses, depending on the function of the element.

appositive
The instructor, *a Southerner*, has an interesting accent.

modifiers
The instructor, *Southern and aristocratic*, has an interesting accent.

attribution
The instructor, *she explained*, is from the South.

conjunctive adverb
He is, *in fact*, from Mississippi.

direct address
The instructor, *students*, is from the South.

nonrestrictive relative clause
The instructor, *who is from the South*, has an interesting accent.
The instructor—who is from the South—has an interesting accent.
The instructor (who is from the South) has an interesting accent.

Note that dashes and parentheses make a stronger interruption than do commas. Dashes are often used for emphasis, as here:

The instructor—a real Southerner—has an interesting accent.

Both dashes and parentheses are especially appropriate when the parenthetical material disturbs the grammatical flow of the main clause:

The instructor—what an interesting accent he has!—is from the South.
The instructor (what an interesting accent he has!) is from the South.

Parentheses Versus Brackets

In addition to their use within sentences, *parentheses* can be used to set off whole sentences from the text. Note that the period in a parenthetical sentence is placed within the parentheses:

The instructor has an interesting accent. (He is from the South.)

Unlike parentheses, square *brackets* ([ ]) are used mainly to indicate that material is being added to a quotation (see page 275). They should not be confused with parentheses.

Eliminating Unnecessary Commas

When students punctuate by feel rather than according to grammatical rules, they sometimes insert unnecessary commas into their sentences when they come to *vocal pauses* (points at which they would stop to breathe if they were reading aloud). This results in faulty sentences in which the grammatical structure is improperly broken up:

Incorrect placement

subject   *verb*
The English instructor I had last summer, assigned a lot of homework. (The comma improperly separates the subject from the verb.)

subject   *verb*
Grammar exercises, book reviews, and ten-page research papers, were her favorite assignments. (The comma improperly separates the subject from the verb.)

conjunction
But, I didn't mind because I didn't do any of it. (The comma improperly separates the conjunction from its clause.

verb   *object*
I'm planning not to do this semester, the homework in engineering, physics, and math. (The comma improperly separates the verb from its object.)

In these sentences, commas have wrongly been inserted between subject and verb, verb and object, and conjunction and clause. Although we might pause in reading or speaking these sentences, none of the commas is justified grammatically. To preserve the grammatical flow of the sentences, the commas should be eliminated:

Correct placement

The English instructor I had last semester assigned a lot of homework. Grammar exercises, book reviews, and 10-page research papers were her favorite assignments.
But I didn't care because I didn't do any of it.
I'm planning not to do this semester the homework in engineering, physics, and math.

Optional Comma Between Conjunction and Clause

When parenthetical material is inserted between a conjunction and its clause, the first comma is often omitted:

But since I didn't do most of it, I didn't care.

However, it may be inserted if desired:

But, since I didn't do most of it, I didn't care.

Punctuating Dates and Places

Dates

A comma separates day and year if the month comes first:

June 1, 1990

If a sentence continues after the date, a second comma should follow the year:

She will graduate June 1, 1990, from a small university in Maine.

No comma is necessary if the day precedes the month:

1 June 1990

or if the day is omitted:

June 1990

Places

A comma separates city from state or state from nation:

Los Angeles, California
Paris, France

Like the commas for dates, if a sentence continues after a place name preceded by a comma, a second comma should follow the final place name:

He was born in Djakarta, Indonesia, in 1963.

Introducing a Series or Equivalent Statement

To introduce an item, series, or statement that closes a sentence, a colon (:) may be used:

They serve many beverages: beer, wine, fruit juice, coffee, tea.
They serve only one beverage: champagne.
Alcoholic beverages were not available: they served no liquor, wine, or beer.

Note that colons can be used only when the statements separated by them are actually equivalent—are two ways of saying the same thing. (To test for equivalence, the student might try inserting *that is* after the colon.)

A colon cannot be used when the sentence continues after the item, series, or statement it introduces:

Incorrect

They serve many beverages: beer, wine, and fruit juice, all at a reasonable cost.

A colon also should not separate sentence elements such as subject and verb or preposition and object of the preposition, as does the colon in the example below:

Incorrect

The meal was accompanied by: red and white wines, coffee, and liqueurs.

Colons are often used (as they are throughout this text) to introduce examples. In addition, colons are one of the main punctuation marks used to introduce quotations, as we will see in the following section.

Quotation Punctuation

Special punctuation is needed for quotation. Quotation punctuation is used primarily in two circumstances: quotation of direct speech (dialogue) and quotation of outside sources. It is mainly the second of these, *quotation of outside sources*, that is important for college students, because it figures prominently in the writing of research papers. In citations of other sources, quotation punctuation must be used for any passages, sentences, clauses, phrases, or "apt" words borrowed directly from another text. (For capitalization of quoted material, see page 300.)

Short Quotations

Short quotations (fewer than five typed lines of prose or two lines of poetry) are generally *incorporated* within the writer's own text. Double quotation marks (" ") are used to open and close incorporated quotations:

> According to this text, "Special punctuation is needed for quotation."
> The writer states that "quotation punctuation is used primarily in two circumstances."
> She calls the second of these "important" in regard to college students.

When incorporated quotations include material that is itself enclosed in quotation marks in the original source, single quotation marks are used to indicate the double quotation marks of the original:

> The author writes that "passages, sentences, clauses, phrases, or 'apt' words borrowed directly from the other text" must be enclosed in quotation punctuation.

Long Quotations

Longer quotations (five or more typed lines of prose or two or more lines of poetry) are *extracted* from the main body of an essay without opening and closing quotation marks. They are generally indented 10 spaces from the left margin. (When two or more paragraphs are quoted together, the line that begins a paragraph in the original is indented an extra three spaces.) When such passages include material that is enclosed in quotation marks in the original, the double quotation marks of the original are retained, as in the following example:

> According to the author,
>> Special punctuation is needed for quotation. Quotation punctuation is used primarily in two circumstances; quotation of direct speech (dialogue) and quotation of outside sources. It is mainly the second of these, *quotation of outside sources*, that is important for college students, because it figures prominently in the writing of research papers. In citations of other sources, quotation punctuation must be used for any passages, sentences, clauses, phrases, or "apt" words borrowed directly from another text.

Inserting Material into a Quotation

Brackets ([ ]) are used to insert material into a quotation, either as an addition or a substitution:

> The author writes that "[quoting outside sources] figures prominently in the writing of research papers." (Bracketed phrase is substituted for *it*.)

According to the author, "Miami [Florida] is a city of contrasts." (*Florida* has been added to the quoted material.)

Note that insertions should generally be restricted to material that clarifies a quotation which would otherwise be unclear. Commentary should generally not be delivered in this manner:

Incorrect

According to the author, "Miami is a city of [appalling] contrasts."

The one exception to this is the Latin term "*sic*," which may be inserted to show that a borrowing contains an error in spelling, grammar, or fact:

Correct use

According to the author, "Maimi [*sic*] is a city of contrasts." *Sic* should not be used, however, to express an opinion on a matter of controversy.

Incorrect use

According to the author, "Miami is a wonderful place for a vacation [*sic*]."

Omitting Material from a Quotation

Ellipsis marks of three equally spaced periods (. . .) indicate that something has been omitted from a quotation:

According to the author, "In citations of other sources, quotation punctuation must be used for any passages . . . borrowed directly from another text."

For words omitted from the end of a sentence or between consecutive sentences, the ellipses follow the normal period, resulting in four spaced periods:

The author writes: "It is mainly the second of these, *quotation of outside sources*, that is important for college students. . . . In citations of other sources, quotation punctuation must be used for any passages, sentences, clauses, phrases, or 'apt' words borrowed directly from another text."

These four evenly spaced periods may also be used to indicate longer omissions, such as a whole sentence or paragraph or more of prose.

In quotations of *poetry*, however, omissions of a line or more are indicated by an entire line of ellipses, which extends the length of the longest line of poetry.

> About suffering they were never wrong,
> The Old Masters: how well they understood
> Its human position; how it takes place
> While someone else is eating or opening a window or just
>   walking dully along.
> ....
> In Brueghel's Icarus, for instance: how everything turns away
> Quite leisurely from the disaster. . . .

Ellipses may also be used to indicate dialogue cut off by another speaker or by an interruptive action:

> The teacher began, "Tomorrow there will be a . . ."
> "Oh, no!" a student interrupted. "Not another quiz!"

It should not, however, be used to indicate an incomplete list, as below:

Incorrect use

> They served coffee, tea, milk. . . .

Rather, students should indicate that a list includes unspecified items with *etc., and so forth*, or an explanatory phrase:

Correct use

> They served coffee, tea, milk, etc.
> They served coffee, tea, milk, and other beverages.

Writers occasionally use ellipses to indicate that there is more to a statement than they are expressing:

> The instructor told the students that their failing grades hurt him as much as them. . . .

This stylistic usage is too cute for serious writing and would generally not be appropriate in a college essay.

Introducing Quotations

When quoted material is integrated into the structure of the sentence that includes it, the punctuation should follow the requirements of the sentence:

> The author writes that in certain cases "the punctuation should follow the requirements of the sentence."

When quoted material interrupts textual sentence structure, it is introduced by a comma or colon:

> According to the author, "When quoted material is integrated into the structure of the sentence which includes it, the punctuation should follow the requirements of the sentence."
> The author states: "When quoted material is integrated into the structure of the sentence which includes it, the punctuation should follow the requirements of the sentence."

Although comma and colon may seem to be interchangeable, the colon makes a stronger and more formal pause than does the comma. In essence, the colon fulfills the function of a period; it must follow a complete sentence. Longer passages (of more than one sentence) are generally introduced by a colon, as are extracted quotations such as the one below:

The author states:

> Special punctuation is needed for quotation. Quotation punctuation is used primarily in two circumstances: quotation of direct speech (dialogue) and quotation of outside sources. It is mainly the second of these, *quotation of outside sources*, that is important for college students, because it figures prominently in the writing of research papers.

Closing Quotations

American and British usage differ regarding how punctuation marks are to be handled when closing quotations. The rules here follow American usage:

1. Periods and commas are placed *inside* closing quotation marks:

   According to the author, "American and British usage differ regarding how punctuation marks are to be handled when closing quotations."

   "American and British usage differ regarding how punctuation marks are to be handled when closing quotations," the author writes.

2. Semicolons and colons are placed outside closing quotation marks:

   The author writes that "American and British usage differ regarding how punctuation marks are to be handled when closing quotations"; she chooses to follow American usage in her text.

   The author writes that "American and British usage differ regarding how punctuation marks are to be handled when closing quotations": in American usage, periods and commas are placed inside quotation marks, whereas in British usage they are placed outside.

3. Question marks and exclamation points are placed inside closing quotation marks when they punctuate the quotation itself:

   At last, the author asks, "Are our skies really safe?"
   The author closes: "Such is the working of man's mind!"

   They are placed outside closing quotation marks when they punctuate the text outside the quotation:

   How many students know that "American and British usage differ in regard to how punctuation marks are to be handled when closing quotations"?

   Incredible as it may seem, I had actually forgotten that "American and British usage differ regarding how punctuation marks are to be handled when closing quotations"!

4. Only one punctuation mark is used when closing a quotation. If the quoted material ends in a question mark or exclamation point, the text incorporates this where a period or comma would normally be called for. Otherwise, the text itself determines the punctuation mark used:

   "Are our skies really safe?" the author asks. (The question mark makes a comma unnecessary.)

The author writes that "the rules here follow American usage." (The colon used in the original source is replaced by a period.)

The use of double punctuation marks is incorrect. The author asks, "Are our skies really safe?".

Punctuation of Documentation

Documentation—the crediting of outside sources—may be handled in various ways. The rules for closing punctuation vary with the documentation format as well as with the length of the quotation. The following rules apply to punctuation after *incorporated* quotations:

1. *Parenthetical references* are placed outside quotation marks, but inside a closing period or comma:

   She writes that "American and British usage differ" (20).

   When a quotation ends in a question mark or exclamation point, the parenthetical reference is placed outside all quotation punctuation, and the writer's own closing punctuation must be added:
   The author asks, "Are our skies really safe?" (6).

2. *Footnote numbers* are placed outside any punctuation except a dash, colon, or semicolon:

   It is important to remember that "American and British usage differ regarding how punctuation marks are to be handled when closing quotations."[2]

   In regard to closing punctuation, "American and British usage differ,"[2] and neither is like that of my own country.

   Nothing in English usage—despite the fact that "American and British usage differ"[2]—compares to the closing punctuation rules used in my own country.

3. After *extracted* quotations, parenthetical references and footnote numbers are placed outside all punctuation:

   According to the author,
   Special punctuation is needed for quotation. Quotation punctuation is used primarily in two circumstances. . . . It is mainly the second of these, [*citation*], that is important for college students, because it figures prominently in the writing of research papers.[2]
   According to the author,
   Special punctuation is needed for quotation. Quotation punctuation is used primarily in two circumstances. . . . It is mainly the second of these, [*citation*], that is important for college students, because it figures prominently in the writing of research papers. (Levy 20)

Quotation Marks with Titles

In addition to their use with incorporated quotations, double quotation marks are also used with the titles of brief works (short stories, articles, reports, units or chapters of books, essays and poems that are shorter than book length, and episodes of television series), as in the examples that follow:

> "Velva, North Dakota"   (a short essay)
> "Musée des Beaux Arts"   (a short poem)
> "Grammatical Conventions"   (a unit in this text)
> "J. R. Vacations at the Ranch"   (an episode in a television series)

(For a discussion of quotation marks versus italics with titles, see pages 302–03).

Punctuation Format

Punctuation marks (except for ellipses) are placed directly before or after the word they punctuate:

> "Punctuation marks are placed directly before or after the word they punctuate."

When a word, phrase, clause, or sentence closes at the end of a line, any mark punctuating it must follow it directly. It cannot be moved down to the beginning of the following line:

Incorrect placement

> Periods, question marks, exclamation points, commas, semicolons
> , and colons never appear at the beginning of a line in English
> ; thus, this sentence contains two punctuation errors.

Correct placement

> Periods, question marks, exclamation points, commas, semicolons, and colons never appear at the beginning of a line in English; thus, this sentence is correctly punctuated.

In addition, specific rules determine the spacing used with punctuation marks made on a typewriter or word processor.

1.   Leave two spaces after a period, question mark, or exclamation point:

> Leave two spaces.   Then start the new sentence.

2.   Leave one space after a comma, semicolon, or colon:

> Leave one space; then start the new sentence.

> Similarly, leave one space after closing parentheses, brackets, or quotation marks unless they occur at the end of a sentence (in which case two spaces are required) or unless another punctuation mark follows (in which case no space is required):

Leave one space (as here) after closing parentheses.
(The same rule applies to quotation marks.) Leave two spaces if the parentheses or quotation marks occur at the end of a sentence.
But leave no space between a closing parenthesis and another punctuation mark (such as a comma), as in this example.

3.   Leave no space before or after a dash.

Leave no space—none at all—before or after a dash.

Summary

A sentence is a group of words including at least one independent clause. An independent clause is a subject plus a verb preceded by no joiner or by a coordinate joiner. A group of words punctuated as a sentence that does not include at least one independent clause is a fragment. And a group of words that includes two or more independent clauses without a colon, semicolon, or coordinate joiner in between is a run-on. Special rules apply to punctuation between clauses, phrases and clauses, and words in pairs or series and to the punctuation of quotations.

Exercises

Exercise 1.   Underline word groups incorrectly punctuated as sentences:
  a.   He likes chemistry. Although it is difficult for him.
  b.   He likes chemistry. But it is difficult for him.
  c.   He likes chemistry. However, it is difficult for him.
  d.   He likes chemistry. And he likes physics.
  e.   He likes chemistry. Also, he likes physics.
  f.   He has to take biology. Because he wants to be a doctor.
  g.   He has to take biology. For he wants to be a doctor.
  h.   He has chemistry at ten o'clock. Then he has English.
  i.   He goes to English. After his chemistry class is over.
  j.   After English he has lunch. Which he likes a lot better than English.

Exercise 2.   Identify fragments (F) and run-ons (R) in the following essay. Then rewrite the passage, punctuating correctly.

Tonight I have to read a chapter in our English grammar text, also I have to do a grammar exercise. I have to reread last night's grammar chapter, too. Because I didn't understand it fully after my first reading. I will revise my last essay, then I will start planning my next essay. I have to read my class notes. And study them thoroughly. I'll review spelling words, I'll review punctuation. All this should get me a good grade in English. Although I'll probably fail everything else.

Exercise 3. Punctuate properly each pair of clauses in as many ways as possible, substituting capitals for lower case letters as necessary. (*Note*: Do not change the order of words in the clauses.)

> Example: I must study tonight + otherwise I may not pass the exam
> I must study tonight; otherwise, I may not pass the exam.
> I must study tonight. Otherwise, I may not pass the exam.

a. students must listen   + and they must study
b. students must listen   + also they must study
c. students must listen   + before they can study
d. before they can study   + students must listen
e. students must listen   + however some do not

Exercise 4. Punctuate properly each of the following pairs of word groups in as many ways as possible, as you did the pairs of clauses in the preceding exercise. Substitute capitals for lowercase letters as necessary. (*Note*: Do not change the order of words in the groups.)

a. she works hard   + she gets good grades
b. she works hard   + and gets good grades
c. she works hard   + then she works some more
d. she gets good grades   + for she works hard
e. she gets good grades   + because she works hard
f. because she works hard   + she gets good grades
g. she gets good grades   + however she works hard to get them
h. she gets good grades   + but she works hard to get them
i. by working hard   + she gets good grades
j. she gets good grades   + by working hard
k. she works hard   + to get good grades
l. to get good grades   + she works hard
m. through hard work   + she gets good grades
n. she gets good grades   + through hard work
o. she gets the kind of grades + which are hard to get
p. she gets As   + which are hard to get
q. she works hard   + and she gets good grades
r. she works hard   + therefore she gets good grades
s. she works hard   + so she gets good grades
t. she works hard   + also she has a 185 I.Q.

Exercise 5. Add commas where necessary.

a. Maria is from Ecuador which is a Latin American country.

b. To succeed in the US Maria believed that she had to try to understand North Americans.

c. Thus arriving at the University of Smallville she decided that she would make friends with North American students.

d. At the student center and in her dorm lobby she stood around to see how many North Americans she could meet.

e. But the only students whom she met were from Chile Peru Venezuela and Argentina.

f. Being a student at an American university I need to know good correct English.

g. The problems which are the worst for me are spelling pronunciation and vocabulary.

h. Reading well writing clearly and speaking fluently are all to be sure very important for me scholastically.

i. But to do well in a good American university one must certainly write well.

j. Therefore I am taking English Composition I which is a course in writing.

Exercise 6. Eliminate unnecessary commas.
a. The dormitory in which most foreign students are housed at our university, seems like a huge, impersonal building, from the outside.

b. But, it's really a friendly, residential hall.

c. Students from Asia, Africa, Europe, and South America, live together in great harmony here.

d. Living with people of different customs and cultures, encourages understanding among fellow students.

e. And, since we all speak English as a second language, everyone speaks slowly enough for everyone else to understand.

f. The only problem, is that the residents of the foreign student dormitory learn, probably just as much Spanish, and Chinese, and Arabic as they do English.

Exercise 7. Add punctuation marks, capitalizing appropriately.

I am a foreign student   I was born in Japan   then I moved to Korea because my father got a job with a Korean bank   later I came to the United States   for I wanted to study here   now I am attending college   but I will graduate in June   then I will return to Korea   where my parents are still living   and look for a job   also I intend to spend time in Japan   which is my native land.

Exercise 8. Read through the essay, "Velva, North Dakota" (page 193). Then, referring back to the original, insert quotation punctuation in the following passage where appropriate. In addition to quotation marks, give attention to introductory and closing punctuation and to titles, and insert page references at the end of each paragraph in the passage.

In his essay Velva, North Dakota, Eric Sevareid describes the changes that have occurred in his hometown:
My home town has changed in these thirty years of the American story. It is changing now, will go on changing as America changes. Its biography, I suspect, would read much the same as that of all other home towns. Depression and war and prosperity have all left their marks.
According to Sevareid, such changes have included changes in sights, which show a new precision, and in sounds. Moreover, although the people have not changed, the kinds of people have changed. As Sevareid writes the characters are vanishing in Velva. In addition, Velvans dress differently and eat exotic delicacies they only read about in former times. As Sevareid says modern tastes, manners, philosophies, fears and ambitions have touched his town as indelibly as they have touched New York.

Chapter 22

Sentence Agreement

In addition to being complete and correctly punctuated, a sentence must also be grammatically consistent; that is, each word in the sentence must agree with the rest of the sentence in terms of tense, number, person, and so on. Sentences that are inconsistent may confuse or distract the reader. Student writers should be aware of the inconsistencies that commonly arise in their essays so they can avoid them.

Predication

Inconsistent

During last semester was when I first arrived in the United States.

The sentence above has an inconsistent predicate. *During last semester* is an adverb and therefore cannot be a subject. Thus, the verb *was* has no subject. The real subject–verb pair in the sentence is I . . . . *arrived*. Thus, the sentence should read as follows:

Consistent

During last semester I first arrived in the United States.

Be careful of other inconsistent predicates arising from adverb–verb pairings:

Inconsistent	**Consistent**
In school was where he studied Greek.	School was where he studied Greek.
Because of work is why he learned it.	Because of work, he learned it.
By traveling is how he became fluent.	By traveling, he became fluent.

Number

Inconsistent

Everyone should do their homework on time.

In the sentence above, *everyone* is grammatically singular (even though we colloquially take it to refer to a number of individuals). Thus, the possessive pronoun *their* should be singular. Another way of saying this is that there must be agreement between subject and verb and between a pronoun and its antecedent (the word it stands for). The corrected sentence should read as follows:

Consistent

Everyone should do his (or her) homework on time.

Similarly, all of the pronouns in this list are singular:

each	everybody	somebody
either	everyone	someone
neither	nobody	anybody
	no one	anyone

Even when one of these pronouns is followed by a phrase containing *of* and a plural object (as in *of these pronouns* in this sentence), the pronoun itself remains singular. Thus, the writer should avoid mistakes like the following:

Inconsistent

Neither of the girls ever have their homework.
One of the girls has their homework.

The corrected sentences should read:

Consistent

Neither of the girls ever has her homework.
One of the girls has her homework.

The following adjectives are likewise always singular:

each	either
every	neither

Thus, the sentence below is incorrect:

Inconsistent

Neither girl has their homework (*Their* should be the singular *her.*)

The word *none* is sometimes singular and sometimes plural depending on whether the writer wishes to emphasize the individuality of each member of the group or the group as a whole:

Consistent

None of the students likes the course. (Individuals are emphasized.)
None of the students like the course. (The group is emphasized.)

There is no choice, however, when the writer's subject consists of a singular noun that refers to a body of several members:

Inconsistent

The administration doesn't care; they just keep requiring the same old courses.

In this sentence, *they* is used in a loose way to refer to the members of the administration. But the plural pronoun is inconsistent with the singular noun *administration*. The sentence should read as follows:

Consistent

The administration doesn't care; it just keeps requiring the same old courses.
The members of the administration don't care; they just keep requiring the same old courses.

(Note that the feeling in the two sentences is not exactly the same; the second sentence is more critical of the individual members than is the first sentence.)

Some students incorrectly mix singular and plural forms as a way of avoiding sexism (the favoring of one sex over another) in their writing, as in this sentence:

Everyone should do their homework on time.

However, alternating between singular and plural forms is awkward, inconsistent, and inappropriate for college essays.

Some instructors may still prefer using only the masculine pronoun (*he/him/his*) to indicate a singular indefinite being. However, in general, students can avoid usage that might be considered sexist by using any of the following methods:

1. Use the plural wherever possible.

Students should do their homework on time.

2. Reword the sentence to avoid the use of pronouns altogether.

Everyone should do homework on time.

3. Use *he or she/him or her/his or her* as often as feasible when a singular pronoun is unavoidable.

    Everyone should do his or her homework on time.

4. Alternate between masculine and feminine forms in separate discussions:

    Everyone should do his homework on time. Otherwise, he may be unable to understand the material being discussed in class.

    And later, in another discussion in the essay:

    Similarly, if a student puts off writing a report until the night before it is due, she will not be able to produce a paper that is thoughtfully and carefully written.

    If this alternative is used, students should take care not to adhere to traditional stereotypes:

    The doctor examined her patient.
    The nurse wheeled his patient down the hall.

Inconsistency of number may also arise in the handling of verb phrases. Verb phrases are always singular, regardless of the number of objects they include:

Consistent

Knowing several languages is advantageous in business.
To have two girlfriends is dangerous.

Inconsistent

Knowing several languages are advantageous in business.
To have two girlfriends are fun.

Compound subjects joined by *and* are, of course, plural:

The students and the teacher are late.

But in sentences with compound subjects joined by *or, either . . . or,* and *neither . . . nor,* the number of the verb should be consistent with the number of the last word in the subject whether it is singular or plural. Thus,

Neither the students nor the teacher is on time.

Finally, phrases such as *with, together with, in addition to,* and *as well as* are prepositions and should not be confused with conjunctions. Subjects including such phrases do not become compound subjects and do not require a plural verb. For example,

The teacher as well as the students is always late.

Person

Inconsistent

When someone has work to do, you should do it right away.

In the sentence above, the pronouns *someone* and *you* are inconsistent in person. *Someone* is a third-person pronoun, whereas *you* is a second-person pronoun. The correct sentence would read:

Consistent

When someone has work to do, he should do it right away.

Or,

When you have work to do, you should do it right away.

This problem often arises when the writer wishes to use the imperative mood:

Inconsistent

When someone has work to do, do it!

Consistent

When you have work to do, do it!

A related problem arises when a writer switches from the passive voice in one clause in a sentence to the second person in another clause:

Inconsistent

When a job has to be done, you should do it.
When a job has to be done, do it.

Consistent

When you have to do a job, do it.

Tense

Inconsistent

The teacher said Sam's essay is the best in the class.

Consistent

The teacher said Sam's essay was the best in the class.

The first verb in a piece of writing establishes the tense. All subsequent verbs must be consistent with that tense. Any change in tense must be signaled by an appropriate transitional expression (*before, now, in the future*, and so on).

Although inconsistencies in tense may arise simply out of carelessness, they commonly arise in the reporting of speech (indirect quotation). In the sentence above, the teacher said something in the past. Since the speaker is paraphrasing, not directly quoting, the teacher, the paraphrased words must also be written in the past tense. *The teacher said* can be called the attribution (indicating to whom a quotation is assigned or attributed). What she said can be loosely called the quotation. And these must be grammatically consistent with one another.

A few rules make reporting speech a fairly simple, mechanical process.

1. Make the person of the quotation consistent with the person of the attribution.
    Original (Mrs. Smith talking): I have the essays.

Consistent

  Mrs. *Smith* said *she* had the essays.

Inconsistent

  Mrs. Smith said I have the essays.

2. Make the tense of the quotation consistent with the tense of the attribution.
    Original: Sam's essay is the best in the class.

Consistent

  She *said* Sam's essay *was* the best in the class.

Inconsistent

  She said Sam's essay is the best in the class.

3. For interrogatives (questions), reverse verb–subject order to normal subject–verb order.
    Original (to Sam): Will you read it aloud?

Consistent

  She asked Sam if *he would* read it aloud.

Inconsistent

  She asked Sam would he read it aloud.

4. Add relators according to the type of sentence reported.

If sentence is:	Add:
declarative (regular)	that (optional)

  She said (*that*) Sam's essay was excellent.

yes/no-interrogative	if/whether

  She asked him *if* he had written it by himself.

information-interrogative	interrogative word (where, when, why, how, and so on)

  She asked him *when* he had written the essay.

imperative (command or request)   to (imperatives are reported in the infinitive, without tense)

She told him *to* speak up.

negative imperative   not to

She told him *not to* rush.

5. Eliminate question marks and exclamation points belonging to the original.
   Original: Did you write the essay?

Consistent

She asked him if he had written the essay.

Inconsistent

She asked him if he had written the essay?

6. Make all time adverbs in the original consistent with the tense of the attribution.
   Original: Will you come and see me tomorrow?

Consistent

She asked if he would come and see her the next day.

Inconsistent

She asked if he would come and see her tomorrow. (unless speech is reported on the same day)

The following dialogue further demonstrates the guidelines set forth above:

	Dialogue	*Reported Speech*
Teacher:	I am going to give a grammar lesson today.	The teacher said she was going to give a grammar lesson that day.
Student:	Will there be a quiz on the material?	The student asked her whether there would be a quiz on the material.
Teacher:	Do birds fly?	The teacher asked the student if birds flew.
Student:	What kind of quiz will it be?	The student asked the teacher what kind of quiz it would be.
Teacher:	Come and see, but don't be late.	The teacher told the student to come and see, but not to be late.

All the sentences in the dialogue at the left use present tense verbs (*will* is a present tense auxiliary verb that combines with an infinitive to form the future tense). When the dialogue is reported with past tense attributions (right), the verbs are written in the past tense (with the exception of the tenseless infinitives). When a dialogue includes past tense verbs, these verbs are written not in the simple past, but in the past perfect tense:

Student:	I didn't do my home-work last night.	The student said he hadn't done his home-work the night before.
Teacher:	Why didn't you?	The teacher asked him why he hadn't.
Student:	I didn't get the assign-ment.	The student said he hadn't gotten the assign-ment.

Form

Inconsistent

She liked neither to read the news nor watching it on TV.

In this sentence, *to read* and *watching* are correlatives and should be written in the same form, either as infinitives (to read; to watch) or as participles (*reading; watching*). The sentence should read:

Consistent

She liked neither to read the news nor to watch it on TV.
She liked neither reading the news nor watching it on TV.

This consistency of form is called parallelism. Each of two coordinates (words joined by *and*), each of two correlatives (words introduced by *both . . . and, either . . . or, neither . . . nor, not only . . . but also*), and every item in a series of three or more are considered parallel and must have the same form: noun with noun, participle with participle, and so forth.

Consistency of form also affects how much material must be repeated in each item in a coordinate or correlative construction. For example:

Inconsistent

Not only must you turn off the TV, but also the radio.

In the sentence above, *the radio*, although a noun like TV, is not sufficient as a correlative of *you must turn off the* TV. The corrected sentence would read:

Consistent

Not only must you turn off the TV, but you must also turn off the radio.

Of course, the sentence might also be corrected by a different positioning of *not only* to refer only to *the* TV:

Consistent

You must turn off not only the TV, but also the radio.

Structure

Inconsistent

Walking in the park, the trees looked beautiful.

In the sentence above, the participial phrase *walking in the park* grammatically refers to *the trees*. As a result, the reader may come away with the wrong and rather comical image of trees walking in the park. The writer has simply omitted the proper referent of *walking in the park*. The sentence might be revised by adding an appropriate referent:

Consistent

Walking in the park, I thought the trees looked beautiful.
As I walked in the park, the trees looked beautiful.

In both of these sentences the person doing the walking (I) is made clear.
Like participles, infinitives lend themselves to this kind of error:

Inconsistent

To get an A, all these facts must be mastered.

In this sentence, *facts* (rather than students) are striving to get an A. The corrected sentence would read:

Consistent

To get an A, the student must master all these facts.

The type of error in the inconsistent sentences above is called a *dangling modifier*. The modifier has no real referent to which it can attach itself, so it "dangles" (hangs loosely) from the sentence. A related error is the squinting modifier. The *squinting modifier* is positioned between two words so that it is not clear which of them it is supposed to modify:

Inconsistent

Mrs. Smith teaches grammar only to foreign students.

In this sentence, *only* might refer to *grammar* (thus, the only subject Mrs. Smith teaches) or to *foreign students* (the only students to whom Mrs. Smith teaches grammar as well, perhaps, as other subjects). Assuming that the latter version is the intended one, we might revise:

Consistent

Mrs. Smith teaches grammar to foreign students only.

A modifier generally should be placed directly before or after the word it modifies. In any other position it becomes a misplaced modifier and may create a confusing or awkward sentence:

Inconsistent

Mrs. Smith only teaches foreign students.

In this sentence, Mrs. Smith seems to have rather a monotonous existence: she does not do anything else but teach foreign students. To give Mrs. Smith credit for having any other interests in her life, the writer must revise:

Consistent

Mrs. Smith teaches only foreign students.

Finally, it is incorrect to place a modifier between *to* and an infinitive verb. There are some exceptions, on occasion, but the writer should make all efforts not to *split the infinitive*:

Correct

She never seems *to finish* anything completely.

Incorrect

She never seems *to completely finish* anything.

Comparison

Incomplete

He liked American colleges because he thought they were bigger.

The comparison above is incomplete. The reader asks, "bigger than what?" A writer might try to improve his sentence thus:

Incomplete

He liked American colleges because he thought they were bigger than his country.
He liked American colleges because he thought they were bigger than in his country.

In neither of these sentences, however, is the comparison consistent. In the first, the size of American colleges is compared to the size of the subject's entire country, obviously not what the writer had in mind. In the second sentence, American colleges are compared implicitly to *American* colleges in the subject's own country. To correct the sentence, the writer must make each part of the comparison consistent with the other:

Complete

He liked American colleges because he thought they were bigger than the colleges in his own country.

Similarly, either of the following two sentences would require revision to make the comparisons consistent:

Incomplete

>   I am doing better in English.
>   I am doing better in English than last year.

The correct version would read:

Complete

>   I am doing better in English than I was doing last year.

   With *comparatives*, comparable objects must be clear in the sentence. With *superlatives*, a group or class from which the superlative can stand out must be identified. For example, the sentence below contains an inconsistent or incomplete superlative:

Incomplete

>   This cafeteria serves the worst food.

To be consistent, this sentence must state clearly in what group the food stands out as the worst:

Complete

>   This cafeteria serves the worst food on campus.
>   This cafeteria serves the worst food I've ever eaten.
>   This cafeteria serves the worst food imaginable.

   Similarly, in sentences with *so* and *such* the comparison must be completed:

Incomplete

>   The meat is so tough!

This sentence is common in colloquial speech, but is inconsistent grammatically. Revise this way:

Complete

>   The meat is so tough that it must be cut with an axe.

or, less colorfully:

Complete

>   The meat is very tough.

   Finally, the writer should be careful not to omit necessary words from sentences containing comparisons:

Incomplete

>   I am doing as well or better than I was doing last year.

This sentence omits *as* from the end of the phrase *as well as*. It should be written:

Complete

I am doing as well as or better than I was doing last year.

A comical result can arise from an omission like the one in the following sentence:

Incomplete

Every week I write to my parents and several people I like.

In this sentence, the missing word is *other*. Unless *other* is inserted to modify *people* I *like*, the writer's parents are excluded from that select group. To make his or her parents happy, the writer should revise as follows:

Complete

Every week I write to my parents and several other people I like.

Possession

Generally, possession is indicated in English by one of two devices, as in the sentences that follow:

This is Maria's homework.
This is the homework of Maria.

And occasionally (never with the definite article), both devices are used together in order to emphasize ownership:

This is homework of Maria's.

Although this third usage is colloquial, it is so common that it is generally accepted. And in certain cases, those in which the use of either device by itself might be confusing to the reader, the use of both devices together is not only accepted, but required:

This is a picture of Maria's.

In the sentence above, Maria's ownership of the picture is emphasized. Had the writer used only one possessive device, the matter of ownership would not be clear:

This is Maria's picture.
This is a picture of Maria.

Either of these sentences might indicate that Maria is the subject of the picture rather than its owner. Thus, when a writer wishes to express ownership of a picture (or photograph, thought, idea, and so on), he must use both possessive devices.

Finally, sentence consistency demands the use of the possessive with the gerund (present participle used as a noun) in sentences like the following:

Correct

I don't like the students' talking in class.
I don't like their talking in class.

Since the gerund is a noun, it cannot be modified by another noun or pronoun. In formal essays, the writer should avoid the colloquial construction:

Incorrect

I don't like them talking in class.

Summary

In addition to being complete and correctly punctuated, sentences must also be internally consistent. Each word in a sentence must agree with the other words in terms of predication, number, person, tense, form, structure, comparison, and possession. Errors in consistency of tense (as well as person) often arise in reporting speech. By breaking down the sentence into its parts and by following simple rules, the student can eliminate such errors from his or her writing.

Exercises

Exercise 1.   Correct errors in sentence agreement in groups a, b, and c, below.

- a. 1) The dorms on the university campus should be safer.
  2) Every resident should know that their lives are safe.
  3) But the university doesn't seem to care; they don't take needed security measures.
  4) To improve security, criminals must be stopped before they enter the dorms.
  5) At present, if someone wants to enter a dorm, you just say, "Hi!" and walk in.
  6) During the evening is when this is especially dangerous.
  7) The following procedural change will help so much.
  8) Dorm security guards will ask all visitors their names, addresses, and to tell them the number of the room they are visiting.
  9) The guard will call the resident of the room with the information and send the visitor up only if the resident said it was all right.
  10) The visitor having an ID card will mean nothing without the resident giving his "OK."
- b. 1) When he was first admitted to State University, Robert thought it was such a great place.
  2) However, since arriving here, everything has gone wrong for him.
  3) He hates the campus's crowds, noise, and being impersonal.
  4) He likes his roommate, but hates him blasting his radio until 3:00 a.m. every night.

5) He prefers to starve than eating at the student cafeteria.

6) To make matters worse, the administration has announced that they plan to increase the tuition for the following semester.

7) And to top it all off, while dancing in a local disco, Robert's car was stolen!

8) Now Robert believes that if students want to enjoy college life, you shouldn't come to State.

9) Thus, next term Robert plans to transfer to a school at which student life will be better than State.

10) Last week Robert told me he is applying to my university; I told him I think you are making a mistake.

c. 1) The class met at the library yesterday, but today they are meeting in their usual meeting place.

2) Walking through the library, the huge collection of books and periodicals amazed me.

3) The teacher discussed how to choose a topic, how to find materials, and writing a research paper.

4) Each of the students have to use at least two sources for research.

5) If a student doesn't complete the research paper, an F will be given to him as a final grade.

6) Professors always say, "When one gets an assignment, don't leave it until the night before it's due."

7) By leaving the work until the night before it's due, an assignment may seem confusing when it is finally looked at.

8) But even if the student is confused, you won't have an opportunity to ask for the professor's clarification.

9) Now let's see; are we only supposed to do part of this exercise or all of it?

10) This homework exercise should come as no surprise; last week the teacher said there will be a homework exercise this week.

Exercise 2.   Rewrite the following dialogues in the past tense as indirectly reported speech.

A.   **Anne**:   Who are you going to vote for?

       Bob: I'm not going to vote.

       Anne: Do you believe in the democratic process or not? Don't complain about the candidates; get out and vote!

       Bob: I can't; I forgot to register.

B.   *Teresa*:   I won't be at the party tomorrow night.

      Juan: What are you going to be doing?

      Teresa: I have to go to the library.

      Juan: Didn't you go to the library last night?

      Teresa: Don't even ask!

C.   *Mary*:   Will you look into my mailbox for me?

      John: I don't see anything in it.

      Mary: I can't believe it!

      John: Don't take my word for it; look for yourself.

      Mary: It's empty all right!

      John: What were you expecting?

      Mary: I expected another tuition-increase notice. I seem to get one everyday.

Exercise 3.   Correct errors in sentence consistency in the following paragraphs.

The other day I had a talk with my roommate, Steve. I told him don't wear my sweaters anymore. He said he won't. I asked him will he clean the tub after he uses it. He said he will. I begged him don't play his radio at midnight. He agreed not to do it.

Last night at five minutes after midnight, Steve turned on his radio and started to clean the tub—with my sweaters. Maybe we need to have another talk.

Chapter 23

Other Conventions

U sage varies from one language or culture to another regarding such formal matters as capitalization, italics, abbreviation, numbers and figures, dates and places, and hyphenation. In one country, all nouns are capitalized; in another, only proper ones. In still another, students print exclusively in block-shaped capitals. One country uses hyphens between month, day, and year; another uses commas; a third uses slash marks (/). Foreign student writers must overcome the habits of their native cultures and handle conventions according to American English usage. Only then will their essays meet the standards expected at American colleges and universities. When in doubt about capitalization, italicization, abbreviation, hyphenation, and so forth for a particular word students should consult an American dictionary.

Capitalization

A mixture of lowercase and capital letters is the norm in American English composition. General rules indicating where and where not to capitalize follow.

The First Letter of a Sentence. The first word of a sentence is always capitalized.

> Students must study. Why? The answer is simple.

A capital is also used for the first letter of a sentence in parentheses occurring between complete sentences:

> Students must study. (We all know why.) But do they?

No capital, however, is used in a parenthetical clause embedded *within* a sentence:

Incorrect

> Although students must study (we all know why), they often do not.

Independent Clauses Following a Colon (:). Some style manuals call for a complete sentence following a colon to be capitalized; others do not. Students should decide ahead of time which style they are going to use and should maintain that style throughout their paper.

> The answer is simple: Students must study in order to pass.
> The answer is simple: students must study in order to pass.

It is improper, however, to capitalize a clause following a semicolon (;):

Incorrect

> The answer is simple; Indeed, it is a joke.

Correct

> The answer is simple; indeed, it is a joke.

The First Letter of Quoted Material. Writers should capitalize the first letter of quoted material if the letter was capitalized in the original or if it begins a sentence or a complete remark in the writer's own text:

> He states that "Students must study." (*Students* is capitalized in the original.)
> "Do they?" asks the author. (*Do* begins a sentence in the writer's own text.)
> His answer is clear: "Frequently, they do not." (*Frequently* begins a complete remark in the writer's own text.)

The Word "I." The pronoun I is always capitalized, whether it appears at the beginning or in the middle of a sentence.

> I think I will study now.

Proper Nouns. Proper nouns are specific names of people, places, and things and are always capitalized, as the following examples show:

1. *People*: George Washington, Vladimir Lenin, William Shakespeare
2. *Places*: Earth (the planet), the United States of America, Mexico City, Main Street, the Empire State Building, Macy's Department Store, the South (as a region of the U.S.—I *live in the South*—but not as a direction—*Birds fly south in the fall*)

3. *Businesses and institutions*: General Motors, Sony, Stanford University, the Massachusetts Institute of Technology, the U.S. State Department, the U.S. Congress (*Note*: When these forms are shortened, they generally should be lowercased—the *Department of English* becomes *the department*, for example. Exceptions to this rule are references to federal institutions that have names similar to state institutions. To avoid confusion, the federal title is capitalized even when shortened. For instance, *the* U.S. *Supreme Court* becomes *the Court* to differentiate it from a supreme court of a state.)

4. *Organized groups*: Catholic(s), Moslem(s), Jew(s), American(s), Republican(s), Social Democrat(s), Communist(s) (party member) (*Note*: Looser groupings should be lowercased—blacks, leftists, moderates, capitalists, freshmen, seniors, communists [believer in Marxism].)

5. *Historical periods*: the Middle Ages, the Renaissance, the Industrial Revolution, World War I, the Second World War

6. *Days, dates*: Sunday, Monday, March, September, the Fourth of July, Ramadan, Christmas, Yom Kippur (*Note*: An exception to this is seasons. Lowercase the names of seasons unless they refer to an academic semester—I *like spring better than summer*, I *hope to graduate in the Spring* 1990 *semester*.)

Proper Adjectives Based on Proper Nouns. Proper adjectives, like proper nouns, should be capitalized: Shakespearean, Leninist, Mexican, Christian, Jewish, Moslem.

Ranks and Titles. All ranks and titles accompanied by a name should be capitalized: President Reagan, Queen Elizabeth II, King Hussein I, Colonel Quaddaffi (Most titles unaccompanied by names are not capitalized, e.g., *the president, the professor*. However, even with no accompanying name, certain titles are consistently capitalized, e.g., the *President of the United States*, the *Queen of England*.)

Abbreviations. In general, an abbreviation is capitalized if the noun that it abbreviates is capitalized. Most initials also are capitalized. For example: MIT, U.S.A., J.F.K., USSR, BA, PhD, Pres., VP, Sept., Dec., Mon., TV, VCR. Common nouns, when abbreviated, should be lowercased: a.m., p.m., etc., et al., pp. (For an explanation of when to use periods with abbreviations, see pages 303–06.)

Academic Disciplines. Use lowercase for general fields of learning (biology, mechanical engineering, sociology, mathematics), but capitalize specific college courses (History 101, Mechanical Engineering 202).

Religious Terms. Religious terms generally are capitalized: the Old Testament, the New Testament, the Bible, the Koran, God (or words referring to God, such as *Lord*, He, *Him*, and so forth), Christ, Buddha.

Names of Family Members. Capitalize names of family members *used as names*:

I hope Mother will like this gift.
Please, Dad, may I have the car this weekend?

Put in lowercase names of family members used generically:

I hope my mother will like this gift.
His dad says working is good for him.

Titles of Works. In titles and subtitles of works (books, articles, plays, poems, and so on), capitalize the first word, the last word, and all words in between except articles, conjunctions, and prepositions of four or fewer letters:

> Gone with the Wind
> A Day in the Life of Ivan Denisovich
> To Bus or Not to Bus: A History of Racial Integration in American Schools
> Caught Between Two Worlds: The Story of My Life

With untranslated foreign titles, capitalization should follow the form used in the original language:

> los de abajo
> les misérables

Italics

Italics, the slanting print in which the first word of this section is printed, is used to make particular words stand out on a printed page. Generally, writers indicate italics by underlining words they wish to be italicized (unless they prepare their manuscripts on a word processor equipped with an italics function). Therefore, student writers should take care not to underline indiscriminately; italicizing (underlining) a phrase *does not make a weak statement strong*, and a page *overfilled* with italics is *jarring* and *difficult* to read (as you can see here). Students should restrict the use of italics to those particular instances in which it is warranted.

Titles. Italicize (underline) titles of long works (works that are complete in themselves, such as books, plays, television programs, movies, magazines, newspapers, and book-length poems and essays) when you refer to them:

> *The Pearl* (a novel)
> *Gone with the Wind* (a novel)
> *Hamlet* (a play)
> *Dallas* (a TV series)
> *Time* (a magazine)
> San Francisco *Chronicle* (a newspaper)

(Note that for newspapers and magazines, *places* of publication are generally not italicized. Some exceptions are the *London Times*, the *New York Times*, and the *Washington Post*.)

Titles of short works (short stories, chapters, articles, reports, episodes in series, essays and poems shorter than book length) are *not* italicized. Rather, they are put in double quotation marks. (See page 280.)

Titles of sacred works are neither italicized nor placed in quotation marks:

> the Bible
> Genesis
> the Koran

Note that, in contrast to titles to which you refer, the titles of your own essays should be neither italicized nor put in quotation marks. Rather, your own title should appear by itself, centered on the first printed line of a manuscript, with no end punctuation (unless the title is a question or exclamation), as in this example:

The Story of My Life

Proper Names of Transport Vehicles. Italicize names of ships, aircraft, and trains:

the *Queen Elizabeth* II
the *Challenger*
the *Orient Express*

Foreign Terms. Italicize foreign words that have not yet attained standard usage in English:

The smorgasbord was simply *wunderbar*!
We had a choice of pie à la mode or *gateaux à la russe* for dessert.

But do not italicize words that have become standard in English. This can be checked by seeing whether or not a word appears in a standard American English dictionary. See, for example, smorgasbörd, forte, schlemiel, macho, taco, per se, vice versa.

Latin technical terms are italicized: *homo sapiens*. Latin abbreviations and expressions may or may not be: *sic* (always italicized), *ibid.* (italics optional), etc., e.g., i.e., et al., and so forth.

Note that the English translation of a foreign term is generally put in quotation marks:

She called him *tovarich*—"comrade."

Words as Words. Italicize words that are referred to as words:

The word *democratic* has many interpretations.

Emphasis. Although italics may be used to emphasize particular words or groups of words, student writers should avoid overuse of this device. In particular, italics should not be used to highlight a sarcastic or humorous remark (explanation kills a joke):

Inappropriate use

Calling the reactor safeguards 100 percent foolproof seems like a *slight* exaggeration in light of the disaster.

Abbreviations

Although abbreviations save time and space, they should generally be avoided in nontechnical college essays. The full names of months, days, cities, states, countries, streets, courses of study, and measurements should be written out when they appear in the main text of an essay, as below:

Appropriate use

One Sunday in December, I went to New York City with my roommate and looked at department store windows along Fifth Avenue.
When our English 1 instructor told us to do the exercises on page 112 of our textbook, we had no idea it would take four hours.

Note how much less readable are the same sentences when abbreviations are used:

Inappropriate use

One Sun. in Jan. I went to NYC w/my roommate and looked at department store windows along Fifth Ave.
When our Eng. 1 instructor told us to do the exs. on p. 112 of our textbook, we had no idea it would take 4 hrs.

Abbreviations Permissible in the Main Text. Some abbreviations, however, are permitted within the main text of an essay. These include the following:

etc.	et cetera (and the rest)
i.e.	id est (that is)
e.g.	for example

With numbers

a.m.	before noon
p.m.	after noon
BC	before Christ
AD	in the year of our Lord
m.p.h.	miles per hour

With names

Mr.	mister (title for any man)
Ms.	title for any woman
Mrs.	title for married woman
Dr.	doctor
Sr.	senior
Jr.	junior

With full names

Hon.	Honorable
Rev.	Reverend
BA	Bachelor of Arts
BS	Bachelor of Science
MA	Master of Arts
MD	Doctor of Medicine
MBA	Master of Business
PhD	Doctor of Philosophy
U.S.A./U.S.	United States
USSR	Soviet Union
D.C.	District of Columbia
U.N.	United Nations
CIA	Central Intelligence Agency
FBI	Federal Bureau of Investigation

NATO   North Atlantic Treaty Organization
OPEC   Organization of Petroleum Exporting Countries

In addition, when a long technical term or name of an institution is used repeatedly in an essay, after it has been written out in full and accompanied by the standard abbreviation or acronym (a word formed from the initial letters of a name), it is usually preferable to use the shorter form in subsequent references:

> According to the Health Essentials Lookout Program (HELP), Acquired Immune Deficiency Syndrome (AIDS) is regarded with great alarm by medical professionals in the U.S. In the view of Dr. T. G. Thornton, a HELP researcher, AIDS, a virus, has reached epidemic proportions among certain populations and may threaten the public at large.

Abbreviations Permissible in Citations. Other abbreviations, notably those of words that refer to outside sources consulted in research papers, may be used in footnotes, endnotes, parenthetical references, and bibliographic entries. They are not, however, used in the main text of essays.

anon.	anonymous (by an unknown author)
c.f.	compare
ch./chs.	chapter(s)
ed./eds.	edition(s)
f./ff.	and the following (use *ff.* for multiple lines or pages)
ibid.	the same (as the title and author named in the preceding note)
l./ll.	line(s)
ms./mss.	manuscript(s)
n./nn.	note(s)
n.d.	no date
n.p.	no page, no place
no./nos.	number(s)
p./pp.	page(s)
rev.	revised, review(ed)
sec./secs.	section(s)
tr./trans.	translator, translation
vol./vols.	volume(s)
passim*	throughout
*sic**	thus—used in quotations when the original text contains an error

(*Because *passim* and *sic* are not abbreviations but complete Latin words, neither of them is followed by a period.)

In addition to the abbreviations listed above, it is also permissible in citations to abbreviate the names of publishers and months and places of publication. Naturally, only standard forms should be used. Abbreviations of many publishers' names can be found in the MLA *Handbook*. For other abbreviations, the student should consult the dictionary.

Form of Abbreviations. Abbreviations ending in lowercase letters are generally followed by a period:

Mr.

In abbreviations made up entirely of lowercase letters, an unspaced period follows each letter:

m.p.h.

In general, initials are not followed by periods except in persons' names (W. H. Auden). In a few cases, periods are optional (U.S./US, U.N./UN, J.F.K./JFK). MLA preference, however, is to omit the periods. When periods are used, generally no space is inserted after the period: U.S.A.

In abbreviations of persons' full names, however, spaces are inserted after the periods: B. F. Goodrich.

Writing Numbers

Usage varies from discipline to discipline regarding how numbers are to be written out. However, the following guidelines will be adequate for most college essay writing.

Numbers Versus Figures. In general, single-digit numbers should be written out, and double-digit numbers and higher are expressed by numerals. Thus, we have

one, three, seven

and

10, 52, 101, 1,284.

If numbers are used infrequently in an essay, however, numbers consisting of only one or two words can be written out:

eleven, two hundred, fourteen hundred

Very large numbers should be expressed by a combination of words and figures:

6 million, 1.5 billion

Note that all numbers beginning a sentence, regardless of their size, should be written out:

Forty-four votes were all they needed.

Use figures for the following:
1. All numbers in tables.
2. All single-digit numbers when they are in the same sentence or discussion as larger numbers.

Class size ranges from 9 to 125 students.

3. Sums of money following a dollar sign ($) and percentages.

$15.25, $2.00, 9%, 84%

However, when amounts of money and whole percentages are used infrequently, two-word amounts can be written out.

two dollars, fourteen percent

4. All numbers in addresses, dates, parts of text (pages, chapters, lines, and so forth), and hours followed by *a.m.* or *p.m.*.

On August 8, 1982, we met at 11 Montrose Avenue at 6 p.m. and studied pages 2–27 of the text.

Whole hours not followed by a.m. or p.m., though, are generally written out:

twelve noon
six o'clock
I picked her up at eight.

Commas Versus Periods. In America, commas, *not* periods, generally separate every three digits of whole numbers:

1,000
6,000,000

Commas are not used, however, between the digits of years:

1990

Between whole numbers and a decimal, a period (*not* a comma) is used:

98.6 Fahrenheit

Roman Numerals. Capital Roman numerals may be used for outlines, chapters in a book, the numbering of royalty and wars:

World War I, Carlos II, Chapter V

Lowercase Roman numerals are generally used for introductory pages preceding the main text of a book: p. xi.

Roman numerals are formed as follows:

1	I	i	6	VI	vi	11	XI	xi	50	L	l
2	II	ii	7	VII	vii	15	XV	xv	90	XC	xc
3	III	iii	8	VIII	viii	20	XX	xx	100	C	c
4	IV	iv	9	IX	ix	21	XXI	xxi	500	D	d
5	V	v	10	X	x	40	XL	xl	1000	M	m

Inclusive Numbers. Students need to write inclusive numbers when they are indicating between what pages an article or citation may be found or between what years a certain event occurred. In writing inclusive numbers,

1. Give the full second number for all numbers between 1 and 99: 2–23, 33–34, 45–58.

2. Give only the last two digits of second numbers above 99 unless more are nec-essary for accuracy: 100–02, 1010–12, 212–13, 99–102, 212–301, 1010–100.

3. Give only the last two digits of years, unless they fall within different centuries: 1860–64, 1986–99, 1899–1901.

Word Division (Syllabication)

Unless a writer is preparing a manuscript on a word processor with a justified (perfectly even) right-hand margin, it should rarely be necessary to divide words at the end of a manuscript line. However, if for reasons of appearance a writer does choose to divide a word at the end of a line, he or she cannot do so arbitrarily. Words can be divided only at *syllable breaks* (a *syllable* is a single, uninterrupted sound which forms part of a word or a whole word). Furthermore, in English, unlike in some other languages, it is not always possible to determine syllable breaks from spelling alone. For example, compare the breaks in the words below:

> cho-les-ter-ol
> col-er-ic
> fall-ing
> bid-ding

Thus, students should consult a dictionary if they have any doubt about where syllable breaks occur in a word.

Special Rules. In addition, students should keep in mind several other rules appli-cable to word division:

1. Words of one syllable cannot be divided:

Improper Break

> fill-ed
> frown-ed

2. Word division should not isolate one letter of a word on a line by itself:

Improper Break

> The essay about the instructor's boyfriend didn't seem to a-
> muse the instructor, but the class thought it was very funny.

3. Division of proper nouns should generally be avoided:

Improper Break

> In 1963, the year I was born, the U.S. president, John F. Ken-
> nedy, was assassinated.

4. Hyphenated words—including compound nouns (*land-grabber*), compound adjec-tives (*well-done*), and words formed by a prefix and a root separated by a hyphen (*co-opt*)—should be divided only at the hyphen:

Improper Break

> To understand the revolution, we must look at the socio-eco-
> nomic situation at the time it occurred.

Proper Break

> To understand the revolution, we must look at the socio-
> economic situation at the time it occurred.

Word Division Format. Word divisions are indicated by centering a hyphen (-) between the lines at the end of a line (right-hand margin) of the manuscript:

Not

> hy   -phen

But

> hy-   phen

Articles

Learning how to use articles (*a, an, the*) correctly is often difficult for the student
who is learning English as a second language. The rules for article use are not only
different in various languages, they are also complex and somewhat irregular within
English itself. However, although occasional errors are to be expected, students should
be able to achieve a high degree of correctness in using articles in their writing.

At the most basic level, there are two kinds of nouns between which students
must distinguish in order to use articles correctly: *unspecified* nouns and *specified* nouns.
Unspecified nouns refer to the general idea of a thing without pointing to a particular
example of that thing:

> I am looking for a book. (The particular book is not specified.)

Specified nouns refer to a particular thing:

> I am looking for the book I lost yesterday. (The book is specified.)

A and *an*, called the *indefinite articles*, are used before many unspecified nouns. *The*,
called the *definite article*, is used before most specified nouns. In certain cases, however,
nouns are preceded by no article at all. This may make English article usage seem
arbitrary to the foreign student. But article usage is neither arbitrary nor impossible to
learn. The guidelines below should help the student master the use of English articles:

Unspecified Nouns.

I. A and *an* are used before singular common nouns.

    a. *a* before most consonants and before vowels pronounced as consonants

a mouse
a horse

a university
There is *a* mouse on the teacher's chair.

b. *an* before most vowels and before consonants pronounced as vowels

an owl
an uncle
an hour
There is *an* owl on the teacher's desk.

(Note: The word *one* should not be used in place of the indefinite article unless the writer wishes to focus on the actual quantity of an object:

Incorrect

When I was a child I had *one* dog named Fido.

Correct

When I was a child I had *a* dog named Fido.
When I was a child I had *one* dog. My cousin had two.)

2. No article appears before plural common nouns.

There are mice on the teacher's chair.

Specified Nouns.

1. *The* is used before singular and plural common nouns.

The mouse on the teacher's chair is dead.
The mice on the teacher's chair are dead.

2. No article is used before nouns of indefinite quantity.

Honesty is admirable.
I love nature.
Gasoline is cheap at present.

b. But *the* is inserted if the noun is quantified with a modifier.

The children doubted the honesty of the old woman.
The gasoline I bought today was cheap.

3. No article appears before a noun modified by a possessive.

Correct

his hat
John's car
I borrowed John's car.

Incorrect

    the his hat
    the John's car
    I borrowed the John's car.

4. a. No article is used before most proper nouns used by themselves.

Correct

    I live in New York.
    I want to see Broadway.

Incorrect

    I live in the New York.
    I want to see the Broadway.

  b. But *a/an/the* are inserted before proper nouns used as modifiers of common nouns (*a/an* with unspecified, *the* with specified common nouns).

Correct

    I want to see a California sunset.
    The New York traffic was very heavy.
    I want to see a Broadway show.
    I want to see the Broadway show you told me about.

  c. *The* is used before *some* multiple-word proper nouns in which the first word serves as a modifier of the final word.

I saw
    the University of North Carolina (but, I *saw* UNC)
    the Rocky Mountains
    the Pacific Ocean
    the United States/the U.S.A.
    the Soviet Union/the USSR
    the Empire State Building
    the Schubert Theatre
    the Grand Canyon
    the Rolling Stones

  d. But no article is used before others.

I saw
    Yale University
    Potash Mountain
    Niagara Falls
    Beverly Hills
    Park Avenue
    J.F.K. Airport
    Central Park
    Def Leppard

e. And either *the* or no article is used before others.

I saw
   (the) Grand Central Station
   (the) Los Angeles Airport
   (the) Hartford Civic Center

Since the rule for article use with multiple-word proper nouns is somewhat fuzzy, students might do well to memorize correct usage for the proper nouns they use most frequently. Newspapers, magazines, instructors, and fellow students are the sources to consult when in doubt.

Exercises

Exercise 1.   Change lowercase letters to capitals as appropriate:

my feelings about life at the university of suburbia

before i came to the university of suburbia, a university to the east of new york city, my mother said, "don't worry, maria; it will be like any other university." but for a venezuelan girl who speaks only spanish and has never been more than five miles outside of caracas, the university of suburbia is different.

i arrived at the university on monday, september 1st, at 3 p.m. it took me several hours to get used to the english signs everywhere; it took me several days to get used to the american students in my math and science classes and in my dorm, kingsley hall. it took me several weeks to get used to the american accents of dr. drawl from the south and mrs. twang from the northeast (my instructors in psychology 101 and sociology 100, respectively). it took me several months to get used to the traffic along main street, second avenue, and washington boulevard. it took me all winter— till the middle of march at least—to get used to the cold weather in this part of the u.s.a. and it took me all spring to get used to the panasonic stereos and sony tape decks blasting at all hours of the night and the parties for every holiday from new year's eve to groundhog's day. as for the american food served at johnson dining hall, i don't expect to get used to that before the end of the spring 1991 semester (that is when i am supposed to get my ba degree and get out of here), and god only knows whether i'll survive till then.

the fact is mother was wrong: this university is different. if i had to give a title to the story of my life here so far, i think it would be this: "a year at su is a very long time."

Exercise 2.   underline (italicize) or put in quotation marks the following titles, as appropriate:
   a.   Biology (a book)
   b.   North Toward Home (a book)

   c. Grammatical Conventions (a unit in this textbook)

   d. the Los Angeles Times (a newspaper)

   e. Students Protest Foreign Language Requirement (a newspaper article)

   f. U.S. News and World Report (a magazine)

   g. Olympic Highlights (an article in a magazine)

   h. A Clean, Well-Lighted Place (a short story)

   i. Ba, Fiji (a brief essay)

   j. pensées (a book length essay in French)

   k. Jaws (a movie)

   l. Dynasty (a TV series)

  m. The Colbys Go Shopping (an episode of a TV series)

   n. the Koran (a sacred book)

   o. Exodus (a chapter in the Old Testament)

Exercise 3. Italicize nonstandard foreign words, as appropriate:

Last week I met my girlfriend's fiancé at a local cafe. She is loco en la cabeza about him, but not vice versa. He is very macho and there doesn't seem to be any quid pro quo in their relationship. Nonetheless, I'm sure if she has her way they will be married pronto; there's just no way to fight l'amour.

Exercise 4. Write the standard abbreviations for the terms listed below, looking up in the dictionary any about which you are unsure. Which abbreviations are acceptable in the main text (MT) of an essay? Which are acceptable in citations (C) only?

   a. Mister

   b. Mistress (title for married woman)

   c. Doctor of Philosophy (degree)

   d. Doctor (title of professor)

   e. Medical Doctor (degree)

   f. street

   g. boulevard

   h. company

   i. December

   j. April

   k. Thursday

   l. Wednesday

  m. Saturday

   n. California

   o. United States of America

   p. Soviet Union (or Union of Soviet Socialist Republics)

   q. Federal Bureau of Investigation

r.   Department of the Treasury

s.   etcetera

t.   before Christ

u.   miles per hour

v.   page

w.   pages

x.   number

y.   for example

Exercise 5.   Write out the complete form of any words in the passage below that should not be abbreviated:

On Fri., Nov. 1, 1985, I arrived in the U.S. at J.F.K. International Airport at 11:00 a.m. I had come from Mexico City, Mex., and I was planning to fly to Washington, D.C. that p.m. I had an appointment with a Prof. I had met at the Universidad Nacional de Mexico (UNAM). His name was Dr. Dekatek, and he had come to UNAM to discuss his paper, "Abbreviations Used in the Kookamonga Scroll" (*Journal of Ancient Kookamongan* 4 Jan. 1986).

The Kookamonga Scroll (KOOKS) was discovered in AD 1200, though it is believed to have been written around 500 BC. According to Dr. Dekatek's paper, almost every word in KOOKS is an abbreviation (see the discussion on pp. 1–3); e.g., the abbreviation *bis* seems to stand for the Kookamongan wd. for "cookie," *biskit* (Dekatek 4).

I met the Dr. and his wife, Mrs. Dekatek, at Washington Nat. Airport. We had dinner at a Chinese rest. on Jefferson Ave. We talked about his paper and about his recent trip to the U.K. Dr. and Mrs. Dekatek then took me to see the sights: the Wash. Monument, the White House, and his own favorite, the Dept. of Education. Though we had only a few hrs. together, I feel that during my visit w/ Dr. Dekatek and his wife, I learned a great deal about D.C., the U.K., and KOOKS.

Exercise 6.   Choose the proper form for each numeral used in the following passage:

The international student population at U.S. colleges and universities is large and growing. In the middle of the (20th/twentieth) century, there were roughly (34,000/thirty-four thousand) foreign students at U.S. institutions of higher learning. By (1966/nineteen hundred sixty-six) this population had increased to over (100,000/one hundred thousand). Currently, over (300,000/three hundred thousand) foreign students study at U.S. colleges and universities. Though the rate of increase has slowed—from a peak of (16%/sixteen percent) in the (1970s/nineteen-seventies) to (.9%/nine-tenths of a percent) in 1985—the increase in numbers has continued. And some experts predict that by (1990/nineteen-ninety) the figure might rise to over (1,000,000/1 million) (see *Chronicle of Higher Education* 21 Oct. 1981: (2/two).

The foreign student population at my university is (1/one) good example of this trend. Here, there are over (452/four hundred fifty-two) foreign students among a total student population of under (5,000/five thousand). Last fall alone (120/one hundred twenty) foreign students enrolled in the freshman class, and (57/fifty-seven) more are expected to join them in the spring. Moreover, by January (8th/eighth) the Admissions Office had already received (86/eighty-six) applications from foreign students for Fall (1991/nineteen-ninety-one). The most recent projections estimate total applications to reach between (89/eighty-nine) and (110/one hundred ten).

The trend is a positive one for my university. The university spends only about ($65/sixty-five dollars) per foreign student for special services, and it recovers that easily in the ($9,000/nine thousand dollar) tuition it collects from each student. However, for me, the trend is less positive. Although it is fine to attend a university at which (6/six) staff members devote themselves exclusively to foreign student problems and at which (299/two hundred ninety-nine) other students understand my special situation personally, up to now I have met only (2/two) students at my university who *aren't* foreign.

Exercise 7. Choose the correct form of the number at the left:

a. one thousand
$$\begin{cases} 1000 \\ 1,000 \\ 1.000 \end{cases}$$

b. six thousand two hundred eighty-seven
$$\begin{cases} 6287 \\ 6,287 \\ 6.287 \end{cases}$$

c. one million
$$\begin{cases} 1000000 \\ 1,000,000 \\ 1.000.000 \end{cases}$$

d. three and five-tenths (a decimal)
$$\begin{cases} 3,5 \\ 3.5 \end{cases}$$

e. eighteen hundred (a year)
$$\begin{cases} 1800 \\ 1,800 \end{cases}$$

Exercise 8. Write capital and lowercase Roman numerals for the following:
- a. 3
- b. 4
- c. 5
- d. 6
- e. 9
- f. 15
- g. 19
- h. 25
- i. 58
- j. 120

Exercise 9. Divide italicized words as appropriate:

An interesting pattern has begun to emerge regarding our English *homework*. In our composition class, English 101, our very first homework *assignment* was to write an essay called a narrative. Our teacher said that the *narrative* should be written in the first person. She said also that it should be *about* a personal experience—of our own or of a friend—from which we had *gained* an insight. To write a sense description of a person we knew was our *second* assignment. The teacher said we should try to focus on someone we *loved* dearly. In our next essay we are supposed to analyze the *person-to-person* interactions between members of our families. Often I wonder if our *teacher*, Mrs. Askall, is really interested in our writing skills or if she is just plain *nosy*.

Exercise 10.   Add articles as needed:

_____ Antonio had always wanted to go to _____ good university. At last he was accepted at both _____ University of Connecticut and _____ Connecticut College. He chose _____ his friend's school, _____ U. Conn.

In _____ August _____ Antonio took _____ plane from _____ his country, _____ Portugal, to _____ United States. _____ plane landed at _____ J.F.K. Airport. _____ Antonio took _____ taxi to _____ New York City. He visited _____ Empire State Building. Then he went to _____ Manhattan department store and bought _____ shoes and _____ new suit. He ate in _____ restaurant. He took _____ taxis everywhere. In _____ evening he went to _____ Broadway show. Later, he spent _____ hour in _____ nightclub.

When he finally got to _____ Grand Central Station to catch _____ train to _____ his school, _____ Antonio did not have enough money to buy _____ ticket. Indeed, _____ Antonio's wallet was empty. _____ excitement does not come cheap in _____ U.S.A.

Glossary

abbreviation: a shortened form of a word, usually standard, e.g., *pp.* for *pages.*

absolute term: a word that allows for no degrees, e.g., *everyone, all, unique.* See *overgeneralization.*

abstract term: a word that stands for a concept or idea, e.g., *violence, beauty.* See *concrete term.*

abstracting service: a periodical index that presents recently published abstracts of articles on a given subject.

abstract: a brief summary of the contents of an article.

acknowledgment: a declaration indicating that an idea or quotation derives from another source.

acronym: a word made up of the initial letters of the words in a name, e.g., AIDS for Acquired Immune Deficiency Syndrome.

ad hominem reasoning: an argumentative fallacy in which one attacks one's opponents instead of their position.

adjective: a word that modifies a noun or pronoun, e.g., She speaks *good* English.

adverb: a word that modifies a verb, adjective, adverb, or whole sentence, e.g., She speaks English *well.*

agreement: consistency between subject and verb or between a pronoun and its antecedent.

analogy: an extended comparison between two unlike objects. See *figurative language.*

analysis: an essay pattern in which a whole is broken into its component parts to show how the parts relate to each other and to the whole. There are several types of analyses. See also *cause and effect, classification, comparison and contrast, process, subdivision.*

appositive: a word that renames or defines a word that precedes it, e.g., Juan, *my roommate,* comes from Puerto Rico.

apt word: a particularly well-chosen word.

Arabic numerals: the figures 1, 2, 3, 5, 10, etc. See *Roman numerals.*

argument: an essay pattern in which the writer tries to persuade readers to adopt his or her position on a controversial issue.

article: a word that precedes a noun and specifies its application. The *indefinite article a* or *an* indicates that a noun is unspecified, e.g., *a* man. The *definite article the* indicates that a noun is specified, e.g., *the* man I told you about.

audience: the readers for whom an essay is intended.

author-date system of documentation: a system in which citations include the author of a cited source and the year in which the source was written.

avoiding the question: an argumentative fallacy in which the writer fails to deal with the actual issue, attacking instead either a misrepresentation of the opponents' position or the opponents themselves. See *ad hominem reasoning* and *straw man.*

balanced sentence: a sentence in which words or grammatical structures are repeated, e.g., I *wanted to learn English; I also wanted to learn life.*

begging the question: presenting an argument in terms that allow for no opposition. See *loaded language* and *self-evident reasoning.*

bibliography: a list of books and articles used in writing a research paper; also, a reference work listing the books and articles written on a given subject. See *list of works cited.*

bibliography card: a 3″ × 5″ file card indicating the author, title, and publication information for a source consulted in the preparation of a research paper.

brackets: square punctuation symbols ([-]) used to indicate that material has been added to a quotation.

call number: the number found on the upper left-hand corner of a card in the library card catalogue, indicating where in the library a particular work can be found.

capital letter: a letter larger in size and different in form from regular lowercase letters, e.g., A, B, C, F. See *lowercase letter.*

card catalogue: a set of file card-size cabinets in which are stored author, title, and subject cards for the books held by a particular library.

cause and effect: an analytical essay pattern in which the writer presents the reasons for or results of a phenomenon.

chronological order: an arrangement of events in the order in which they occurred.

circular definition: a definition that uses the term being defined in giving its meaning, e.g., A *circular definition is a definition that goes in a circle.*

citation: an indication that a particular quotation or idea derives from another source. See also *documentation.*

classification: an analytical essay pattern in which the writer assigns an object to a particular group by showing that it shares the characteristics common to all members of the group. See *subdivision.*

clause: a subject + verb combination; clauses may be either *independent* (I *passed*) or *dependent* (*because* I *studied*).

cliché: an expression that has been used so often that it has lost its freshness, e.g., *old as the hills.*

cognates: words that share a common ancestry and have a similar meaning, e.g., English *night* and German *nacht*.

colloquialism: a word or expression appropriate for conversation but not for a composition requiring the middle level of diction, e.g., *guy* or *kid* for *child*. See *diction*.

colon: a punctuation symbol (:) used to introduce a list or quotation or to show the equivalence of a following utterance to a preceding one.

comma: a punctuation symbol (,) used to separate items in a series, coordinate modifiers, a phrase and a clause, a clause and a clause, and a parenthetical element from a surrounding utterance.

common knowledge: facts or ideas that need no documentation because they are generally known, e.g., T*here are nine planets in our solar system.*

comparison and contrast: an analytical essay pattern presenting the similarities or dissimilarities between two related objects.

common noun: a noun that stands for a general representative of a class that contains more than one member, e.g., *a* man, a *language.* See *proper noun.*

concession: the granting of an objection against the writer's position in an argument. See *objection, refutation.*

concrete term: a word that represents a sensually perceived object or quality, e.g., *blood, sunlight, red, bright.* See *abstract term.*

conjunctive adverb: an adverb (sometimes called a *sentence adverb*) that relates one sentence, clause, or paragraph to another, e.g., I think; *therefore,* I am. Conjunctive adverbs differ from conjunctions in that, like other adverbs, they can move within the clause of which they are a part. See *conjunction.*

conclusion: the logical result of two argumentative premises; also, the end of an essay. See *premise.*

conjunction: a word that joins two words, phrases, clauses, or sentences and that must stand at the head of the element it introduces; conjunctions can be either *coordinate (and, but, or, nor, for, so, yet),* correlative *(both . . . and, not only . . . but, either . . . or, neither . . . nor)* or *subordinate (although, because, until,* etc.).

connotation: the associations carried by a word. See *denotation.*

controlling idea: the main idea that determines what should or should not be included in an essay. See *thesis.*

convention: a rule established by common practice.

coordinate modifiers: two or more modifiers each of which modifies another term, e.g., He is a *bright, hard-working* student.

copyright page: the reverse side of the *title page,* listing a book's copyright and printing history. See *title page.*

core thesis: the main idea, expressed in a main clause, within a thesis statement, e.g., Although it is expensive, *free medical care should be provided to all citizens,* because health is a right that the government should guarantee. See *thesis statement.*

cross-indexing: a system of indicating where in a catalogue or index additional references on a given subject may be found.

cut-and-paste effect: a term used to describe the way an essay using outside sources sounds to the reader when the writer has failed to integrate material from the sources into his or her own writing.

dangling modifier: a participle or infinitive that has no proper referent, e.g., W*alking along,* the trees look beautiful.

dash: a punctuation symbol(—)used around parenthetical elements.

definition: statement of the meaning of a word. A classical definition includes the *term* being defined, the *class* to which the term belongs, and the *differentiae* which distinguish it from other members of the group. Dictionary definitions also include spelling, pronunciation, syllabication, the part of speech to which a word belongs, the etymology or history of origin, and examples of usage.

denotation: the explicit meaning of a word without its connotations. See *connotation*.

dependent clause: See *clause*.

description: an essay pattern in which the features of an object are delineated.

diction: level of speech (informal, middle, or formal).

direct paragraph structure: paragraph structure that begins with the theme sentence and continues with supporting sentences.

document delivery service: a service that provides copies of journal articles to researchers for a fee, e.g., ERIC.

documentation: an indication that an idea or quotation is borrowed from an outside source.

draft: the written or typed form of an essay.

either/or reasoning: reasoning that allows for only two possibilities when more actually exist.

ellipsis/es: a symbol used to indicate an omission from a quotation (. . .).

endnote: a documentation device using numbers or symbols to refer to citations of sources included at the end of an essay, chapter, or book.

essay: a unified piece of writing on a single theme.

essay patterns: various patterns on which an essay can be organized; also called *rhetorical modes*. See *analysis, argument, definition, description, illustration,* and *narration*.

essay question: an exam question that calls for an answer to be written in essay form.

etymology: the history or origin of a word.

euphemism: a figure of speech in which a less negative term is substituted for a more negative one, e.g., *senior citizen* for *old person*.

evidence: statements and facts supporting a writer's argumentative position.

example: See *illustration*.

explicit thesis: an outright statement of an essay's main idea within the essay itself.

exclamation point: a punctuation symbol (!) used to indicate emphasis. Exclamation points in English are used only at the *end* of a sentence, word, or group of words, e.g., Eureka!

fallacy: an error or fault in logic.

false cause (*post hoc ergo propter hoc* reasoning): an argumentative fallacy in which there is an assumption that, because two incidents occurred in succession, they are causally related.

false cognates: words that look like but are not cognates, e.g., *embarrassed* and *embarasada*.

fascicle: a separately bound installment of a larger volume.

figurative language: language that clarifies an idea or image by making a comparison that is not literal. Common figures include *similes*, which make a comparison using *like* or *as* (e.g., *green as grass*); metaphors, which make a direct comparison (e.g., *the blushing rose*); and analogies (see *analogy*).

footnote: documentation device using numbers or symbols to refer to citations of sources printed at the bottom of pages in the text.

fragment: an incomplete sentence; a group of words punctuated as a sentence, but consisting of less than one independent clause.

grammar: the set of rules governing correctness in a given language.

hyphen: a symbol (-) used to divide compound nouns and modifiers, prefixes and roots, and words between their syllables at the end of a line.

illustration: an essay pattern demonstrating an idea by showing an instance of it.

implicit thesis: a thesis that, though it does not actually appear in an essay, is apparent to the reader through the supporting detail provided by the writer. See *thesis*.

indention: the starting of a line of text a certain number of spaces to the right of the left margin to indicate the beginning of a paragraph or an extracted quotation.

independent clause: See *clause*.

index: a publication that lists the articles (and sometimes books) published yearly in a given subject area; also, an alphabetically arranged listing appearing at the end of a book indicating on what pages in the book material on particular subtopics can be found.

intensifier: a modifier that adds strength to the word it modifies, e.g., *very, really*.

interjection: a word or phrase, generally exclamatory, that interrupts or stands outside of normal syntax or word order, e.g., *alas, oh*.

interlibrary loan: a procedure for obtaining from another library a book or periodical not held by one's own library.

interrogative: a question form.

italics: slanted print used to make words stand out on a printed page, indicated in a manuscript by underlining, e.g., A *zapateado* is a Mexican dance step.

jargon: special vocabulary particular to a given discipline, e.g., She has trouble shifting out of the office *mode* (computer jargon).

joiner: used in this text to refer to any word that can join two clauses and that must stand at the head of the clause it introduces. The joiners are divided into *coordinate joiners* (coordinate and correlative conjunctions) and *subordinate joiners* (subordinate conjunctions and relative pronouns). Though conjunctive adverbs are relators (see *relator*), they are not joiners because they can occupy various positions within the clauses they introduce.

journal: a publication, such as a magazine, that appears on a regular basis, e.g., weekly, monthly, etc.

limiting material: material that does not support the theme sentence in a paragraph. See *objection*.

list of works cited: a list of the articles and books used in the writing of a research paper. See *bibliography*.

loaded language: emotionally charged words that allow for no reasonable opposing argument, e.g., Nuclear testing should be banned because it is *murder*.

loose sentence structure: sentence structure that begins with a main clause followed by modifying elements, e.g., I *came to the* U.S. *because I wanted to learn English*. See *periodic sentence structure*.

lowercase letter: the regular form of a letter, e.g., a, b, c, f. See *capital letter*.

margin: a column of space to the left and right and on the top and bottom of the writing on a sheet of paper.

metaphor: see *figurative language*.

microfiche: a special type of microfilm shaped like an index card. See *microfilm*.

microfilm: a film on which documents are photographed and greatly reduced in size for purposes of library storage.

misplaced modifier: a modifier placed in a position in which it seems to refer to a word other than the one it is supposed to modify, e.g., *Hungry from hard work*, the food looked wonderful to the man.

modifier: a word or word group that describes another element, e.g., a *warm* day, a day *that I will always remember.*

narration: an essay pattern in which a series of events is recounted.

nonrestrictive element: an element that does not limit the term it describes, e.g., William Shakespeare, who wrote plays, was also an actor. See *restrictive element.*

noun: the name of a person, place, thing, or idea, e.g., *man, city,* New York, *book, food, fear.* See *common noun* and *proper noun.*

number: in English, the singularity or plurality of a noun, verb, etc., e.g., *book/books.*

number system of documentation: a system that refers to the works cited in a research paper by numbers assigned to particular works.

object: the receiver of an action (*direct object*), the receiver of a direct object (*indirect object*), or the receiver of the direction of a preposition (*object of the preposition*), e.g., I wrote a *letter* (direct object); I wrote my *parents* a letter (indirect object); I wrote a letter to my *parents* (object of the preposition).

objection: argument that favors the position of one's opponents on an issue of controversy; in an argument, objections must be recognized and either conceded or refuted. See *concession, refutation.*

online catalogue: a computerized card catalogue.

outline: a plan that guides the writing of an essay. Outlines can be either *informal* (scratch) or *formal* (subordinated). The entries in a formal outline can consist of either topics (*topic outline*) or sentences (*sentence outline*). See *paragraph outline.*

overgeneralization: the use of absolute terms where they are not warranted. See *absolute term.*

oversimplified causes (catchall reasoning): an argumentative fallacy in which only one cause of a phenomenon is recognized although several may actually exist.

paragraph: one or more sentences that relate in the same way to the thesis of an essay and thereby constitute a unit of thought; generally, the largest subdivision in an essay. New paragraphs are indented.

paragraph outline: an outline in which a reader writes one sentence to express the idea of each paragraph or group of related paragraphs in a writer's work, for the purpose of better understanding the work.

parallelism: two or more elements that are similar in structure or idea, e.g., He likes *skiing* and *skating.*

paraphrase: a sentence-by-sentence summary.

parentheses: curved symbols (-) used to enclose qualifying material.

parenthetical documentation: a citation system in which references to the sources used in writing a research paper are included in parentheses within the text itself.

parenthetical element: a word or group of words that interrupts the syntax of a sentence, e.g., Mr. Bard, *the professor of English 101F,* loves grammar.

parts of speech: the general classes to which words are assigned with regard to their capabilities to perform certain sentence functions, e.g., verb, noun, pronoun, etc.

passive voice: see *voice.*

period: a symbol (.) used to indicate the end of a sentence. Periods are also used with some abbreviations (e.g., *i.e.*).

periodic sentence structure: sentence structure in which modifying material precedes the main clause, e.g., *Because I wanted to learn English, I came to the United States.* See *loose sentence structure.*

periodical: a publication, such as a newspaper or magazine, the issues of which appear at regular intervals, i.e., daily, weekly, monthly, etc.

person: a grammatical term indicating the relationship of the person speaking to the person being spoken about. There are three persons in English: first (I, *we*); second (*you*); and third (*he/she/it, they*). Verbs as well as pronouns are inflected for person.

persuade: to move another to adopt one's position in an issue of controversy.

phrase: a group of words that does not include a subject and a predicate.

pivoting paragraph structure: paragraph structure that begins with limiting material before introducing and supporting the theme sentence. See *direct paragraph structure.*

plagiarism: using another writer's words or ideas without acknowledgment; stealing.

plural: more than one person, object, or instance. See *number.*

predicate: the part of a clause or sentence that expresses an action or feeling about the subject; the *complete predicate* consists of the verb and all words that go with it; e.g., Hans *studies engineering.* The simple predicate consists of the verb by itself, e.g., Hans *studies* engineering. See *verb.*

prefix: a letter or group of letters which, placed before the root or main element of a word, creates a new word with a distinct meaning, e.g., *prefix.*

premise: in logic, one of two propositions on which a conclusion is based. See *conclusion.*

preposition: a word that relates the *object* of a phrase to another sentence element, e.g., She is studying *for* an exam. See *object (of the preposition).*

prewriting: a composition technique, also called *free writing* or *brainstorming,* in which one writes freely and continuously, without regard to proper form or logical organization, in order to collect ideas and to formulate a thesis for a writing topic.

primer English: writing in which sentence structure is so simple, repetitive, and lacking in subordination that it resembles the sentence structure of textbooks from which children learn to read.

process: an analytical essay pattern that presents the steps required to reach a goal.

pronoun: a word that substitutes for a *noun;* there are several types of pronouns including *personal* (e.g., I, *me, it*), *possessive* (e.g., *my, mine, its*), *indefinite* (e.g., *everyone, all*), *reflexive* (e.g., *myself, themselves*), *reciprocal* (e.g., *each other, one another*), *demonstrative* (e.g., *this, those*), *interrogative* (e.g., *who, which*), and *relative* (e.g., *which, that*). See *relative pronoun.*

proper noun: the name of a particular person, place, or thing, e.g., *Albert Einstein, Paris, English.*

punctuation: a system of marking written text with symbols that clarify the meaning of the text and that separate textual elements from one another.

qualifier: a word that restricts the application of another sentence element, e.g., It is a *fairly* hot day.

question mark: a punctuation symbol (?) used to indicate a question. Question marks in English are used only at the *end* of sentences.

quotation: a word or words borrowed exactly from another source; sometimes called *direct quotation.*

quotation marks: a punctuation symbol used to indicate a quotation inserted within a text. Quotation marks are generally double (" "), but single quotation marks (' ') are used to indicate a quotation within a quotation.

redundancy: unnecessary repetition; a word that is unnecessary because its meaning is expressed by another word or words, e.g., a *happy* smile, a *loud* shout.

refutation: the denying of an objection made by opponents against one's position in an argument. See *objection, concession.*

relative pronoun: pronoun that serves as both relator and joiner of one clause to another. Relative pronouns can be either *restrictive* (e.g., The student who rooms with me is from Italy) or *nonrestrictive* (e.g., Lina, who rooms with me, is from Italy).

relator: used in this text to refer to a word which relates or refers one sentence element to another. The relators include *prepositions, conjunctions, relative pronouns,* and *conjunctive adverbs.*

reported speech: the indirect recounting of conversation (sometimes called *indirect discourse*), e.g., T*he professor said there would be no exam that day.* See *quotation.*

restrictive element: an element that limits the term it describes, e.g., The person *who wrote that play* is from Spain. See *nonrestrictive element.*

research paper: a paper for which a student researches a topic, using outside sources and integrating them into the text with formal documentation.

revision: a rewriting of a paper to correct errors in form and content.

Roman numerals: the figures I, II, III, V, X, etc. See *Arabic numerals.*

run-on sentence: a group of words punctuated as a sentence but containing more than a single sentence (more than one *independent clause* without the insertion of a colon, semicolon, or a coordinate joiner). The two types of run-on sentences are the *fused sentence* (I *got up then* I *went to class.*) and the *comma splice* (I *got up, then* I *went to class*).

self-evident reasoning: an argument expressed in such a way that it says only that $a = a$, e.g., *Nuclear testing must be stopped because we cannot allow it to continue.*

semicolon: a punctuation symbol (;) used to separate independent clauses or items in a series in which commas are used within individual members of the series.

sentence: a complete thought unit beginning with a capital letter containing a subject and a predicate, and closed by a period, question mark, or exclamation point. A sentence consists of at least one independent clause.

sentence fragment: See *fragment.*

sentence outline: See *outline.*

series: in grammar, a listing of three or more items, e.g., She never eats *cake, cookies,* or *candy.* Items in a series should be parallel. See *parallelism.*

simile: see *figurative language.*

simple sentence: a sentence consisting of one independent clause.

singular: one person, object, or instance. See *number.*

slang: colloquial vocabulary, not appropriate for writing that requires the middle level of diction, e.g., *jerk* for "stupid person." See *diction.*

specific term: a word that is particular rather than general, e.g., *sunflower seeds* rather than *snack, soccer* rather than *activity.*

specified noun: a noun identified as a particular member of a class, e.g., *man* in "the man in the green jacket." See *unspecified noun.*

squinting modifier: a modifier placed between two elements that can refer to either element, e.g., She studies *only* on weekends.

straw man: an argumentative fallacy in which the opponent's position is represented in exaggerated terms which makes it easy to refute.

style sheet: printed guidelines detailing a particular system of formal documentation, e.g., MLA *Handbook.*

subdivision: an analytical essay pattern in which a class is divided into its subgroups. See *classification.*

subject: the actor (generally a noun) in a sentence or clause, e.g., The *student* slept through class. The *simple subject* is the subject by itself; the *complete subject* consists of the subject plus its modifiers, e.g., T*he student from Argentina* slept through class. See *predicate.*

subordination: the process of making one element less important than and/or dependent on another.

summary: a brief restatement in one's own words of the ideas expressed in another, longer version.

supporting details: details that help to reveal the thesis of the essay to the reader.

suspended paragraph structure: a paragraph structure in which the theme sentence is reserved for the final position, for the purpose of teasing or intriguing the reader. See *direct paragraph structure.*

synonyms: words of like or very similar meaning, e.g., *talk* and *speak.*

tense: the time expressed by a verb (past, present, future).

theme sentence: the sentence that expresses the main idea of a paragraph.

thesis: the main idea of an essay; the thesis can be expressed only in a complete sentence. Also called *theme.*

thesis statement: a complicated sentence combining the *core thesis* with subordinate clauses, used in the planning of an essay (especially an argument) to express the main idea, the major supporting points, and the most important objections; e.g., *Although it is expensive, free medical care should be provided to all citizens, because health is a right that the government should guarantee.* See *core thesis.*

title page: the page at the beginning of a book listing the book's title, author, publisher, and place of publication.

tone: the manner of expression in a written passage; tone may be light, angry, moderate, restrained, etc.

topic: the subdivision of a subject area about which an essay is written.

topic outline: See *outline.*

transition: movement from one thought to another in an essay; transition can be either in the direction of continuity or change.

transitional expression: an expression that helps the reader move from one thought to another by showing how the thoughts are related to one another, e.g., *however* (contrast), *moreover* (addition).

unity: the quality of oneness, of belonging together as part of a unit. Unity in an essay is achieved when all details included in the essay support the theme.

unspecified noun: a noun identified as a general representative of a class, e.g., *a man.* See *specified noun.*

usage: customary and accepted way in which the elements of a language are used in speech or writing.

verb: a part of speech and a sentence element that expresses the action performed by or the state of being of the subject, e.g., *run, speak, be, appear.* See *predicate.*

voice: a verb form indicating the relationship between the subject and the action expressed by the verb. If the subject performs the action, the voice is *active,* e.g., He *wrote* the essay. If the subject receives the action, the voice is *passive,* e.g., The essay *was written* by him.

weaseling thesis: an argumentative fallacy in which the thesis slips between two positions rather than taking a stand.

word: the basic building block of writing or speech; the smallest unit of composition.

Copyrights and Acknowledgments

Index

a, an, 309–10
Abbreviation, 301, 303–6
  capitalization with, 301
  in citations, 305
  form of, 305–6
  in main text, 303–5
  of repeated term, 305
Absolute phrase, 153
Abstract (of article), 212
Abstract language
  avoiding, 32–33
  in conclusion, 113
  vs. concrete language, 12–13, 172–77
  defined, 173
  degree in, 177–78
  sample essay demonstrating, 172
  as sign of sophistication, 174
Academic disciplines, capitalization of, 301
Accuracy
  literal vs. literary, 21–22
  in summary, 193–95
Acknowledgment
  of ideas, 224
  vs. plagiarism, 223
  in research paper, 203
  See also Documentation; Textual acknowl-
    edgment
Active voice, 156. *See also* Passive voice
actually, as false cognate, 183
Addition, as transitional relationship, 163
Addresses, numbers in, 307
Ad hominem argument, 85–86
Adjective, demonstrative, as transitional de-
  vice, 161
Adverb, conjunctive, 162–64, 264–65, 271–72
Afterword, in list of works cited, 222
Agreement, 284–96. *See also* Comparison; Form;
    Number; Person; Possession; Predica-
    tion; Structure; Tense

"Alienation and Affection," 199–202
Alphabetization, in card catalogue, 204
Alternating pattern, in comparison and con-
    trast, 65
Alternative, as transitional relationship, 163
Analogy, 182
  invention of words by, 183
Analysis, 50–72
  natural vs. mechanical, 57–58, 62
  thesis in, 55
  types of, 55
  See also Cause and Effect; Classification;
    Comparison and Contrast; Process; Sub-
    division
and
  in balanced sentence, 151
  as coordinate conjunction, 264
  as transitional word, 161–62
Anthology, in list of works cited, 221
anybody, number of, 285
anyhow, as transitional word, 164
anyone, number of, 285
anyway, as transitional word, 164
appear, as nonaction verb, 174
Applied Science and Technology Index, 213
Appositive
  punctuation of, 271
  as subordinating structure, 153
Apt word
  plagiarism and, 224, 227
  quotation of, 275
Arabic numerals, 101
archaic, 170
Argument, 75–87
  defined, 75
  elements of, 77–81
  example of adequate, 83–84
  example of inadequate, 76
  example of researched, 234–50

Argument (*continued*)
  guidelines for revision of, 121
  objections in, 77, 80–81
  organization of, 84
  purpose of, 75, 76
  qualities of, 76
  supporting evidence in, 76, 77, 79–80
  testing, 86–87
  thesis in, 77–79
  tone in, 81–82
  words indicating in an essay question, 253
  See also Controversy; Fallacy, argumenta-
    tive; Persuasion
Article, 309–12
  with common noun, 309–11
  definite, 309
  indefinite, 309
  with noun of indefinite quantity, 310
  with possessive, 310–11
  with proper noun, 311–12
Articles (in periodicals). *See* Periodical
as, in comparison, 294–95
aspect, as abstract noun, 175
Attribution, punctuation of, 272
Auden, W. H., 29–30
Audience, 5–6
  in argument, 75–76
Author
  in list of works cited, 219–220, 221
  multiple, 220
  of multiple sources, 221
Author card, 204, 208
Author–date system of documentation, 222
Authorities
  in argument, 80
  biased, 80
Avoiding the question, 85

Balanced sentence, 151
basis, as abstract noun, 175
be
  as nonaction verb, 174
  in participial phrase, 175
  in passive voice, 175
  in *there is/there are* constructions, 175
  wordiness and, 156
Begging the question, 85
Bibliography, 204, 209–10
  of bibliographies, 209–10
  card catalogue entry for, 209
  select, 210
  specialized, 209

Bibliography card, 214–15
  preparation of, 209
  samples of, 215
Books
  citations of, 222
  gathering titles of, 204–10
  listing titles of, 208
  in list of works cited, 219–20, 221–22
  obtaining, 208–9, 210
Books in Print, 210
both . . . and
  in balanced sentence, 151
  as correlative conjunction, 264
Brackets
  for insertion into quotation, 275–76
  in note taking, 224
  vs. parentheses, 272
Brevity, in summary, 193, 195
Bureaucratese. *See* Jargon
Business Index, 213
Business Periodicals Index, 213
but
  in balanced sentence, 151
  as coordinate conjunction, 264
  as transitional word, 162

Call number
  of bibliography, 214
  of book, 205
  in online card catalogue, 206
  of periodical, 213
Capitalization, 299–302
  of abbreviations, 301
  of academic disciplines, 301
  of independent clause, 300
  of names of family members, 301
  of proper adjectives, 301
  of proper nouns, 300–302
  of quoted material, 300
  of titles and ranks, 301
  of titles of works, 302
  of religious terms, 301
  of sentences, 300
  of the word I, 300
Capital letters
  abbreviations consisting of, 306
  mixed with lowercase letters, 299
  in subordinated outlines, 101
Card catalogue, 204–8
  alphabetization in, 204
  author card in, 204, 208
  bibliography card in, 209

cross-indexing in, 208
main entry in, 208
online, 204, 205–6
periodicals, 213
subject card in, 204–5
subject headings in, 206–8
case, as abstract noun, 175
Cataloguing, changes in procedures, 211
Catch-all reasoning. *See* Oversimplification
Cause
   false, 69, 86
   immediate, 69
   multiple, 69
   underlying, 69
Cause and effect, 68–69
   defined, 68
   example of, 68
   words indicating in essay question, 253
Change, indicating. *See* Transition
character, as abstract noun, 175
Chicago Manual of Style, 219
Chronological order, 22
Circular definition, 50
Circumstance, as abstract noun, 175
Citation, 223
   abbreviations in, 305
   of multiple sources, 203
   See also Parenthetical documentation
Clarity, of summary, 193, 195
Class, in definition, 47–48, 49
Classical definition, 48, 51
Classification analysis, 56–58
   combining with subdivision, 58
   defined, 56
   example of, 56
   example of mechanical, 57
   organization of, 57–58
   outline of, 57
   words indicating in essay question, 253
Clause
   dependent, 267–68
   independent, 150, 152, 263, 266–68
   main, 152
   punctuation with, 266–68
   relative, 267–68, 272
   subordinate, 153
Cliché. *See* Figurative language
Cognate, 182
   defined, 182
   false, 182–83
colloquial, 169, 170
Colloquial language, 170
   in conversation, 168
   occasional use of in essays, 171
   See also Diction

Colon
   in balanced sentence, 151
   capitalization following, 300
   for introducing equivalent statement, 274
   for introducing quotation, 277
   for introducing series, 274
   with quotation punctuation, 278
Comma
   in balanced sentence, 151
   between clauses, 266–67
   between coordinate modifiers, 270–71
   in dates, 273
   eliminating unnecessary, 272–73
   for introducing quotation, 277
   between items in a series, 270
   with numbers, 307
   with parenthetical elements, 271–72
   between phrases and clauses, 268–69
   with place names, 274
   with quotation marks, 278
   between words or phrases, 269–71
Common knowledge, 224
Common noun, 309
Comparison, complete vs. incomplete, 293–95
Comparison and contrast analysis, 64–66
   compared to subdivision and classification, 64
   defined, 64
   examples of, 64–66
   organization of, 65–66
   words indicating in essay question, 253
   See also Analysis
Completeness, of summary, 193
Compound subject, number of, 287
Computerized index, 213
Computerized listing, of periodicals in libraries, 213
Concession, 77, 80–81
   as transitional relationship, 163
Conclusion, 112–14
   argumentative, 86–87
   completing a circle with, 113–14
   with example, 113
   focus in, 112–13
   with question, 113
   with quotation, 113
   repetitive, 112
   strong, 113–14
   with summary, 113
   with suspended paragraph, 138
Concrete language
   vs. abstract language, 12–13, 42–43, 172–77
   defined, 173
   in introduction, 111–12

Concrete language (*continued*)
   lack of, 32–33
   and word number, 174
Concreteness, degree of, 177–78
Concrete noun, 175–76
Concrete verb, 175
Conjunction
   in comparisons, 294–95
   coordinate, 162–63, 264
   correlative, 264
   subordinate, 264
Conjunctive adverb
   differentiated from joiners, 264–65
   punctuation and, 271–72
   in transition, 162–64
Connotation, 178–80
   vs. denotation, 169, 178
   defined, 178
   indicated in dictionary, 169
   insensitivity to, 179
   negative vs. positive, 178–79
   relationship to meaning, 178
   synonyms and, 180
   variations in, 179
Context
   clues to connotation in, 170
   defined, 169
   vs. dictionary entry, 170
Continuity, indicating. *See* Transition
Contrast, as transitional relationship, 162, 163
Controlling idea, 3. *See also* Thesis
Controversial statement, 79
Controversial term, 180
Controversy, as subject matter of argument,
   75, 78
Conventions, 299–312
   questions for revision of, 121
   See also Abbreviation; Article; Capitaliza-
   tion; Italics; Numbers; Word Division
Conversation
   colloquialism in, 168, 170
   nonsentences in, 148
   vague modifiers in, 176
Coordinate conjunction
   punctuation and, 264
   in transition, 162–63
Coordinate joiner, 263–64
Coordinates, parallel form of, 291
Copyright page, 219
Core idea. *See* Main idea
Core thesis, 96. *See also* Thesis statement
Correlative conjunction, 264
Correlatives, parallel form of, 291
Cover sheet, in final draft, 122
Criteria, in classification, 56

Criticism
   by inner and outside critics, 120
   revision after, 122
Cross-indexing. *See* Card catalogue; Library of
   Congress Subject Headings; *Readers' Guide*
   to Periodical Literature
Cross-reference, 169
Cumulative Book Index, 210
Current Index to Journals in Education, 213
Cut-and-paste effect, 227
Cutting, in revision, 120

Dash, 271–72
Dates
   numbers in, 307
   punctuation of, 273
Deduction, 86
Definition, 47–52
   broadness of, 50–51
   circular, 50
   classical, 48, 51
   common errors in, 50–51
   dictionary, 48
   examples of, 49, 51–52
   extended, 49
   length of, 48–49
   parenthetical, 48
   parts of, 47–48
   in vocabulary list, 169
   words indicating in essay questions, 253
Demonstrative adjective, as transitional device, 161
Demonstrative pronoun, as transitional device, 161
Denotation
   compared to connotation, 169, 178
   defined, 169
Dependent clause, punctuation with, 268
Description, 29–37
   advantages of foreign student in writing, 35
   arranging details in, 34–35
   compared to narration, 4, 29, 32, 34
   defined, 29
   examples of, 35–37
   selecting details for, 29–34
   spatial order in, 34–35
   vague modifiers in, 33–34
   words indicating in essay questions, 253
Detail
   abstract, 12, 32–33
   concrete, 12, 33–34
   elimination of in summary, 195
   irrelevant, 13, 14, 22, 32–33, 254

selection of, 13
thesis and, 3
vivid, 173
Development, of paragraphs, 139–40
dial (dialectal), 170
diction, 170–72
colloquial, 168, 171
formal, 170, 171
labels of, 170
level of in dictionary entry, 169
middle level of, 170
occasional variations in, 171
Dictionary
college, 169
definition in, 48
false cognates and, 183
standard English vs. foreign language, 169
unabridged, 169–70
and vocabulary building, 169
Dictionary definition
examples of, 169–70
information provided in, 48
parts of, 169
Differentia, in definition, 47–48, 49
Direct address, 272
Direct paragraph, 134–35
overuse of, 135
Direct speech, 274
Dissertation
as long essay, 3
and research paper methodology, 203
Divided pattern, in comparison and contrast, 65–66
Documentation
in essay questions, 255–56
of evidence in argument, 84
formal, 219–23
informal, 218
parenthetical, 223, 279
punctuation with, 279
reasons for, 218
in research paper, 203, 218–27
variations in format for, 219, 223
See also Textual acknowledgment
Draft, revision of rough, 119–25. *See also* Final draft; First draft

each, number of, 285
Ear, development of, 172
Edited English, 170
Edition number
for a book, 221
for a newspaper, 222

Education Index, 213
either, number of, 285
either . . . or
in balanced sentence, 151
as correlative conjunction, 264
Either/or reasoning, 86
element, as abstract noun, 175
Ellipsis, 276–77
in dialogue, 277
with incomplete list, 277
for a line or more of poetry, 276
with a period, 276
in quotation, 276
Emphasis
italics for, 303
position in series and, 152
as transitional relationship, 163
Endnotes, 223
Engineering Index, 213
Enumeration, as transitional relationship, 163–64
Equality of elements
in balanced sentence, 151
in series, 152
ERIC, 213
Errors, correction of in final draft, 124
Essay, 2–14
definition of, 2
examples of adequate and inadequate, 3
impersonal, 4
length of, 3
patterns of, 4
personal, 4, 6
subject matter of, 4
Essay question, 251–57
considering, 251–56
content in answering, 254–55
documentation in, 255–56
as an essay, 257
as an exam, 251
example of adequate answer to, 255
example of inadequate answer to, 254
guidelines for revision of, 121
key words in, 253
length of answer to, 256
pattern(s) required in answering, 252–53
planning of answer to, 257
rewriting, 254
selectivity in answering, 254
vs. summary, 254
time and point value of, 256
Etymology, 49, 169
Euphemism, 171
and connotation, 179–80
as vague language, 179

every, 285
everybody, 285
everyone, 285
Evidence, supporting. *See* Supporting evidence
Example
  in argument, 80
  in concession, 113
  in introduction, 111
  as transitional relationship, 163
Exams, essay questions as, 256
Exclamation point
  with closing quotation marks, 278–79
  in indirect quotation, 289
exist, as non-action verb, 174
Explanation, as transitional relationship, 163
Explicit thesis, 11
  in analysis, 55

Fable, 41
facet, as abstract noun, 175
fact, as abstract noun, 175
Fact, in argument, 79
the fact that, as wordy construction, 155
factor, as abstract noun, 175
Fairness, in argument, 76
Fallacy, argumentative. *See also* Ad hominem argument; Avoiding the Question; Begging the Question; Either/or Reasoning; False cause; Loaded language; Overgeneralization; Oversimplification; Self-evident reasoning; Straw man
False cause, 86
  in cause and effect essays, 69
False cognates, 182–83
Family members, capitalization of names of, 301
Fascicle, 210–11
Feminine, alternating with masculine, 287
field, as abstract noun, 175
Figurative language, 180–82
  clichés in, 180–81
  defined, 180
  guidelines for, 181–82
  overuse of, 182
  in translation, 181
Figure. *See* Numbers
Final draft
  example of, 234–50
  guidelines for appearance of, 122–25
  neatness of, 125
First draft, 109–110

Focus
  in conclusion, 112–13
  in essay, 94
  in introduction, 111–12
Footnotes, 223
  numbers of with quotation punctuation, 279
for, as coordinate conjunction, 264
Foreign language/English dictionary, 169
Foreign language sources, 227
Foreign titles, capitalization of, 302
Foreign words, italics with, 303
Foreword, in list of works cited, 221
Form
  consistency of, 291
  inflectional, 48
Formal diction, 171
Fragment, 265–66
  independent, 265
Future tense, 290

General Science Index, 213
Gerund, possessive with, 295–96
Goal, in process analysis, 71
Goodwin, Michael, 199–202
Grammar and conventions, 262–312
  questions for revision of, 121

Handwritten draft
  appearance of paragraphs in, 139–40
  revision of, 120–21
he or she, 287
however
  as conjunctive adverb, 264
  as transitional word, 162
Humanities Index, 213
Hyphenated word, division of, 308–9

Ignoring alternative possibilities, 86
Illustration, 41–43
  defined, 41
  example of adequate, 43
  example of inadequate, 42
  extended vs. brief, 41
  relationship to thesis, 42
  words indicating in essay question, 253
Imperative mood
  in indirect quotation, 290
  and sentence agreement, 288

Impersonal essay, 4
  title of, 115
Implicit thesis, 11
  vs. explicit thesis, 55
Implied repetition, as transitional device, 161
Indefinite pronoun, number of, 285
Indefinite quantity, noun of, 310
Indention
  in final draft, 122
  of paragraphs, 131
Independent clause
  definition of, 263
  main idea and, 150, 152
  punctuation with another clause, 266–68
  punctuation with a phrase, 268–69
Independent fragment, 265
Index
  computerized, 213
  newspaper, 212–13
  periodical, 210–13
Index Medicus, 213
Indirect quotation
  examples of, 290–91
  punctuation of, 290
  and sentence agreements, 289–91
Infinitive, split, 293
Infinitive phrase, 268
  punctuation of with a clause, 268
Inflectional forms, 169
Information service, 222
Initials
  abbreviation consisting of, 301
  to indicate own ideas, 224
instance, as abstract noun, 175
Intensifiers, overuse of, 177
Interlibrary loan, 210
International Index to Periodicals, 213
Introduction, 110–12
  announcing issue in, 112
  concreteness in, 111–12
  focused vs. unfocused, 111
  in list of works cited, 221
  quotation in, 111–12
  strong, 111–12
  suspended paragraph as, 138
  weak, 110–11
Issue, controversial. *See* Controversy
Issue number, 222
Italics, 299, 302–03
  for emphasis, 303
  with foreign words, 303
  with proper names of vehicles, 303
  with titles, 302
  with words as words, 303
-ize, 175

Jargon, 171, 174
Joiner, 263–64
  coordinate, 263–64
  vs. conjunctive adverb, 264–65
  definition, 263
  subordinate, 264
Journal. *See* Periodical
Journalism, 141

Landscape with the Fall of Icarus, 31
Language
  concrete vs. abstract, 12–13, 32–33, 42–43, 173–74
  figurative, 180–82
  loaded, 77, 85
Length
  of essay, 3, 95
  of paragraph, 138–42
  of sentence, 152
less than, in balanced sentence, 151
Letter, capital. *See* Capital letter
Letter, lowercase. *See* Lowercase letter
Library
  and interlibrary loan, 210
  newspaper, 214
  periodical room in, 213
  request slip, 209
  reserve desk, 208
  stacks, 204
  trace, 209
Library of Congress Subject Headings, 206–8
  cross-indexing in, 207–8
  symbols in, 206–7
Limiting material
  position of, 136
  purpose of, 135–36
List of works cited, 219–22
  author in, 220–21
  date in, 220
  example of, 247–50
  format of, 220–21
  information required in, 219–20
  page numbers in, 220
Loaded language, 77, 85
Logic, model of, 86
London Times, 213
Loose sentence, 150
Los Angeles Times, 213
Lowercase letter
  abbreviations with, 305
  with capitals, 299
  in subordinated outlines, 101

Main clause, 152. *See also* Independent clause;
   Main idea
Main entry, 207
Main idea, 150–51, 152
   independent clause and, 150, 152
   function in sentence, 152
   position of in sentence, 150–51
Margins, 122
Marking systems, 122–23
Masculine, alternating with feminine, 287
Master's thesis
   as essay, 3
   and research paper methodology, 203
Matched elements, 151
Medicalese. *See* Jargon
Medical writing, paragraphs in, 141
Metaphor, 180, 181–82
   dead, 180
   extended, 181
   mixed, 181–82
Microfiche, 213
Microfilm, 213
Middle level of diction. *See* Diction
MLA *Handbook*, 218, 219, 223
Modifier
   concrete vs. abstract, 176–77
   coordinate, 270–71
   dangling, 292
   linked with noun, 177
   misplaced, 292–93
   punctuation of, 270–71
   redundant, 177
   as subordinating structure, 152–53
   squinting, 292
   subordinate, 271
   vague, 33–34, 176–77
Mood, imperative, 288
more than, in balanced sentence, 151
Morris, Willie, 10–11
"Musée des Beaux Arts," 30

Nacht, Craufurd, 199–202
Narration, 20–22
   arranging details in, 22
   contrasted with description, 4
   defined, 20
   example of, 21–22
   selecting details for, 21–22
   words indicating in essay question, 253
National Union Catalogue, 210
nature, as abstract noun, 175
the nature of, as wordy construction, 155

neither, number of, 285
neither . . . nor, in balanced sentence, 151
Neologism, 170
nevertheless, as transitional word, 162
Newspaper
   indexes to articles in, 212–14
   locating back issues of, 214
New York Times Index, 212–13
nobody, 285
none, 286
Nonrestrictive relative clause, 267–68
Nonsentence
   in conversation, 148
   vs. sentence, 262–66
   in writing, 148
no one, number of, 285
nor
   in balanced sentence, 151
   as coordinate conjunction, 264
not . . . but, as correlative conjunction, 264
Note cards, 215–17
not only . . . but also
   in balanced sentence, 151
   as correlative conjunction, 264
Noun
   combined vs. single, 176
   common, 309
   concrete vs. abstract, 175–76
   of indefinite quantity, 310
   proper, 300, 311–12
   specified vs. unspecified, 309–10
Number
   and avoiding sexism, 286–87
   of compound subject, 287
   consistency of, 285–87
   of indefinite pronouns, 285–86
   of verb phrase, 287
Numbers, 299, 306–8
   comma vs. period in, 307
   vs. figures, 306–7
   inclusive, 307–8
   ordinal, 162, 164
   in percentages, 306–7
   in sums of money, 306–7
Number system of documentation, 223

Objection
   answer to in argument, 77, 80–81
   recognition of in argument, 77, 80
Online card catalogue, 205–6
   author search in, 206
   examples of entries from, 205, 206

subject search in, 205
or
  in balanced sentence, 151
  as coordinate conjunction, 204
Order
  chronological, 22
  rank, and ordinal numbers, 163–64
  spatial, 34–35
Ordinal numbers, as transitional words, 162, 164
Organization, 99–106
  of argument, 84
  of classification analysis, 58
  of comparison and contrast analysis, 65–66, 101
  in description, 34–35, 101
  in narrative, 22, 101
  questions for revision of, 121
  of summary, 193, 195
  types and uses of, 99
other, with members of a group, 295
Outline, 106–9
  for classification analysis, 57
  combining formats in, 104–5
  errors in structure of, 105–6
  formal, 101–6
  informal, 99–101
  paragraph, 106, 197
  revising, 104
  scratch, 100–101, 257
  sentence, 102–4, 197
  for subdivision analysis, 61
  subordinated, 101
  for a summary, 197
  topic, 101–2, 197
Overgeneralization, 85
Oversimplification, 86
  in cause-and-effect analysis, 69

Padded paragraph, 141
Page numbers, in final draft, 124
Paragraph, 130–42
  art of writing, 141
  compared to unit or chapter, 130
  defined, 130
  general guidelines for, 131
  in handwritten essay, 139–40
  indention of, 122, 131
  length of, 138–42
  limiting material in, 136–37
  order in, 134–38
  padded, 141

  questions for revision of, 121
  relationship of to thesis, 130
  theme sentence in, 133–34
  transitional, 140
  unity of, 131–33. *See also* Theme sentence
Paragraph outline, 106, 197
Parallelism, 291
Paraphrase vs. plagiarism, 224
Parentheses
  vs. brackets, 272
  capitalization of clauses in, 300
  with parenthetical elements, 271–72
  punctuation with, 281
Parenthetical definition, 48
Parenthetical documentation, 223
  with quotation punctuation, 279
Parenthetical elements, 271–72
Participial phrase, 268
  punctuation of with a clause, 269
  and wordiness, 175
Part of speech, 169
  labeling, 48
Passive voice
  function of, 155–56
  and sentence agreement, 288
  and wordiness, 155, 175
Patterns for essays, 4, 19–87
  combination of, 5, 32, 55
  predominating, 5
Period
  in abbreviations, 306
  at end of sentence, 262
  between independent clauses, 266
  with numbers, 307
  with quotation marks, 278
Periodic sentence, 150–51
Periodical, 210–14
  articles in list of works cited, 220–21, 222
  citation of articles in, 223
  computerized listing of, 213
  finding articles in for research paper, 210–13
  listing titles of articles in for research paper, 213
  obtaining, 213–14
Periodical room, 213
Person
  agreement of, 288–89
  in indirect quotation, 289
Personal essay, 4, 6
Personal pronouns
  and sexism, 286
  as transitional device, 161
Persuasion, 75, 76

phenomenon, as abstract noun, 175
Phrase
    infinitive, 268
    participial, 268–69
    prepositional, 268–69
    as subordinating structure, 153
    verb, 287
Pivoting paragraph, 135–37
    limiting material in, 135
    order of material in, 135–36
Place
    punctuation in name of, 274
    as transitional relationship, 164
Plagiarism
    intentional vs. unintentional, 223
    in research paper, 224–27
    vs. summary and paraphrase, 224–26
    ways to avoid, 224
Planning the essay. *See* Outline
Plaudit, 176
Plural
    use of in avoiding sexism, 286
    See also Number
Possession
    combining devices of, 295
    consistency of, 295–96
    the gerund and, 295–96
Predication, 284–85
Premise, argumentative, 86–87
Preposition, vs. transitional relators, 162
Prepositional phrase, 268
    punctuation of, with a clause, 269
Prewriting, 97
Primer English, 152–53
Process analysis, 71–72
    defined, 71
    example of, 71–72
    goal in, 71
    outline of, 72
    words indicating in essay question, 253
Pronoun
    demonstrative, 161
    number of indefinite, 285
    personal, 161
Pronunciation, in dictionary definition, 48, 169
Proofreader's marks, 124–25
Proper noun
    articles with, 311–12
    capitalization of, 300
Punctuation, 262–81
    between clauses, 266–68
    with closing quotations, 278–79
    of dates and places, 273–74
    with documentation, 279

format for, 280–81
    in indirect quotation, 290
    of items in series, 270
    of modifiers, 270–71
    of quotations, 274–81
    of parenthetical elements, 271–72
    of relative clauses, 267–68
    on typewriter or word processor, 280–81
    between words, phrases and clauses, 268–70

Questions, in indirect quotation, 289
Question mark
    in indirect quotation, 289
    with quotation marks, 278–79
quite, as intensifier, 177
Quotation
    American vs. British usage, 278
    of balanced sentences, 151
    capitalization of, 300
    closing, 278–79
    in conclusion, 113
    extracted, 275, 279
    incorporated, 275
    indirect, 289–91
    introducing, 277–78
    in introduction, 111–12
    material inserted into, 275–76
    omitting material from, 276–77
    of outside sources, 274–75
    punctuation of, 224, 274–81
    within quotation, 275

Readers' Guide to Periodical Literature, 210–212
    cross-indexing in, 211
    key to symbols in, 212
    sample entries from, 211–212
    subject entry in, 211
Reading, 168–69
really, as intensifier, 177
reason
    in cause and effect analysis, 68
    as transitional relationship, 163
Reasoning, 76
Reference work, in list of works cited, 221
References to research sources, 204, 210
Refutation, 77, 80–81
relationship, as abstract noun, 175
Relative clause
    as parenthetical element, 272
    punctuation with, 267–68

restrictive vs. nonrestrictive, 267–68
Relative pronoun, 264
Relators, comparison of functions of, 162
Religious literature, 41
Religious terms, capitalization of, 301
Religious works, titles of, 302–3
Repetition
  in the balanced sentence, 151
  implied, as transitional device, 161
Repetitiousness
  of conclusion, 112
  of sentence structure, 149, 150, 151
Reprint, in list of works cited, 221
Request slip, 209
Research paper, 203–28
  acknowledging sources in, 203, 224
  documentation in, 203, 218–223, 224
  finding articles for, 210–14
  finding books for, 204–10
  finding a topic/thesis for, 204
  gathering information for, 203, 204–17
  guidelines for revision of, 121
  overdocumentation in, 227
  sample, 233–50
  sample bibliography cards for, 215
  sample note cards for, 216, 217
  taking notes for, 214–17
  using foreign language sources in, 227
  See also Plagiarism; Textual acknowledgment
    Reserve desk, 208
Restrictive relative clause, 267–68
Result
  in cause and effect analysis, 68
  as transitional relationship, 162, 163
Revision, 119–25
  by categories, 121–22
  cutting in, 120
  deciding what needs, 121–22
  according to inner critic, 119–20
  on longhand or typewritten drafts, 120–21
  marking systems for, 122–23
  according to outside critic, 120, 122
  of paragraphs, 139–140
  proofreader's marks in, 124–25
  stages in, 120
  taking time for, 120–21
  See also Final draft
"Richard Cory," 186–87
Robinson, Edwin Arlington, 186–87
Roman numerals
  form of, 307
  in subordinated outlines, 101
ROM *Catalogue*, 213
run-on, 265–66

Scholarly Journals, indexes of, 213
Scratch outline, 100–101
  ordering ideas in, 101
  variations in form of, 100
seem, as nonaction verb, 174
Self-control, in argument, 76, 81–82
Self-evident reasoning, 85
Semicolon
  in balanced sentence, 151
  capitalization of a clause following, 300
  between clauses, 270
  with items in a series, 270
  with quotation marks, 278
Senses, 173–74
Sentence, 147–57
  aims in writing, 148
  balanced, 151
  capitalization of first letter of, 300
  clarity of, 147
  completeness of, 148
  defined, 147, 262–63
  economy of, 154–56
  emphatic structure in, 150–51
  length of, 152
  loose, 150
  vs. nonsentence, 262–66
  periodic, 150–51
  questions for revision of, 121
  See also Agreement; Sentence structure
Sentence outline, 102–4
  sample of, 103–4
  for a summary, 197
Sentence structure
  judgment vs. rules in determining, 148
  and meaning, 154
  possibilities of, 149
  and relationship of ideas, 149
  repetitive pattern of, 149, 150, 151
  variety in, 150–52
Series
  citation of book in, 220, 221
  emphatic order in, 152
  introducing, 274
  parallelism in, 291
  punctuation of items in, 270
  in sentence structure, 152
Sevareid, Eric, 193–95
Sexism, 286–87
Similarity, as transitional relationship, 163
Simile, 180
Singular
  article with noun in, 309–10
  See also Number
slang, 169, 170

Slur, 176
so
  in comparison, 294
  as coordinate conjunction, 264
  as transitional word, 162
Social Science Index, 213
somebody and *someone*, 285
Spatial order, 34–35
Specificity
  excessive, 177–78
  vs. generality, 173, 177–78
Spelling
  indicated in dictionary definition, 48
  revision of, 121
Split infinitive, 293
Stacks, library, 204
Statistics, in argument, 79
Steps
  in process analysis, 71
  and ordinal numbers, 163–64
Stereotypes, avoiding, 287
Straw man, 85
Structure, consistency of, 292–93
Subdivision
  illogical, in outline, 105–6
  of subject into topics, 95–96
Subdivision analysis, 60–62
  contrasted with classification analysis, 60
  defined, 60
  example of, 60–61
  outline for, 61
  words indicating in essay question, 253
Subject
  number of compound, 287
  relation of, to topic, 95–96
Subject card. *See* Card catalogue
Subject headings. *See* Card catalogue
Subordinate clause, 153. *See also* Dependent
    clause
Subordinate conjunction
  vs. coordinate conjunction, 264
  vs. transitional relators, 162
  punctuation and, 264
Subordinate joiner, 264
Subordination, 152–54
  defined, 153
  in formal outline, 101
  function of, 153–54
  omitting words through, 155
  vs. primer English, 152
  structures of, 153
Subtitle
  capitalization of, 302
  as reflection of thesis, 115
  relationship to title, 115

such, in comparisons, 294
Summary, 192–98
  accuracy of, 193, 195
  acknowledgments in, 196
  aims in writing, 192–93, 197
  brevity of, 193, 195
  checking against original, 197
  clarity of, 193, 195
  completeness of, 193, 195
  concluding, 113
  defined, 192
  examples of, 195–96
  formal, 192
  guidelines for revision of, 121
  importance of, 192
  method for writing, 197
  organization of, 193, 195
  vs. plagiarism, 224
  transition in, 193
  as transitional relationship, 163
  use of own words in, 193, 195
Superlative, 294
Supporting detail
  concreteness of, 12–13, 32–33
  ordering of, 22, 34–35
  relationship to thesis, 10–14, 42–43
Supporting evidence, 76, 77, 79–80
  to back up concession, 81
  vs. supporting detail, 79
Suspended paragraph, 137–38
  in introduction and conclusion, 138
  suspense in, 137
Syllabication. *See* Word division
Symbols
  in dictionary entries, 169
  in *Library of Congress Subject Headings*, 206–7
  of subordination in formal outline, 101
Synonym
  defined, 167
  as definition, 48
  dictionary of, 179
  in dictionary entry, 169
  inequality of, 168, 180

Technical language, 171
Technical writing, paragraphs in, 141
Term
  in dictionary entry, 169
  in definition, 47–48, 49
Tense, consistency of, 288–91
  in indirect quotation, 289
Textual acknowledgment, 218
  and overdocumentation, 226

in summary, 196
than, in comparisons, 294–95
Theme. *See* Thesis
Theme sentence
  checking for, 134
  compared to thesis sentence, 133
  defined, 133
  implicit vs. explicit, 134
  and paragraph unity, 138
  position of, 134–38
  implicit vs. explicit, 134
  vs. topic sentence, 133
  See also Direct paragraph; Pivoting para-
    graph; Suspended paragraph
there is/there are, as wordy construction, 155, 175
Thesaurus, 179
Thesis
  in analysis, 55
  in argument, 77–79
  deciding on, 95–97
  defined, 2
  development of, 43, 139
  in essay question, 254
  explicit vs. implicit, 11, 55
  expressed as a complete sentence, 10, 96
  in outlining, 100–101
  limiting the, 78
  questions for revision of, 121
  reflected in title, 114–15
  relationship of to supporting details, 10–
    14, 42–43
  relationship of to topic, 95–96
  for a research paper, 204
  in a summary, 197
  vs. theme, 2
  vs. topic in outlining, 100
  weaseling, 78
  See also Master's thesis
Thesis statement
  in argument, 79
  compared to core thesis, 96
  use of, 96
Time, as transitional relationship, 164
Title, 114–16
  in final draft, 124
  of foreign works, 302
  form of one's own, 303
  italics vs. quotation marks with, 302
  length of, 115–16
  listing article, 213
  listing book, 208–9
  misleading, 116
  narrowing, 114–15
  phrase vs. sentence in, 116
  playing on words in, 115

quotation marks with, 280
and rank, capitalization of, 301
as reflection of thesis, 114–15
of religious work, 302
with subtitle, 115
See also Subtitle
Title card. *See* Card catalogue
Title page, 219
Tone, 5–6
  in argument, 81–82
  consistency of, 172
  in definition, 51
Topic
  change of as transitional relationship, 164
  limiting, 96–97
  relation of to subject and thesis, 95–96
  for a research paper, 204
Topic outline, 101–2
  for a summary, 197
Topic sentence. *See* Theme sentence
Trace, library, 209
Transition, 160–65
  continuity vs. change in, 160
  defined, 160
  with demonstrative adjectives, 161
  with pronouns, 161
  faulty use of, 165
  for indicating change, 161–65
  for indicating continuity, 160–61
  overuse of expressions of, 165
  between paragraphs, 162
  questions for revision of, 121
  with a short paragraph, 140
  with repetition, 161
  in summary, 193, 195, 197
  table of indicators of, 163–64
Translation
  of foreign language sources, 227
  of words in vocabulary list, 169
Typewritten essay
  and appearance of paragraphs, 140
  punctuation in, 280–81
  revision of, 120–21

Union List of Serials, 213
Units of the essay, 129–83
Unity
  of the essay, 2
  of paragraphs, 131
  of sentences, 148
Usage
  in dictionary entry, 48, 49, 169
  in vocabulary list, 169

Variety
  of sentence length, 152
  of sentence structure, 150–52
"Velva, North Dakota," 193–95
Verb
  concrete vs. abstract, 174–75
  formed with -ize, 175
  guidelines for choosing, 175
  vs. verb-plus-noun combinations, 175
Verb phrase, number of, 287
very, as intensifier, 177
Vocabulary
  building, 168–70
  difficulty for foreign student, 167–68
  listing, 169
  and word choice options, 168
Voice, active. See Active voice
Voice, passive. See Passive voice
Volume
  bound, 213
  citation of book with number of, 219–20, 222
  citation of periodical with number of, 220

Weaseling thesis, 78
whether . . . or, in balanced sentence, 151
White, E. B., 155
will, 290
Word choice, 167–83
  cognates in, 182–83

concreteness in, 172–77
connotation in, 178–80
and diction, 170–72
and the dictionary, 169–70
figurative language in, 180–82
specificity in, 177–78
questions for revision of, 121
and synonyms, 167–68
and vocabulary building, 168–70
Word division, 299, 308–9
  in dictionary definition, 48
  special rules regarding, 308–9
Word origin. See Etymology
Word processor
  punctuation with, 280–81
  revision with, 120
Words
  division of, 299, 308–9
  omitting needless, 154–55
  reduction of in summary, 195
  use of own, 193, 195, 225
  See also Word choice
Wordiness, 155–56
Works cited, list of. See List of works cited
Writer as critic, 119–20
Writer's block, 109
Writing, methodology of, 93–125

yet, as coordinate conjunction, 264